Robert M Stitt

Boeing B-17 Fortress
in RAF Coastal Command Service

STRATUS

Published in Poland in 2010
by STRATUS s.c.
Po. Box 123,
27-600 Sandomierz 1, Poland
e-mail: office@mmpbooks.biz
for
Mushroom Model Publications,
e-mail: rogerw@mmpbooks.biz
© 2010 Mushroom Model
Publications.
http://www.mmpbooks.biz

All rights reserved. Apart
from any fair dealing for
the purpose of private
study, research, criticism
or review, as permitted
under the Copyright,
Design and Patents Act,
1988, no part of this publication may be reproduced,
stored in a retrieval system,
or transmitted in any form
or by any means, elec-
tronic, electrical, chemi-
cal, mechanical, optical,
photocopying, recording
or otherwise, without
prior written permission.
All enquiries should be
addressed to the publisher.

© Author: Robert M Stitt
© Colour profiles
& scale drawings
Juanita Franzi

ISBN
978-8389450-88-3

Editor in chief
Roger Wallsgrove

Editorial Team
Bartłomiej Belcarz
Robert Pęczkowski
Artur Juszczak
James Kightly

Colour profiles
& scale drawings
Juanita Franzi

DTP
Robert Pęczkowski
Artur Juszczak

Printed by
Drukarnia Diecezjalna,
ul. Żeromskiego 4,
27-600 Sandomierz
tel. +48 (15) 832 31 92;
fax +48 (15) 832 77 87
www.wds.pl
marketing@wds.pl
PRINTED IN POLAND

*Dedicated to the remarkable young men
of Royal Air Force Coastal Command.*

F/Sgt Frederick W J Hedges, 220 Sqn, RAF Coastal Command

This book is based on a series of articles that appeared in the now-discontinued British aviation history journal, AIR Enthusiast. The original content has been fully revised and substantially expanded for this publication.

Cover and title page: Fortress IIA FK186 'S' of 220 Sqn in its maritime element, mid-1943. IWM CH.11146

Table of Contents

Introduction

Unlikely as it may seem, the origins of this book date back to April 1977 and a chance visit to a crash site near the township of Wau in Papua New Guinea. At the time I was working for an international development agency and had stopped with a colleague to spend a few days with a family on their coffee plantation before driving inland on the Highlands Highway. Knowing I was a life-long aviation enthusiast, a trek to "the bomber" was proposed and three young members of the Benson family, plus some residents from the local village, guided us up the bush trail to Black Cat Pass.

I had no idea what we were about to see but recognized the imposing B-17 Fortress immediately – I had seen the same aircraft illustrated years earlier in a *Profile* publication, captioned as a 'Mystery Ship'. Appearing mid-grey overall, its USAAF insignia had mostly eroded away to reveal RAF markings, a puzzling reversal that had caused much speculation over the years. I took a number of colour transparencies and made notes on what markings and colours I could see, including an RAF serial number – then, except for having a few images published, I left these materials untouched for the next 20 years.

But I often thought back to that memorable visit and around the year 2000 resolved to learn as much as I could about the Black Cat B-17. I was fortunate to be linked with Pacific B-17 researcher Janice Olson and together we were able to chronicle its full history. The mysterious Fortress proved to be one of a number earmarked through Lend-Lease for RAF Coastal Command's aerial campaign against the U-boats but subsequently retained by the USAAF for service in the Pacific. Most gratifyingly, our research resulted in a reunion for the three surviving American crew members, some 60 years after their crash-landing near Wau on January 8, 1943.

By the time the story was published, the answer to the question: What shall I write about next? had become obvious. I had become fascinated by what had happened to those Fortresses that, unlike the Black Cat example, had been delivered to Britain. How were they acquired? What role did they play in the Second World War? Who flew them? What were their fates?

So began a six-year journey to research and write a complete chronicle of the Boeing B-17 Fortress in service with Coastal Command. One fact quickly became clear: the Fortress had received little coverage in texts about the Battle of the Atlantic yet a few dozen of these aircraft had played a critically important role in protecting Britain's convoy lifeline and, later in the war, helped provide invaluable meteorological data for Allied weather forecasting. And as I made contact with a

Boeing B-17E Fortress 41-9234 where it came to rest on January 8, 1943. Phillip Bradley

growing number of former Fortress squadron members, the story became as much about the extraordinary contribution they had made to Britain's survival as it was about an aircraft type.

As it turned out I had begun my project at the very last moment. Many of the former Fortress airmen and ground crew I located during my research have since passed away. I feel privileged to have shared their memories and friendship and to tell their story. I have also been fortunate to have made contact with the sons and daughters and brothers and sisters of many former Fortress squadron members and to have been given access to logbooks, photographs and other mementos. On several occasions I have been able to fill in historical gaps in return. In many ways, these exchanges have been the most affecting and rewarding of all.

Coastal Command operations were a new area of study for me and a large number of fellow aviation researchers have given generously of their time and materials to help make this book a reality – those who have contributed are listed in the Sources and Acknowledgement section. Contributing artist Juanita Franzi of Aero Illustrations, prepared the outstanding colour profiles and scale drawings. Roger Wallsgrove and Robert Pęczkowski of Mushroom Model Publications were a pleasure to work with and remained committed throughout to realizing my vision for this volume. Great care went into researching and checking the information presented in this book – at the end of the day, any errors or omissions are those of the Author.

Two people deserve special mention. My wife Susan has been wonderfully supportive throughout the preparation of this book. Former 220 Squadron flight engineer Ted Hedges has, through the wonder of the Internet, been 'at my side' throughout, contributing, checking and encouraging.

A heartfelt thank you to you all.

It is my hope that this book goes some way towards illuminating the important role played by Coastal Command's Fortresses and the young men who crewed and maintained them.

I would welcome any feedback on the contents of this book. Please forward correspondence to the publisher.

Robert M Stitt
Cowichan Bay, British Columbia
Canada
February 2010

A Lockheed Hudson shepherding a convoy through the Western Approaches in June of 1941. The primary role of Coastal Command's patrol aircraft was to keep the U-boat packs submerged so they could not launch a co-ordinated attack. via Joe Griffith

Foreword I

The story which follows describes the vital role played by RAF Coastal Command's Boeing B-17 Fortresses in countering the U-boat threat during the Battle of the Atlantic. Much has been written about the importance of long-range aircraft in this war-long campaign and the limelight has invariably fallen on the Consolidated B-24 Liberator. Yet during the most critical period of the Battle, from the autumn of 1942 to the spring of 1943, a few dozen Fortresses spread over two, and for a brief period, three Coastal Command squadrons performed a major share of the long-range convoy protection role in the North Atlantic.

This book is the product of years of dedicated, detailed research and presents an accurate record of the immense effort and many sacrifices made by Fortress crews to keep the convoy lanes clear of U-boats. This facet of the Atlantic battle has often been overlooked by chroniclers – even Sir John Slessor, commander-in-chief of Coastal Command during height of the campaign, makes scant reference to the Fortress in his memoirs. These omissions have finally been rectified in this most authoritative work.

While the Liberator possessed greater range and load carrying capability, squadron crews were proud to operate the Fortress. The Boeing product was a great aircraft: easy to fly, stable, dependable and with a good service reputation. It did, however, have one major flaw which prompted almost daily discussion among crews: it possessed inadequate forward firepower to suppress return fire from surfaced U-boats during attack runs. Even the late arrival in the Azores of a handful of 'G'-model Fortresses fitted with chin turrets still left the 'Fort' at a disadvantage and crews tended to believe this arrangement would still leave them going into action with one hand tied behind their backs.

We young aircrew were thrown into the Battle as little more than boys. Many of us were still in our 'teens' yet we were given a level of responsibility that would be inconceivable today. Most of us were driven by childhood dreams of flying and I recall standing underneath a Fortress for the first time, believing that nothing could possibly happen to it. But flying on operations would reveal ever-present dangers – weather, mechanical failure, fatigue and loss of concentration – and we each had to overcome fear and inexperience so we could react to immediate threats for the sake of the aircraft and the entire crew. We roamed the Atlantic wastes, navigating by compass, watch, sextant, drift meter and the faith that our navigator would keep awake for the long hours of our operational flight. Tedious hour followed tedious hour over sorties lasting up to 14 hours. Then, in an instant, a U-boat sighting. We had only seconds to drop down to between 50 and 150 feet and position for a 10 degree angle of track over the conning tower. When possible, our captain weaved the aircraft to avoid return fire from up to six 20 or 30 millimetre guns. But in the end there was no option but to fly through the hail of shells and bullets. This happened hundreds of times during the Battle and by the end of hostilities between 350 and 400 U-boats had been sunk by Coastal Command's aircraft while hundreds of aircraft and thousands of aircrew were lost. Two Fortresses and one full crew are known to have been lost to return fire from their intended prey.

With the North Atlantic convoy routes secure by mid-1943, vital supplies flowed mostly un-hindered from the United States and Canada and, as later models of the Liberator became available with vastly improved radar, greater weapons carrying capability and even longer range, the Fortress passed to another important role, meteorological reconnaissance. We aircrew tasked with defeating the U-boats had done our work and our Fortresses had served us superbly.

A final thought. I would ask the reader to give thought to those who backed the men at the 'sharp end'. I owe my life to those who worked on servicing my aircraft, in all weathers, out in the open day and night, for months on end. They were, each and every one, true heroes.

Frederick W J 'Ted' Hedges
Former flight engineer, 220 Squadron, RAF Coastal Command

Foreword II

Soon after the start of WWII, it became obvious that there was an essential requirement for regular and reliable weather intelligence. It was particularly important for chart analyses and forecasts issued for Bomber Command bases and for Combined Operations. The necessary data could only be provided by long-range reconnaissance aircraft with specially trained crews, operating over the Atlantic and other data-sparse areas, including the Norwegian Sea and North Sea.

In the Spring of 1941, the first Met Reconnaissance flights commenced operations, using Blenheim aircraft of limited range. These aircraft were superseded by Lockheed Hudsons, Handley Page Hampdens (briefly) and Lockheed Venturas and although extra fuel tanks were fitted, their range was still somewhat restricted. Modified four-engined aircraft, with bomb-bay tanks and special instrumentation were needed to launch long-range sorties and this requirement was finally met with the introduction of modified Halifaxes and Boeing B-17 Fortresses, the latter operating with USAAF weather squadrons and with RAF Coastal Command as the Fortress IIA, II and III.

The Author has produced an admirable and well-researched account of operations carried out by the long-range Met reconnaissance squadrons equipped with the Fortress. With these aircraft it was possible to extend the range of Met sorties and carry out soundings up to the 400 millibar level (about 7,300m) The Fortress was ideally suited to the task and could cope with the severe turbulence and icing often encountered on these long and arduous operations. The principal enemy for Met crews was weather; they had a 'licence to operate' when all other flying had been cancelled. It is worth paraphrasing a paragraph written by Lt Cdr (A) E E Barringer of the Fleet Air Arm, ex-CO of 835 Squadron and an airman very familiar with maritime operations:

"I often remember the weather, and the fact that in our operations over the North Atlantic and Arctic oceans we had two enemies, the Germans and the elements. The elements were the more dangerous; we lost more aircrew through incidents caused by bad weather than through enemy action."

This book is a most valuable addition to the history of wartime operations by Fortress crews of the RAF's Coastal Command. It serves as a tribute not only to the aircrew, but also to the Boeing Aircraft Company who produced this famous aircraft, and to the dedicated ground crews, working in adverse conditions to maintain it.

Peter G Rackliff, DipGeog MCMI FRMetS
Ex- No. 518 Squadron & Radar Met Flight.

Sources and Acknowledgements

The National Archives, Kew, Surrey, England

ASV Installation in Fortress IIA aircraft, 1943. File: AVIA 7/1708.

British Air Commission Aircraft Programme. File: AVIA 38/510.

Camouflage and Marking Instructions (Coastal Command) – January 1942 to November 1943. File: AIR 15/285.

Coastal Command: Aircraft operational requirements: policy. File: AIR 15/46

Coastal Command: Expansion and re-equipment June 1941 – September 1943. File: AIR 15/340.

Coastal Command: Policy on air and war plans. File: AIR 15/27.

Coastal Command Development Unit. File: AIR 15/555.

D-54 Report No.25 (Sept. 23, 1942), The British Air Commission, Statistics Branch, Washington, DC. Includes listing of 'Army Release' B-17Es allocated to Britain but taken back by the USAAF. File: AVIA 38/594.

Handling reports for Fortress II aircraft by the Aeroplane and Armament Experimental Establishment (A&AEE), Boscombe Down, Report A&AEE/770,a. File: AVIA 18/721.

Lend-Lease accounting for Boeing B-17Es. File: AVIA 15/various and AVIA 38/various.

Liberator Aircraft: Release to service. File: AIR 20/1774.

LRASV Installation in Fortress IIA Aircraft, 1943. File: AIR 6/12306.

Movement and Deliveries of Aircraft. File: AVIA 38/594.

Operations Record Book, No. 15 Group, RAF. File: AIR 25/254.

Operations Record Book, No. 19 Group, RAF. File: AIR 25/453.

Operations Record Book, No. 29 Maintenance Unit, RAF: AIR 29/991

Operations Record Book, No. 53 Squadron, RAF. File: AIR 27/505.

Operations Record Book, No. 59 Squadron, RAF. File: AIR 27/555.

Operations Record Book, No. 86 Squadron, RAF. File: AIR 27/708.

Operations Record Book, No. 90 Squadron, RAF. File: AIR 27/731

Operations Record Book, No. 111 Operational Training Unit, RAF: AIR 29/689

Operations Record Book, No. 120 Squadron, RAF. File: AIR 27/911.

Operations Record Book, No. 206 Squadron, RAF. File: AIR 27/1223.

Operations Record Book, No. 220 Squadron, RAF. File: AIR 27/1366-1367.

Operations Record Book, No. 224 Squadron, RAF. File: AIR 27/1388.

Operations Record Book, No. 247 Group, RAF. File: AIR 25/1044.

Operations Record Book, No. 251 Squadron, RAF. File: AIR 27/1506.

Operations Record Book, No. 519 Squadron, RAF. File: AIR 27/1989 & 1990.

Operations Record Book, No. 521 Squadron, RAF. File: AIR 27/1995.

Operations Record Book, RAF Coastal Command. File: AIR 24/364-365

Surplus Lend-Lease Aircraft: Disposal. File: AVIA 38/1259.

The RAF Narrative. The RAF in the Maritime War. Vol. III. July 1941 - February 1943. File: AIR 41/47.

RAF Museum, Hendon, London, England

Air Ministry Form 54 and Form 78 Movement Cards for Fortress I aircraft and Air Ministry Form 78 Movement Cards for Fortress IIA, II and III aircraft in RAF Coastal Command service.

Air Ministry Form 1180 Accident Cards for Fortress IIA and II aircraft in RAF Coastal Command service. (Accident Card for Fortress II FA708 acquired from the Air Historical Branch, London, England).

Air Publication 2544A A.S.V. Mk. II Equipment and Ancillaries, Air Ministry.

National Archives of Australia

Service Record for F/O J E Delarue, 402322. Series A9300, control symbol DELARUE J E.

Casualty – Repatriation file for F/O J E Delarue, 402322. Series A705, control symbol 163/27.163. Includes Proceedings of Court of Inquiry or Investigation, Flying Accidents. Fortress IIA FL454 'J' of 206 Squadron, crashed Benbecula October 6, 1942.

Other Primary Sources

Air Ministry Air Diagram 1161: Camouflage Scheme for Four Engined Monoplanes (courtesy Paul Lucas)

Air Ministry Bomb Disposal – Report on an incident at RAF Benbecula, 28.10.42 (courtesy Chris Ransted)

Air Publication 2099B C,D,E,F-PN Pilot's Notes for Fortress GR. IIA, GR. II & III, BII & BIII. Air Ministry (courtesy Ted Hedges).

Aircrew assignment cards, RAF Ferry Command. Directorate of History and Heritage, Ottawa, Canada. Information extracted by Bob Bolivar.

General Arrangement Drawings – Models B-17E and B-17F. Boeing Archives, Seattle.

Progress Report on the Modification of B-17 Aircraft at United's Cheyenne Modification Center from the Date of Its Inception on January 9, 1942 Through June 30, 1943. United Airlines, Chicago, Illinois.

RAF Coastal Command – The Unseen Films. Imperial War Museum. Ref. IWM AV00993

USAAF aircraft movement cards for Boeing B-17 Fortress aircraft (microfiche loan courtesy David Osborne).

Wireless log, RAF Nutts Corner, August 10/11, 1942 (courtesy Richard Gates)

Aircrew Logbooks

Bass, Kenneth B – pilot, 206 Sqn. (courtesy John Lowe, grandson)

Baxter, Edward L – pilot, RAF Ferry Command (courtesy Diane Harvie, daughter)

Beaty, David – pilot, 206 Sqn (courtesy Betty Beaty, wife)

Blackwell, William S - WOP/AG, 206 Sqn (courtesy owner)

Boudreault, J E Roch – WOP/AG, 220 Sqn (courtesy Laurette Chagnon, sister)

Cairns, George W - WOP/AG, 206 Sqn (courtesy Moira Edge, daughter)

Croft, Laurence H – pilot, 220 Sqn (courtesy owner)

Forrest, James W S – pilot, 220 Sqn (courtesy Rod Forrest, son)

Fox, W George – pilot-in-training, 1674 Heavy Conversion Unit (courtesy owner)

Fretwell, Eric – flight engineer, 220 Sqn (courtesy owner)

Gates, Richard T F – commanding officer and pilot, 220 Sqn (courtesy of Richard Gates, son)

Glazebrook, James – pilot, 206 Sqn (courtesy owner)

Griffith, Joe E – navigator, 206 Sqn (courtesy 206 Sqn Archives)

Haggas, Gerald R – pilot, 220 Sqn (courtesy owner)

Hedges, Frederick W J – flight engineer, 220 Sqn (courtesy owner)

Knowles, Eric – pilot, 59 Sqn (courtesy Roger Knowles, son)

Langdale, Russell – WOP/AG, 519 (Met) Sqn (courtesy owner)

Longmuir, Hervey R – navigator, 59 Sqn (courtesy Lorenzo del Mann, grandson)

Machin, William A – copilot, 220 Sqn (courtesy owner)

Major, Follett K – pilot, 220 Sqn (courtesy Alan Wells, researcher)

Marshall, Nigel G S – pilot, 519 (Met) Sqn (courtesy owner)

Meech, Lloyd – co-pilot, 206 Sqn (courtesy Martin Meech, brother)

Nelson, Edward H – WOP/AG, 206 Sqn (courtesy owner)

Nelson, Lawrence M – pilot, 206 Sqn (courtesy Simon Nelson, son)

Pinhorn, Anthony J – pilot, 206 Sqn (courtesy Wendy Hopkins, sister)

Pullan, George H – pilot, 519 (Met) Sqn (courtesy owner)

Ramsden, Kenneth L H – pilot, 220 Sqn (courtesy Edward Ramsden, son)

Roberson, G Peter – pilot, 220 Sqn (courtesy Jesse Roberson, granddaughter)

Roxburgh, William – pilot, 206 Sqn (courtesy 206 Sqn Archives)

Rutherford, John T – navigator, 206 Sqn (courtesy Ray Rutherford, son)

Smith, Eric H – pilot, 220 Sqn (courtesy Roger Smith, stepson)

Speirs, Kenneth – pilot, 220 Sqn (courtesy Brian Speirs, son)

Stone, Eric A – pilot, 220 Sqn (courtesy of Lynda Matthews, daughter)

Towell, Gordon – pilot, 220 Sqn (courtesy of Dennis Towell, son)

Travell, Wilfred R – pilot, 220 Sqn (courtesy of Newark Air Museum)

Wardill, Lesslie E – WOP/AG, 90 Sqn and 90 and 220 Sqn Detachments, Middle East (courtesy Edward Wardill, cousin)

Secondary Sources
Books

Beaty, Betty Campbell. Winged Life. Airlife, 2001.

Christie, Carl A. Ocean Bridge – The History of RAF Ferry Command. University of Toronto Press, 1997.

Cooper H J and Thetford, O G. Aircraft of the Fighting Powers – Vols I-VII. Harborough, 1941-1947.

Dunmore, Spencer. In Great Waters – The Epic Story of the Battle of the Atlantic. McClelland & Stewart, 1999.

Franks, Norman. Search, Find and Kill – The RAF's U-boat Successes in World War Two. Grub Street, 1995.

Freeman, Roger A. Fortress at War, Ian Allan, 1977.

Freeman, Roger A, with Osborne, David. The B-17 Flying Fortress Story. Arms and Armour, 1999.

Glazebrook, James. A War History of No. 206 Squadron, Royal Air Force. Self-published, 1946.

Goss, Christopher. Bloody Biscay. Crécy, 1997.

Green, William. Famous Bombers of the Second World War. MacDonald, 1959.

Gunn, Peter B. Naught Escapes Us. The 206 Squadron Association, 2004.

Hart, Leslie. From Bicycles to Boeings. Unpublished autobiography.

Hendrie, Andrew W A. The Cinderella Service. Pen and Sword, 2006.

Hughes, Mike. Hebrides at War. Birlinn, 2001.

Jay, Alwyn. Endurance - A history of RAAF aircrew in Liberator operations of Coastal Command 1941 -1945. Banner Books Australia, 1995.

Meekcoms, Ken J. The British Air Commission and Lend-Lease. Air-Britain, 2000.

Kington, John A & Rackliffe, Peter G. Even The Birds Were Walking – The Story of Wartime Meteorological Reconnaissance. Tempus, 2000.

McVicar, Don. Ferry Command. Airlife, 1981.

Pearcy, Arthur. Lend-Lease Aircraft in World War II. Airlife, 1996.

Pitt, Barrie and Frances. The Chronological Atlas of World War II. MacMillan, 1989.

Price, Alfred. Aircraft versus the Submarine. William Kimber, 1973

RAF Museum (John Tanner, General Editor). British Aviation Colours of World War Two. Arms and Armour Press, 1986.

Richards, Denis. Royal Air Force 1939-1945, Volume I. The Fight At Odds. HMSO, 1953.

Richards, Denis, and Saunders, Hilary St. George. Royal Air Force 1939-1945. Volume II. The Fight Avails. HMSO, 1954.

Robertson, Bruce. British Military Aircraft Serials 1912-1966. Ian Allan, 1966.

Saunders, Hilary St. George. Royal Air Force 1939-1945. Volume III. The Fight Is Won. HMSO, 1954.

Slessor, Sir John. The Central Blue. Frederick A Praeger, 1957.

Sturtivant, Ray with John Hamlin Flying Training and Support Units Since 1912. Air-Britain, 1979.

Thetford, Owen G. Aircraft of the Royal Air Force since 1918. Putnam, 1968.

Thomas, Richard. Towards the Sun. Self-published, 2000.

Vintras, Roland E. The Portuguese Connection. Bachman & Turner, 1974.

Magazines, Booklets and Newsletters

No. 206 Squadron Association Newsletter, various.

Baker, Ian. The First RAF Fortresses. Ian K Baker's Aviation History Colouring Book 54, Questions & Answers. Self-published, 2006.

Gover, Lee (Freeman, Roger A). First in the Fight. FlyPast Special B-17 Tribute. Key Publishing, July 1999.

Jones, Eric R. The Recipe. 519 Squadron Ex Members' Newsletter, 2003, Parts I and II.

Lucas, Paul. B-17 in RAF service, 1941-1942. Model Aircraft Monthly, August 2007.

Thomas, Andrew. For King and Country. Classic Aircraft Series No. 22. B-17 Flying Fortress, Key Publishing, 2005.

Thompson, Charles D. The Boeing B-17E & F Flying Fortress – Profile Number 77. Profile Publications, 1966.

William Green and Gordon Swanborough (editors). Royal Air Force Yearbook 1981. Royal Air Force Benevolent Fund, 1981.

Acknowledgements

Correspondence with former Fortress aircrew
(in addition to those listed earlier who supplied copies of their logbook):
Ayling, Joseph F – WOP/AG, 220 Sqn
Banks, Leslie F – pilot, 206 Sqn
Graham, John C – pilot, 206 Sqn
Grant, Stuart T – pilot, 519 (Met) Sqn
Hobbs, Jack P – pilot, 220 Sqn and past president, 220 Sqn Association
Jones, Eric R – navigator, 519 (Met) Sqn
Lockwood, Charles H – pilot, 220 Sqn
MacNeil, Donald S – pilot, 519 (Met) Sqn
Monaghan, Allan – instrument fitter, 206 Sqn
Smith, Alan D B – pilot, 206 Sqn
Thomas, Richard – WOP/AG, 206 Sqn
Willis, Derek – Meteorological Air Officer, 519 (Met) Sqn

Other Correspondence
Ashdown, John – nephew of Ronald Stares, WOP/AG, 206 Sqn
Beaty, Betty – wife of David Beaty, pilot, 206 Sqn
Clarke, David – nephew of John Owen, pilot, 206 Squadron
Hawkins, Margaret – daughter of Patrick E Hadow, Commanding Officer, 220 Sqn
Hopkins, Wendy – sister of Anthony J Pinhorn, pilot, 206 Sqn
Hart, Joan – wife of Leslie Hart, pilot, 519 and 521 (Met) Sqns
McIlwrick, Maurice – brother of Eric B McIlwrick, pilot 220 Sqn
Roxburgh, William 'Willis' – letters to Allan Monaghan, both 206 Sqn
Roxburgh, William – son of William 'Willis' Roxburgh, pilot, 206 Sqn
Travell, Barbara – wife of Wilfred Travell, pilot, 220 Sqn

Assistance from Researchers and Writers
A special 'thank you' to the following researchers and writers who generously shared their time and
materials:
Chris Ashworth, Malcolm Barrass, Peter Berry, Steve Birdsall, Bob Bolivar, Brian Booth, Peter M
Bowers, Steve Bowsher, Michael J F Bowyer, Martin Briscoe, Ian Brown, Phil Butler, John Carter, Carl
Christie, Peter Clare, David Clarke, Simon Coles, Gus Coutts, Peter Davies, Mike Diprose, David Earl,
Howard Eastcott, Ken Ellis, Gary Fowkes, Norman Franks, Roger Freeman, Stuart Grant, Norman
Groom, Peter Gunn, Jim Halley, Hugh Halliday, Richard Hankins, Jo Harris, Marion Hebblethwaite,
Terry Hissey, Mike Hughes, Phil Listemann, John Lowe, Paul Lucas, Norman Malayney, Tim Mason,
Paul McMillan, Ross McNeill, Jeff Noakes, David Osborne, Matt Poole, John Rabbets, Peter Rackliff,
Chris Ransted, Pierre Renier, Neil Robinson, Jak Showell, Ray Sturtivant, David Thomas, Pavel Turk,
Chuck Varney, Jerry Vernon, Tim Vincent, Richard Ward, John Withers and Bryan Yates. Also,
numerous additional members of the RAF Commands Forum, a web-based forum.

Historical Organisations
No. 59 Squadron Association. (Roger Sheldrake)
No. 206 Squadron Archives. (Tom Talbot & Alex Sell)
No. 206 Squadron Association. (Derek Straw)
Air Historical Branch, Whitehall, London, England.
Boeing Archives, Seattle, Washington State, USA. (Tom Lubbesmeyer)
Burtonwood Association, Warrington, Lancashire, England. (Les Granfield)
Canadian Aviation Museum, Ottawa, Ontario, Canada. (Stuart Leslie)
Directorate of History and Heritage, Ottawa, Ontario, Canada. (Charles Rhéaume)
Imperial War Museum, London, England. (Dave Parry)
Mission Community Archives, Mission, British Columbia, Canada.
Museum of Flight, Seattle
New Zealand Defence Force Personnel Archives, Wellington, New Zealand.
Newark Air Museum, Nottinghamshire, England (Mike Smith)
North Atlantic Aviation Museum, Gander, Newfoundland, Canada. (Brian Williams)
Provincial Archives, Government of Newfoundland and Labrador, St. John's, Newfoundland, Canada.
Royal Air Force Museum, Hendon, London, England.
The National Archives, Kew, Surrey, England.

On-line Resources
No. 206 Squadron: Coastal Command: http://www.coastalcommand206.com
No. 269 Squadron RAF: http://www.oca.269squadron.btinternet.co.uk/index.htm
Air of Authority – A History of RAF Organisation: http://www.rafweb.org/Index.htm
Commonwealth War Graves Commission: http://www.cwgc.org
Kriegstagebücher (KTB) & Stehender Kriegsbefehl Des Führers/Befehlshaber der Unterseeboote (F.d.U./
B.d.U.) – War Diary and War Standing Orders of Commander in Chief, Submarines: http://www.
uboatarchive.net/BDUKTB.htm
London Gazette: http://beta.gazettes-online.co.uk
National Archives of Australia: http://www.naa.gov.au
Navy-History.net: http://www.naval-history.net
RAF Commands Forum: http://www.rafcommands.com/forum/index.php
The National Archives: http://www.nationalarchives.gov.uk
U-boat.net: http://uboat.net/index.html
World War 2 Ex-RAF: http://www.worldwar2exraf.co.uk

By the end of September 1940 it was clear that Germany had failed to take control of the air during the Battle of Britain. This unexpected defeat forced Hitler to postpone invasion plans and refocus his strategy on a slow strangulation of Britain's oceanic lifelines. Britain depended on its trade routes from North America and the Empire, with nearly one million tons of food, raw materials and arms needing to arrive in British ports every week for the country to survive and for there to be any chance of launching a second front in Europe.

The resulting Battle of the Atlantic is without parallel in the history of warfare. Fought over thousands of square miles of featureless ocean, it spanned years rather than days, weeks or months, and pitted ships and aircraft, sailors and airmen, and Britain's best scientific minds against an array of threats. Germany marshalled battleships, battle cruisers, aircraft and mines to sink Allied merchant shipping. But by far the greatest threat came from submarines, better known as U-boats (from the German *unterseeboot*). Prime Minister Winston Churchill would later write: "*The only thing that ever really frightened me during the war was the U-boat peril.*"

The availability of continuous air cover for transatlantic convoys was to prove one of the decisive factors in defeating the U-boat packs and accounts of the campaign rightfully identify the Consolidated B-24 Liberator as the most numerous and effective long-range type used by RAF Coastal Command. Often forgotten is a relatively small number of Boeing B-17 Fortresses which, although less capable than their eventual successor, made an indispensable contribution to minimising shipping losses to U-boats during the most critical phase of the Battle.

Attacker's view of a U-boat, in this case Type XIC/40 U-534. This submarine was sunk by a Liberator VIII of 86 Sqn on May 5, 1945. It was raised in 1993 and put on display at the Nautilus Maritime Museum near Liverpool, England. In early 2008 it was cut into four sections to form a walk-through display at the Woodside ferry terminal on the River Mersey. via Bryan Yates

PAST LESSONS

German submarines sank nearly 6,000 ships during the First World War, one quarter of the world's total tonnage. The experience demonstrated that clustering vessels in convoys was a powerful countermeasure to the U-boat threat – especially when supported by air cover – and most Allied shipping moved in convoys from mid-September 1939. In practice, convoys were difficult to find in the vast Atlantic Ocean. The U-boat arm commanded by then *Konteradmiral* Karl Dönitz depended on shadowing U-boats to report convoy positions, but once forced to dive by the presence of escorting aircraft, the U-boat's low submerged cruising speed meant they were soon left behind and contact was lost.

Moreover, the U-boat was not a submarine as we understand it today – able to travel submerged over vast distances for extended periods – but a submersible boat that needed to surface for four hours in every 24 to recharge its running batteries and purge the foul air from its cramped hull. The workhorse of the U-boat fleet, the Type VIIC, could cover only 80 miles (130km) at 4 knots (7.5km/h) before resurfacing and, although capable of around 18 knots (33km/h) while on the surface – faster than any convoy – it was vulnerable to sudden attack from the air.

U-boat commanders were therefore extremely wary of surfacing and attacking ships when aircraft were thought to be in the vicinity.

The principal role of aircraft was to patrol around and ahead of convoys, keeping threatening U-boats submerged and frustrating their efforts to track and attack the ships. It followed that the greater the range and load carrying capability of an aircraft, the longer its crew could maintain this harassment and carry out attacks when conditions allowed. All other factors being equal, an aircraft with an endurance of ten hours, for example, could escort a convoy located three hours from base for four hours while one with eight hours endurance could provide an escort for only two hours, 50 percent of the first type.

On the eve of war, Coastal Command could muster ten squadrons of Avro Ansons plus one of partially operational Lockheed Hudsons, six with flying boats – including two of Short Sunderlands and four using ageing Saro Londons and Supermarine Stranraers – and two strike squadrons of outdated Vickers Vildebeest biplanes. Of these, only the Sunderland and Hudson could be considered up-to-date combat aircraft. The more numerous Anson boasted a range of 800 miles (1,290km) and could provide cover over a 250-mile (400km) radius. It carried four 112-pound (51kg) anti-submarine bombs, a dangerous weapon that was prone to skipping and exploding under the attacking aircraft.

By May 1940, U-boats had sunk 560,000 tons (568,985 tonnes) of Allied shipping, an uncomfortable but not yet critical total. But with the fall of France in June 1940, and the operation of U-boats from the Atlantic coast beginning late the following month, the threat to Allied convoys increased dramatically. From June to the end of December 1940, U-boats sank 343 ships totalling more than 1,700,000 tons (1,727,280 tonnes), forcing convoys to abandon the route to the south of Ireland and take the longer northern passage to Britain. This major impact was achieved with just 26 operational U-boats. For its part, RAF Coastal Command, charged with providing aerial escorts to Allied shipping, could show little for tens of thousands of hours of flying.

U-boats sank 1,400,000 tons (1,422,265 tonnes) of merchant shipping during the first six months of 1941. By the end of this period Coastal Command had replaced the Anson with the more effective Hudson, with a range out to 500 miles (800km) from base, while British types such as the Armstrong Whitworth Whitley and the Vickers Wellington could spend some two hours on patrol at this distance. Better still, the Sunderland was able to patrol for two hours at 600 miles (970km) out and the newly-available Consolidated Catalina was capable of two hours at more than 800 miles (1,290km). But with no larger, long-range types available and no bases in neutral Eire, there remained a yawning gap in mid-Atlantic where U-boats could operate without fear of attack by patrolling aircraft.

The one cause for hope in closing this gap was the Consolidated Liberator, which promised a two-hour endurance at more than 1,000 miles (1,610km) from base. Britain had purchased 20 Liberator Is and the type was soon to come on strength with 120 Sqn. But the number of aircraft was small, introduction to service still some way off, and the type as yet untried.

LONG-RANGE OPTIONS

The shortage of long-range maritime reconnaissance types was finally addressed following passage of the Lend-Lease Act on March 11, 1941. This crucial initiative allowed the United States to circumvent its isolationist policy and support Britain with a massive supply of desperately needed military equipment. In terms of aircraft, Coastal Command was to be the major early beneficiary in the form of Hudsons and Catalinas but there remained a critical need for long-range types.

At the time Britain had few long-range, land-based aircraft in service. The Short Stirling had only become operational in February 1941, while the Handley Page Halifax entered service the following month. The first Avro Lancaster squadrons would not take to the air until October. The Air Ministry had already ordered and paid for 20 Boeing B-17C Fortresses for the high-level bombing role, together with 165 Consolidated B-24 Liberators, comprised of the 20 Liberator Is plus

139 Liberator IIs and six LB-30s. But these so-called 'heavy bombers' were not sufficient to build a long-range, land-based maritime reconnaissance capability in addition to the planned strategic bombing offensive. In the event, both types proved to have a common drawback for night bombing in that their powerplants exhausted through turbo-superchargers on the underside of the engine nacelles, an arrangement that created flame damping problems. In the case of the Liberator, this meant the type was dropped by Bomber Command for operations in Europe with deliveries switched to Coastal Command.

Representatives from the British Air Commission (BAC) and their American counterparts lost no time in acting on the intent of the Lend-Lease Act. By March 25, 1941, they had drawn up a list of requirements under the 'Aircraft Programme' comprised of three categories: those aircraft covered by existing British orders, those to be acquired under Lend-Lease contracts, and those to be released to Britain by the US Army and US Navy. The idea of Army and Navy releases was to give advanced delivery of types needed by Britain from existing American military orders while orders under Lend-Lease were still being placed or, in some cases, still being authorised. The planned total for Lend-Lease acquisitions and American military releases was an impressive 11,904 aircraft, including single- and twin-engined pursuits, transports, trainers, flying boats, observation and liaison types, dive bombers, and light, medium and heavy bombers. It was this last category that most closely fitted Coastal Command's needs.

The US Army indicated it would release 255 heavy bombers – 135 B-17s and 120 B-24s, or an estimated 40 percent of planned production – between May 1941 and June 1942 and a further 1,000 heavy bombers were to be acquired by the end of 1943 through Lend-Lease contracts. This total was based on '300 latest US/British standardized B-17', nominally B-17Es covered by Lend-Lease requisition BSC 149, and 700 similarly described B-24s, nominally B-24Cs.

New-built Boeing B-17E Flying Fortress 41-9131 poses for Boeing's cameras in April 1942, prior to delivery to the US Army Air Force. With good endurance and straightforward flying characteristics, the type proved to an excellent addition to Coastal Command's anti-submarine resources. via Peter M Bowers

Fortress I AN531 during type performance and handling trials at A&AEE, Boscombe Down, April to August 1941. It is finished in USAAF Dark Olive Drab and Neutral Gray. Two months of preparation for service at Burtonwood Repair Depot followed after which it served with 90 Sqn as 'WP-O'. It joined 220 Sqn at Nutts Corner, Northern Ireland, in mid-February 1942 , becoming 'NR-O' (see photo page 23), and was one of two examples, the other being AN537 'NR-L', modified to carry depth charges and used for convoy patrols. In August 1942, it became a type trainer and hack with 206 Sqn at Benbecula coded 'VX-X' (see colour profile page 228) and from March to July 1943 underwent an overhaul with Marshall of Cambridge (see colour profile page 229) prior to a period of storage at 51 MU at Lichfield. via Peter Davies

The two models were due to begin coming off their respective production lines in June and July of 1941. Coastal Command's 'New Expansion Program' envisaged six Liberator squadrons and three Fortress squadrons in operation in the United Kingdom by March 1943 with the B-24 judged, because of its greater load carrying capability, to be "*the more desirable airplane*". The BAC, led by Sir Henry Self, was pragmatic in its approach to procurement, stating, "*…we should accept any B-17s and B-24s we can get and modify them as necessary to meet our needs.*"

The order for 300 B-17Es was placed on June 2, 1941, under Defense Aid contract DA-16. The aircraft were allocated US Army Air Corps (USAAC) serials 41-24340 to 41-24639 and assigned Air Ministry serials FA675 to FA823 and FH467 to FH617 (149 and 151 serials respectively). Unforeseen events would dictate that none of these USAAC or Air Ministry serials would be applied to B-17Es delivered to Britain, although, in a confusing twist, some of the FA-series would be applied to other Coastal Command-bound Fortresses under the same contract.

It was hoped that Britain would receive as many as 50 B-17Es per month over the period September 1941 to March 1943, but this expectation was quickly tempered by a revised Boeing production schedule that predicted maximum output would not be achieved until July 1942. Then, on November 5, 1941, the US Army Air Force (USAAF) – as the US Army Air Corps was renamed on June 20 of that year – announced that, since President Theodore Roosevelt had authorised a substantially larger 84-group Air Force, it would reduce the number of heavy bombers released to Britain from 255 to just 99: 15 B-17s and 84 B-24s.

In the meantime, RAF Bomber Command had placed its Fortress Mk Is (B-17Cs) in service on a trial basis with 90 Sqn based at Polebrook, Northamptonshire, in July of 1941. Poor results, primarily due to equipment failures at high altitude, and several losses resulted in the withdrawal of the Fortress from the strategic bombing role by late September. This was an opportune development for Coastal Command, as by late January 1942 the decision had been made to allocate some of the remaining Fortress Is and any B-17s that could be acquired through Lend-Lease to the maritime reconnaissance role, although this diversion from high-level bombing was not well received by senior USAAF commanders.

MIDDLE EAST SIDE SHOW

While Coastal Command's use of the Fortress is most often associated with anti-submarine operations over the Atlantic, a handful of Fortress Is had flown with the Command prior to the start of operations from the United Kingdom.

The remains of Fortress I AN521 'WP-K' of 90 Sqn Detachment are stripped for spare parts after being abandoned during a fuel consumption flight test on January 10, 1941. Two crew members lost their lives and the rest of the aircraft was completely destroyed. *Andy Thomas via Phil Listemann*

Crew members await rescue behind enemy lines in Libya after AN529 'WP-C' ran out of fuel while returning from a daylight bombing raid to Benghazi on November 8, 1941. Standing to the left is the aircraft's captain, F/O James C Stevenson, DFC, and to the right, Sgt Thomas J Gwynn. Seated, clockwise, starting near left, are F/Sgt Stephen F 'Dick' Pannell (facing the camera), squadron medical officer F/O Antony J 'Doc' Barwood, Sgt Colin S Barber, Sgt Lesslie E Wardill and co-pilot Sgt Kenneth H Brailsford. The photo was taken by P/O William M Struthers. Stevenson, Wardill, Struthers and Gwynn lost their lives with four other crewmates when Liberator II AL526 'G' of 159 Sqn failed to return from a one-aircraft Army cooperation flare-dropping operation along the Arakan coast of Burma on April 6/7, 1942. *via Matt Poole*

Waist gunner Sgt Colin Barber re-enters AN529 as he prepares to destroy the Sperry 0-1 bombsight, the dark object in the foreground. Moments later Barber fired three machine gun bursts, demolishing the classified equipment. via Matt Poole

to evade the fighters for 20 minutes and the Bf 110s finally broke away after the battle had reached 23,000ft (7,010m). The Fortress received a number of hits, though no major damage, and was later flown to 107 MU for repairs. Meanwhile, Stevenson had set off in AN532 thirty minutes after Stokes but found nothing and landed at 18:15.

The final bombing operation by an RAF Fortress took place on March 9 when F/O Stevenson took AN532 on a sortie against an Italian convoy, again with Lt Spademan on board to observe. The Fortress was intercepted by a lone Bf 110 and slightly damaged, while the bomb load was dropped prematurely. The rest of the month was taken up with various systems and bombsight tests and the test-dropping of an emergency supply canister designed by the squadron Medical Officer, F/O Antony J Barwood – unfortunately the parachute failed to open. Any chance of further operations was frustrated by unserviceability and lack of spare parts, and the detachment was wound down with the intention of sending the two surviving Fortresses to join those now with 220 Sqn at Nutts Corner in Northern Ireland – the last surviving ORB entry was for an abandoned test flight by AN518 on March 31, 1942, and the last confirmed logbook entry for an air test in AN532 on April 18. For reasons unknown, this decision was reversed and AN518 and AN532 were flown to India in late April 1942. Found to be in very poor condition, they were turned over to the Tenth Air Force, USAAF, in late September.

SEARCH TOOL

British scientists began developing radar in 1935 and in September of the following year work began on aerial radar direction finding. This effort naturally led to the idea of applying the new technology to detect surface vessels and in July 1937 trials began using an Anson fitted with a forward-looking system. The equipment worked reasonably well – with a range of over 5 (8 km)miles when used for detecting large surface ships – and evolved into ASV Mk I (Air-to-Surface Vessel) radar for the detection of surfaced submarines. Trials began in December 1939 using a Hudson and, although the sets were barely effective in locating submarines, with a range of only 3-½ miles (5.6km) at 200ft (60m), three Hudson squadrons received 12 systems and used them for rendezvousing with convoys and detecting coastlines as an aid to navigation. Work then began on ASV Mk II with the objective of producing a more robust and reliable system of greater range.

Scientists at the Telecommunications Research Establishment (TRE) at Hurn in Hampshire took the opportunity to add a sideways-looking capability that employed four 'stickleback' transmit aerial masts on the fuselage top and eight dipole receiving elements on each side of the rear fuselage. This enhancement allowed patrolling crews to perform 24-mile (40km) wide sweeps, 12 miles (20km) each side of the aircraft, and then turn 90 degrees to use the forward-looking homing aerials to home in on a contact. Trials of the sideways looking capability in mid-1940 using a Whitley demonstrated that a submarine could be detected at 12 miles (20km) bows-on from 2,000ft (610m) and at seven miles (11km) from 1,000ft (305m). Long Range ASV (LRASV) was subsequently installed on a variety of Coastal Command types including the Liberator I, Wellington, Whitley, Sunderland and Catalina. The large dorsal masts created considerable drag and the introduction into service of later types, including the Fortress, came with an operational requirement to use common transmit and receive aerials on the fuselage side, thereby eliminating the need for the masts.

Conflicting Demands

One of the most vexing conundrums of WWII revolved around the conflicting equipment needs of Bomber Command and Coastal Command. In order to survive, Britain had to protect its vital convoy routes and needed multi-engine, long-range aircraft to do this. Conversely, Britain's leadership was committed to an aggressive bombing policy that would hopefully crush German industry and open up the possibility of invading continental Europe, a strategy that needed the same type of aircraft.

The obvious counter argument was that without sufficient long-range aircraft to protect Allied convoys against U-boats, Britain might be brought to its knees before the bomber offensive could yield results. The outcome was a constant struggle by Coastal Command to secure equipment against the overwhelmingly strong views of those, including Churchill, who promoted a decisive victory by bombing. This situation was compounded when Germany invaded Russia in June 1941. Britain and the United States now needed to demonstrate to Stalin that they were doing everything they could to launch a second front, including taking the war to Germany through heavy bombing.

The much-anticipated Liberator Is began arriving in the spring of 1941. With a range of 2,400 miles (3,860km) they held the promise of escorting convoys across the 300 mile-wide (485km) Mid-Atlantic Gap in the North Atlantic. But there were to be many delays as decisions were made about equipment to be fitted and it would be August 1941 before 120 Sqn took delivery of its first aircraft at Nutts Corner, and September 20 before the first Liberator I patrol was flown. By early October, wastage, loans, and the allocation of aircraft to RAF Ferry Command and British Overseas Airways Corporation had reduced the squadron's pool of aircraft to just ten, and it would be another year before the squadron could move to Iceland and finally cover the Gap.

The entire bomber procurement plan, including British-funded contracts, then came under close scrutiny following Japan's attack on Pearl Harbor on December 7, 1941. In terms of heavy bombers, the result was an immediate re-evaluation of priorities for aircraft destined for Britain, with 50 of the 139 Liberator IIs already purchased being retained by the USAAF as LB-30s. Of the remainder, 71 were transferred to Britain but only a small proportion was available to Coastal Command and, with a range of only 1,800 miles (2,900km) and lacking ASV radar, they were less than ideal for Coastal Command's needs. A further supply constraint would emerge as some American military leaders, most notably Admiral Ernest King of the US Navy, favoured allocating resources to the Pacific Theatre, despite agreement between the Allies that winning the war in Europe was the first priority. This resulted in delayed release and periodic blocking of long-range aircraft earmarked for Britain.

Meanwhile, production of the first of 512 B-17Es for the USAAF had begun at Seattle, on September 5, 1941. The new model incorporated a large number of improvements to mitigate the B-17C's shortcomings, the most significant being a massive fin and rudder assembly with a long dorsal spine to improve directional stability at high altitude and greatly improved defensive armament, including the addition of an upper turret and ventral ball turret and two machine guns in the tail. Early deliveries went to the Pacific Theatre to help counter sweeping advances by Japanese forces – the 7th Bombardment Group began operating the B-17E in Java in January 1942 – while the first examples for the 8th Air Force in Europe would not arrive in Britain until July.

Given the pressing needs of the USAAF it is perhaps surprising that it released the first seven B-17Es to Britain early that same January as part of an initial batch of 30 aircraft destined for RAF Coastal Command under Army Release 10552. These were covered by the same requisition as the planned block of 300 Lend-Lease aircraft, BSC 149, and were accounted for under the original USAAC contract AC-15677 placed on August 30, 1940, for 277 B-17Es valued at US$70,449,955. For reasons unknown, B-17Es received by Britain were designated Fortress Mk IIA – rather than, as might be expected for the first variant delivered, Fortress Mk II – and allocated Air Ministry serial numbers from a new block, FK184 to FK213. (The official designations were Fortress GR Mk IIA and GR Mk II, the initials GR standing for General Reconnaissance. Fortress IIA or Mk IIA etc. are used throughout the rest of this text).

EARLY OPERATIONS

Three RAF Coastal Command squadrons were destined to operate the Fortress on general reconnaissance and anti-submarine duties, each having previously flown the Hudson. They were, in order of receiving the type, 220, 206 and 59 Sqns.

Previously based at Wick in Scotland, 220 Sqn (code letters 'NR' and motto, in Greek script, 'We Observe Unseen') was declared non-operational on January 1, 1942, and posted to Nutts Corner where it was to re-equip as part of 15 Group covering the Western Approaches into the port of Liverpool. On January 24, the squadron learned it would reform on the Fortress I, pending delivery of the first Fortress IIAs, and on January 29 a detachment arrived at Polebrook to begin conversion using four former 90 Sqn Fortress Is (AN527, AN530, AN531 and AN537). The two weeks of type familiarisation, general flying and emergency procedures under the command of S/Ldr Richard D Williams concluded with the Fortresses being flown to Nutts Corner by 220 Sqn personnel on February 13.

Training continued throughout February, March and April with, according to the squadron ORB, "*unabated zeal*". The newly-qualified squadron pilots were able to quickly check out their fellow pilots thanks to the docile handling characteristics of the Fortress. Typical training sorties included navigation exercises, descent through cloud (DTC) practice, low-level bombing (LLB) and night flying as well as dinghy and ditching drills and pigeon release. Between March 10 and 24, the squadron undertook a series of fuel consumption tests to establish the optimum boost and RPM settings for the predominantly low-level reconnaissance role to be undertaken by the former high-level bombers.

Fortress I AN537 narrowly escaped disaster during training on April 19 while being flown by F/Sgts Neville Carpenter and Ernest W Bristow. A swing to the right developed during the take-off roll for which Carpenter overcorrected, sending the Fortress off the runway to left. Carpenter elected to continue and just managed to clear the airfield boundary, the tailwheel snagging barbed wire atop the perimeter fence — the tailwheel subsequently burst on landing. Sadly, Bristow would lose his life just four months later.

Although the Fortresses were not yet operational, Air Vice-Marshal Ralph S Sorley advised his superior, Air Chief Marshal Sir Charles Portal, in a note dated March 4, 1942, that: "*In spite of the fact that the Fortress is not the best type as far as range and capacity for depth charges is concerned, I think we should still ask the Admiralty to accept the Fortress, with which C-in-C Coastal Command*

[Air Chief Marshall Sir Philip Bennet Joubert de la Ferté] *feels satisfied, provided there is a long* [production] *run of aircraft to provide the Squadron he requires."*

The note recorded that the Liberator III – a slightly modified version of the B-24D which followed the stop-gap Liberator II into service with Coastal Command in July 1942 – could be modified to carry twelve 340-pound (154kg) depth charges over a range of 2,070 miles (3,330km), while the Fortress could carry eight similar weapons over 1,860 miles (2,995km). In practice these figures proved to be overly optimistic for both types. Sorley also stated that work had begun in the United States to fit the Fortress with ASV Mk II radar and that it was hoped installation of the new 10-centimeter radar, called ASV Mk X in the United States, would begin later in the year. Fortresses already delivered to Britain were to be modified at the Burtonwood Repair Depot at Warrington in Lancashire.

The Liberator was not, however, without its drawbacks, as an early-1942 Coastal Command planning document reveals: *"The Liberator very decidedly does not meet the bad weather requirements as it has a particularly long landing run."*

220 Sqn's first operational flight with the Fortress took place on April 26, 1942, when F/Sgt Stanley J Houghton captained AN520 'D' in the search for B-24D Liberator 41-1119, intended for service with Coastal Command but missing over Donegal Bay at the end of its transatlantic delivery flight. Meanwhile, two of the squadron's other Fortress Is – AN531 'O' and AN537 'L' – were now considered ready for anti-submarine work, having been adapted to carry eight 250lb (113kg) Torpex-filled depth charges. The first escort operation was flown using AN531 on May 9, 1942, although the crew led by F/Sgt Kenneth L H Ramsden failed to meet up with Convoy 'L'. The squadron flew 140 patrol hours out of a total 308 hours flown during the month.

A fourth squadron aircraft, AN530 'F', was assigned to parachute depth charge experiments and was slightly damaged on May 12 while operating from Aldergrove when a weapon exploded on hitting the sea surface. The aircraft was struck by splinters but none of the crew, led by F/Lt Robert B Fleming, was hurt. AN530 was also used for an air-sea rescue operation on May 24 with F/O Kenneth W J Tarrant at the controls. Tarrant was also in command of AN537 when it was fired on by a destroyer off the coast of Ireland while returning from a convoy escort on June 6 – fortunately, no hits were sustained.

A base change to nearby Ballykelly took place on June 20 and on July 18, F/O John Wright and crew took Fortress I AN537 on its final anti-submarine patrol while AN531 performed its last operational flight with 220 Sqn on July 27 with F/Sgt George D Gamble as captain. The Fortress I sorties were comparatively uneventful, the only attack taking place on May 18, 1942, when the crew of AN537 under F/O Gerry R Haggas dropped depth charges on a school of porpoises mistaken for

Fortress I AN531 'WP-O' at Nutts Corner, Northern Ireland, shortly after transfer from 90 Sqn to 220 Sqn on February 13, 1942. Camouflage colours are believed to be Dark Green and possibly Dark Sea Grey with blue under surfaces. It became 'NR-O' in service with 220 Sqn. IWM HU.96589

This well-known portrait of Fortress I AN537 'NR-L' escorting a convoy has appeared in two forms: with and without its 220 Sqn codes and Air Ministry serial. Examination of both versions suggests that they have been airbrushed by censors to conceal the various ASV Mk II aerial arrays.

AN537 was allocated to 220 Sqn on February 12, 1942, and was one of two Fortress Is with the unit – the other being AN531 – to be modified to carry depth charges and flown on convoy escorts from Nutts Corner and Ballykelly. Former 220 Sqn pilot Gerry Haggas, who flew both aircraft on operations, confirmed to the Author that neither was equipped with ASV Mk II radar while with the unit.

According to its movement card, AN537 was next assigned to Coastal Command Development Unit (CCDU), also based at Ballykelly, on June 20, although the aircraft continued to fly with 220 Sqn until mid-July, suggesting that the unit's Fortresses were pooled with CCDU. Quite when and where ASV Mk II was installed is not known but it seems likely that the modification took place at the end of July and that the aircraft flew trials with CCDU still in 220 Sqn markings. AN537 suffered Cat. B damage on August 17 and was flown to Marshall at Cambridge for repairs – whether it returned to Ballykelly for further trials with CCDU is not known but, as noted below, the Fortress was airworthy in November.

The lower version of the photograph held by the Imperial War Museum is dated October 1942. If accurate, this date would tend to confirm that AN537 was fitted with ASV Mk II radar shortly after leaving 220 Sqn and subsequently used for testing. As described in the main text, ASV Mk II trials using Fortress IIA FK190 were completed on August 14, 1942 with the response to the test report stating that the dorsal 'stickleback' installation was unsatisfactory not appearing until September 18.

John Rabbets was an air cadet in the Lichfield area during the latter part of World War Two, and made a sketch of AN537, still equipped with ASV Mk II radar and wearing 220 Sqn markings 'NR-L', while visiting 51 MU at Lichfield in late 1942. "I clearly remember seeing this Fortress I in a hangar, illuminated by the greenish-white lights so characteristic of the time. The duty RAF corporal told me I should not have seen it and hastily closed the hangar door but I had seen enough to make a drawing and to note the colours (see following page). What struck me so forcibly was the spiky nature of the ASV aerials and their profusion. AN537 was striking in her green and grey/white finish, particularly when seen against a hangar full of Wellington IIIs and Xs in their sombre Bomber Command green and brown/black." *(see colour profile page 228).* Well-known author and wartime enthusiast Michael J F Bowyer noted AN537 at Cambridge following overhaul by Marshall on February 28, 1943. It was in Temperate Sea and White finish but now without ASV Mk II radar and code letters, suggesting that the ASV installation was removed by Marshall. AN537 departed Cambridge for 29 MU at High Ercall on March 27 and in November moved to 51 MU at Lichfield.

The aircraft was subsequently allocated to 1674 HCU at Aldergrove on December 24, 1943, and assigned to 214 Sqn as a trainer on March 19, 1944. It was struck off charge on September 1 of that year. via Andy Thomas and Phil Butler

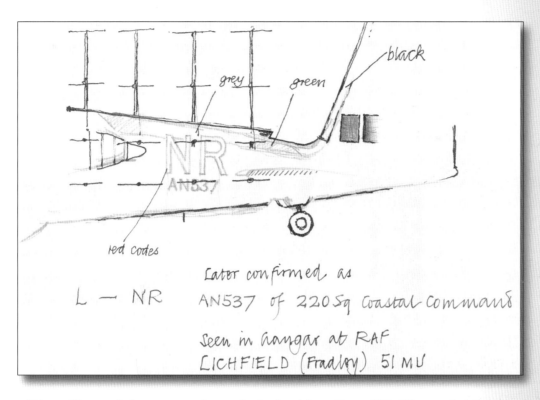

grey

green

black

NR

AN537

red codes

L — NR

Later confirmed as AN537 of 220 Sq Coastal Command

Seen in hangar at RAF LICHFIELD (Fradley) 51 MU

John Rabbets' original pencil sketch of Fortress I AN537 'NR-L' at 51 MU, Lichfield, late 1942, inked over by John for clarity and with his additional notes. John Rabbets

a U-boat. The attack drew a somewhat sardonic signal from Group HQ: "*Congratulations to crew of "L" 220 for successful attack on enemy in which 50 were destroyed.*" All told, 220 Sqn's Fortress Is flew 30 operational sorties, establishing the type as a reliable long-range maritime reconnaissance platform.

Following their use by 220 Sqn, three of the four Fortress Is originally assigned to the unit – AN530, AN531 and AN537 – together with AN520 'D' which joined the squadron in April 1942, were allocated to the Coastal Command Development Unit (CCDU), also based at Ballykelly from June 20. The Unit's purpose was to test new equipment being introduced to Coastal Command and to advise on tactical deployment of the equipment and the aircraft in which it was installed. Given that 220 Sqn continued to use AN531 and AN537 on convoy patrols until mid-to-late July, it seems likely that the aircraft were operated in a pooling arrangement with CCDU. According to their movement cards, the Fortress Is remained with CCDU for between one and two months each before being assigned to other units, most notably Coastal Command's second operational Fortress unit, 206 Sqn. As previously noted, AN537 was an exception as it was at some point fitted with ASV Mk II radar and likely used by CCDU for trials. The fifth example allocated to 220 Sqn, AN527 'A', remained at Ballykelly until June 1943, three months before the unit flew its last United Kingdom based Fortress 'op'.

King George VI inspects a 220 Sqn detachment during a visit to Nutts Corner on June 26, 1942. The King is accompanied by the unit's commanding officer, W/Cdr Richard T F Gates. The Fortress I, one of three flown in from Ballykelly for the inspection, retains the high-level bombing camouflage worn during service with 90 Sqn. via Richard Gates (son of W/Cdr Gates)

Above: Six newly-minted Sgt pilots, four of whom would become Fortress captains with 220 Sqn. F/Sgt Kenneth L H Ramsden, front right, captained the first convoy patrol by a Coastal Command Fortress when he took Fortress I AN531 'O' aloft on May 9, 1942. On February 3, 1943, he sank U-boat U-265 while in command of Fortress IIA FL456 'N'. Like Ramsden, F/Sgt George D Gamble, front centre, flew Hudsons with 220 Sqn before the arrival of the Fortress Is. He was awarded the British Empire Medal for twice entering a burning aircraft to rescue crew members after being compelled by weather to force-land Hudson AM670 on January 4, 1942, while flying from Wick to Nutts Corner. Gamble disappeared on November 24, 1944, after ditching a Mitchell while serving with 111 OTU at Nassau in the Bahamas. F/Sgt Wilfred R 'Pip' Travell, front left, also initially flew Hudsons with 220 Sqn. After a brief period flying Miles Martinet target-towing aircraft at Long Kesh, he was re-posted to the squadron in February 1943 to fly Fortresses. On March 13, 1944, he contributed to the sinking of U-575 while flying Fortress IIA FL459 'J' from the Azores. F/Sgt Neville 'Chips' Carpenter, centre rear, flew Fortress Is from their earliest days with 220 Sqn at Nutts Corner and flew from both Benbecula and the Azores on Fortress IIAs and IIs. Of the other two, F/Sgt George R Heppell, DFM, left rear, also flew Hudsons with 220 Sqn and was later killed on April 6, 1942, when Hudson III AE565 struck a tree and crashed near Saxthorpe in Norfolk. The sixth pilot, rear right, is an otherwise unidentified F/Sgt Ramsey. Newark Air Museum

B-17F modification line at the Cheyenne Modification Center in May 1943. All 64 of Coastal Command's B-17Es and B-17Fs passed through this facility between January and October 1942. United Airlines

CHEYENNE MODIFICATION CENTER

It became obvious to the American government shortly after declaring war against the Axis that it would need to retain at least some aircraft ordered by friendly powers for its own use, and these aircraft would require modification before they could be operated by the USAAF. It was also realised that adding modifications to new aircraft after they had left a prime contractor's facilities was far more efficient than introducing changes on the production line. Army Air Force Materiel Command therefore began planning a series of modification centres throughout the United States to make modifications, additions and adjustments to aircraft that had left their parent factory.

United Air Lines Transport Corporation had operated a repair base at Cheyenne Municipal Airport, Cheyenne, Wyoming since 1928. On January 9, 1942, the company received authorization from Materiel Command to modify two unidentified Boeing B-17B Fortresses for an undisclosed special mission. The two former training aircraft were stripped of all armament and bombing equipment and fitted with a variety of cameras and long-range fuel cells at a cost of $40,789.99. Both were delivered to the USAAF on February 15, 1942, and moved to Alaska. One of the high-flying B-17Bs would later fly over Japan to secure reconnaissance photographs in preparation for the famous Doolittle Raid on April 18 of that year.

Meanwhile, United Air Lines had begun its second B-17 project following receipt of a Letter of Intent from Materiel Command dated January 24, 1942. It authorised the company to modify the 30 'Army Release' B-17Es for Britain under the provisions of the Lend-Lease Act at an estimated cost of $31,800.00.

Initial modifications were largely based on the RAF's experience with the Fortress I, the final details being worked out by representatives from Boeing, United and the BAC. Specified changes included installing brackets for the British Mk IX bomb sight (of no value for low-level attacks against U-boats), bomb rack adapters and wiring for nose and tail fusing, recognition lights, demand oxygen regulators and system charging adapters, a British-style Verey pistol, a flare launching chute and racks for flares and drift markers, a ground start cart plug fitting, electrical sockets for heated clothing at crew stations (never used on Coastal Command operations) and a dinghy transmitter for the SCR-578 'Gibson Girl' air-sea rescue radio. In addition, provision was made for fitting R.3003 (IFF Mk II) and R.3090 (IFF Mk III) receiver/transmitters and an SCR-287 low frequency radio system comprised of a BC-348 receiver, a BC-375 transmitter and a trailing aerial system was completed. Finally, the radio compass was modified, the pilot's compass changed to a Type B-16, the fuel systems protected against aromatic fuels, and the fuel tank labels marked in Imperial gallons.

B-17Es 41-2610 and 41-2611 at Seattle February 13, 1942, painted in Dark Olive Drab and Neutral Gray with RAF markings. Allocated to 'Britain' under Lend-Lease, they were among 16 examples transferred back to the US Army Air Force, later serving together in the Pacific with the 5th Bombardment Squadron, 11th Bombardment Group. 41-2610 crashed at Espiritu Santo on August 24, 1942, while 41-2611 was returned to the United States in January 1944 and sold for scrap in June 1945. Boeing via Peter M Bowers

The first ten or so Fortress IIAs (B-17Es) delivered to Britain wore Type A1 fuselage and Type B wing roundels applied over the standard USAAF Dark Olive Drab and Neutral Gray scheme, all applied by Boeing at Seattle. The USAAF serial, 12516, can still be discerned on the tail of FK187, seen flying over the United Kingdom during performance and handling trials with the A&AEE at Boscombe Down. MAP

The first aircraft, 41-2513, arrived at Cheyenne on January 26, 1942, while three more reached Cheyenne on February 5, followed by a further three on February 10. Each arrived from Boeing's plant in Seattle wearing standard USAAF Dark Olive Drab and Neutral Gray finish with so-called Type A1 RAF fuselage roundels, equal-banded fin flash, Type B upper wing roundels and the five-digit USAAF serial in yellow on the tail.

The influx of new work in the middle of winter required construction of two temporary canvas hangars to house the nose and wings of each Fortress, with heating provided by blowing warm air through the fuselage from furnaces located at the tail. Work began on February 5 under contract W535 ac 25500 while the original Letter of Intent was replaced on February 9 to recognize higher than anticipated costs, the total contract now amounting to $79,500.

The first Fortress IIA for the RAF, now marked FK184, was inspected by Royal Air Force representatives at Cheyenne on March 11 and handed over to USAAF Ferrying Command. It was subsequently flown to Dorval, Quebec to await delivery to Britain by RAF Ferry Command. The last of the initial batch of 30 aircraft was completed by the end of May 1942.

Of related interest, United received a request from Materiel Command on March 11, 1942, that it establish a permanent modification centre to modify large numbers of B-17s since Boeing felt, unlike other major manufacturers, that it could not undertake such work. The result was Modification Center #10, built on 90 acres (36ha) on the northeast corner of the Cheyenne Municipal Airport and destined to become the engineering hub for all B-17 modification centres. At peak throughput, eleven B-17s emerged from the Cheyenne facility each day and by April 1945, United Air Lines had processed 5,680 Fortresses.

On May 27, 1942, United received a second Letter of Intent authorizing modification of a further 23 B-17Es for Britain, for a total of 53 aircraft. The second batch was allocated Air Ministry serials from another new block of 54 serials, FL449 to FL502, although, as with the balance of the first batch of 30 aircraft, the Air Ministry serials were not allocated in sequence with their corresponding USAAF serials and unforeseen events would dictate that not all 54 Air Ministry serials would be used. (See Appendix A for individual aircraft histories).

According to United's records, the Cheyenne Modification Center delivered six RAF-bound B-17Es by the end of March with eleven following in April, 14 in May, 20 in June, seven in July and four in August, for a total of 62 – the Air Ministry actually received 45. The reason for the three different totals – 53 authorised, 62 recorded by United as modified and 45 B-17Es actually delivered – was the reallocation of aircraft destined for Britain to the USAAF as the latter scrambled to build its strategic bombing forces in Europe and the Pacific. According to records maintained by the BAC's statistics branch, 16 B-17Es over and above the 45 delivered were 'taken back' by the USAAF over April and June 1942 for a total of 61 aircraft – another example appears in USAAF records as having originally been allocated to Britain for a total of 62. (See notes in Appendix A for a listing of aircraft allocated to Britain).

The first Fortress IIAs were delivered to Britain without the nose astrodome and ASV Mk II radar required by Coastal Command. However, the eighth aircraft delivered, FK193, is known to have been fitted with an astrodome – almost certainly at Cheyenne since it was not a standard feature of the B-17E – while, from around the fifteenth example, aircraft were delivered with ASV Mk II and early search and homing aerial arrays installed.

Camouflage and markings applied to Fortress IIAs prior to delivery fell into three categories. The first ten or so aircraft delivered from Cheyenne to Dorval wore the standard USAAF Dark Olive Drab and Neutral Gray scheme with Type A1 fuselage roundels, equal-banded fin flashes and Type B upper wing roundels. These were followed by aircraft finished in Coastal Command's then standard Temperate Sea scheme of Extra Dark Sea Grey and Dark Slate Grey on the upper surfaces and fuselage sides, Sky under surfaces and, with at least one known exception, Type C1 fuselage roundels and unequal-banded fin flashes. The third scheme, formerly introduced in July 1942, was the definitive Coastal Command Fortress scheme of Temperate Sea upper surfaces with White fuselage sides, under surfaces, and the fin and rudder assembly. This finish was applied to all squadron-bound Fortress IIAs, either at Burtonwood following delivery across the Atlantic Atlantic or in the United States in the case of later deliveries. (See Appendix L for a broader discussion of Coastal Command Fortress camouflage and markings and Appendix M for examples of nose artwork).

In compliance with what are assumed to have been Lend-Lease requirements, aircraft continued to display their original USAAF data block stencil below the rearmost nose window on the port side, regardless of the paint scheme applied, while those that did not have their fins painted White prior to delivery still wore their yellow USAAF serial.

Air Ministry serial numbers were applied to the Fortress IIAs at Cheyenne just prior to delivery and one of the 16 examples allocated to Britain but retained by the USAAF, 41-9234, had already been modified, painted and marked as FL461 when it was reassigned to the 5th Air Force in the Pacific. This is the only known example of a 'wasted' Air Ministry serial applied to a B-17E reclaimed by the USAAF. (See Appendix K for the full history of this aircraft).

Termination of B-17E production on May 28, 1942, prevented the Air Ministry from receiving more Fortress IIAs and the 512th and final B-17E, 41-9245, became the last example allocated to Britain. Because the Air Ministry serials were not allocated in sequence with the USAAF serials, it was 41-9238 that received the last Air Ministry serial number to be allocated from the FL series, FL464. All 45 B-17Es delivered to Britain were classified as 'Army Release' although they were still covered by Lend-Lease requisition BSC 149.

Scene at Dorval Airport, Quebec, mid-May 1942. More than a dozen Lockheed Venturas are visible, together with two North American B-25D Mitchells, Consolidated B-24D Liberator 41-1124 and Fortress IIA FK193/41-2526. The Fortress was the tenth of its type delivered to Dorval on its way to the United Kingdom and is finished in USAAF Dark Olive Drab and Neutral Gray. It served with 220 Sqn throughout the entire campaign against the U-boats. The Liberator, 41-1124, was one of eleven unmodified B-24Ds rushed to the UK to bolster Coastal Command's anti-submarine capabilities – it became Liberator IIIA FV345. All aircraft wear Type A1 fuselage roundels, officially replaced by the Type C1 on April 30, 1942. National Archives (Canada) PA114763

FORTRESS II

The first example of the improved B-17F came off Boeing's production line at Seattle on May 30, 1942. Externally almost identical to the B-17E, the B-17F could be distinguished by its moulded, frameless nose cone and broader propeller blades for the improved Wright R-1820-97 Cyclone engines. The first six examples for Coastal Command were delivered to Cheyenne at the end of August 1942, again covered by requisition BSC 149 but this time under Lend-Lease contract DA-AC16. These aircraft, 41-24594 to 41-24599, were drawn from the USAAF serial number block originally allocated to the 300 B-17Es planned for delivery to Britain through Lend-Lease but, with the termination of B-17E production, these serials had been applied to the first 300 production B-17Fs. A further six B-17Fs arrived at Cheyenne in September followed by another seven in October for a total of 19 Boeing-built B-17Fs for the RAF – the latter 13 aircraft were covered by Army Release contract AC-20292. The B-17Fs received the same modifications as later deliveries of the B-17E, including an astrodome and the homing aerials for ASV Mk II radar but not the fuselage-mounted search aerials.

The first 12 aircraft featured B-17E-style cheek windows in the nose, while the remaining seven were modified at Cheyenne with the larger staggered cheek gun windows normally associated with the B-17F. Some examples were also fitted with additional fuel cells near the wingtips known as 'Tokyo Tanks' (or 'Tokio Tanks' as they are referred to in the Air Ministry's Pilot's Notes for the Fortress). The B-17F became the Fortress II in Coastal Command service and all were painted in the Temperate Sea and White scheme prior to delivery to the United Kingdom.

The 19 Fortress IIs were allocated Air Ministry serials FA695 to FA713 from the series FA675 to FA823, part of the block of 300 serials originally allocated to RAF-bound B-17Es. The first 20 serials from the series were apparently skipped. However, three early B-17Fs are known to have been marked as FA678, FA683 and FA684 and painted with Type A1 roundels. No records have been found to indicate that these aircraft were allocated to Britain, passed through Cheyenne or were taken back by the USAAF. It is also unknown if the remaining Air Ministry serials from the range FA675 to FA694 were applied to B-17Fs that went on to serve with the USAAF. But the fact that some serials were applied strongly suggests that possibility and further complicates confirming how many B-17Es and B-17Fs were at least nominally allocated to Britain. And to compound

Fortress II FA711 at Wayne County Airport, Detroit, on December 19, 1942, prior to being ferried to Prestwick via Houlton, Maine and Gander, Newfoundland by a crew led by Arthur G Sims. It is fitted with British-designed under-wing and nose-mounted Yagi homing aerials for ASV Mk II radar but not the ineffective American-designed sideways-looking wire aerials installed at Cheyenne on the RAF-bound Fortress IIAs. FA711 served with 206 Sqn as '1-E' in the Azores before being struck off charge in August 1944 while assigned to Scottish Aviation for repairs. via Boeing

Poor quality but interesting photocopy image of Fortress II FA705 at Burtonwood on December 17, 1942, en route to 29 MU, High Ercall for modification. It later became FA705 '1-U' of 206 Sqn in the Azores and was lost on January 6, 1944, when shot down while attacking U-boat U-270 (see photo page 110, colour profile page 232 and aircrew profile for her last captain, S/Ldr Anthony J Pinhorn, DFC, page 178). Burtonwood Association

Left, centre: Example of an early B-17F assigned an Air Ministry serial but retained by the USAAF, 41-24368 The Maverick of the 352nd BS, 301st BG based at Tafaraoui, Algeria, is marked FA683 and shows remnants of a Type A1 fuselage roundel (see Appendix A for listing of other known tie-ups for serials FA675-FA694). 301st Veterans Association via Steve Birdsall

Left: Close-up from image below of B-17F *Special Delivery* showing Air Ministry serial FA684 and Type A1 roundel to the extreme right. via Peter M Bowers

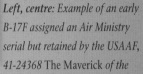

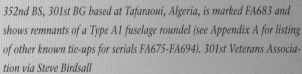

Below: Early 1943 scene at a salvage yard in North Africa as two early production B-17Fs are stripped for spare parts. The nearer aircraft, 41-24442 *Little Eva*, was damaged by Luftwaffe bombing on December 23, 1942. The other is 41-24369 *Special Delivery*, damaged on December 15, and sporting the 'unused' Air Ministry serial FA684 and a Type A1 roundel overpainted with USAAF markings (see detail above). via Peter M Bowers

the issue further, B-17F 41-24363 is known to have been marked as FA672, a serial allocated and applied to a Martin Baltimore V.

Certainly the Air Ministry intended to use some of the remaining FA series serials, FA714 to FA823, and the BAC later requested additional B-17s. But Coastal Command would receive only a few additional Fortresses in the form of three B-17Gs, of which more later.

Further complicating the analysis of modifications versus deliveries, United Air Lines' records indicate that a total of '74 [B-17s] were modified and delivered to the British', ten more than the 64 Fortress IIAs and IIs actually delivered. Unfortunately, no breakdown by model appears to have survived.

TRANSATLANTIC DELIVERY

Fewer than one hundred aircraft had crossed the Atlantic by 1939, while around another fifty had been lost in the attempt. Given these discouraging statistics, it is perhaps understandable that initial deliveries of desperately-needed Hudsons, purchased by Britain prior to the start of World War Two to bolster its maritime reconnaissance capabilities, were made by sea.

The need to place aircraft in service as soon as possible, a shortage of shipping capacity, and the threat of losing precious aircraft to sinkings by U-boats naturally spawned the idea of delivering aircraft by air. There was much resistance to the scheme – most especially from Britain's Air Ministry who had ordered the aircraft in the first place – and it was not until November 10, 1940, that seven Hudson IIIs, led by the indomitable Capt Donald C T 'Don' Bennett, took off from the new airfield at Gander, Newfoundland, to arrive safely at Aldergrove, Northern Ireland the following day. At one stroke, the delay from manufacturer's test flight to delivery to Britain had been reduced from three months to less than ten days.

The autumn of 1941 saw the completion of the huge Royal Canadian Air Force (RCAF) base at Dorval airport, Montreal, Quebec. Dorval would become the main collection point for aircraft flown across the North Atlantic and the centre of operations for the newly-created RAF Ferry Command. Coastal Command would be the major beneficiary of early deliveries from Dorval, their Hudsons and Liberators arriving in increasing numbers at the transatlantic air terminus at Prestwick in Ayrshire, Scotland.

Impressive view of Gander airfield with dozens of Prestwick-bound Liberators and Fortresses awaiting delivery - all but one of Coastal Command's Fortress IIAs and IIs passed through Gander. The wide runway in the foreground, 09/27, measured 4,800 by 1,200 feet (1,463 by 366m), reputedly to ease identification and landings for pilots weary at the end of an east-to-west Atlantic crossing. North Atlantic Aviation Museum

Fortress IIA FK184 photographed at Prestwick on April 1, 1942, just after shut-down at the end of its overnight ferry flight from Gander, Newfoundland, Canada. FK184 was the first of its type converted for RAF Coastal Command and the first to arrive in the United Kingdom – it is painted in Dark Olive Drab with Neutral Gray undersides. It is recorded as serving in the training role with 206 Sqn at Benbecula as 'VX-K' in August and September of 1942 but then 'disappears' from operational records until resurfacing as 'AD-A' with 251 (Met) Sqn at Reykjavik, Iceland, in March 1945. IWM CH.17922

Fortress IIA FK184, now painted in Coastal Command's Temperate Sea and White scheme but without squadron code letters. The photograph was presumably taken after the aircraft had passed through Burtonwood in preparation for Coastal Command service but prior to entering service with 206 Sqn as 'VX-K'. Like other early deliveries, it is not fitted with an astrodome. IWM CH.8619

Fortress IIA FK209, alias 41-9203, photographed at Dorval, Quebec on August 24, 1942, while en route to Britain. In this view the Temperate Sea upper camouflage scheme consists of Dark Slate Grey (the darker hue in this photograph, actually a muted mid-green) while the lighter hue is Extra Dark Sea Grey – the undersides are Sky. The letters 'AVD' or 'AVO' visible in front of the Air Ministry serial are likely a Cheyenne Modification Center code. The aircraft is fitted with British-designed Yagi homing aerials in the nose and under the wings and American-designed search aerials on the rear fuselage.

Delivered to 59 Sqn in December 1942, FK209 'J' was shot down by a Junkers Ju 88C on March 23, 1943, while based at Chivenor, Devon. The event is described in the main text and in the aircrew profiles for pilot F/O Richard J Weatherhead and his adversary, Oblt Hermann Horstmann. Identifiable aircraft to the rear include Fortress IIA FL450 (see colour profile page 230), Noorduyn-built Harvard IIB FE275 and Douglas A-20C Havoc 41-19198. Department of National Defense Photo Unit PL-11069

One of Ferry Command's older pilots, 37-year-old Robert E Perlick of Houston, Texas, arrived at Dorval after a term with the Air Transport Auxiliary (ATA) in the United Kingdom – he wears the organisation's uniform in the accompanying photograph. During his term with the ATA, Perlick delivered a diverse range of RAF types including the Anson, Battle, Blenheim, Botha, Henley, Hereford, Hurricane, Lysander, Roc, Spitfire, Wellington and Whitley. As a captain with Ferry Command, he delivered Fortress IIA FL450 (see above and profile page 230) in addition to a wide variety of other types, including no less than 16 Consolidated PBYs of various models. Directorate of History and Heritage

The RAF's Fortress IIAs and IIs received a minimum of testing at Cheyenne before being ferried onward by military crews from USAAF Ferrying Command. In most cases the aircraft were delivered to Dorval via Wayne County Airport on the outskirts of Detroit, Michigan, although, as Dorval became congested and an overflow location was required, several were delivered to Houlton Airport in Maine, again via Wayne County. Both Houlton and Wayne County were home to USAAF Ferrying Command ground support bases, the 314th Materiel Squadron (Special) and the 308th Materiel Squadron (Special) respectively, and Wayne County Airport would later become Willow Run Airport. Following handover to RAF Ferry Command at Dorval or Houlton, each Fortress was tested by the Flight Test Department before being assigned a crew and flown to Gander. Here each aircraft received a final inspection before the long ferry flight to Prestwick.

The first Fortress IIA to be ferried to Britain, FK184, arrived at Gander from Dorval via Dartmouth, Nova Scotia on March 28, 1942. Unfortunately the pilot's name does not appear on crew assignment records, although the civilian co-pilot is known to have been George Insley Bliss of Pasadena, California (see aircrew profile page 156). Interestingly, no less than 21 Hudsons, three Liberators, one LB-30 and one Catalina arrived at Gander the same day, all destined for Coastal Command. After final checks, the Fortress departed three days later on March 31 and arrived at Prestwick the following morning.

There were a couple of other exceptions to the standard Dorval-Gander-Prestwick routing. Dillon M Teel and crew set off for Prestwick from Goose Bay, Newfoundland, rather than Gander in Fortress IIA FK186 on June 9, 1942, and remained grounded at Reykjavik, Iceland for over two weeks. Fortress II FA709, flown by British pilot Arthur G Sims, was inexplicably delivered via the South Atlantic ferry route: West Palm Beach in Florida, Trinidad, Belem and Natal in Brazil, Bathurst and Yundum in Africa, Gibraltar, and Portreath in Cornwall. Other aircraft touched down at Bangor, Maine and Sydney, Nova Scotia en route to Gander, likely due to poor weather en route.

A typical Gander-Prestwick leg took around 9½ hours and the majority were overnight flights to ensure a daytime arrival. Designated alternate destinations included Silloth in Cumberland, Squires Gate Airport at Blackpool, Lancashire, and Aldergrove in Northern Ireland. While most crews completed the planned direct flight to Prestwick, four aircraft are known to have been involved in diversions: Fortress IIAs FK196 to Eglinton and FL449 to Ballykelly, both in Northern Ireland, Fortress IIA FL459 to Silloth, and Fortress II FA705 to Limavady, also in Northern Ireland.

Co-pilot F/Sgt Eric Stone, second from the right, and the crew that ferried Fortress IIA FK196 to the United Kingdom, enjoy the sights of Washington, DC, with a USAAF guide. The photograph is believed to have been taken by the crew's captain, F/Lt Walter E Edser. via Lynda Matthews

PIONEERING CREWS

RAF Ferry Command crews were made up largely of contracted civilians recruited from Britain, Canada, the United States, France and other Allied countries. Trainee pilots received $10 Canadian per day while co-pilots received $800 per month and captains $1,000. A five-man Fortress ferry crew consisted of a captain, co-pilot, navigator, engineer and radio operator, while a few passengers were carried on occasions. For example, early delivery FK185 departed Dorval with five passengers, three of whom were dropped off at Gander while the other two, including USAAF officer Lt Col Ellis, continued to Prestwick.

A review of known Fortress ferry captains reveals an amazing range of experiences among a virtual who's who of Ferry Command personalities. The pilot of Fortress II FA704, Ralph E Adams of Emorry, Texas, was captain of one of the seven Hudson IIIs that took part in the first Gander-to-Aldergrove ferry flight. San Francisco native Robert E Perlick, who delivered Fortress IIA FL450, held the record for the 'fastest' delivery of a Consolidated PBY-5A Catalina from Bermuda to Scotland: 19 hours 50 minutes.

Famous Canadian Arctic pilot Louis Bisson ferried Fortress IIA FK199 while W L Sheldon Luck, a future stalwart of specialty aviation in Canada, delivered Fortress II FA695. Another well-known Canadian aviator and author of several books on his Ferry Command experiences, Donald M

Fortress IIA FK197 alongside a Scottish Aviation hangar at Prestwick in late August 1942. Ferried to Prestwick by a crew led by Robert E Coffman that May, it is about to be modified by Scottish Aviation "for trial installation of special wireless" – in fact ASV Mk II radar – and would spend the next 2½ years based at Prestwick. A relatively early delivery to Britain – it was the 12th Fortress IIA delivered to Dorval – it likely received its Temperate Sea and White camouflage scheme at Burtonwood following the transatlantic flight. FK197 served with 251 (Met) Sqn from May 1945, coded 'AD-E' (see page 136). Provincial Archives of Newfoundland and Labrador B 21-186

McVicar, captained Fortress IIs FA699 and FA710 and would later receive the Order of the British Empire for his many special contributions to the delivery of Lend-Lease aircraft.

American Robert E Coffman was captain of Fortress IIAs FK197 and FL452. He and two Canadian crewmembers would later miraculously survive an eleven-day ordeal, marooned on a large rock off the Greenland coast after ditching Handley Page Hampden I AE309 on a west-bound flight to Canada. Arthur G Sims delivered Fortress IIs FA709 and FA711 and later successfully belly-landed de Havilland Mosquito B.25 KA970 at Prestwick after a pneumatic system air bottle exploded and blew a seven-foot-long (2.13m) hole in the rear fuselage. (See Appendix B for profiles for three Ferry Command pilots who delivered Fortresses to Britain, including Arthur Sims).

Following arrival at Prestwick, most crews boarded a Liberator of the Return Ferry Service for the return trip to Dorval. Less frequently, and certainly less popularly, they were assigned to a transport ship destined for a port on the Eastern Seaboard from where they returned to Dorval by train. Amazingly, not a single Ferry Command pilot was lost at sea while returning to North America.

The delivery of FK196 was something of an exception in that it was crewed by squadron personnel. Effective February 21, 1942, a detachment of six 220 Sqn aircrew led by F/Lt Walter E Edser and including co-pilot F/Sgt Eric Stone, squadron gunnery leader F/O William E Nicholas, DFC, P/O Christopher E Lewis, and Sgts Hall and House were sent to the United States to advise American technicians on the development of the Fortress for Coastal Command operations and to pass on low-level bombing skills to USAAF pilots. Sailing on the SS *Strategist*, they underwent type training on USAAF B-17Es at Hendricks Field, Sebring, Florida, under the tutelage of US Army pilot, 1st Lt Perna, from March 26 to April 11. On April 12, Edser and crew were reassigned to RAF Ferry Command at Dorval and, after three flights in temporarily resident Fortress IIA FK192/41-2615, ferried FK196 to the United Kingdom. As noted earlier, the usual flight time from Gander to Prestwick for a Fortress was 9½ hours but on this occasion a fuel-stretching 11½ hours were needed, with the aircraft departing Gander on May 7 and landing at Eglinton the following morning.

According to the 220 Sqn ORB, the Fortress arrived *"with not too much petrol to spare"*. Edser and his crew flew on to Prestwick on May 9 and then rejoined their unit at Nutts Corner.

Of related interest, crew member William Nicholas received the Order of the British Empire in January 1944 for his outstanding contribution to training 220 Sqn air gunners while also undertaking 130 operational sorties over a three-and-a-half-year period.

Fortress deliveries continued at a steady rate with all but four of the 45 Fortress IIAs arriving at Prestwick by late September 1942. Of the exceptions, FK189 was assigned to the US Army Air Force's flight test facility at Wright Field, Dayton, Ohio on March 24, 1942. It is believed that the Fortress, like a pair of RAF-bound LB-30s, was engaged in ASV radar trials and by the time it left for Wayne County, Detroit on October 10 on its way to Prestwick it had accumulated 308.6 flight hours. FK205 is recorded as having been 'on special duty' in the United States and moved between a number of sites from June 14, 1942 – including Wright Field – until it was finally delivered to Prestwick in early January 1943. After passing through Cheyenne, FK198 remained, for reasons unknown, at Wayne County from mid-May 1942 until it proceeded to Dorval in mid-October. The first Fortress II to be completed, FA697, was ferried to Dorval and on to Britain in early November 1942, while the last, FA710, arrived at Prestwick in March 1943.

The last Coastal Command Fortress to be ferried to Britain, Mk IIA FK192, arrived at Dorval in mid-April 1942 but did not touch down at Prestwick until May 16 of the following year. There is no record, as suggested elsewhere, that the Fortress was taken on charge by the RCAF. However, aircrew assignment cards indicate FK192 undertook numerous 'special flights' from Dorval to USAAF Ferrying Command headquarters at Presque Ile in northern Maine, while several records, including a logbook, refer to the Fortress being used for training. Its captain for the flight to Prestwick was William J Vanderkloot, perhaps the most famous of all Ferry Command pilots. The 28-year-old American had just completed an assignment as Churchill's pilot, flying his personal Liberator II AL504 *Commando* – still in its original twin-tail configuration – to Cairo, Tehran, Moscow and Casablanca among other famous destinations. Vanderkloot would also become a recipient of the Order of the British Empire.

On arrival at Prestwick the Fortresses were put into the custody of Scottish Aviation Ltd, the company designated by the Ministry of Aircraft Production as a 'sister firm' to Boeing regarding design, modification and airworthiness issues for the Fortress, among other types. The company also carried out modifications, manufactured spare parts and later performed overhauls.

Following servicing, each Fortress was delivered, typically within two days, by crews drawn from Prestwick-based 4 Ferry Pilots Pool, Air Transport Auxiliary, to one of two destinations for final modification. The Fortress IIAs – with the exception of FK185 and FK192 – were flown to the new Burtonwood airfield near Warrington in Lancashire. Burtonwood was home to both 37 Maintenance Unit and Burtonwood Repair Depot Ltd., a civilian assembly and modification centre managed by Fairey Aviation and the Bristol Aeroplane Co and dedicated to preparing American-manufactured aircraft for RAF service. Each Fortress IIA remained at Burtonwood for two to three weeks to receive final modifications and finishing for service with Coastal Command. Burtonwood was handed over to the USAAF on July 15, 1942, so the Fortress IIs were dispatched from Prestwick to either 12 Maintenance Unit at Kirkbride, Cumberland, or 29 Maintenance Unit at High Ercall, Shropshire, and then on to Air Service Training (AST) at Hamble in Hampshire for preparation for service.

Robert E Coffman of White Castle, Louisiana, was captain for the delivery flights of Fortress IIAs FK197 (see previous page) and FL452. In October 1943, he and two fellow crew members survived a desperate eleven-day ordeal after ditching Canada-bound Hampden I AE309 off the coast of Greenland. Despite this harrowing experience, he returned to Ferry Command after a period of leave and had flown as co-pilot on five transatlantic flights on Liberator Is of BOAC and delivered 21 aircraft by the time he resigned in mid-1944. Directorate of History and Heritage

Toledo, Ohio native Richard B Stophlet was captain for the delivery of Fortress IIA FK187 from Dorval to Prestwick. He joined Ferry Command in October 1941 with 2,800 hours of flying experience and went on to deliver 31 aircraft, including 15 Liberators, to the United Kingdom, Middle East and India. Directorate of History and Heritage

TESTING

Like all new types destined for RAF service, the Fortress underwent extensive testing to evaluate its suitability and readiness for operations. The Aeroplane and Armament Experimental Establishment (A&AEE) at Boscombe Down and the Royal Aircraft Establishment (RAE) at Farnborough therefore each received a number of Fortresses.

First to be allocated was the second example ferried across the Atlantic, Fortress IIA FK187. Delivered to Boscombe Down on April 24, 1942, and wearing its original Dark Olive Drab and Neutral Grey finish, it was destined to become the principal test vehicle for the type. Trials began with an evaluation of the Norden automatic flight control system. This advanced equipment allowed the aircraft to be flown from the bomb aimer's position in the nose and it was found possible to make co-ordinated turns at all speeds and to hold a heading with two engines on one side at idle.

Fuel consumption, range and endurance trials followed, to help the Air Staff evaluate the type's suitability for the low-altitude maritime reconnaissance role. These indicated that at 1,000ft (305m) and an economical cruise speed of 145 mph (233km/h), the Fortress had a practical still air range of 1,620 miles (2,610km) when equipped with standard fuel tanks totalling 1,416 Imp gal (6,440l). This increased to 2,360 miles (3,800km) with the installation of a hypothetical 600 Imp gal (2,730l) bomb bay fuel tank. The actual range proved to be less, in part because FK187 was not fitted with ASV radar aerials. Climb and performance trials in late May produced a time to 20,000ft (6,100m) of 21.78 minutes at a take-off weight of 48,700lb (22,090kg) and a true airspeed cruise of 286mph (460km/h), although this information was not of any direct application to the maritime reconnaissance role.

Starting May 9, FK187 was used extensively to test defensive gun positions, an area of weakness on the earlier Fortress I. The first month of firing trials was conducted on the ground while flight trials ran from June 22 until a collapsed tail wheel halted flying on August 1. Another test conducted in late June found carbon monoxide contamination to be non-existent.

Gunnery trials resumed with the arrival on August 12 of recently delivered Fortress IIA FL458, resplendent in Coastal Command's Temperate Sea and White scheme. The Sperry upper turret was found to work well, with a rotation rate of 50° per second at airspeeds up to 300mph (483km/h) – although it was possible to shoot the aircraft's fin – while the twin hand-held Browning machine gun installation in the tail and the single beam guns were also found to be satisfactory. The innovative ventral Sperry ball turret came in for a lot of criticism, because the search view between the

Fortress IIA FK187 at A&AEE, Boscombe Down shortly after arrival in April 1942. This was the main test and evaluation airframe for the Fortress IIA and II, hence the yellow prototype marking. Note that it is not fitted with an astrodome or ASV radar aerials. A&AEE via Tim Mason

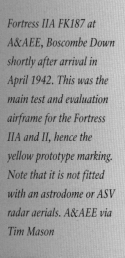

Fortress IIA FL458 replaced FK187 for gunnery trials at Boscombe Down after the latter suffered a collapsed tail wheel – it is equipped with the early aerial arrangement for ASV Mk II radar. On June 6, 1943, a 220 Sqn crew led by S/Ldr Hugh L Warren damaged U-boat U-450 while flying this aircraft from Benbecula. Coded 'A' at the time, it was re-coded as '2-Q' for service with 220 Sqn in the Azores. A&AEE via Tim Mason

Left: Fortress IIA FK211 undertook several trials at Boscombe Down from November 1942 to June 1943. These included attitude measurements for a plan to fit the Fortress with rocket projectiles, a test Mk IIN Identification Friend or Foe (IFF) installation, testing of the Mk IC gyro gun sight for the Sperry upper turret, and an improved ammunition feed for the ball turret. via Mike Diprose

Fortress II FA706 was the only example of the mark to undergo trials at Boscombe Down and these were limited to an evaluation of the nose-mounted astro-dome for navigation purposes. The nose features B-17E-style windows and the under wing and nose homing aerials for the ASV Mk II radar have been erased by the censor. FA706 'S' served with 220 Sqn from Benbecula and the Azores and was struck off charge on February 2, 1944, after colliding with an unidentified aircraft while being taxied at Lagens. A&AEE via Tim Mason

gunner's knees being very restricted while the ammunition feed suffered many failures. It was also found to be extremely cramped.

Curiously, the single .30 calibre Browning machine gun in the nose was not replaced by a larger calibre weapon, and the lack of forward suppressive firepower, notwithstanding restricted use of the upper turret, would become a contentious issue for Fortress crews.

FK187 was airworthy again by mid-October and between November 1942 and the spring of 1943 was used for high- and low-altitude flame damping and exhaust pipe shrouding trials, supercharger tests, navigation flights, carbon monoxide tests after gun firing, and determining static vent position errors. Prototype exhaust pipe shrouds were discarded because of their drag effects on range, although one operational aircraft, FK202 'B' of 59 Sqn, is known to have been fitted with the modifications, most likely by the Bristol Aeroplane Co. FK187 was later modified to carry Long Range ASV radar, but saw no squadron service and was struck off charge in July of 1945.

Other Fortresses passing through Boscombe Down included Fortress IIA FK211, which arrived in November 1942 and in March of 1943 was used for preliminary attitude measurements for a still-born plan to fit the Fortress with rocket projectiles. The following month it took part in trials to confirm that the Mk IIN Identification Friend or Foe (IFF) installation worked satisfactorily on the Fortress, and in May and June was engaged in testing of the Mk IC gyro gun sight for the Sperry upper turret and an improved ammunition feed for the ball turret.

The Fortress II was not considered sufficiently different from the Fortress IIA to warrant separate testing, the only example to pass through Boscombe Down, FA706, arriving on December 31, 1942, for evaluation of the astrodome installed in the upper nose.

By 1940, it had become apparent that the factors affecting high altitude flight – both the impact on aircraft and their systems and the aircrew who were required to operate them – were not fully understood. It was therefore decided to establish a High Altitude Flight at the A&AEE to conduct a wide variety of research projects, the unit being formed on December 30, 1940. Since the Fortress' raison d'être was high-altitude bombing, it was a natural candidate for such work and on June 8, 1943, Mk IIA FK192, the last example to arrive in Britain, joined the Flight for 15 months of high altitude and meteorological research.

Second view of FA706 at Boscombe Down. The USAAF data block has been masked off as individual lines rather than as a single block. The American-designed ASV Mk II nose and underwing aerials have been deleted by the censor. IWM ATP.12047B

Other known testing involving Coastal Command Fortresses included Mk II FA695, which served with the Signals Flying Unit at Honiley, Warwickshire, following delivery on October 1, 1944, for "*secret tests*" related to new radio equipment.

LONG RANGE ASV SAGA

As noted earlier, it was an operational requirement that Coastal Command's Fortresses be fitted with Long Range ASV radar, the sideways-looking search enhancement of ASV Mk II (also referred to as 'broadside'). However, since the rapid delivery of aircraft was critically important, it was planned that the first 18 examples delivered from the United States would not have the radar and associated aerials installed. This was eventually improved to around the first 14 aircraft.

The British had given the ASV Mk II design to the United States, complete with nose- and underwing-mounted Yagi-type homing aerials. The Americans repackaged the system, substituted locally-made components and designated the system SCR-521. Development of the long range component then proceeded in parallel in the two countries, resulting in different designs for the fuselage-mounted search arrays. The American design, installed on Fortress IIAs delivered to the United Kingdom with the ASV Mk II system, consisted of a wire beam array mounted above the rear fuselage for transmitting and a collinear array of four wire dipoles on each side of the rear fuselage for receiving. An August 1942 dispatch from HQ Coastal Command to the TRE branded the American search arrays as "*useless*" and these were finally removed from all Fortress IIAs in the spring of 1943. They were never installed on Fortress IIs.

The RAE at Farnborough was therefore tasked with developing, in collaboration with the TRE, a replacement aerial system. The Air Ministry allocated Fortress IIA FK190 to the task and it arrived at Farnborough on May 3, 1942. Since several key components were not yet available to implement the transmit and receive ('T & R') switch that would allow one aerial to be used for both transmitting and receiving, the prototype installation proceeded using the familiar drag-inducing 'stickleback' masts for the search transmit function. The receiving array consisted of two collinear arrays of four rigid dipoles mounted on the fuselage sides.

The homing receiving arrays were installed under the nose rather than under the wings outboard of the engine nacelles as had been earlier practice. The under-nose installation solved a fading problem that occurred when homing on large targets at close range with the under-wing aerial location. To give sufficient left-right discrimination for homing, the aerials were toed in 18° from

Fortress IIA FK192 with the High Altitude Flight at A&AEE Boscombe Down during the latter half of 1943. It is fitted with Mk II (aft) and Mk VI psychrometers for comparison tests. via Peter Rackliff

Fortress IIA FK197, to the left, at Prestwick on June 30, 1943. Assigned to Scottish Aviation, it can seen to be fitted with LRASV radar plus a unique aerial array forward of the fin. It remained at Prestwick until March 1945. The Mk IIA to the right coded 'Z' is unidentified but may be FK188. via Phil Butler

The first trials for LRASV
employed Fortress IIA
FK190, seen here at
the RAE Farnborough.
Non-availability of critical
electrical switching gear
meant that the instal-
lation included a large
drag-inducing 'stickleback'
array for the search
transmit function with
four pairs of dipoles on
each fuselage side for
receiving the signals. (see
colour profile page 229).
National Archives (UK)

the line of flight (the left aerial thus gave maximum response to targets 18° right of the line of
flight and the right aerial to targets 18° left of
the line of flight). The relocation of the receiving arrays required moving the DF loop in its
bullet-shaped fairing back five feet (1.5m) and
to a position slightly starboard of the aircraft's
centreline.

Flight trials began on July 21 and were completed on August 14 following a ten-day delay
due to engine magneto problems. While the
aerial systems were generally an improvement
over the American versions, the reaction to the
continued use of the large dorsal masts was extremely negative – one squadron commander

was quoted as being "*horrified*" at the installation – and there was concern that the American part-
ners would not be impressed, particularly as they were known to have already developed a suitable
T & R switching unit.

Fortress IIA FK202 undertook four LRASV-related flights from Farnborough between July 15
and September 15, 1942 – presumably with the original aerial fit as it was still in this configuration when it entered service with 59 Sqn in late 1942 – and was later used for radio trials recorded
as 'RT – Bombers'. FK204 was posted to Farnborough for ten days that July as a backup but does
not appear to have been used.

As a consequence of the unsatisfactory 'stickleback' installation, a second Fortress IIA, FL455,
was assigned as the LRASV 'first production model' and allocated to Scottish Aviation at Prestwick
for modification on November 11, 1942. On December 23, an instruction was issued that all
Fortresses fitted with the British LRASV installation would receive the common T & R unit.

The modifications to FL455 were tested by RAE representatives at Prestwick on February 22,
1943, and the aircraft duly arrived at Farnborough for ground tests on March 18. The flight trials
were conducted by F/Lt Hood over the Bristol Channel and Lundy Island on April 8. Test results
for both the homing and search arrays were good, but a plan to eliminate the homing transmitting aerial in the nose cone was dropped since it was a standard component to which the T.3040D
transmitter could easily be tuned. The receiver was designated R.3039A.

Testing complete, FL455 was flown to AST at Hamble on April 20 and later to 218 MU at RAF
Colerne so both organizations could become fa-
miliar with the modifications. The plan was for
38 aircraft to be modified by 218 MU and another
18 by AST, but 51 aircraft were eventually modified, all, with the exception of FL455 and FK197,
by 218 MU, with the majority passing through
Colerne from June to September 1943 in advance
of 206 and 220 Sqns moving to the Azores.

The work included Mods 121 and 140 for
LRASV as well as installation of a Distant
Reading (DR) Compass under Mods 132

*The revised homing aerial configuration included new aeri-
als mounted below the nose to replace the earlier underwing
arrangement. The installation required that the ADF loop
fairing be moved back approximately five feet (1.5m).
National Archives (UK)*

The first production model
of LRASV was installed
and tested on Fortress IIA
FL455 in the early months
of 1943 – the homing
aerial arrangement was
the same as that tested
on FK190. Although
well-worn looking, FL455
had not yet seen squadron
service. It was lost on
February 1, 1945, when it
flew into marshy terrain
near Wick, Scotland,
while operating with
519 (Met) Sqn as 'Z9-A'.
National Archives (UK)

Dual purpose transmit-
and-receive dipoles
mounted each side of the
fuselage allowed deletion
of the dorsal search transmission masts tested on
FK190. National Archives
(UK)

and 146. The first aircraft, former 59 Sqn Fortress IIA FK198, arrived as early as April 2, 1943, and was air-tested following conversion on June 17. The opportunity was also taken to add other modifications, including some changes to the IFF system.

Meanwhile, Mk IIA FK197 had been assigned to Scottish Aviation at Prestwick for ASV Mk II trials. These included testing the improved LRASV aerials with an additional dorsal array

The protracted development of LRASV was to incur an unfortunate penalty as, by mid-September 1942, U-boats were being equipped with the simple Metox detector, primarily as a countermeasure to sudden night-time attacks in the Bay of Biscay by Leigh Light-equipped Wellingtons. The detector rendered ASV Mk II generally ineffective for finding U-boats as it could pick up an aircraft's 1.5m radar transmission at greater than 50 miles (80km), more than twice the distance at which the radar could provide a return from a submarine.

INTO SERVICE

220 Sqn crews began collecting their first Fortress IIAs from Burtonwood during July 1942 and by month's end the unit had eleven on strength. The first operational flight was undertaken by S/Ldr Richard Williams and his crew on July 24 in FK207 'J', a 10-hour convoy escort sortie. By the beginning of August, three more aircraft were operational – FK206 'K', FK200 'B' and FK185 'E' – and in total the squadron had completed nine uneventful missions. Apart from 120 Sqn, also based at Ballykelly from July 27 with a mixed complement of Liberator Is, IIs and IIIs, 220 Sqn was the only Coastal Command unit operating four-engined, land-based aircraft in the campaign against the U-boats.

The squadron experienced its first mishap with a Fortress IIA in the early hours of August 1, 1942. F/Sgt George Gamble had elected to fly a high approach to ensure avoiding tree tops on the flight path to a 1,400-yard (1,280m) runway. Landing too long, FK196 'C' ran off the end of the runway in the darkness and fell into a ditch. There is no record of FK196 undertaking operational flights with 220 Sqn and from a study of logbooks against squadron records it appears to have been common practice for selected aircraft to be dedicated to training and general transportation duties for extended periods.

Meanwhile a second Coastal Command squadron had begun converting to the Fortress. Previously based at Aldergrove in Northern Ireland, 206 Sqn (code letters 'VX' and Motto '*Nihil nos effugit*' or 'Naught escapes us') had moved to Benbecula in the Scottish Outer Hebrides with their Lockheed Hudsons on July 1, 1942. Benbecula was well placed as a location from which to provide air cover for convoys navigating the Western Approaches but it was not the most popular wartime base in Coastal Command. Bill Blackwell served as a Wireless Operator/Air Gunner (WOP/AG) with 206 Sqn:

"*To reach Benbecula you either had to fly or take a boat from Oban or Mallaig to Lochboisdale. On arrival at the aerodrome you were confronted by a very bleak, open space with huge hangars, some Nissen huts and one or two larger mess buildings. The wind never seemed to drop below 30mph and frequently gusted up to 100mph. I witnessed hangar doors blown down and remember that the B-17s had to be anchored to the ground. Life there was very dull with nowhere to go except the mess. The one highlight was the monthly binge when we spent our mess fees on a big blow-out. Transport was*

Benbecula airfield was a frontline base for Fortress operations from September 1942 until the campaign against the U-boats in the North Atlantic was won in mid-1943. Located in the Scottish Outer Hebrides, it was home to the Fortresses of 206 Sqn from July 1942 and these were joined in March 1943 by those of 220 Sqn. It was generally considered too confined for accommodating two squadrons of large aircraft and this proved to be a contributing factor in the crash of FL454 'J' of 206 Sqn during an early morning take-off on October 6, 1942. via John Lowe

The operations room at RAF Benbecula. via Ted Hedges

Below: *Fortress IIA FL451 'D' of 206 Sqn, shortly after arrival at Benbecula from Burtonwood at the end of July 1942. It is equipped with ASV Mk II, rendered partially ineffective by the American-designed and -installed search aerial arrays visible above and on the side of the rear fuselage. Squadron code 'VX' was painted out after Coastal Command dropped unit codes, effective November 1, 1942. P/O Robert Cowey sank his second U-boat, U-710, while flying this aircraft on April 24, 1943. 206 Sqn Archives via Tom Talbot*

206 Sqn personnel at Benbecula with newly-arrived Fortress IIA FL451 'D'. Left to right are: F/O William 'Willis' Roxburgh, F/O 'Tom' Pearse, F/O 'Freddie' Wills and S/Ldr Richard C 'Butch' Patrick. Note the original USAAF data block below the rearmost window of the Fortress, retained as required by the Lend-Lease agreement. 206 Sqn Archives via Tom Talbot

45

Armourers install 250lb (113kg) Torpex-filled Mk XI depth charges in a Fortress bomb bay at Benbecula. The type initially carried 14 of these weapons but this was reduced to seven in October 1942 to allow installation of a 341 Imp gal (1,550l) fuel tank on the port side of the bay. When 206 and 220 Sqns moved to the Azores in October 1943, their aircraft were fitted with two bomb bay fuel tanks for maximum range and endurance leaving a complement of just four depth charges on underwing racks. IWM CH.11102

sent around the island to bring all the maidens to a dance… I'm sure they only came for the food!"

Joe Griffith, a Canadian navigator with 206 Sqn, recalls that one station commander, G/Cpt Douglas L Blackford, did his best to introduce some levity to counter the steady stream of complaints:

"Blackford held regular meetings to allow crews to let off steam. He would dutifully record their complaints on a roll of toilet paper for 'filing and future consideration'. Interestingly, the Canadian crewmembers, who were generally more used to isolated locations, complained much less about their surroundings."

On July 20, 206 Sqn flew a detachment of 19 personnel to Ballykelly for a Fortress conversion course and to take delivery of three 220 Sqn Fortress Is, AN520, AN530 and AN531. Training consisted of dual instruction provided by 220 Sqn pilots on the Fortress I followed by familiarisation and solo flights on the Fortress IIA.

The detachment departed for Benbecula in their newly-acquired Fortress Is on July 29, the aircraft being flown by 206 Sqn's commanding officer W/Cdr Alfred Hards, S/Ldr Richard C Patrick and F/Lt William Roxburgh. The following day, F/Lt Roxburgh flew AN520 to Burtonwood with 17 crew members as passengers to pick up the first of the squadron's Fortress IIAs, FL451 'D', FL453 'A' and FL457 'F'.

The squadron began converting to the Fortress on August 1, primarily under the tutelage of F/Lt Roxburgh. The Fortress Is were used as trainers for a matter of days until sufficient Fortress IIAs arrived. Training continued throughout the month with new aircraft collected from Burtonwood by squadron crews every few days. The final Hudson operation took place on August 27 using AM734 'O' and all operational flying ceased for the first 18 days of September while conversion to the Fortress was completed.

Following their brief service as trainers, the Fortress Is became squadron hacks, their use including occasional runs to Stornoway to pick up ice cream and other luxury items for the mess. The last documented flight by a Fortress I of 206 Sqn occurred on March 24, 1943, when F/Lt Frederick S Wills, DFC, delivered AN520 'X' from Benbecula to Marshall's facilities at Cambridge for repairs and subsequent storage. A fourth Fortress I, AN519, is recorded as briefly allocated to 206 Sqn, from July 16 to August 10, 1942, but is believed to have remained stored at Burtonwood until issued to 59 Sqn, the third Coastal Command unit to operate the Fortress.

F/Lt Roxburgh recorded: *"The Fortress I was quite a pleasant aircraft to fly. Our main problem was with the brakes. They had a peculiar expanding oil bag system on to the drum. No matter how carefully and gently one used the brakes, there were endless cases of the bags breaking under heat and friction and having to be replaced. The Fortress II was a completely different proposition and a real tough and pleasant aircraft to fly in every way."*

Two of the Fortress Is were subsequently allocated elsewhere. After a period of storage, AN520 joined 214 Sqn, Bomber Command as a trainer in support of its ECM operations based on the Fortress III (B-17G), while AN531 moved to the RAE at Farnborough. AN530 was not so fortunate – it was recategorised as a write-off at Benbecula on September 11, 1943, as 206 Sqn prepared to move to the Azores, and buried in a large hole dug by local civilians at one end of the airfield.

The first accident involving a 206 Sqn Fortress occurred during crew training on September 9, 1942, when FK194 'M' was damaged while landing at Stornoway en route to Burtonwood. After returning to Benbecula two days later, it was flown to Prestwick for repairs by Scottish Aviation, which according to the aircraft's record card, were not completed until October 1944.

206 Sqn undertook its first Fortress sortie on September 19 when F/Lt Roxburgh took FL453 'A' on a Creeping Line Ahead (CLA) reconnaissance that ended at the remote island of Rockall. The squadron resumed full anti-submarine work on October 1, at which time flights 'A' and 'B' were merged into one under the command of S/Ldr Richard Patrick.

A Fortress crew initially consisted of seven members: captain and co-pilot, navigator, and four WOP/AGs, one of whom was the senior wireless operator. By late 1942, the crew complement had increased to eight with the addition of a fifth WOP/AG and from late 1943 the eighth crew member was a qualified flight engineer and air gunner. Former WOP/AG Bill Blackwell remembers the diminutive Sperry ball turret and tail gun positions:

"My first encounter with the ball turret was quite a frightening experience. You sat as a baby in its mother's womb. The controls were not as stable as in other types of turret and you could find yourself upside down in the foetal position, facing the nose while trying to operate the guns. If you rotated too fast, you simply spun around and I think we were all glad when this turret was removed from our B-17s. As for the tail turret, one had to crawl into position on hands and knees and sit on something akin to a bicycle seat. I remember on one trip with the cloud base down to 500ft, the wind was blowing the tail around with such ferocity that I continually banged my head from side to side and could do very little about it."

The Fortress IIA was initially armed with twelve 250lb (113kg) depth charges and two 250lb (113kg) anti-submarine bombs. This was changed in late October 1942 to fourteen depth charges due to the risk of damage to the aircraft during low-level drops of the anti-submarine bombs. Towards the end of the month, HQ 15 Group Coastal Command issued a signal requiring all Fortresses to be fitted with a jettisonable bomb bay fuel tank of 341 Imp gal (1,550l), leaving room for only seven depth charges on the starboard side of the bomb bay but giving the Fortress an official endurance of 10.7 hours.

Following service with 90 Sqn, Fortress I AN520 was allocated in turn to 220 and 206 Sqns for crew training. After a period of storage it was allocated to 214 Sqn in early 1944 for training Fortress III crews at RAF Oulton where it is seen here, with an almost all-white finish on the fuselage. J Southgate via Bryan Yates

THE LIBERATOR

Liberators in Coastal Command service are often collectively categorised as Very Long Range (or VLR) and therefore thought of as uniformly capable. In fact, the Liberator I was the only true VLR mark, equipped from the outset with long-range tanks to give a range of 2,400 miles (3,860km) and an endurance of around 16 hours. Follow-on Liberator IIs and IIIs were configured by the manufacturer as high-altitude bombers and needed de-modification and weight reduction to be suitable for the maritime reconnaissance role. The Liberator I possessed 33 percent greater range than the Liberator II at 1,800 miles (2,900km) and 43 percent more than the Liberator III at 1,680 miles (2,705km). (Ranges are based on a take-off allowance followed by economical cruise in 'still air' to 'dry tanks'. Range for operational planning purposes was 20-25% less.)

Compounding this lower endurance and range was the painfully slow pace of supply from the United States, despite constant requests by Sir Philip Joubert for long range aircraft. The Air Ministry recognised that promised deliveries of Liberators and Fortresses would not be met and in

The Liberator I was among Coastal Command's most valuable assets during the early Battle of the Atlantic but only ten were available to 120 Sqn when operations started and that number quickly dwindled. AM916/G is seen at Prestwick prior to service and following installation by Scottish Aviation of ASV Mk II and a ventral gun pack. AM916 'L' remained with 120 Sqn until 1944. In March 1952 she was sold for scrap for just £20 following an aborted conversion for BOAC's Ceylon-Australia route. via Peter Clare.

August 1942 revised its New Expansion Plan to reduce the planned Liberator squadrons from six to four and Fortress squadrons from three to the two then working up, 206 and 220. It was now hoped that three of the Liberator squadrons would be formed by November, but this failed to happen due to allocation of aircraft elsewhere by American authorities, changing priorities for fitting aircraft out at the manufacturer's plant at Fort Worth, Texas, and conflicts over the allocation of ASV equipment.

120 Sqn was now down to just six Liberator Is, together with two non-ASV-equipped Liberator IIs and three Liberator IIIs. They were to be stretched even thinner when seven squadron aircraft – a Liberator I, three Liberator IIs, two Liberator IIIs and one Liberator IIIA – were detached to Reykjavik on September 4, 1942. To address this critical shortage, the Air Ministry contracted Scottish Aviation in November 1942 to modify all 33 Liberator IIIAs to Long Range configuration with a range of 2,300 miles (3,700km), a program that would take three months to complete. On top of this, there was a two-month lag from allocation to delivery and only two Liberators were received in January 1943 against the already meagre four allocated.

The Fortress with a single bomb bay tank could manage a more modest still-air range after take-off of around 1,825 miles (2,940km) and was regarded as a medium-range reconnaissance type. But from September 1942 to March 1943, among the most critical months of the Battle of the Atlantic, the Fortress was available in greater numbers than the Liberator, with an establishment of 24 aircraft between 206 and 220 Sqns. They would play a key role in keeping the U-boats at bay by escorting convoys for the last third of their voyages while the precious Liberators were deployed further out into the Atlantic.

SERVICE, LOSS AND SUCCESS

By the beginning of August 1942, 220 Sqn had settled into a steady routine of escorting convoys – and to a lesser extent, single troopships and naval task forces – and conducting anti-submarine sweeps of the Western Approaches. The escort missions were typically around ten hours long with the convoy or individual troopship being met, when weather permitted, between one-and-a-half to three-and-a-half hours into the flight, or 225 to 525 miles (360 to 845km) from base. Because of their superior speed, troopships – or 'monsters' as they were known – such as the converted ocean liners *Queen Mary*, *Durban Castle* and *Franconia* travelled alone, although they still came under the watchful eye of Coastal Command whenever they were close enough to a shore base and the

206 Sqn's commanding officer W/Cdr James Romanes (left) with co-pilot P/O Alan Marriott, to his left, and crew at Benbecula in late 1942 with Fortress IIA FK210 'E'. Third from the left is W/O Ron Stares who was lost in the shooting down of Fortress II FA705 '1-U' on January 6, 1944. Other crew members from left to right are Sgt J H Norris and F/Sgt S Bickell on the wing and to the right of Stares, F/Sgt D L Baldwin, Sgt W H S Clough and W/O George W Cairns. 206 Sqn Archives via Tom Talbot

weather permitted. As an example, 220 Sqn's Fortress IIA FK203 'M', captained by F/Sgt Stanley Houghton, departed Ballykelly at 08:30 on August 3, 1942, to escort the liner *Franconia*. The Fortress arrived over the vessel at 10:59 but at 12:14 contact was lost due to poor weather. The crew searched in vain for over three hours before returning to Ballykelly, to land at 18:54.

Bad weather was a constant challenge during winter maritime reconnaissance operations and sorties were often cut short by crews because of poor visibility or by operations control at base due to deteriorating weather at Ballykelly. Normal alternates included Tiree and Stornoway in Scotland, while landings were also made at Limavady and St. Angelo in Northern Ireland. Very poor weather was the main cause of two losses by 220 Sqn on the same night.

Fortress IIA FK204 'N' had departed Ballykelly at 14:27 on August 10 with W/Cdr Richard T F Gates in command to escort convoy SC 94. As the aircraft returned to base, a series of factors conspired to prevent the crew from fixing their position. The prevailing very low and widespread cloud meant that obtaining a visual fix was out of the question while heavy static made radio communication almost impossible. When contact with 15 Group flying control was made, the controller failed to provide diversion instructions for three hours and, when assistance was most urgently needed, the trailing aerial winch jammed. At 00:15 the aircraft was diverted to Prestwick but by 00:45 the Fortress had overshot its destination by eight miles to the east and had only an estimated 30 minutes of fuel remaining. Gates was then instructed to fly due west and at 00:53 was reported to be trying to land at Drem. The crew finally took to their parachutes at around 01:35 on August 11, just before the aircraft ran out of fuel. All eight landed safely while their Fortress came down at Doddington quarry near Acklington in Northumberland.

The crew of FK207 'J' captained by 23-year-old W/O Gordon A Sanderson was not so fortunate. They departed Ballykelly at 19:46 on August 10 to escort convoy ONS 120. At 23:30 the aircraft was seen flying below low cloud and very close to rising ground near Nutts Corner

Graves of Australian crew members who died in the crash of 206 Sqn Fortress IIA FL454 'J' on October 6, 1942. Left to right: Sgt John F Guppy, F/Sgt John B Taplin and captain P/O Jack E Delarue. They are buried in Nunton Old Church yard, close to Benbecula airfield. Martin Briscoe

Sgt Jim Hunt was seated in the radio compartment when FL454 crashed at Benbecula. He survived to paddle ashore with the other survivor, Sgt David Strang Coutts. Hunt's only injuries were a small cut over his right eye and a large bruise on his left side. (via John Lowe)

Damage to hangar at Benbecula following the winter storms of December 13, 1942. via Chris Ransted

airfield. Moments later the Fortress appeared to lose speed in a left turn towards the airfield and dived into the ground, its load of depth charges exploding on impact. All six on board died. (See Appendix C for a listing of all aircrew lost in Coastal Command Fortress accidents).

220 Sqn's first offensive action took place at 08:15 on September 19, 1942, when P/O Stanley Houghton flying FK186 'S' dropped depth charges on a 15-foot (4.6m) diameter patch of bubbles coming from a submerged object at 55°03'N 12°42'W. No results were observed and there were no U-boat losses for this date.

206 Sqn's first confirmed U-boat attack took place just over two weeks later on October 5, when F/O A Eric Bland in command of FK208 'B' dropped five depth charges on a submarine without any results at position 58°37'N 21°12'W. The squadron's first loss of a Fortress occurred in the early hours of the following morning.

Three aircraft had been assigned by HQ 15 Group to conduct anti-submarine sweeps around Halifax-to-Liverpool 'fast' convoy HX 209. First away at 05:57 was FL453 'A', captained by 206 Sqn's commanding officer, W/Cdr James R S Romanes, DFC, on that day leading F/Lt Roxburgh's usual crew. P/O Robert L Cowey in FL457 'F' was delayed by a chock stuck beneath his starboard mainwheel so his take-off slot was taken by 26-year-old Australian P/O Jack E Delarue in FL454 'J'. It was his first operational flight on the Fortress. Delarue was well into his take-off run when Cowey's aircraft emerged out of the darkness, taxiing straight towards him along the runway. Although still below take-off speed, Delarue and co-pilot Sgt James C H R Jaeger managed to haul the fully-laden Fortress into the air and leapfrog Cowey's aircraft, miraculously without making contact. But the effort was at the expense of precious airspeed and the doomed Fortress hit the runway before staggering into the air again, flipping over, and crashing into the sea off the end of the runway.

While a small rescue boat was available, the oars were missing due to an earlier accident involving a Sunderland. Anxious to help, Acting F/Lt Roxburgh and his then co-pilot, F/O John Owen, stripped off their clothes and began swimming out to the wreck, one wing of which was clearly visible in the light provided by an ambulance's headlights and a Chance Light (a large floodlight) but the distance was too great and they reluctantly returned to shore. Delarue's four WOP/AGs were seated in the radio compartment at the time of the crash and two of them, Sgts Jim Hunt and David S Coutts, miraculously survived the crash with only minor injuries, to paddle ashore in a rubber dingy. But pilots Delarue and Jaeger, navigator F/Sgt Frederick A Robinson and the two

Australian WOP/AGs, F/Sgt John B Taplin and Sgt John F Guppy, had died. The three Australians were buried in nearby Nunton Cemetery while Robinson's body was never found.

Meanwhile, a no-doubt-shaken Cowey and his crew took off at 07:00, as demanded by operational requirements, to complete their patrol while F/O Lawrence M Nelson was airborne in FL451 'D' at 09:05 to fill the gap left by the loss of Delarue's aircraft.

Sgts Hunt and Coutts returned to 206 Sqn after three months leave, based again at Benbecula and later in the Azores. Hunt survived the war but Coutts was not so fortunate, losing his life in the crash of Fortress IIA FK208 'B' off Gibraltar in November of 1943.

P/O Cowey, as pilot-in-command of FL457, was held primarily responsible for the loss of FL454 but, as with most aviation accidents, there were a number of contributing factors. The Court of Inquiry revealed that it was common practice to use Benbecula's runways for taxiing at night as the perimeter track was considered too confined for use by Fortresses due to encroaching buildings. A lack of adequate hard standings meant that the Fortresses were parked on grass verges close to the runways, further encouraging pilots to shun the perimeter track.

Crews were not permitted to use radio communication within four hours of an operation and relied on visual signals, with flying control using a combination of Aldis lamps and identification lights. Flying control had given Delarue a red light when it observed Cowey's aircraft taxi onto the runway but this was evidently missed by Delarue's crew as they focused on their first operational take-off. The poor communications structure was complicated by the presence of a crofter's cottage in the middle of the airfield, which obstructed vision between flying control and the intersection of two of the three runways. Further compounding these deficiencies was the absence of a handover between the outgoing and recently arrived replacement Senior Flying Control Officers, while it emerged that standing orders related to flying control had not been enforced and in some cases not even read by station personnel. Both the senior flying control officer and the duty officer on watch were singled out for failing to enforce and carry out flying orders. Finally, there was a suggestion in testimony by Cowey's navigator, P/O John Duns that, because of the delay they had experienced due to the stuck chock, there was a possibility Delarue had already taken off. This may have made Cowey and his crew less guarded about another aircraft being on the runway.

The crash of the fully-armed Fortress presented a major risk of an explosion from the load of twelve depth charges and two anti-submarine bombs, amounting to some 3,000 pounds of Torpex. The Air Ministry's bomb disposal group, Organisation 10, was therefore requested to find a way to neutralise the weapons. (See Appendix D for the full report on the disposal of the weapons carried by FL454. Profiles for Jack Delarue, as well as four other Fortress aircrew and one Luftwaffe pilot, are to be found in Appendix E).

There was another unfortunate, albeit less tragic, outcome from this operation. The 206 Sqn ORB records that W/Cdr Romanes' crew in FL453 sighted a U-boat three hours into their sortie and suggests that navigator F/Sgt Joe Griffith set the depth charge release lever to 'Safe' instead of 'Operate', precluding a successful attack. Joe Griffith had a very different recollection:

"As we went into the attack, I was well aware that it took at least 30 seconds for the electrically-operated bomb bay doors to open, so I immediately asked for permission to open them. This permission was not forthcoming and when the order was finally given there was insufficient time to open the doors before we reached the drop point."

It became normal practice for the crewman on watch in the nose to open a Fortress' bomb doors as soon as the action bell sounded.

Bob Cowey was to be involved in a more positive event three weeks later on October 27, the first sinking of a U-boat by a Fortress and only the second by a land-based four-engined Coastal Command aircraft. Cowey and his crew departed Benbecula in FL457 'F' at 06:30 to fly cover for convoy SC 105. At 11:25 his crew spotted a U-boat travelling at conning tower depth at 59°14'N 22°49'W. Cowey attacked, dropping all seven depth charges 25ft (7.6m) ahead of the swirl as the U-boat

P/O Robert Cowey was the only Coastal Command Fortress pilot to sink two U-boats. He is pictured, rear centre, with part of his 206 Sqn crew in front of Fortress IIA FL452 'G'. Identified are, rear right, Sgt J H Morris; front centre, P/O D E Bryan; and, front right, F/Sgt N H Wright. Robert Cowey via Norman Franks

dived. This produced a patch of light oil 100 yards (91m) long but little other evidence of a kill. In fact, U-627, captained by *Kapitänleutnant* Robert Kindelbacher, had been destroyed on its first patrol of the war with the loss of all 44 on board.

U-627 had been part of Group 'Puma', charged with intercepting what Dönitz's war diary – *Befehlshaber der Untersee-Booten Kriegstagebuch* (or *B.d.U.* War Diary) – referred to as 'Convoy 61'. Together with U-606, U-627 had been added to the intercept line and the crew had reported spotting the convoy in the early hours of October 27. There was no further report from the U-boat though, as late as October 31 U-627 was tasked with attacking another convoy. Dönitz's war diary concluded: *"After close of operation no reports were received in spite of many calls... On 27.10 U-627 reported convoy in* [grid reference] *AL 2559 at 03:25 on easterly course and gave chase after which no further report was received. Loss of both* [including U-412] *must be reckoned with."*

(The first sinking by a long-range, land-based aircraft had occurred on October 12, 1942, when Liberator I AM929 'H' of 120 Sqn sank U-597 while operating from Reykjavik, Iceland.)

206 Sqn went on to fly 523 operational hours during October 1942, a major achievement considering the squadron had only 19 of its establishment of 36 fitters. This total increased to 676 operational hours in November with one sighting and attack made.

Fortress IIA FL452 'G' of 206 Sqn lifts off from Benbecula. The view is interesting for a couple of reasons. It confirms that some Fortresses were fitted with underwing depth charge racks as early as mid-1943, when this view was recorded. In addition, while the ineffective American-designed search ASV aerials on the rear fuselage have been removed, the censor has not deleted the underwing homing ASV aerials, likely because the full image was over-exposed on one side and not suitable for general distribution. This was the aircraft in which then P/O Leslie G Clark made the first of three successful U-boat attacks when he damaged U-632 on January 15, 1943. IWM CH.11133

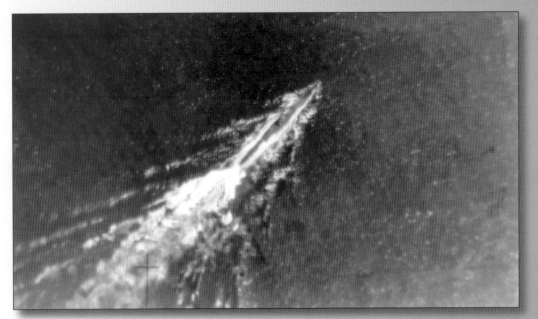

U-boat caught on the surface by a Bristol Blenheim IV of 1404 Met Flight on June 30, 1941. via Peter Rackliff

Middle: *Fortress IIA FK186 'S' of 220 Sqn during the mid-1943 air-to-air photo session out of Benbecula. The aircraft later served with 206 Sqn as 'X', though only very briefly operationally, and then returned to 220 Sqn with the same code when the former unit left the Azores. via Sid Banks*

FK186 'S' of 220 Sqn near its Benbecula base, mid-1943. IWM CH.11140

FK186 'S' pulls up and away from the camera ship during the mid-1943 photo session. IWM CH.11147

Fortress IIA FK186 'S' of 220 Sqn during an air-to-air photo sortie from its Benbecula base, mid-1943. It later served with both 206 and 220 Sqns in the Azores. IWM CH.11137

F/O Leslie 'Knobby' Clark, DFC, was one of the most successful Fortress captains with one U-boat destroyed and two damaged during four engagements – his name has been misspelled on the photograph. Clark stands centre rear on handing over his 206 Sqn crew to Canadian captain F/O Laurence Croft, to Clark's left, and co-pilot F/O Alex R Chisholm to Clark's right. Four of the remaining airmen – from left to right, W/O A Garnham, F/Sgt F W Allison, Sgt W E Pollard and, on the far right, New Zealander P/O John D Ackerman – had been part of Clark's crew during each attack. Ackerman, who went on to fly 71 sorties with 206 Sqn, was awarded the Order of the British Empire in June 1945 for his contribution to target and bomb sight development. He became a Weapons Specialist and flight tested aiming devices for the Valiant, Vulcan and Victor and later models of the Canberra. He was later associated with the introduction of the THOR missile system and eventually rose to the rank of Wing Commander. via Laurence Croft

'OPERATION TORCH'

By the latter part of 1942, a joint British-American force was preparing to land in French North Africa with the primary goal of clearing the Axis from North Africa. This would in turn lead to improved naval control of the Mediterranean and allow an invasion of Southern Europe the following year. 'Operation Torch' required reliable meteorological forecasts throughout the invasion and Coastal Command was asked to provide long-range aircraft to collect the necessary data. Three Fortresses from 220 Squadron were detached to St Eval in Cornwall on November 6 under the command of S/Ldr Walter Edser, F/Lt John Wright and F/O Gerry Haggas. The participating aircraft were FK193 'H', FK199 'R' and FK203 'M' and each had a Met Air Officer (MAO) attached to its crew. Prior to the three-week detachment, the pilots were sent to RAE Farnborough to spend time in the decompression chamber so they could immediately recognise the onset of oxygen starvation at altitudes up to 30,000ft (9,144m). A typical sortie included an outbound leg to Gibraltar via Cape Finisterre on Spain's Atlantic coast, with climbs up to 21,500ft (6,553m), and a similar return leg to St Eval the following day. The lower portions of the flights over the Bay of Biscay were flown as U-boat sweeps.

The success of the Met sorties for 'Operation Torch' prompted a request for more flights and on January 18, 1943, Fortress IIA FL459 'J' with F/O Haggas as captain was attached to 1402 Met Flight at Aldergrove for a planned series of flights over the Atlantic. Unfortunately, the severe weather and icing conditions prevalent during the winter of 1942/43 caused the flights to be abandoned after just four sorties.

Anti-submarine and Met flights were not the only ways in which Coastal Command's Fortresses proved their worth. Airborne search and rescue (ASR) was a natural component of their far-ranging over-water operations and a downed RAF crew could wish for nothing more than to be spotted by a vigilant Fortress crew member. As an example, on November 14, 1942, Mk IIA FL459 'J' was dispatched from Ballykelly at 07:15 to provide anti-submarine escort for convoy KMS 3. The convoy was duly met at 12:42 at position 48°35'N 18°30'W. Three-and-a-half hours into the patrol, at 16:19, a crew member spotted a dingy with three occupants, half of the crew of ditched Whitley V Z6725 of 10 OTU, on detachment to St Eval.

The captain of FL459, W/O George Gamble, promptly ordered the dropping of emergency rations, Verey cartridges and flame floats and had radio fixes reported to base. After receiving instructions, the Fortress crew signalled the survivors to fire Verey cartridges every 30 minutes. The Fortress stayed on station until 18:00 when it was instructed to land at St Eval. Short on fuel, Gamble elected to divert to Predannick where the Fortress landed at 20:40, some 13 hours 25 minutes after taking off from Ballykelly, substantially more than the official endurance of 10 hours 40 minutes. All six Whitley crew members were eventually rescued.

BATTLING THE ELEMENTS

Returning to the campaign against the U-boats at the end of 1942, December had brought terrible weather to the Outer Hebrides with very high winds. The runways at Benbecula were short for the operation of heavily-loaded Fortresses and crews were required to bring back unused depth charges. Shortly after dark on December 4, P/O Leslie G Clark of 206 Sqn found himself attempting to land Mk IIA FL452 'G' in continuous heavy rain following an eleven-hour anti-submarine sweep. His difficulties were compounded by a misunderstanding over the altimeter setting, a high landing weight, a short runway, and a low approach that resulted in the starboard wheel touching the water. Clark responded instantly by opening up the engines and completing a safe circuit before landing.

On December 11, F/O John Owen was covering convoys HX 217 and SC 111 in Fortress IIA FL460 'H' when at 13.50 the crew sighted a U-boat at 56°58'N 23°32'W making six knots on a heading 250 degrees, slightly on the port side and one mile away. Owen delivered an attack on

F/O John Owen and his regular crew on December 13, 1942, the day before Fortress IIA FL453 'A' disappeared without trace. Left to right: WOP/AG Sgt Eric Crowe, co-pilot Sgt Robert N Hildred, WOP/AGs Sgt Don Bryan and Sgt Walter 'Jock' Shanks, F/O John Owen, WOP/AG Sgt William 'Jimmy' Parnell and observer Sgt Charlie Neill in the darker blue uniform of the RAAF. Sgts Bryan and Neill were replaced by Sgts Rupert Bentley and Garfield C Wilson, RNZAF, for the fateful December 14 mission. To the rear is Fortress IIA FL452 'G'. Cpl Tom Blue via Tom Talbot and 206 Sqn Archives

the submarine's port quarter at 20 degrees to its track with the periscope and stem still visible. Explosions to the port side of the swirl from six depth charges resulted in the unidentified U-boat surfacing with a jagged hole through the forward end of the conning tower.

Half an hour later, at 14:19, and in the same position, the crew sighted a second U-boat dead ahead at four miles making ten knots (18km/h) on a heading of 260 degrees. This time Owen made an attack from dead astern and dropped his last depth charge from 30ft (9m) as the submarine submerged. The weapon exploded in the front portion of the 'greenside' water caused by the swirl and produced a greater water disturbance than in his first attack, with bubbles rising to the surface for three minutes. Photos taken by the crew showed the U-boat surfacing with its periscope bent into a loop. Two hours later, at 16:08 and in position 57°34'N 20°28'W Owen's crew sighted a third U-boat but, with no depth charges remaining, he could only make a mock attack.

The terrible weather continued with gusts of up to 100mph (160km/h) damaging hangars and aircraft at Benbecula on December 13. The following morning, three Fortresses departed in very poor weather to provide cover for convoys ONS 152 and TA 29. Fortress IIA FL453 'A' with 21-year-old F/O John Owen as captain failed to return. Three aircraft were dispatched the following day to search for the missing crew, hopefully still alive in a dinghy. But despite everyone's best efforts, during which FK210 'E' was struck by lightning, nothing was found.

The barometric pressure could vary considerably between base and the area being patrolled and crews routinely descended to around 100ft (30m) above the sea once on station and set their altimeters to zero feet. This gave them some reassurance that their altimeter was correctly set while providing a small margin of 'padding'. It is believed that Owen may have flown into the sea while attempting this procedure in the prevailing terrible conditions.

Two less serious mishaps involving 206 Sqn followed in December and January. On December 28, Fortress IIA FK191 'N' was damaged at Aldergrove following low level bombing practice. F/Lt Roxburgh had delegated co-pilot F/O Alexander T Lovell to make the landing on a runway that was being extended. Lovell landed long, skidded on a surface made greasy with mud by left by work trucks and ran off the end into banks of rubble, causing the port undercarriage to collapse and the propellers to churn up the ground. The Fortress was repaired on site by 26 MU.

A few days later, on January 9, 1943, 206 Sqn pilot F/O Frederick S Wills was making an approach to Hawarden in Fortress II FA708 while en route to AST at Hamble. Knowing the runway was short, Wills attempted to land as early as possible using a low-power approach while believing that a waiting Hawker Hurricane – Mk IIB JS358 of 41 OTU – was clear of the threshold. However, the Hurricane pilot apparently moved his aircraft forward, its propeller striking the underside of the Fortress' wing. FA708 was repaired on site and moved to AST for modifications prior to formerly joining 206 Sqn in mid-February.

The next attack on a U-boat by 206 Sqn took place on January 15, 1943. The crew of Fortress FL452 'G', captained by P/O Leslie Clark, was tasked with conducting anti-submarine sweeps around convoy ON 160. A surfaced submarine was sighted at six miles (9.7km) in position 57°40'N, 27°10'W and Clark attacked with all seven depth charges, although three failed to explode. U-boat U-632 was seen to slip backwards below the surface at a steep angle but had in fact sustained only minor damage. It would be sunk on April 6 by Liberator III FL930 'R' of 86 Sqn.

Short Commission

59 Sqn (code letters 'TR' and motto '*Ab uno disce omnes*' or 'From one learn all') was the third Coastal Command unit to operate the Fortress, albeit briefly and, uniquely, between operating different marks of Liberator. The squadron was released from operations using Hudsons on August 17, 1942, to begin training on Liberator IIIs, the first operation with the type taking place from Thorney Island, Hampshire, on October 24. Just weeks later, and to the consternation of squadron

Liberator IIIA LV337 'E' of 120 Sqn. Formerly B-24D 41-1087, it also served with A&AEE, RAE and the ATA. It was sold on July 31, 1947, and became G-AHDY. via Peter Clare

personnel, the unit was advised it was to re-equip with the Fortress in advance of moving to Chivenor in Devon as part of 19 Group's coverage of U-boat transit routes in the so-called 'Outer Zone' of the Bay of Biscay.

The main reason for the change of equipment was the critical shortage of Liberators. This had created a pressing need to increase 120 Sqn's establishment so it could maintain a detachment in Iceland to cover the critical North Atlantic convoy routes and had further resulted in a decision to concentrate long-range Liberator Is and modified Liberator IIIAs with 120 and 224 Sqns. 59 Sqn's Liberator IIIs were therefore withdrawn and among those sent to Scottish Aviation for conversion to Long Range configuration.

The initial plan was to re-equip 59 Sqn with new Halifaxes as they became available, but this was subsequently changed to the Fortress of which there were now enough to equip three squadrons. The Inspector-General, Air Chief Marshal Sir Edgar R Ludlow-Hewitt, would later visit Chivenor to placate 59 Sqn's commanding officer W/Cdr Geoffrey C C Bartlett, AFC, and subsequently wrote to Coastal Command's new commander, Air Marshal Sir John Slessor: "*Ultimately of course we shall have to re-equip one of the Fortress squadrons to Liberators again... it is all a little bit of a mess.*"

59 Sqn, who for a number of weeks had no aircraft at all, began converting to the Fortress at Thorney Island on December 13. In the meantime, two officers and one crew were detached to 206 Sqn at Benbecula for a Fortress conversion course on December 8, returning to Thorney Island ten days later. During the work up Fortress IIA FK188 was badly damaged when, on December 30, it was struck by Handley Page Hampden I AE370 of 415 Sqn after the latter swung off the runway while taxiing. The Hampden was written off while the Fortress would require more than six months of on-site repairs by Marshall of Cambridge.

Meanwhile, Fortress I AN519 had joined 59 Sqn at Thorney Island on December 28 after service with 206 Sqn at Benbecula. It was employed as a hack until it passed to 1 OTU at Thornaby at the beginning of October 1943.

The first Fortress left Thorney Island for Chivenor on January 21, 1943, and the first anti-submarine patrol was undertaken by FK205 'B' two days later with F/O Alexander R Neilson, RCAF, in command. Of the three Coastal Command Fortress units, 59 Sqn was the most likely to meet enemy aircraft due to the proximity of its operations to Luftwaffe bases in France. The first encounter took place on January 24 when FK205, with F/O Howard A L Moran, RAAF, at the controls, was involved in an "*inconclusive combat.*"

Taking off at 10:06, Moran reached his patrol starting position of 46°10'N, 08°15'W at 13:05. Five minutes later, while on track at 2,500ft (762m), a Junkers Ju 88 was sighted off the starboard beam, some 800 yards (732m) away and flying on a parallel course. Both aircraft immediately climbed for the cloud base some 500ft (152m) above while the Ju 88 worked its way around to make an attack. As it bore in towards FK205's starboard nose, it fired a long burst starting from 400 yards

Fortress IIA FK202 'B' of 59 Sqn wearing a variation on the Temperate Sea and White scheme – it had previously spent two months at RAE Farnborough engaged in LRASV, auto-pilot and radio transmitter trials. It is equipped with the American-designed search aerials and shrouds and waste gate extensions on the exhaust systems. The upper leading edges of the wings and the sides of the nacelles have been painted White (see colour profile page 230). FK202 crashed off the Azores on October 25, 1943, while flying with 220 Sqn as '2-L'. 59 Sqn via Andy Thomas

(366m) but scored no hits. In return, Moran's rear gunner managed to get off a 5 to 6 second burst of some 160 rounds as the Junkers passed under the Fortress and then entered cloud, but no hits were observed. Moran then took evasive action and the Ju 88 was not seen again. The undamaged Fortress landed at Chivenor at 16:41, its load of 14 depth charges still intact. FK205 was apparently not fitted with a bomb bay fuel tank. The fact that the Ju 88 was a singleton indicates it was most likely either a reconnaissance aircraft of 3 *Staffel (Fern)/Aufklaerungsgruppe* 123 based at Rennes or a weather reconnaissance Ju 88D-1 from *Wekusta* 51 based at Toussus-le-Buc.

The move to Chivenor was completed on February 6, by which time the squadron had eleven Fortresses on strength, including the first Fortress IIs to enter Coastal Command service, FA698 'V', FA703 'T' and FA704 'R'. That same day P/O Stephen G Duplooy attacked a U-boat while flying Mk IIA FL463 'D'. Airborne at 09:33, the Fortress had reached its Prudent Limit of Endurance (PLE) at position 47°18'N, 18°47'W, and the planned patrol was cut short. At 16:20 hours, at position 46°59'N, 16°42'W while returning to base at 3,300ft (1,006m), the nose look-out spotted the wake of a U-boat three points on the starboard bow and four miles (6.4km) away. At two miles (3.2km) it was seen to be fully surfaced and travelling at an estimated 6 knots (11km/h). Duplooy turned to starboard for an up-sun attack while attempting to rapidly lose height but, too close to the target when it was sighted, he could not descend fast enough to make the run.

When 1,000 yards (914m) away, the upper turret gunner opened fire and numerous hits were seen on the U-boat's conning tower, with three or four men seen scrambling for cover. When 800 yards (731m) away, the U-boat returned fire with what was believed to be a cannon, although FL463 sustained no hits. As the Fortress passed overhead, the rear gunner opened fire, again scoring hits on the conning tower, and as Duplooy turned the aircraft to starboard, the beam gunner also fired, just as the U-boat was diving. The Fortress completed a 200-degree turn to drop five depth charges from 50 feet (15m) across the U-boat's track from port to starboard, some 30 seconds after the U-boat had submerged and three swirl lengths ahead of the swirl. The beam gunner saw the depth charges explode in a straddle across the vessel's track but, beyond the usual depth charge 'scum', no further results were observed.

On March 1, FL463 'D' was to be involved in a second attack, this time while being flown by F/O Neville Barson. The Fortress was five hours into its sortie when the beam gunner sighted a surfaced U-boat one to two miles (1.6 to 3.2km) on the starboard beam in position 47°N 18°W. Barson altered course by 180 degrees to starboard, losing height rapidly to make an up-sun attack, 15 degrees to the target's track. As FL463 approached, U-223, commanded by *Oberleutnant* Karl-Jürgen Wächter, opened fire with red and blue tracer and continued firing for a few seconds after the aircraft had passed overhead. The Fortress sustained considerable damage with the hydraulic system hit, causing a large spurt of oil on the flight deck and in the navigator's compartment, the No. 4 engine throttle control severed, and the automatic pilot rendered unserviceable. Despite the numerous distractions, including the aircraft filling with smoke, Barson managed to drop five depth charges from 60 to 80ft (18 to 24m), aimed to fall from the U-boat's port bow to its starboard quarter. Three explosions were observed, the nearest being 20ft (6m) from the starboard side of U-223's hull and two-thirds the distance from conning tower to the bow.

At least six men were seen on the U-boat, four in the conning tower and two on the aft deck. FL463's rear gunner raked the deck but no casualties were seen. U-223 appeared to lose way and stop after the attack while Barson flew out of range for a minute to assess damage to the aircraft.

On his return, the U-boat had submerged and a patch of depth charge 'scum' was seen merging into the swirl. Baiting tactics carried out for the next 17 minutes failed to reveal the U-223's position so Barson set course for base. The aircraft landed back at Chivenor without incident at 18:37. The U-boat had sustained only minor damage

59 Sqn's final recorded action with the Fortress took place on March 3 when F/O Henry D Kelvin and crew attacked an unknown U-boat in Fortress IIA FL462 'C' at 46°55'N 19°05'W. Kelvin attacked 'up track' from 200ft (60m) and at 10 degrees from port to starboard, dropping five of his seven depth charges. The U-boat lost all way and a further attack was attempted but the aircraft was turning too steeply when it next passed over the target. The submarine then sank very slowly, stern first, leaving just the bows above water, but there is no record of a U-boat being damaged or lost that day.

On March 23, 1943, FK209 'J' departed Chivenor for a patrol over the Bay of Biscay with 30-year-old Canadian pilot F/O Richard J Weatherhead as captain. At 13:10 the radio operator was heard stating that they were being attacked by an enemy aircraft and five minutes later FK209 was shot down at 47°42'N 06°55'W by *Oblt* Hermann Horstmann of 13/KG 40 flying a Junkers Ju 88C. All eight on board, including seven Canadians, were lost (see aircrew profiles pages 177 and 182).

Three days later, on March 26, Fortress II FA698 'V' was lost when it flew into a hillside at Luscott Baton in low cloud while preparing to land at Chivenor at night at the end of a ten-hour patrol. Three crew members died while another was injured. The court of enquiry determined that the pilot, Australian-born F/Lt James L Heron, had erred in not carrying out a "*full and correct*" Blind Approach Beam System (BABS) procedure and had begun his descent outside the centreline of the beam.

The last 59 Sqn operation using the Fortress was flown by P/O Stephen Duplooy, DFC, on March 27, FL463 'D' reaching 47°N 11°W. The squadron moved back to Thorney Island the same day to begin converting to the Liberator V equipped with the improved ASV Mk III radar.

An unusual postscript concerning 59 Sqn and the Fortress focused on the idea of using artificial lighting to camouflage Coastal Command aircraft. The concept involved installing an array of forward-facing lights below the leading edge of an aircraft's wing so that the aircraft's light level matched the sky when viewed from a U-boat. Photo-electric sensors calculated the intensity of the lightning required. Preliminary trials at A&AEE Boscombe Down using a Whitley had shown "*very promising results*" and on December 1, 1942, an immediate service trial was requested "*... as it seems probable that aircraft so fitted would achieve an appreciable increase in the number of sightings of U-boats and even more in the number of attacks.*" The Fortress was considered "*... the aircraft best suited for the purpose and as 59 Sqn is to be re-equipped with this type of aircraft, it was suggested that they should be fitted with this system of lighting camouflage.*" It was requested that the system be made an operational requirement but the idea was quickly abandoned due to excessive battery weight and the promise of ASV radar.

Whitley VII, possibly Z9529, was assigned to trials of an artificial lighting system considered for installation on Fortresses of 59 Sqn. The idea was to blend the aircraft's head-on silhouette with the brighter ambient lighting. Although, the concept did allow the aircraft to get closer to an observer before being spotted, it was not adopted for operations against U-boats due to the weight of the system's batteries and, no doubt, the drag created by the array of underwing lights. via Peter Clare

However, the concept of reducing aircraft visibility while approaching a target appears to have been explored further by 59 Squadron as two unit aircraft, Fortress IIA FK202 'B' and Fortress II FA704 'R', are known to have been painted with White bands on the upper wing leading edges with the White undersides extending further than normal up the sides of the engine nacelles (see pages 58 and 68).

Crew of Fortress IIA FL464 'E' of 59 Sqn while based at Chivenor, Devon, March 1943. The captain, second from the front left, is F/O Howard A L 'Tim' Moran, RAAF, while the poodle mascot is Stinker. In the centre of the window group is WOP/AG Sgt Kenneth R 'Titch' Regan, father of the contributor of this photograph. Of technical note is the clear view of the upper RC-143 search transmit aerial for the ASV Mk II radar. Both it and the partially-visible side-mounted RC-147 receive array were removed from operational Fortresses shortly afterwards. Chris Regan

BATTLE FOR THE

WESTERN APPROACHES

Shipping losses for the second half of 1942 averaged an unsustainable 500,000 tons (508,025 tonnes) per month and the first six months of 1943 proved to be the most precarious and ultimately most crucial period in the Battle of the Atlantic. By the end of January 1943, there were 37 U-boats operating in the Mid-Atlantic Gap and when Sir John Slessor took over as C-in-C Coastal Command on February 5, 1943, his only resources to cover the vital Western Approaches into Liverpool – later described as "...*the pivot on which the Allies' whole European war effort has turned*" – were the five Liberator Is and twelve Liberator IIIAs (Long Range) of 120 Sqn, shared between Aldergrove and a detachment in Iceland, and the two dozen Fortresses of 206 and 220 Sqns based at Benbecula and Ballykelly respectively. Of the other Liberator units, 86 Sqn was non-operational at Thorney Island with six modified Liberator IIIAs while 224 Sqn was operational at Beaulieu in Hampshire with unmodified Liberator IIIAs covering the outer Bay of Biscay. The equipment situation appeared desperate yet there were signs that the tide of shipping losses could be turned, beginning with a string of successful attacks by Fortress crews.

220 Sqn's first two U-boat sinkings took place in early February. On February 3, Fortress IIA FL456 'N' was providing a daytime sweep for convoy HX 224 when the crew, captained by P/O Kenneth Ramsden, spotted a U-boat at four miles (6.4km) through a gap in the clouds while 29 miles (47km) from the convoy. Ramsden descended from his 3,000-foot (914m) patrol altitude and positioned the aircraft with the sun behind him to attack from 50ft (15m) with all seven depth charges. The detonations produced some oil but, according to the Admiralty assessment, "*Insufficient evidence of damage.*" In fact, U-265 had been sunk at 56°35'N, 22°49'W with all hands on its first patrol with *Oberleutnant zur See* Berhhard Auffhammer in command. Ramsden would not learn of the revised 'U-boat sunk' assessment until receipt of a letter from Headquarters, Coastal Command dated September 17, 1945. The German authorities were more certain about what had happened, the war diary stating: "*U-265 was probably lost in this operation. There is a report of an attack by an English aircraft with bombs on a U-boat N. of the convoy.*"

Four days later, P/O G Peter Roberson was sweeping around convoy SC 118 in Fortress IIA FL459 'J' when, at 56 miles (90km) from the convoy, a submarine was sighted on the surface. Roberson climbed into cloud and approached through a rain squall to ensure a surprise attack and the submarine's conning tower was still partially above the surface as he released his seven depth charges from 50ft (15m). These produced a 12-foot (3.7m) long round object, various issues of oil and a variety of debris. U-624, a veteran of seven merchant ship sinkings, had been destroyed at 55°42'N 26°17'W on her second patrol under *Kapitänleutnant* Ulrich Graf von Soden-Fraunhofen.

206 Sqn then achieved a partial success two days later when, on February 9, S/Ldr Richard Patrick and the crew of Fortress IIA FK195 'L' attacked a U-boat at 56°12'N 20°59'W while flying escort to a destroyer towing a corvette. A stick of six depth charges straddled U-614 forward of its

220 Sqn's FL459 'J - Johnnie' was the most successful of Coastal Command's Fortresses with three U-boats sunk. It also appears to have been one of the most photographed examples while in the anti-submarine role. This view well illustrates the nose and underwing 'Yagi' aerial arrays for the ASV Mk II's homing function. For unknown reasons, the cold air intake for the outboard engine's supercharger – inboard of the de-icing boot and landing light – has been blanked off and painted in under surface White. The cowlings appear to have a slightly glossy appearance and may be painted with the required stoving enamel. FL459 later served with 519 and 251 Met Sqns before being struck off charge in December 1945. IWM CH.11131

FK186 'S' of 220 Sqn flares for a classic three-point landing at Benbecula. Flying the big-winged Fortress has been likened to piloting a Piper Cub, a nod to its stable and predictable handling qualities. via Mike Hughes

220 Sqn flight personnel at Benbecula with Fortress IIA FK193 'H', May 1943. At the centre is Sqn commanding officer, W/Cdr Patrick E Hadow. via Edward Ramsden

P/O G Peter Roberson and the crew of Fortress IIA FL459 'J' achieved 220 Sqn's second success when they sank U-boat U-624 on February 7, 1943. After the war, Roberson became an airline pilot with British European Airways and British Airways. IWM CH.11068

conning tower, causing the U-boat to lift out of the water and sink, although she was able regain St Nazaire on February 26.

Because of the difficulty of confirming which actions had resulted in which U-boat losses, the results of a number of engagements have been the subject of reassessment over the years. One such case involved an attack made on March 7, 1943, by a 220 Sqn crew led by F/O William Knowles. Knowles was flying Fortress IIA FL459 'J' as escort to convoy SC 121 when he spotted a submarine at 57°14'N 26°30'W. He attacked, dropping seven depth charges from 80ft (23m), and was subsequently deemed to have sunk U-633. However, U-633 is now judged to have been sunk three days later on March 10 after being rammed by the merchant vessel SS *Scorton* and it is thought that Knowles' target was in fact U-641, which did not sink.

The climax of the convoy battles was about to take place. On March 5, 60 ships sailed from New York to Liverpool as convoy SC 122 and behind these were another 40 ships forming the faster convoy HX 229. The German command positioned eleven U-boats in the path of the convoys plus two further patrol lines of 18 and ten U-boats respectively. Severe weather made them late into position to intercept SC 122 but they did find HX 229. Recognising that a major battle was at hand, Coastal Command moved 220 Sqn to Benbecula on March 13 to operate its Fortresses alongside those of 206 Sqn.

The U-boats moved in on March 16, torpedoing eight ships of which two sank almost immediately. They then located SC 122 and on March 17 more than 40 U-boats were ordered to move in. 120 Sqn's Liberators arrived just in time, sighting eleven U-boats and attacking six. From March 18, the Liberators were constantly overhead, resulting in no losses to SC 122 and only two to HX 229. By the early morning of March 19, the two convoys were within 600 miles (965km) of Benbecula and the protective coverage of 206 and 220 Sqns. Relays of Fortresses now took over providing close escort over the sea lanes into Liverpool and were to carry out two effective attacks that day.

P/O Leslie Clark of 206 Sqn, who had earlier damaged U-632, was captain of Fortress IIA FK208 'B' when his crew spotted a U-boat hiding in a rain squall behind HX 229. An excellent straddle produced a heavy oil patch that would later prove to mark the end of U-384, commanded by *Oberleutnant zur See* Hans-Achim von Rosenberg-Gruszczynski and sunk on its second patrol at position 54°18'N 26°15'W. Clark subsequently received the DFC.

Making his second attack in less than two weeks, F/O William Knowles of 220 Sqn damaged U-666 while escorting SC 122 in Fortress IIA FK203 'M'. Two separate runs left the submerged

Staged view of FL459 'J' and FK212 'V' of 220 Sqn while operating from Benbecula in mid-1943. Coastal Command's Fortresses invariably patrolled alone. IWM CH.11142

U-boat surrounded by oil, forcing its captain *Oberleutnant zur See* Herbert Engel to cut short the submarine's first patrol and return to St Nazaire with its No. 5 ballast tank and bow tubes leaking and its speed restricted to 10 knots. Later in his patrol, Knowles guided escort vessels to lifeboats and rafts from the sinking MV *Luckenbach*.

There were no further losses to SC 122 and HX 229 and Dönitz called off the U-boats on March 20. His war diary states: *"Many [U-]boats were bombed on the 19th and some depth-charged for a long time and it is probable therefore that more escort forces joined the convoy after the first big coup in the night 16/17 and above all it was surrounded by a very strong air escort. Operation by day on the 20th would already bring the boats too far into the area covered by English shore-based aircraft, they were ordered to break off at first light on the 20th. Any opportunity to make a day submerged attack after dawn was to be taken and the boats were then to move off to the S.W. in case there should be stragglers and damaged ships left on the convoy route."*

In all, 21 merchantmen had been lost totalling 141,000 tons (143,265 tonnes) and only one U-boat had been sunk – but the carnage would have been far greater without continuous air support.

The next major U-boat action was to have focused on convoy ONS 1. A bad storm meant that the 30 U-boats ended up pursuing convoys SC 123 and HX 230 and when the storm abated, they were constantly harassed by aircraft from the escort carrier *Bogue* until within range of 120 Sqn's Iceland-based Liberators. The operation ended in failure for the Germans with only one straggler sunk, while escorting Fortresses of 206 Sqn sank two of their number.

The first sinking took place on March 25 with F/Lt William Roxburgh in command of Fortress IIA FK195 'L' (see colour profile page 231). F/Sgt Joe Griffith was his navigator:

"We had left Benbecula in the dark for our search area between the Faeroe Islands and Iceland. The area was to be only 60 nautical miles square and since it was still dark when we arrived I suggested to Roxburgh that we move up closer to Iceland, some 100 miles to the northwest. He agreed and we began our search from over a lighthouse on the southeast corner of Iceland, flying the north-south tracks ten nautical miles apart. It was daylight by then and we settled into flying at 3,500ft with little bits of cloud below us."

Jaunty mid-1943 view of FK190 'J' of 206 Sqn at Benbecula. It wears a predominantly all-white finish on the fuselage with a narrow band of Temperate Sea camouflage running along the upper centreline (just visible on top of the nose) and aluminium paint on the de-icing boots. FK190 was used exclusively for training and transportation flights and, for reasons unknown, retained the now obsolete sideways-looking 'stickleback' array installed for the earlier LRASV trials at RAE Farnborough. IWM CH.11130

F/Lt Lawrence 'Slug' Nelson in the cockpit of a 206 Sqn Fortress at Benbecula. His last flight with the squadron took place from the Azores on January 18, 1944, following which he was posted to the Empire Central Flying School at RAF Hullavington in Wiltshire. On March 19, Nelson was on final approach in Mosquito VI HJ665 following a local type familiarization flight when he experienced failure of the port engine. A sharp veer to left was corrected by shutting down the starboard engine with the intention of gliding into a field. All went well until both wings were torn off as the Mosquito passed between some trees. Nelson, still attached to his seat, was ejected through the canopy of the shattered Mosquito but miraculously survived. He was discharged on medical grounds after the end of the war. via Simon Nelson

F/Lt William Roxburgh and the 206 Sqn crew that sank U-boat U-469. From left to right: WOP/AG Sgt Jock Rimmer, navigator F/Sgt Joe Griffith, WOP/AG Sgt Richard E Thomas, Roxburgh, WOP/AG Sgt Ray L Simpson, co-pilot Sgt Lloyd R Meech, and WOP/AGs F/Sgt Douglas Eley and Sgt Jack K Churchill. Taken at Benbecula with Fortress II FA709 'B' of 220 Sqn as backdrop. Note that the fuselage is painted White with a narrow band of Temperate Sea camouflage along the upper centreline. via Joe Griffith

Sgt Richard Thomas was monitoring the ASV radar set in the radio compartment:

"For some 15 miles or so I had been passing instructions to 'Willis' about a blip on the radar screen and he had turned to home in on the return. The orange blip grew as we made a descending approach through a layer of cloud but we expected to see nothing more than a fishing trawler out of Reykjavik."

Joe Griffith resumes his account:

"Then there, straight in front of us at between one-and-a-half and two miles, was a surfaced U-boat, cutting across our second south-to-north track. We were close enough that there was no hesitation in making a direct attack. I opened the electrically-actuated bomb bay doors, which took more than 30 seconds to open, and Roxburgh put the aircraft into a dive to lose the 3,500ft. As we got closer, Doug Eley opened fire from the top turret and we could see tracers going down into the conning tower."

Despite the spur-of-the-moment attack, Roxburgh's aim from around 200ft (60m) proved to be deadly accurate with three depth charges falling on either side of the U-boat. He and co-pilot Sgt Lloyd Meech then just managed to pull the Fortress out of its dive before making a steep turn to assess the results of the attack. Joe Griffith:

Well-known view of a Fortress in landing configuration over a croft located within the airfield boundary at Benbecula. The aircraft appears to be rather high to be on approach and close examination reveals that the Fortress has been cut out from another image and pasted onto a photograph of the building. via Sid Banks

"As we came around in the turn, we saw the U-boat with maybe a third of its hull out of the water and headed stern down at an estimated 30-degree angle. We learned later from photographs taken by Richard Thomas that Roxburgh and Meech had pulled the Fortress out of the dive just 20ft above the water."

In what Roxburgh described in his logbook as a 'double attack', a second run was made to drop the seventh depth charge. This produced a film of light oil, followed by an ominous stream of dark bunker oil. U-469 was on her first patrol under the command of *Oberleutnant zur See* Emil Claussen when sunk by Roxburgh's crew at 62°12'N 16°40'W. The German war diary entry for March 30 stated: *"U-469 left Kiel on 16.3 and has not reported since then. According to a Radio Intelligence report, English aircraft reported a U-boat in AF 7122 on 22.3 and one in AE 84 on 25.3. In both cases it could have been U-469* [it was the latter]. *Possibly she was attacked and sunk by the aircraft."*

The second attack took place two days later on March 27. F/O A C Ian Samuel was captain of the same Fortress, FK195 'L', and flying a Creeping Line Ahead search when his co-pilot P/O Lewis G Healy spotted a U-boat three miles off the starboard nose. Samuel dived from 2,000ft (610m) to drop his first cluster of depth charges in the face of return fire from the U-boat. The submarine was seen to roll over and then reappear with its bows up at a sharp angle. A second attack resulted in the U-boat crew emerging from the conning tower and the boat rapidly sinking at 60°54'N, 15°25'W. U-169, commanded by *Oberleutnant zur See* Hermann Bauer, was also on its first patrol. The German war diary for April 2 states: *"U-169 has not yet reported since her departure from Kiel... The boat must be considered lost."*

WINNING FORMULA

These engagements represented the beginning of the end of easy pickings for U-boats in the North Atlantic. The growing use of escort carriers, expansion of the long-range Liberator force to around 30 aircraft, and the outstanding work of Fortress and Sunderland squadrons meant it was now increasingly difficult for U-boat packs to concentrate their attacks against Allied shipping. But building a larger Liberator force was presenting new challenges, reinforcing the value of the Fortress. On April 4, three of 206 Sqn's most experienced Fortress crews, headed by F/Lts William Roxburgh and Eric Bland, and F/O Ian Samuel, were urgently transferred to 86 Sqn, then based at Aldergrove in Northern Ireland. Previously equipped with short-range, twin-engined Bristol Beauforts, 86 Sqn's navigators had no long-range experience, leading to cases of near fuel exhaustion and one non-fatal loss following 16-hour-plus missions. 220 Sqn also provided crews to assist with the transition.

April 1943 proved to be a relatively quiet month in the North Atlantic but it did offer F/O 'Bob' Cowey of 206 Sqn the chance to dispatch a second U-boat on April 24. Cowey was flying Fortress IIA FL451 'D' on a sweep for convoy ONS 5 when a submarine was spotted some ten miles (16km) ahead. Cowey attacked at right angles to the U-boat's track, the first six depth charges lifting the vessel almost clear of the surface, and then made a second attack after which some 25 survivors were seen in the water. U-710 had been sunk at 61°25'N, 19°48'W on its first cruise while captained by *Oberleutnant* Dietrich von Carlowitz. Once again, the German war diary records that a new vessel had disappeared: *"U-710 has not reported since it sailed from Kiel on 15.4. There have been numerous sighting and attack messages recently from the area of the Iceland Passage, so that its loss through aircraft must be presumed."* With Benbecula closed in and fuel running low, Cowey diverted to Iceland. He was later awarded the DFC.

There were still more than 90 U-boats operating in the North Atlantic in early May and, from May 10, 36 were in position to engage eastbound fast convoy HX 237 and associated slow convoy SC 129. But 86 Sqn was now fully operational, its Liberators equipped with homing torpedoes, and the escort carrier HMS *Biter* was in attendance with its Fairey Swordfish and Grumman Wildcats. The U-boat force failed to develop a co-ordinated attack and lost four of their number for the sinking of five ships. The next eastbound convoy, SC 130, was detected on May 18 and, although not protected by an escort carrier, benefited from continuous air cover which made repeated surprise

220 Sqn crew boarding Fortress IIA FL462 'W' at Benbecula. It is painted with a variation on the Temperate Sea and White camouflage scheme believed applied by its previous operator, 59 Sqn (see also FK202, pages 58 and 230). via Ted Hedges

attacks on the U-boats from the low cloud base. Six U-boats were lost with no sinkings or hits on ships. Over the two-week period starting May 10, ten convoys totalling 370 ships passed through mid-Atlantic, losing only six of their number, of which three were unescorted stragglers.

A combination of continuous air cover, the introduction of escort carriers and homing torpedoes, the ability to locate the source of U-boat radio transmissions using high-frequency direction finding equipment – known as 'Huff-Duff' – and the routine deciphering of these coded transmissions had combined to tip the balance in favour of the Allies and make U-boat losses unacceptable. Coastal Command's Fortresses had played a key part in the victory by providing convoy escorts for the last third of their North Atlantic crossings, freeing the limited number of Liberators to cover the Mid-Atlantic Gap. Over the period January to mid-May 1943, the Fortresses had sunk six U-boats and damaged three while Liberators had sunk a further four.

By the end of May, the U-boat force had been squeezed out of the North Atlantic and relocated to the area around the Azores through which the Americans were moving vast quantities of men and materials to the Mediterranean for the forthcoming invasions of Sicily and Italy. At the time, there were no land bases available to provide long-range aerial protection.

Ken Bass' crew from 206 Sqn, clockwise from back left: Ken Bass (captain), Jim Hunt (WOP/AG), Ranald Anderson (co-pilot), Kenneth Roberts (navigator), Bill Morgan (WOP) and Dusty Miller (WOP/AG). via John Lowe

SUPPLY AND MODIFICATIONS

The supply of Liberators and Fortresses remained well below needs and expectations throughout the critical phase of the Battle of the Atlantic and led to the curious notion that Coastal Command's precious Fortresses be replaced by a shorter range type. In a revealing letter dated April 24, 1943, Sir John Slessor expressed his displeasure to Air Chief Marshal Sir Christopher L Courtney, Air Council Member for Supply and Organization at the Air Ministry:

"I am horrified to see the idea is that 206 and 220 Sqns should be re-equipped at the end of this year with Wellingtons. Except that it has not quite the range of the Liberator, the Fortress is the best aircraft in Coastal Command and it would be a disaster if these two excellent squadrons had to be re-equipped with a type of aircraft so inferior to the Fortress as the Wellington. I know only too well

Fortress II FA702 'P' of 206 Sqn returning to Benbecula from St Eval on May 11, 1943, with F/O Ken Bass in command. The ASV Mk II aerial arrays have been removed from the nose and below the wings by the censor. Following installation of Long Range ASV by 218 MU at Colerne in September 1943 and a period of storage with 51 MU, FA702 served with 1674 HCU at Aldergrove for 18 months. It was then stored again and later scrapped. Note the deployed port beam gun. via John Lowe

Two views of Fortress II FA704 'R' of 206 Sqn, the aircraft in which W/Cdr Ronald B Thomson and his crew were shot down by U-boat U-417 on June 11, 1943. The camouflage scheme differs from the definitive Temperate Sea and White scheme in that the fuselage is almost completely White except for a thin band of Temperate Sea camouflage along its spine while there are White bands spanning the entire upper leading edge of the wing and up the nacelle sides. Also of note are the undersize Type B upper wing roundels. The nose and underwing ASV aerials have been deleted by the censor. via John Lowe

the difficulty of screwing Fortresses out of the Americans. On the other hand the position in the beginning of 1944 will surely be very different to that when I last argued the subject with the Americans in November, 1942. I do hope you will do your best to get the Americans to let us have Fortresses at wastage rates, which as you know are not heavy in Coastal Command, to keep these two good squadrons going on the Fortress. I find it very hard to believe that it would be beyond the capacity of the United States to let us have 50 Fortresses through 1944 to keep these two squadrons going.

If it is impossible to get Fortresses, I hope you will do all you can to get Liberators in their place. As you know, the Liberator has a much better range but there are very definite limitations in the way of aerodrome facilities and aerodrome surfaces which make the Fortress easier to accommodate than the Liberator."

Courtney evidently acted on Slessor's urgings as a May 1943 review of requirements included a bid for 40 Fortresses as attrition replacements for 206 and 220 Sqns, although these were never received. As if to prove the continued efficacy of the Fortress, S/Ldr Humphrey L Warren of 220 Sqn attacked and badly damaged U-boat U-450 on June 6 while piloting Fortress IIA FL458 'A'.

Related to the supply issue was the growing concern over the number of projects and modifications requested by or being implemented on behalf of Coastal Command and the resources these required. At the same time, numerous modifications were adding weight to already heavy aircraft at the expense of precious range and endurance. Consideration was even given to reducing the amount of ammunition carried. All current projects and modifications had come under review at meeting held on February 18, 1943, and the minutes reveal plans for the Fortress. These included the addition of external under-wing racks for depth charges, installed on some aircraft by June 1943 according to attack records for that month, a variety of signals and navigation equipment, 'tail parachutes', and a Leigh Light. A single Leigh Light was allocated for trial installations in both the Liberator and the Fortress but in the case of the Fortress the installation never took place.

VULNERABLE FROM BELOW

Fortress IIAs and IIs were delivered to the squadrons with just a single .30 calibre Browning machine gun in the nose cone. Ted Hedges served as a flight engineer with 220 Sqn and recalls that this weapon was woefully inadequate when attacking a surfaced U-boat:

"The user was expected to locate the weapon in one of the ball sockets in the Perspex panels in the nose but it would be an unusual attack for a front gunner to have time to then correct his aim. In any case, the gun usually jammed after firing just one round, most often the fault of a cartridge case split at the rim. We didn't know how to adjust them and never did get it right."

This lack of forward offensive capability became a major issue after a Fortress II of 206 Sqn was shot down by a U-boat on June 11, 1943. Recently-delivered FA704 'R' had departed Benbecula at 07:10 with new squadron commanding officer W/Cdr Ronald B Thomson at the helm. Four hours later a U-boat was spotted from 1,500ft (455m) at seven miles (11km). Co-pilot F/Sgt Anthony F Chisnall recalled the attack.

"The U-boat made no attempt to dive and when we were about 50ft above the surface and three or four hundred yards from the submarine she opened fire with her guns. As we passed over her the captain dropped the depth charges and we realised we were being hit as the bullets made an awful rattle along the fuselage of the aircraft."

S/Ldr Humphrey L Warren of 220 Sqn attacked and badly damaged U-boat U-450 on June 6, 1943, while piloting Fortress IIA FL458 'A' during a search for a missing Sunderland. IWM CH.11065

FK185 was withdrawn from service with 220 Sqn in mid-January 1943 and in March fitted with a Vickers 40mm 'S' gun in a new nose section. The A&AEE conducted firing trials in early 1944 but the modification never entered service. The USAAF serial '12514' and original Dark Olive Drab finish are visible beneath the weathered white paint on the tail as are the overpainted 220 Sqn code letters 'NR' on the fuselage side, to the right of the roundel. The individual 220 Sqn code letter 'E' was retained and repainted on the new nose section, albeit in a darker shade of grey (see colour profile page 232). Photographed at Boscombe Down in February 1944. via Boeing

Right: W/Cdr Ronald B Thomson was 206 Sqn's commanding officer during its Fortress years. He was noted for his strong leadership and tenacious attitude, characteristics that no doubt helped him and his crew survive being shot down by a U-boat while flying FA704 'R' and drifting in a dinghy for three days. The photograph was taken at Benbecula in mid-1943. IWM CH.11063

W/Cdr Robert B Thomson and the crew of ditched Fortress II FA704 'R', about to be rescued by Catalina IB FP102 'L' of 190 Sqn flown by S/Ldr Jack A Holmes, DFC. 206 Sqn Archives via Alex Sell

Crew of Fortress II FA704 'R' about to climb aboard the Catalina after being shot down by U-417. The U-boat was sunk during the engagement. via Andrew Sweetlove

Close-up of FK185 with installation gear for the Vickers 'S' gun in place. Note the stiffener below the life raft compartment, one of two added to each side of the fuselage to accommodate the extra weight of the nose modification and recoil from the large gun. via Boeing

Right: Operator's position for the Vickers 'S' gun installed in FK185. The gun weighed 295lbs (134 kg) and was fed from the 15-round drum. Each weighed 4lbs (1.8 kg). Boeing Archives

Below: Ammunition locker for the 40 mm rounds. Boeing Archives

The U-boat's bows rose out of the water until the hull was vertical and then slid backwards into the sea. U-417 under the command of *Oberleutnant zur See* Wolfgang Schreiner had been sunk on its first patrol at 63°20'N, 10°30'W but the Fortress had also been mortally wounded. Tony Chisnall continues:

"We were making our second circuit when I noticed the number three engine was pouring out a lot of smoke. I told the Wing Commander who throttled it back and attempted to feather the airscrew… then number one and two engines started giving trouble and petrol and oil was pouring from the wing. The navigator gave the captain a course for home but we were losing height very quickly and only one engine seemed to have any life in it."

Thomson ditched a minute later and the eight crew members took to a single dinghy. Fortunately, the wireless operator had been able to transmit an SOS but the subsequent rescue operation was hampered by heavy seas and the fact that the ditching had taken place in a minefield. Later that evening a Catalina from VP-84 Squadron, United States Navy, captained by Lt Douglas S Vieira spotted their dinghy but was split open by a wave while attempting a rescue. It was not until 12:46 on June 14 that the Fortress crew was taken on board Catalina IB FP102 'L' of 190 Sqn flown by S/Ldr Jack A Holmes, DFC. Remarkably, only one Fortress crew member, former jockey F/Lt Jack F Clark, suffered any injuries. His back was hurt during the ditching and his feet became frozen while in the dinghy but his feet, less a few toes, were saved. The only survivor from the nine USN Catalina crew members, ARM1c Lionel F Pelletier, was rescued from a dinghy four days later. His companions had all died from exposure.

The nose-mounted .30 Browning was subsequently replaced by a .50 calibre weapon but 206 Sqn continued to make strenuous efforts for additional armament until it converted to Liberators in March 1944.

Underside of Fortress IIA FK185 equipped with the 40mm Vickers 'S' gun. The effectiveness of the white finish against the sky is apparent, as are the exhaust stains emanating from the exhaust-driven turbo superchargers. via John Rabbetts

Big Gun

The need for hard-hitting nose armament for the Liberator and Fortress had been recognised by Coastal Command from the arrival of the first Liberators. The answer for the Liberator I was the installation of a ventral gun pack consisting of four 20mm Hispano cannon. A different concept was envisaged for the Fortress in the form of a single turret-mounted 40mm cannon in place of the normal Perspex nose cone. The project was subsequently cancelled by Coastal Command as early as July 25, 1942, the command's ORB stating: "…*in view of the greatly reduced number of Fortress aircraft to be received by Coastal Command, the installation of a 40mm gun in this aircraft could be cancelled as an operational requirement for this Command.*"

Nevertheless, the Ministry of Aircraft Production decided to proceed with a trial installation based on former 220 Sqn Fortress IIA FK185. This Fortress had served on operations for just three months, from late July to late September 1942, and was then used exclusively by the squadron for training flights until dispatched to the Bristol Aeroplane Company at Filton, Gloucestershire in March 1943. Modifications took place over the latter part of 1943 and comprised a 40mm Vickers 'S' gun installed in a Bristol B.16 nose turret. The ball turret, tail guns and upper turret guns were removed, presumably to compensate for the weight of the new weapon. The gun was remotely controlled from a cupola beneath the gun mounting and could be traversed 30° horizontally and 40° vertically. The addition of the heavier nose section and recoil from the large calibre gun required the addition of external stiffeners along fuselage section 4 to the catwalk strut and to the longeron

Rear port quarter view of FK185 showing the degree of weathering to the White finish and emergence of the Dark Olive Drab upper camouflage and USAAF serial number. The large spilt flaps show up well in this view as does the added stiffener on the fuselage side, below the upper turret. Boeing

Below: Another view of FK185 at Boscombe Down in early 1944. Boeing

73

in the bomb bay area, fuselage section 5, high on the fuselage. The reinforcements were made in consultation with Boeing. Marshall of Cambridge may also have played a role as the aircraft briefly visited their facilities following modification.

FK185 arrived at Boscombe Down for flight trials on January 28, 1944. Earlier ground firing trials, undertaken elsewhere, and handling trials undertaken during February proved to be satisfactory, with no adverse affects on stability when the gun was moved, although the aircraft itself was dogged by unserviceabilities most of the time. The A&AEE's maximum take-off weight for the Fortress was raised from 48,700lb to 52,000lb (22,090kg to 23,587kg) for the trials and tests were limited to an indicated airspeed of 220mph (354km/h) because planned strengthening of the tailplane and elevators had not taken place. The installation did not proceed beyond the prototype phase and FK185 was subsequently returned to standard configuration by a Civilian Repair Organization in mid-1944, to later serve with 251 (Met) Sqn.

WIND DOWN IN UK

Fortress operations from the United Kingdom continued for the remainder of June and throughout July and August of 1943, although the opportunities for attacks on U-boats in the North Atlantic were now almost non-existent. 206 and 220 Sqns were therefore detached to the southwest of England to better cover U-boat transit routes in the southern Bay of Biscay. On the evening of June 14, Fortress IIA FK212 'V' of 220 Sqn departed St Eval in Cornwall for a 'Musketry 3' patrol with F/O Charles F Callender as captain. Early the following morning the radio operator transmitted a position, course and speed report from 46°03'N 10°55'W. Nothing further was heard from the aircraft. The second Fortress to fall to a German aircraft over the Bay, FK212 was shot down by Lt Lothar Wolff of 15/KG 40 flying a Junkers Ju 88C.

Two days later, on June 17, F/O Leslie Clark, DFC, of 206 Sqn added a second damaged U-boat to his run of successes, the last documented attack on a U-boat by a Coastal Command Fortress in the North Atlantic. Also on a 'Musketry' patrol out of St. Eval in Fortress IIA FL457 'F', Clark's front lookout spotted a surfaced U-boat at about seven miles (11km). The commander, *Kapitänleutnant* Manfred Kinzel, elected to engage the Fortress rather than dive and manoeuvred his craft to bring his rear gun to bear, resulting in a strike on the Fortress' starboard wing. The U-boat's signals

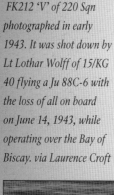

FK212 'V' of 220 Sqn photographed in early 1943. It was shot down by Lt Lothar Wolff of 15/KG 40 flying a Ju 88C-6 with the loss of all on board on June 14, 1943, while operating over the Bay of Biscay. via Laurence Croft

officer was killed and three other seaman were injured during the exchange of gunfire. Clark made two attacks in position 43°42'N 09°37'W, dropping a total of eleven depth charges, of which four were carried on recently installed underwing racks. U-338, which three months earlier shot down Halifax GR Mk II BB314 'B' of 502 Sqn, was forced to return to St Nazaire only two days into her second cruise.

Fortress crews typically flew an operational sortie every two or three days. Since it was rare to see, let alone attack U-boats, they would maintain their operational proficiency by flying regular training sorties, practising those skills most needed in the maritime reconnaissance environment: low-level bombing, gunnery, instrument flying and blind approaches. These flights naturally carried their own level of risk and there were the inevitable mishaps. One such incident befell F/O Donald A Clarke and Canadian co-pilot P/O Alfred W Dungate of 220 Sqn while landing at Benbecula on June 26, 1943. Their Fortress, Mk IIA FK206 'K', undershot the runway and the undercarriage collapsed on striking the runway end, which stood proud of surrounding ground. Two months later, on August 21, FK206 passed to 218 MU for modifications and was then reissued to the unit prior to service in the Azores.

With the North Atlantic convoy routes now secure, 206 and 220 Sqns were temporarily stood down at the end of August 1943. 206 Sqn's last Fortress sortie from the United Kingdom was flown on August 31 by S/Ldr Richard Patrick, DFC, when he captained Fortress II FA699 'O' on an operation to drop a container of W/T equipment to a destroyer escorting convoy ON 199. The final 220 Sqn operation took place on September 3, a 'Moorings Four' anti-submarine patrol in "*the customary area between Iceland and the Faeroes Islands*" by an unidentified crew in Fortress IIA FA708 'D'.

The Fortress squadrons had made an inestimable contribution to Britain's survival. Over their 13-month operational term, from late July 1942 to the end of August 1943, 206 and 220 Sqns had sunk eight U-boats while damaging another five, all without benefit of a fully effective ASV radar system. This compares with eleven sunk and eight damaged over the same period by Liberators of 120 Sqn and, from March 1943, 86 Sqn. What can never be known is the number of occasions on which a U-boat commander elected not to attack a tanker, troopship or straggler due the presence of a shepherding Fortress.

Two Fortress IIAs of 220 Sqn with FL459 'J' in the foreground and likely FK212 'V' behind. The American-designed search aerials for ASV Mk II have been removed from the rear fuselage leaving only a homing capability until the fitting of improved LRASV aerial arrays in mid-1943. Newark Air Museum

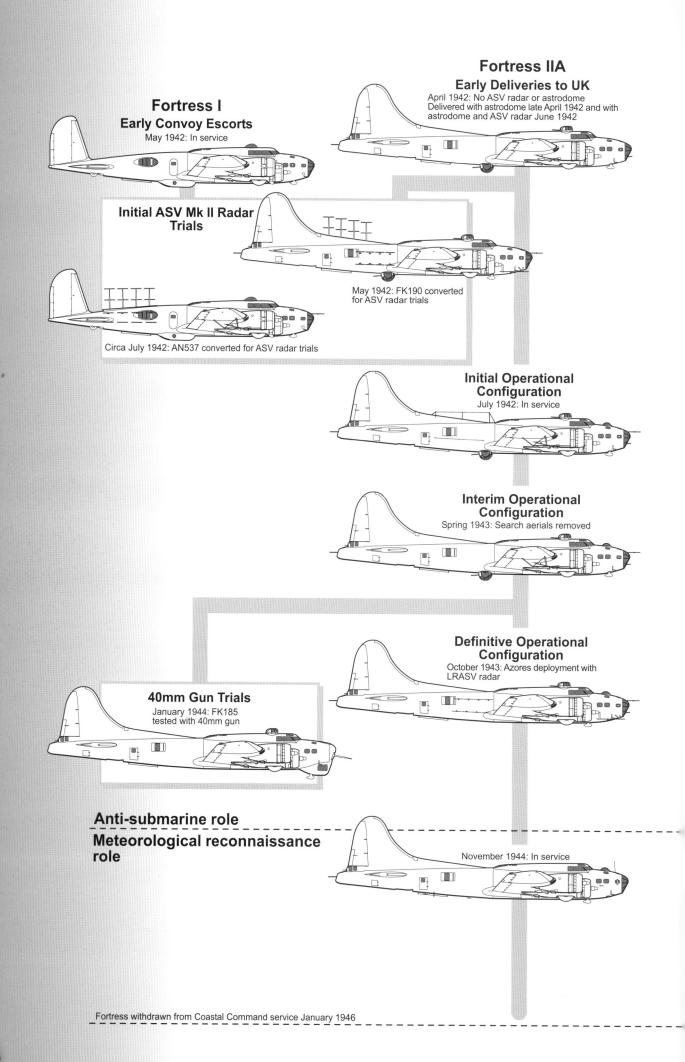

Fortress I
Early Convoy Escorts
May 1942: In service

Fortress IIA
Early Deliveries to UK
April 1942: No ASV radar or astrodome
Delivered with astrodome late April 1942 and with
astrodome and ASV radar June 1942

Initial ASV Mk II Radar Trials

May 1942: FK190 converted
for ASV radar trials

Circa July 1942: AN537 converted for ASV radar trials

Initial Operational Configuration
July 1942: In service

Interim Operational Configuration
Spring 1943: Search aerials removed

Definitive Operational Configuration
October 1943: Azores deployment with
LRASV radar

40mm Gun Trials
January 1944: FK185
tested with 40mm gun

Anti-submarine role
Meteorological reconnaissance role

November 1944: In service

Fortress withdrawn from Coastal Command service January 1946

RAF Coastal Command Fortress Configuration Changes
1942-1946

220 Sqn briefly flew two Fortress Is on convoy escort operations – they were fitted with internally-mounted depth charges and did not differ externally from the high-level bombing configuration. One of these aircraft, AN537, was fitted with ASV Mk II radar following squadron service.

The first few Fortress IIAs were delivered to the United Kingdom without an astrodome or ASV Mk II radar. The eighth example is known to have been fitted with an astrodome while deliveries from around the fifteenth example were fitted with the radar system. This became the initial operational configuration for anti-submarine operations, as flown by 59, 206 and 220 Sqns.

The ineffectiveness of the early fuselage-mounted aerial system for the sideways-looking search function led to its removal in the spring of 1943. This resulted in an interim operational configuration with the homing aerials retained in the nose and under the wings.

All Fortress IIs were delivered with an astrodome and nose- and wing-mounted homing aerials but without the ineffective search aerials installed on the Fortress IIA.

The definitive operational configuration for both the Fortress IIA and Fortress II comprised of British-designed nose-mounted homing aerials and fuselage-mounted search aerials. The improved sideways-looking component was known as Long Range ASV (LRASV).

The Fortress IIIs were delivered directly to 220 Sqn in the Azores fitted with ASV Mk III radar.

The Fortress IIA, II and III were assigned to the meteorological reconnaissance role with 251, 519 and 521 Sqns after retirement from anti-submarine operations. All were fitted with additional probes and antenna for their new role and progressively stripped of their machine gun armament. Representative armament combinations are illustrated along the bottom row.

See the scale drawings for full details of the various Fortress IIA and II modifications.

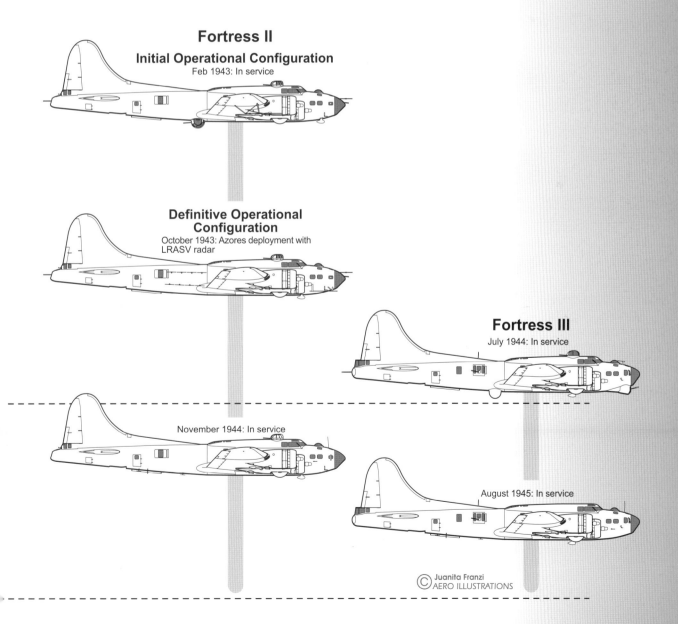

Fortress II
Initial Operational Configuration
Feb 1943: In service

Definitive Operational Configuration
October 1943: Azores deployment with LRASV radar

Fortress III
July 1944: In service

November 1944: In service

August 1945: In service

© Juanita Franzi
AERO ILLUSTRATIONS

77

TRAINING UNITS

As with the introduction of any new type, Coastal Command's Fortresses required the training of a substantial number of aircrew and 1 (Coastal) Operational Training Unit at Thornaby in North Yorkshire was selected for the task, albeit just as the type's United Kingdom-based anti-submarine role came to an end. Previously dedicated to training Hudson crews, 1 (C) OTU was assigned three former 220 Sqn Fortress IIAs on August 30, 1943 – FK196, FK199 and FL450 – as the squadron was stood down in preparation for deployment to the Azores. The Fortress Flight was formed in late September and commanded by former 220 Sqn captain, F/Lt Gerry R Haggas. Fortress I AN519 is recorded as joining the unit on October 1.

The OTU allowed pilots to build dual and solo experience, while exercises included crew familiarisation, navigation, air-to-surface photography, low-level bombing, air-to-air firing, night flying and fighter affiliation. Instructors were usually aircrew 'on rest' from operational squadrons and each was required to complete a one-month instructor's course on Airspeed Oxfords.

1 (C) OTU was disbanded on October 19, 1943, its Fortresses passing to 1674 Heavy Conversion Unit (HCU) at Longtown in Cumberland for the pilot conversion role. The unit moved to Aldergrove in Northern Ireland in mid-January 1944. Other Fortresses allocated to 1674 HCU included Mk IIAs FK201, FK205 and FL463, Mk IIs FA702 and FA703, and Mk I AN537, which was used for transportation duties. Like many aircraft pressed into the training role, they were already well-used and regarded by instructors and trainees alike as 'clapped out'.

Four Fortresses remained on strength with 1674 HCU as late as September 1945 to provide training for crews preparing for the Fortress' final role, meteorological reconnaissance, of which more later. One example, Fortress IIA FK201, was damaged on two occasions in mid-1945, the second incident occurring on June 22, 1945, while the aircraft was engaged in circuits. F/Sgt G Tough was taxiing between landings when he attempted to turn on a locked port mainwheel. The port undercarriage collapsed due to the stress imposed on a fatigue crack in the scissors bracket and the Fortress was subsequently written off.

Canadian F/O Ken Speirs, extreme right, and his new 220 Sqn crew with ASV-equipped Fortress IIA Lucy Lastic *between May and July 1944, prior to their posting to the Azores. The aircraft is believed to be a trainer with 1674 Heavy Conversion Unit at Aldergrove, Northern Ireland. If so, this would suggest FK196, FK199, FK201 or FL450 as the most likely aircraft serials. via Brian Speirs*

Fortress IIA FK205 'D' of 1674 Heavy Conversion Unit at Aldergrove, 1945. It had previously served with 59 Sqn. via George Fox

W/O George Fox and crew with a training Fortress IIA of 1674 HCU at Aldergrove, 1945. The aircraft is fitted with ASV Mk II and carries nose art featuring a 'Scotty' dog clenching a U-boat in its teeth. Left to right are: flight engineer F/Sgt Mitch Livingstone, co-pilot F/Sgt Mackie, WOP/AG Sgt Les Chambers, pilot George Fox, Sgt WOP/AG Jake Burford, MAO Sgt Ron Pretty, navigator F/Sgt Derek Wright and Flight Engineer W/O Robbie Roberts. via Andy Thomas

'FORGOTTEN' CREW MEMBER

The flight engineer was a critically important and often forgotten member of a Coastal Command crew. Ted Hedges was 18 years old when he began his training with eight months of intensive courses at RAF Cosford, a shortened air gunnery course at Pembrey in Wales and a further eight weeks at 4 School of Technical Training at RAF St Athan, also in Wales.

"I was in the very first Fortress entry trained at St Athan. It was a great place. In those days before simulators, we had examples or mock ups of everything you could imagine, including engines, bombsights, autopilots... in fact anything related to Fortresses, Liberators, Lancasters and Halifaxes. We were introduced to the Fortress through a retired Fortress I [formerly AN526 of 90 Sqn, then 4449M]. It was in Coastal Command colours and we crawled all over it though it was very firmly stuck to the ground. There were no manuals available and one's memory assumed huge importance.

Flight engineers normally spent 10 to 14 days of any course at a manufacturer's site but there was no chance that they would send us to Boeing! So I spent ten days at the American repair base at Burtonwood where damaged aircraft that couldn't be repaired in the field were flown or transported in for repair. The huge hangars were full of aircraft and the damage, especially the results of a hit by a 20mm cannon shell, was something to see... or not, depending on your point of view.

On August 16, 1943, I was one of just two trainees who successfully completed what had been a year and twelve days of training. I was given the rank of Sgt and posted to 220 Sqn at RAF Benbecula in the Outer Hebrides, just before the squadron was to go to the Azores."

THE AZORES

The air coverage gap in the North Atlantic had effectively been closed by mid-1943. This left one important void in the Atlantic, the so-called Azores Gap or, as it was known by German submariners, the 'black pit'. U-boats operating between the Azores and the Bay of Biscay and from the Azores to beyond the Canary Islands and to the west coast of Africa constantly threatened convoys plying routes from the United States and West Indies to the Mediterranean, the West Indies and South America to the United Kingdom, and from the United Kingdom to the Mediterranean, West Africa, the Cape of Good Hope and eastwards. As an example, 27 U-boats operating 400 to 600 miles (645 to 965km) north of the Azores sank a crippling 108 ships totalling 627,377 tons (617,460 tonnes) during March of 1943, severely affecting the supply of men and materials to campaigns in North Africa and the build-up for the invasion of Italy and Sicily.

Sgt Frederick 'Ted' Hedges, shortly after joining the RAF at age 19. By the time he was 21, Ted was a veteran of 35 operational flights from the Azores and was training flight engineers on Fortresses and Liberators at 1674 HCU, Aldergrove. Ted provided invaluable assistance throughout the six years the Author spent preparing this book. Ted Hedges

Fairey Swordfish IIs, an example of which is shown being refueled at Lagens, and Supermarine Seafire I and IIs of 842 Sqn from HMS Fencer conducted anti-submarine patrols from the new airstrip until the first Fortress patrols were flown on October 21. IWM CA.38

In early 1941, Portugal – which had colonised the Azores in the mid-15th Century – offered to take up arms against Germany under the terms of the Anglo-Portuguese Treaty of Alliance and Friendship, signed in London nearly six centuries earlier on June 16, 1373. If accepted, Britain faced the possibility of Germany overrunning the Iberian Peninsula, an unacceptable risk given Britain's dire situation and the plan for landings in North Africa. Nevertheless, talks began in early March 1941 with British negotiators hedging on the possibility of Portugal going to war. The sole output from the talks was an agreement to allow Britain to help develop airfields in the Azores – the Portuguese were to carry out the work with technical advice provided by Britain. The Portuguese project coordinator was Staff-Major Humberto Delgado while his contact within the Joint Planning Committee in Britain was Roland Eugene de Trevières Vintras. The Committee worked on projects for the Joint Planning Staff who in turn prepared papers addressing problems or ideas for consideration by the Chiefs-of-Staff Committee, itself a subcommittee of the War Cabinet.

Lagens airfield looking east on November 17, 1943, with the steel planked runway about half complete. Visible at the base of the hill are the tented encampments and serviceable Fortresses of 206 and 220 Sqns with Hudsons of 269 Sqn in the far distance. To the right is the servicing area containing more Hudsons and Fortresses. via Jim Glazebook.

The underlying objective for the Azores initiative was to build airfields suitable for long-range reconnaissance aircraft, thereby providing previously unavailable coverage to convoys crossing the Central Atlantic. There was already a small airstrip at Lagens on the island of Terceira, together with a reasonable port at Angra, plus a second airstrip on the island of São Miguel. Work on the primary airfield at Lagens progressed slowly but steadily over the following months, with only hand tools and ox-drawn wagons available to local workers. Other tasks included demolition of buildings to make way for the beaten earth runway together with surveys for water supplies, sewage disposal and electrical installations.

In August 1942, it was brought to Vintras' attention that, while the Portuguese Prime Minister, His Excellency Dr. Antonio D'Oliveira Salazar, was fully supportive of the development of Lagens airfield to meet Britain's reconnaissance needs, no formal request had been made to use the facilitates under the terms of the Alliance. The first response from the Admiralty was surprisingly unenthusiastic and it was not until February 22, 1943, that the First Sea Lord, Admiral of the Fleet Sir Dudley Pound, prepared a memorandum for the Chiefs of Staff promoting the Azores as base for extended air cover to "...*greatly increase the security of the lines of supply to all our overseas forces.*"

Pound laid out a number of benefits, including increased scope for evasive routing of convoys, increased carrying capacity by allowing more direct routes and increased harassment of U-boats while they were resting, refuelling and recharging their batteries. Refuelling facilities in the Azores would enable the Navy to make better use of the inadequate number of escorts, while allowing blockade runners between Germany and Japan to be more easily attacked. In addition, German warships, raiders and tankers would have greater difficulty in breaking out into the Atlantic while the islands would provide an invaluable staging point for air supply routes from the United States to the Mediterranean theatres of operations. Presumably because he was not privy to the genesis of the project, Pound held the misconception that Prime Minister Salazar would have to be browbeaten into allowing use of the islands.

On March 16, Churchill, who, according to Vintras, was still unaware of the airfield project at Terceira, reintroduced a year-old scheme to take control of the Azores, while in another twist, the US Army and US Navy presented a memorandum for Roosevelt and Churchill on May 18 entitled 'Use of the Portuguese Atlantic Islands.' These independent efforts began to coalesce when the Combined Chiefs of Staff met at the Washington Conference later that month but the proposed solution was still a small expedition by the British to capture the islands.

The airfield on Terceira was nearing completion when on June 16, 1943, a dispatch was delivered to Dr. Salazar formally requesting, under the intent of the Treaty of 1373, use of the Azores. Salazar replied in the affirmative the following day and formally responded on June 23.

Fortress II FA710 'M' just after the first landing by the type at Lagens in the Azores on October 18, 1943. Flown by 206 Sqn's commanding officer, W/Cdr Robert B Thomson, it beat out Fortress IIA FK206 'K' flown by W/Cdr Patrick E Hadow of 220 Sqn. Note the aft port depth charge rack just to the rear of the ADF loop fairing. IWM CA.4

A British delegation met with the Portuguese Chiefs of Staff on July 5, at which time they presented a memorandum detailing the facilities required. Unfortunately, the subsequent negotiations became bogged down by the demanding and not always sympathetic Portuguese delegation, to the point where, on July 24, Churchill sent a note to his Foreign Secretary, Anthony Eden, stating that the Azores must be in use by August 15 or an expedition would be launched on August 20 to take them. This was in turn leaked to the Portuguese authorities at which point the pace of the negotiations picked up markedly, although much valuable time and effort was expended addressing Portugal's demands for military equipment that could not be utilised by the Portuguese armed forces.

An agreement was finally signed on August 17 and provided, among other concessions, unrestricted use by aircraft of the British Commonwealth of Lagens airfield on Terceira and emergency diversions to Santa Ana airfield at Rabo de Peixe on the island of São Miguel.

OBVIOUS CHOICE

With its role in the North Atlantic now taken over by the Liberator, the Fortress became the obvious choice for longer range anti-submarine patrols from the Azores. Besides its availability, the Fortress' tailwheel configuration and shorter take-off and landing runs made it far better-suited to operations from the grass airfield at Lagens. The airfield itself was little more than 2,000 yards (1,830m) long and about 1,500 yards (1,372m) across at its widest point and located in a narrow valley some four miles (6.4km) long and varying in width from a few hundred yards to two miles (3.2km). It was bounded by the lower slopes of a 3,000-foot (914m) mountain to the west and separated from the sea to the east by a ridge four miles (6.4km) long which varied in height from 200 to 400ft (60 to 120m).

The move to the Azores by 206 and 220 Sqns began in earnest at the beginning of September 1943, although 220 Sqn had ferried ten of its aircraft to the assembly and preparation point at RAF Thorney Island as early as July 28. Prior to leaving Benbecula, the Sperry ball turrets were removed from each aircraft, freeing up around 1,400 pounds (635kg) for additional fuel. In general the two squadrons' aircraft were similarly equipped but, as Ted Hedges recalls, there were minor differences:

F/O Wilfred R 'Pip' Travell (second from the left, rear) and his crew with the only known view of FA708 'D' of 220 Sqn. This aircraft was written off on landing at Lagens on November 30, 1943, during a training flight. via Newark Air Museum

"206 Sqn had American headsets with throat mikes while 220's aircraft were fitted with RAF helmets with earphones and oxygen masks with fitted mics. Of course, I would not have been seen 'dead' in a 206 Sqn 'kite'!"

Ted describes the interim move to Thorney Island:

"On September 5, the rest of 220 and 206's Fortresses at Benbecula took to the air, loaded solid with all the crews' worldly possessions and as much squadron gear as could be stuffed in, to the extent that in no way could any member of the crew move to another part of the aircraft. After unhurried take-offs and careful spacing, all of which took a considerable time, the entire group flew over in a stream, beating up flying control... I experienced my first real 'g' force in the pull up. We then dispersed and set off on various courses for Thorney Island on the south coast, next door to the Portsmouth naval base.

I was part of a scratch crew for the ferry flight with S/Ldr [Harry A A] Webster as pilot of FK191 'P'. We took off at 12:30... four hours later we left a lot of Fortress 'P for Peter' spread out on RAF Benson's main runway. We had developed a major oil leak in the No. 3 engine which shed little red bits now and again. Webster soon found that we could not maintain height – which tells you how loaded we were – and since Benson was right on our course, we went for a straight-in landing. At this point the 'bod' in the tail gun position, who had no ammo, said: 'There's an Fw 190 starting an attack run on our tail!' We were on final approach so Webster called 'undercart' and pulled back on the throttles. The warning horn blew out our eardrums and it turned out that tailwheel did not fully extend. The Fw 190 proved to be a captured one that was being demonstrated to pilots of the PRU squadrons at Benson. We were God's gift to a demonstration pilot: a big Fortress leaving a miles-long smoke trail and with wheels coming down."

On arrival at Thorney Island the Fortresses were placed in the care of 3502 Servicing Unit (SU) which serviced and fuelled aircraft as required. To help differentiate the aircraft of the two units, those of 206 Sqn were marked with the unit code '1' while those belonging to 220 Sqn were marked '2'. Each Fortress was fitted with a second 341 Imp gallon (1,550l) fuel tank in the bomb bay, giving a nominal endurance of 15 hours and a still air range after takeoff of around 2,200 miles (3,540km) to dry tanks. To restore some of the lost offensive capacity, all aircraft not already so equipped were fitted with two tandem bomb racks under each wing, inboard of the inner engines and in total capable of carrying four 250-pound (113kg) Torpex depth charges.

Fortress IIA – either FK193 'H' of 220 Sqn or FL460 'H' of 206 Sqn – lands at Lagens following an anti-submarine patrol. The ASV aerial arrays have been deleted by the wartime censor. IWM CA.9

Viscount Trenchard, known as the 'Father of the Royal Air Force', visiting Lagens shortly after the start of maritime reconnaissance operations in the Azores. Although by then no longer a member of the Royal Air Force, Trenchard took it upon himself to visit RAF bases in Britain and overseas to give advice and encouragement. 247 Group's commanding officer AVM Geoffrey R Bromet stands to Trenchard's left in the foreground. Ted Hedges recalls of the visit: "Trenchard flew into Lagens in a 'Dak' in bad weather. He was very affable, humorous and required no ceremony. He talked with all he could, which was good for morale. He praised our flying effort and record, and joked that, as a Marshall of the RAF, it was his privilege to sleep all the way from the UK to Lagens." via Charles Lockwood

Ted Hedges recalls:

"Our depth charges were cylindrical in shape with an inset concave nose which prevented skipping when they hit the surface. The rear portion consisted of a cylinder of light metal with internal fins which prevented handling damage. They were painted various shades of green or dark grey and were always very weathered-looking. The normal method of removal was for the armourer to drop all four onto the deck from the nearest release point, either the button on the right hand side of the pilot's control column or from the nose bombing position. This was very disconcerting the first time you were in the vicinity as it was invariably done without warning. It was a certain cure for constipation and proof-positive that the Torpex filling didn't explode too easily!"

Ted continues:

"I was crewed up with P/O Brian Reuter and we then went on 14 days leave, as did all crews. Between September 20 and October 15, we spent our time flying between Thorney Island and St Davids Head on the west coast of Wales, doing fuel consumption tests, DF loop swings and other training details. At one point we were transported to the naval and Fleet Air Arm base at Gosport where we were issued with additional kit for going overseas, including Khaki uniforms, revolvers and much else."

One aircraft came to grief at Thorney Island during the preparations. On October 1, W/O Norman H Wright of 206 Sqn was taking Fortress IIA FK198 'W' for an air test. The engine-driven hydraulic pump failed while taxiing and Wright ordered his co-pilot to operate the emergency system. Due to the time lag the aircraft ran into a ditch. The aircraft was repaired on site by Marshall of Cambridge and reallocated to 206 Sqn in the Azores on December 24, 1943.

220 Sqn maintained a detachment at Thorney Island in support of operations from the Azores from October 1943 until the end of the war, with a handful of its aircraft regularly stationed there.

OPERATION ALACRITY

The move to the Azores – code name Operation Alacrity – was the first of its kind undertaken by the RAF and by Coastal Command in particular. The combined British force came under the direction of AVM Geoffrey R Bromet, CB, CBE, DSO, and consisted of two ocean-going elements: a leading supply convoy and the main convoy carrying 2,791 servicemen from the RAF, Royal Navy and Army. They embarked on HMT *Franconia* at Liverpool on October 1, 1943, and were escorted by HMS *Inconsistant* and HMS *Garland* as convoy HT A14. The three vessels left Liverpool on October 2 at noon and put into Belfast to await the main escort. This was picked up off the Mull of Kintyre at 14:30 on October 3 and consisted of the escort carrier HMS *Fencer* and the escorts *Havelock*, *Burza*, *Whitehall* and *Volunteer*.

Rough weather and heavy seas protected both convoys from possible attack by U-boats until October 6, with two Asdic warnings picked up on October 5 and other shadowing known to be taking place. There were also several contacts on October 8 prior to reaching the bay at Angra on Terceira, so HMS *Fencer* sent up Supermarine Seafires on patrol. The main convoy anchored at 14:30 and from then on Swordfish and Seafires began continuous patrols from HMS *Fencer* and Lagens airfield pending arrival of the Fortresses and a detachment of Hudsons from 233 Sqn. The main disembarkation began on October 9 and included 2710 Field Sqn of the RAF Regiment, tasked with protecting the airfield against potential German raiding parties landed by submarines.

In the spirit of partnership, one aircraft from each squadron was assigned to make the first transit flights to the Azores on October 18. W/Cdr Ronald B Thomson, 206 Sqn's commanding officer, flew Fortress II FA710 'M' while his counterpart from 220 Sqn, W/Cdr Patrick E Hadow, took Fortress IIA FK206 'K'. Ted Hedges remembers that there was more than history resting on these positioning flights.

"They took off from RAF St. Mawgan in Cornwall together at around 06:15 to race to the Azores. Thomson of 206 arrived first, approximately one hour before Hadow... I still remember the whole of 220 lost money on it. But Thomson 'cheated' by flying at 12,000ft all the way while Hadow flew it as an anti-submarine patrol at low level. Thomson was a 'certain type' of chap and would go hell-for-leather for anything. Somehow we all knew he would get to the Azores first or bust!

All 206 and 220 Sqn aircraft deployed to the Azores that October set off from St Mawgan. The reasons, as we understood them, were that we had the benefit of experienced servicing personnel at our departure point – our own ground crew were already in the Azores having travelled aboard the convoy

The first U-boat 'kill' by an Azores-based aircraft, U-707, fell to F/Lt Roderick P Drummond and crew flying Fortress IIA FL459 'J' on the night of November 9, 1943. Left to right are: Sgt L S C Parker, WOP/AG F/Sgt F L Fitzgibbon, co-pilot F/O Robert D Thompson, navigator F/Lt G A Grundy, Drummond, WOP/AGs P/O J B Brodie and Sgt F D Galloway, and flight engineer F/Lt J B Fitzpatrick. Fortress II FA706 'S' provides the backdrop. IWM CA.3

– and we were heavily loaded with maximum fuel plus a variety of gear for use at Lagens. Take-off took us straight out to sea, St Mawgan being, to all intents and purposes, on a cliff top."

The first anti-submarine sweeps from the Azores were flown on October 21 using the aircraft delivered by Thomson and Hadow. P/O James B Taylor of 220 Sqn captained FK206 'K' while F/O Frank W Rigg of 206 Sqn flew FA710 'M'. Delivery of the rest of the aircraft was delayed by bad weather, the next batch having to wait five days for a suitable break. Ted Hedges:

"There were no radio aids on Terceira at that time and we could not afford to chance any losses… this ruled out any prospect of a mass flight. So each crew was allocated a flight date and on October 20 our crew took off from Thorney Island for St Mawgan. On each of the mornings of October 21 and 22 we sat at the end of the runway at 6:30 waiting for a 'green' but each time the flight was scrubbed because of teeming rain at both St Mawgan and our destination. Finally, at 06:37 on the 23rd, we got off and 9 hours and 45 minutes later landed on the grass at Lagens.

The route was to fly due west from the north coast of Cornwall, thereby minimizing any likelihood of interception by Ju 88s operating from France over the Bay of Biscay. Then at a point well clear and north of the Azores, we turned south. The navigation was all done with pencils, dividers, rulers, a watch, drift calculations, really tight flying and me calculating the fuel just in case the others got it wrong! That counted as my first operational flight, a transit and anti-sub patrol."

The balance of the initial 15 aircraft allocated to each squadron for service in the Azores arrived at Lagens over October 23, 24 and 25, the Fortresses and the Hudsons of 233 Sqn taking over all patrols on October 24. Just a day later FK202 'L' of 220 Sqn failed to return. Ted Hedges was part of the search mission:

"My first flight from the Azores took place two days after we arrived. We were in our tented living area, just finishing lunch, when our CO, Wing Commander Hadow drove on site and called out for Brian Reuter's crew. He ordered us to collect our flying kit and took us straight out to Fortress FK193 'H' in his Jeep while our captain and navigator went to 'ops' for a briefing. We were off the ground in 20 minutes.

It turned out that S/Ldr Harry Webster from the Benson 'episode' in FK191 had gone off on an early morning flight and not returned. We were to fly his course while two other aircraft were to fly out on diverging courses. Webster's task had included taking meteorological readings on each hour following take-off as part of an anti-submarine sweep. To do this he had to drop down to sea level to take the readings. We found the wreckage spread over a large area, exactly one hour's flying time from the runway. The crew of eight was lost and S/Ldr Webster left a wife and new-born baby. He was a good man.

'Sea level' for most pilots meant that the man in the tail turret could see the aircraft's slipstream on the wave tops. This was always dicey as we had no radio altimeter. The angle of the sun plus the waves, wind and weather could cause height perception problems for the pilot but I must admit, even after finding the wreckage of Webster's aircraft, it never worried me when we went really low. I always thought it thrilling at 150-plus knots!

The old practice of flying down to sea level for setting the altimeter was never used in the Azores. We were always given the QFE barometric setting on approach to the airfield and I would check on the altimeter reading set by the pilots. Self interest ruled and though the Skipper knew I did this, he never commented. I guess he approved."

247 Group, as the combined air resources in the Azores were named, was officially declared operational on October 27. This coincided with the first sighting of a U-boat by the crew of Mk II FA701 'F' of 220 Sqn at 47° 17'N 35°29'W, but the submarine dived within 15 seconds and the Fortress, piloted by F/Lt Roderick P Drummond, could not lose height in time from 3,500ft (915m) to make an attack.

F/O Frank Rigg, third from the right, led the first patrol by 206 Sqn from the Azores on October 21, 1943. The LRASV aerial arrays on the aircraft involved, FA710 'M', have been crudely deleted. *via Laurence Croft*

Local labourers carry steel planking for the new runway at Lagens. IWM CA.29

Officers and men laying steel planking at Lagens. The resulting mat was covered with red volcanic earth which turned to choking dust during dry weather. IWM CA.30

BUILDING A BASE

Although the grass runway was immediately usable, there was little else at Lagens to support intensive patrol operations by the two Fortress squadrons and detachments from other units. Ted Hedges:

"Following the gentlemanly arrival of the aircrew in the Fortresses, our squadron 'erks' soon realised it was 'all right for some'. Prior to disembarking from their transport ship, they were told to change into their Best Blue uniform and then had to scramble down netting into open boats while draped with .50 ammo belts and their personal kit.

The airmen were then directed to walk over the mountains to the airfield site… 18 miles, I believe… while still carrying ammo and kit. There was nothing at the airfield site except one stone building that looked like a small barn [a former distillery]. Over the next 14 days the Royal Engineers built various compounds consisting of the standard British 12-man ridge tents while larger tents were erected to provide operating facilities. When I arrived the cooks were still doing their job using fuel stoves in the open and all food was served from its original tin onto an enamel plate… we ate standing up, sitting on the ground or in our tents if it was raining."

The highest priority after establishing the tent encampments was to install a more durable runway surface. By the beginning of November, hundreds of tons of interlocking Pressed Steel Plank (PSP) – or Marston matting as it was called by its American suppliers – together with thousands of gallons of aviation fuel, had been brought ashore and transported over the island to the airfield via the badly rutted road. In the meantime the Royal Engineers worked on preparing the existing runway surface for the 2,000 yard-long (1,830m) PSP runway. Their work was frequently interrupted by heavy rain when the ground became waterlogged in sections and exceedingly soft, but by dint of careful levelling and draining, the surface was ready for laying the planking on November 3. Ted Hedges:

"The overall task took weeks. Hundreds of personnel, including all officers, NCOs and airmen – no one was excused except hospital patients – worked four hours on and four hours off until the runway was completed. Air Vice-Marshal Bromet did at least one four-hour stint to my certain knowledge and I did a night shift with our CO, Wing Commander Hadow, because I remember him cutting his hand rather badly. He refused aid as he said he would have been accused of doing it deliberately!

Each piece of steel plank measured 10 feet long and 15 inches wide and weighed 60 pounds. I can still remember the effort required to lift and carry those sheets of steel from the stacks to the Royal Engineers who then clipped it into place and how tired I was after each stint."

Aircraft operating from Lagens meanwhile landed and took off on the grass to either side of the planking as the resident and detached squadrons got into their stride. The Azores were of great strategic value in closing the last gap in anti-submarine coverage but their remote location presented

View of Lagens airfield with Fortress IIAs FL459 'J and FK200 'B' ready for operations in 220 Sqn's dispersal area. Eleven Fortresses of 220 and 206 Sqns are visible in the servicing area across the airfield. The Pressed Steel Plank (PSP) runway is still under construction with piles of dirt and stacks of planking visible at the centre and to the left of the photograph. Progress on the runway indicates the image was taken in mid-to-late November 1943. IWM CA.1

some serious operational challenges to aircrew, particularly the shortage of diversion options. The first confirmation of this occurred on November 8 when P/O James Taylor of 220 Sqn was obliged to divert to Casablanca in Fortress IIA FK206 'K'. It was subsequently determined that an unauthorised eight-degree correction had been made to the Distant Reading Compass.

The following day, a 220 Sqn crew led F/Lt Roderick Drummond achieved the first of three sinkings involving Azores-based Fortresses. Fortress IIA FL459 'J' was on its way to meet convoy MKS 29A at dawn on November 9 when the flight engineer spotted a surfaced U-boat at position 40°31'N 20°17'W.

Drummond attacked with four depth charges from 40ft (12m) in the face of heavy fire, leaving the submarine stopped and down by the stern. A second attack with the three remaining depth charges – FL459 was apparently not yet fitted with a second bomb bay tank and underwing bomb racks – sent U-boat U-707, commanded by *Oblt* Günter Gretschel, to the bottom down by the stern. The Fortress crew later spotted a man in the water and dropped a dinghy and rations. Drummond was awarded an immediate DFC.

The German war diary recorded the following chilling entry: *"U 707, a submarine belonging to Group 'Schill', reported an aircraft attack at 08:25 on 9.11. Subsequently, the submarine did not reply in spite of frequent requests for position. She must be considered lost. [Unidentified U-boat] after returning to base, reported hearing a loud detonation with a very clear ring, similar to a torpedo detonation, followed by sounds of sinking. The sounds of diesels, which had been heard previously, had disappeared."*

Day-and-Night Team

The Fortresses provided the required long-range patrol and escort capability from the Azores but were somewhat limited for night operations as crews lacked the ability to illuminate a surfaced U-boat. A third reconnaissance type was therefore added to 247 Group during November in the form of Leigh Light-equipped Wellington XIVs of 172 and 179 Sqns, both on detachment from Gibraltar. These began night patrols on November 11, as recalled by Ted Hedges:

"The Wellingtons kept the U-boats down at night after we had been over them all day. We did some full night patrols when the moon was out, otherwise most of our night work was transits to and from patrol areas. Full moonlight was actually better than a sunny day as there was no glare and, with the great contrast, the silhouette effect was very dramatic."

After all the development effort that had gone into ASV Mk II radar it proved to be of very limited value in its intended role. Ted Hedges:

"ASV II with its improved aerial design would at least pick up a sub echo in good conditions but it had very limited range. The official figure for sideways-looking range was out to 12 miles each side. The look forward range, depending on height, was 10 to 20 miles, if you were lucky. At 3,000ft one might pick up a conning tower but a periscope was very unlikely. Even a visual sighting of a periscope would have to be in the form of a wash moving at variance to all other surface movement.

By the autumn of 1943, the U-boats had the Metox detection device which gave them ample warning of our appearance in the area. This made it useless for attack purposes and it was not normally used for searching. In all my operational flying from the Azores, ASV II was only used when the convoy commander told us to turn it on in the hope that the enemy would submerge, thus preventing them from tracking the convoy. The only use my captain ever had for the set was for navigating and homing in on beacons during bad weather. It was said that at height and with a bit of luck one could pick up beacons at 60 miles."

The effectiveness of the new aerial convoy escorts around the Azores was amply demonstrated by 247 Group between November 18 and 20, when it provided continuous cover to convoys SL 139 and MKS 30 as a formidable U-boat pack tried to get into position for a concentrated attack. The Group's Fortresses, Hudsons and Wellingtons flew 49 sorties totalling 470 hours, the only convoy casualty being the sloop HMS *Chanticleer*, damaged by a U-boat.

Fortress IIA FL 459 'J' of 220 Sqn taxies past a local oxcart of the type used during preparation of the expanded runway at Lagens. Note the covered inner engine. IWM CA.36

However, there was one incident on November 19 that had the potential to ruin this success. F/Lt Walter L Vickerstaff of 206 Sqn met the convoy in Fortress IIA FL452 'F' at 13:14Z in position 42°16'N 19°38'W. The squadron ORB describes what happened next:

"At 18:30 an aircraft emerged from cloud and found itself over wing ships of a convoy. The captain at once informed the SNO [Senior Navigation Officer] that he had broken cloud cover over convoy. The SNO acknowledged, but almost immediately the wing ships opened fire, followed almost immediately by most of the other ships. The [aircraft] Captain requested the SNO by R/T to stop ships firing, and fired recognition signals. The SNO informed all ships to cease fire, but after a slight lull heavy fire from all ships was resumed. The aircraft took violent evasive action asking the SNO repeatedly to stop ships firing. Aircraft was holed in the rear fuselage and the elevator cable broken. There were no injuries to the crew. The SNO made repeated efforts to stop the ships firing without effect. At 18:43 in position 42°55'N 19°25'W the aircraft left the convoy and set course for base which was reached safely."

This proved to be FL452's last operational flight with 206 Sqn. It was subsequently assigned to Scottish Aviation for six months of repairs before being overhauled and placed in storage. It later flew with 521 (Met) Sqn.

Lagens airfield viewed from the 500-foot (152m) hill that paralleled the north side of the runway. 206 Sqn's tented encampment is in the foreground while visible on the airfield are two Walruses of 269 Sqn coded 'A' and 'B', a transiting Dakota and Catalina, and a Hudson. Hudsons of 269 Sqn and six Fortresses occupy the servicing area to the rear. via Jim Glazebrook

Rare unofficial photo of Fortress IIA FK200 'B' of 220 Sqn about to touch down at Lagens. The American flying control tower is visible to the left of centre. via Dennis Towell

Coincidentally, a crew from 220 Sqn was to experience live firing, albeit of a very different kind, on the same day. F/Lt Peter Roberson, DFC, lifted FA706 'S' off the Lagens runway at 11:00 to provide escort for convoys SL 139 and MKS 30. The normal crew of eight was augmented by the commanding officer of 247 Group, Air Vice Marshall Geoffrey Bromet. Shortly after taking up position at very low level ahead of the convoys at 14:43, the crew sighted a surfaced U-boat. Roberson climbed to 100 feet (30m) to gain cloud cover but his quarry had dived, its swirl lost in the rough sea before he could make an attack. Escort vessels subsequently dropped depth charges on the U-boat's estimated position as FA706 returned to the convoy.

At 17:40, the Fortress crew received a transmission from the convoy's SNO: "*Enemy aircraft in Sector Dog*" and, after 30 minutes of searching, spotted a Junkers Ju 290 long-range maritime patrol aircraft. Roberson went into the attack and hits were claimed by the upper and nose gunners, mainly on the Junkers' tail, while a beam gunner reported scoring hits on its port wing. The beam and tail gunners both reported return tracer fire from the Ju 290 passing over the Fortress from port to starboard but FA706 was not hit. Roberson left the convoy in darkness at 18:30, landing back at Lagens at 21:12. This is believed to have been the only deliberate attack on a German aircraft by a Coastal Command Fortress. Interestingly, though not surprisingly given his rank, AVM Bromet's name, while noted in Roberson's logbook, does not appear in the squadron ORB.

By month-end 247 Group had attacked seven U-boats, including the one sunk by the crew of FL459 'J', and flown 2,490 flight hours over 286 sorties. This impressive performance was to

220 Sqn personnel settle in at Lagens after erecting their eight-man tents. Ted Hedges

Group of 220 Sqn engine, airframe, radio and radar fitters at Lagens, proudly displaying their home-made bamboo wash stand with biscuit tin basin. Left to right: Bill Reynolds, Bill Strang, 'Taff' Howell, Chas Hassett, 'Spike' Kelly and Bill Buchan. All worked with unrelenting cheer and determination. Ted Hedges

All maintenance work on Fortresses based in the Azores was performed in the open, regardless of weather conditions. IWM CA.17

Group of 206 Sqn fitters pose in front of FL455 'N' at Lagens (aircraft serial is conveniently visible in the crook of the left-hand fitter's arm). Second from the left is Corporal Electrician Reginald Choyce. Again, the cold air intake for the supercharger – to the left of the landing light – has been blanked off. via Lee Linley, grandson of Reginald Choyce

The RAF Standard and a Portuguese flag support a tape across the runway as ministers of three denominations bless the new runway at Lagens during opening ceremonies, December 15, 1943. IWM CA.75

be marred on November 30 when Fortress IIA FK208 'B' of 206 Sqn crashed ten miles south of Gibraltar. The crew, led by 21-year-old F/Sgt Denis J A Mitchener, was tasked with providing escort to convoy SL 140. Two-and-a-half hours after departing Lagens mid-afternoon on November 29, they were instructed by base to land at Gibraltar on completion of their sortie and nearly eleven hours into the flight, Lagens received a transmission from FK208: "*Changing alternative frequency Gibraltar station.*" Some six hours later, at 05:00 in the morning, Gibraltar advised: "*Airfield closed down with fog.* [Fortress] *Baker/206 insufficient endurance to make Port Lyautey and believed crashed near Gibraltar. Air and surface search being made first light.*" At midday Gibraltar advised: "*Regret B/206 crashed off Carnero Point early this morning. Three bodies so far recovered.*" In fact there were no survivors among the crew of seven, including W/O David S Coutts who had survived the crash of Fortress IIA FL454 'J' at Benbecula a year earlier.

Later that day saw the write-off of Fortress II FA708 'D' of 220 Sqn during a dual training exercise, happily without casualties. F/Lt Peter Roberson, DFC, was the instructor while the two trainees were his American co-pilot, Lt Theodore W Case, who was occupying the left seat, and Canadian F/O William G Cameron who sat to his right. Also on board were Cameron's captain, F/O John M Ireland, and five passengers. FA708 took off at 16:35 and ten minutes later Case made an approach. The Fortress began to undershoot close to touchdown, too late for Roberson to respond, and the aircraft hit a bank of earth short of the runway, the port undercarriage collapsing as the aircraft came to a stop. The Station Commander, G/Cpt Roger C Mead, commented that the "*risk was to be expected on* [an] *inadequate* [air]*field and* [given the] *serious shortage of captains.*" Roberson and Case flew two more convoy escorts together, following which Roberson departed Lagens as pilot of Mk IIA FL459 'J' on December 18 at the end of his tour. Like many experienced Coastal Command captains, he joined 1674 HCU at Longtown as an instructor. Lt Case left Lagens by air for the United Kingdom on December 31 on release to the USAAF while Cameron continued as Ireland's co-pilot.

The damaged FA708 was towed to the maintenance area where it was propped up and presumably picked apart for spares, as there is no record of it flying after the accident and its code letter 'D' was allocated to another aircraft in March 1944. It was eventually struck off charge on November 7, 1944.

One possible explanation for this unusual accident – given the calibre and experience of the instructor – was the method of flap selection on the Fortress. The three-position switch for the electrically-operated flaps was located on the right side of the throttle console between the pilots and was normally operated by the co-pilot on an order from the captain. Without any mechanical detents to positively engage the switch in the 'up', 'neutral' and 'down' positions, it was not unknown for the control to be flipped through the 'neutral' position after selecting flaps 'down',

220 Sqn's commanding officer W/Cdr Patrick E Hadow beats up the new steel planked runway at Lagens during the opening ceremonies. IWM CA.77

thereby inadvertently selecting flaps 'up'. If this happened during the final stages of the approach, it was likely the aircraft would develop a sink rate from which it was difficult to recover due, in part, to the relatively slow operating characteristics of the electrically-driven flaps.

LIFE AT LAGENS

At the time the British force landed on Terceira, the airfield area was absolutely bare with the exception of the one stone building. It was obvious to the servicemen that they were going to spend some time living and sleeping in the open so, in the 14 days prior to the arrival of the first aircraft, great effort was put into erecting the tented encampments and making them more comfortable. Ted Hedges:

"We lived in tents, four officers, eight NCOs or twelve other ranks to a tent and was a tight squeeze for some of us. The officers' tents are located on top of the 500-foot range of hills while those of the NCOs and other ranks were arranged in squadron areas a few hundred yards from the runway, parallel to its length. The runway was in constant use and the noise level from aircraft operating off the steel planking was very high, day and night."

Wireless Operator and Air Gunner Bill Blackwell adds his reminiscences:

W/Cdr Patrick E Hadow oversaw 220 Sqn's Fortress operations from becoming commanding officer on September 5, 1942, until he was tragically lost on December 25, 1943 while returning to the Azores from a meeting in the United Kingdom. Universally liked and admired, he is pictured at Benbecula in mid-1943. IWM CH.11062

"Food came from field kitchens and considering the primitive conditions it was quite palatable. With the town being within walking distance, we also did a bit of dining out and pineapples, bananas and most fruits were in abundance. Wines and spirits were quite cheap and off-duty hours were spent in the local drinking places. After the black-out restrictions at home, lights were a welcome luxury. I remember going to the local hairdresser in town, very similar to the ones at home with periodicals to read while waiting. There were no English newspapers but plenty in German as U-boat crews were apparently using the same shop only weeks earlier.

Rats were quite a problem in camp. One could walk between the lines of tents and often meet one. I remember doing so with a friend who took a kick at it and propelled it over a tent - it was twice as big as a cat. Water was in short supply and we were rationed so much a day… and not a lot at that. I remember having a bath in a biscuit tin, one of the old square ones. You could put one foot in at a time."

Ted Hedges continues:

"The water shortage was so acute that we were sometimes excused shaving. The ubiquitous square biscuit tin was placed on a 'home-made' bamboo table outside each tent and having collected perhaps two inches of water, tent occupants were given a number. If you were an NCO for example, you were numbered one to eight and then washed and shaved in order, moving up one position each time you collected enough water. It can be

appreciated that after the first three or four washed, soap was not required. We even shaved in the coffee remaining in our eight-man Thermos flask following an anti-submarine patrol!"

With no hangars available, squadron maintenance crews performed all routine servicing in the open. Ted Hedges remembers their incredible contribution:

"It should never be forgotten that the role of the groundcrews who worked on our aircraft was as important as any aircrew duty. Without those people – their dedication, devotion and sheer 'stickability' – we would not have survived. Every bit of servicing had to be done outdoors, in all weather conditions. Yet not once did I ever find cause to question the work done."

When the time came for Major Inspection – every 800 flight hours – the Fortresses were ferried to Thornaby, a practice that would only apply to 220 Sqn aircraft since 206 Sqn's aircraft would leave the Azores before accumulating the necessary hours. The first example scheduled for inspection was Fortress IIA FK206 'K'. F/O Desmond E Morris lifted FK206 off the planked runway at Lagens at 03:26 in the early morning of December 4, 1943, en route to Thorney Island (see photo page 174). Thirty seconds later the Fortress was seen to begin a turn to starboard and plunge into the Atlantic with the loss of all on board. The official likely cause was loss of control following the change from visual flight to instruments on a very black night. The bodies of three crewmembers were recovered, two Canadian and one Australian, to be buried in the civil cemetery at Angra and later moved to the Lajes War Cemetery. Among those missing was W/O Michael Patrick Campion. He had received the Empire Gallantry Medal, later re-awarded as the George Cross, after helping rescue the pilot of a crashed Blenheim at Uphaven, Wiltshire, on March 12, 1940.

Lagens' steel plank runway was virtually complete by the end of November, despite rains that regularly turned the airfield's red volcanic dust surface into thick mud, and on December 15 the upgraded airfield was officially opened by the military governor, His Excellency *Brigadeir* Tamagnini Barbosa. Two green and red flares, the Portuguese national colours, signalled his arrival and three padres of different denominations blessed the new runway prior to the governor cutting tapes stretched across the runway using a mallet painted with the Portuguese and British flags. A low-level display flown by W/Cdr Patrick Hadow of 220 Sqn in a Fortress II brought the ceremony to a close.

TYPICAL MISSION

Since their arrival at Lagens in the Azores in October, 206 and 220 Sqns had been engaged in a steady regime of patrols to drive U-boats away from the convoy routes. Ted Hedges begins a description of a typical mission:

"There were 18 crews per squadron, each of eight men. They ranked from Sgt to Wing Commander with the pilot usually the captain, irrespective of rank. Each crew was known by the captain's name

F/O Peter Roberson, second from the right, and his crew atop Fortress II FA706 'S' at Lagens. To his left is co-pilot Lt Theodore W Case, an American citizen who trained in Canada and who flew for several months with 220 Sqn before being released to the USAAF. via Susan Case Sciarretta, daughter of Theodore Case

and these names were listed on the operations board... each would be called in turn for an operational flight, starting from the top of the list.

Let's say our captain's name has reached the top of the board and we are next to fly. We are now on immediate standby and stay together near the operations room... if an aircraft out on 'ops' calls for assistance, we can be airborne within 20 minutes. But that doesn't happen so at about 18:00 another crew takes over immediate standby and, after a meal, we go to bed. We can expect to be called at any time and at 03:00 we're roused by the duty military policeman who shakes us until we are fully awake. He may make each of us initial his call sheet because, if we do not do all the things required of us, we could be deemed to be refusing to fly, a major offence subject to court martial.

But we are up and very much awake. We dress, pick up our shaving gear and go out under the dark open sky, rain or shine, to wash and shave at what looks like a horse trough full of cold water. After gathering our flying gear, it's down to the mess for the operational meal of bacon and eggs, tea, and bread and butter... even breakfast is completed to a pre-set time. Next we move to the 'ops' room where we sit on hardwood benches as we learn what we are about to do and the position of every U-boat in the area. We are also given the German colours of the hour and day and can always match these as we carry every colour of Verey cartridge you can imagine, from straight colours to all forms of stars.

We learn that our mission is to provide cover for a convoy sailing from Freetown, Sierra Leone, to the United Kingdom. It's a 'fast' convoy with ships of all types and we're going to relieve the previous escorting Fortress. Briefing complete, we're taken with all our gear to our aircraft where we do our in-dividual checks and tasks, bearing in mind that our wheels have to leave the ground two-and-a-half hours after our wake-up call – the only thing that can change this is a decision from 'ops'. We are even expected to move all our equipment and gear to another aircraft if ours develops a fault and still be flying on time.

The doors are shut so here we go. Our captain, Brian Reuter, checks in with all the crew and then taxies to the active runway. As flight engineer I stand entirely unsecured between the pilots with my arms looped around the shaped armour sheet fitted to their seats. My destination in the case of accident is 200 yards straight ahead through the windshield. Brian lines up on the centreline and then locks the tail wheel with the brakes hard on. He checks with the crew once more, then pushes the throttles for-ward, staggered slightly to allow for a crosswind.

We weigh 56,000 pounds... we are 6,000 pounds overweight... and have four engines of just over 1,000hp each for a total of 4,100 hp. Of our 26 tons, a little over ten tons is our full load of fuel and about five tons is weapons and explosives. As we occupy our take-off positions we know that if an en-gine fails we are likely dead... so until we all hear the reassuring 'clunk' of wheels locking in their hous-ings, we each ponder the possibilities.

We circle base according to procedures and set course as determined by the navigator. We have no set height on patrol or transit but never fly at more than 3,000ft. Our parachute bags remain stacked against the rear wall of radio cabin on the port side and we never bother putting on our parachute harnesses. There is no 'chute servicing facility at Lagens and if we are ever called on to use these things we doubt they will open. For months, un-til the Nissen huts are built, our flight equipment bags sit on the bare earth in our tents.

From now on the navigator will not cease his calculations until just before we land. The two pi-lots remain in their seats all the way while the re-maining crewmembers, including the flight engi-neer, change positions every hour - some captains use a two-hour rotation, as does 206 Sqn. This rotation between the nose, beam and tail guns, upper turret, radio set – with the exception of the flight engineer – and, if qualified in its use, the

220 Sqn flight personnel in the Azores with Fortress IIA FK193 'H'. via Bryan Yates

Future Fortress captain
Brian Reuter occupies
the co-pilot's seat of a
220 Sqn aircraft. via Ted
Hedges

ASV radar, ensures some measure of relief for the eyes from the constant scanning and for general body
strain. Each crewmember also has a one-hour rest period, although this can include a stint monitoring the radar. The rotation is drawn up by the senior radio operator and starts as soon as the aircraft
is established on course and only ends as the crew takes up landing positions. The roster has to ensure
that the flight engineer is at the upper turret position for the fuel transfer 'hour' since his controls are
located at the base of the turret.

   The beam gun positions are always ready for action with guns unlatched, loaded and cocked. If
the ASV radar is in use, one of the crewmembers allocated to the beam guns sits at the set for a 'rest'
period... if not, he is free to do anything he wants, including sleep, the only time sleep is permitted or
tolerated. When the ball turret was still fitted, one of the beam men would have been in the turret, with
the benefit of all-round vision and keeping a target in constant view.

206 Sqn pilot F/Lt Walter
L Vickerstaff scans the
Atlantic Ocean from the
port beam gun position.
Note the stowed .50
calibre Browning machine
gun. IWM CA.80

Fortress IIA FL464 '2-C' of 220 Sqn in full operational configuration while flying from the Azores in early 1944. Equipment fit includes LRASV radar and four underwing depth charges mounted in tandem pairs.

Close-up of FL464 carrying four 250lb depth charges.

Above: Underside view of FL464 showing the relative position of the four depth charges.

Detail shot of FL459 '2-J' of 220 Sqn under maintenance showing open rear crew entrance door, lowered flaps and fuselage mounted transmit-and-receive search aerials for the LRASV radar.

220 Sqn Fortress IIA FK193 '2-H' receives attention in the often-present mud at Lagens.

Fortress II FA706 '2-S' of 220 Sqn climbs out at Lagens.

206 Sqn's dedicated trainer, Mk IIA FK190 '1-J', shortly after takeoff. It is still fitted with its original dorsal 'stickleback' LRASV search transmit array but lacks tail guns.

A Fortress navigator squints into his drift sight, located on the starboard side of the nose compartment. Estimating drift by measuring wave patterns was one of several methods used to check drift during the long over-water patrols. IWM CH.11113

In the event of an anti-submarine action or an emergency, the senior WOP/AG takes over the radio as soon as is practical while the flight engineer does whatever is called for by the captain and the gun positions are manned appropriate to the situation... the top turret gunner is designated the 'fire controller' in the event the aircraft is attacked by enemy aircraft.

We took off at 05:00 and it is still dark, the only light coming from the navigator's blacked-out position and the ultraviolet illumination of the cockpit instruments. The 'nav' calls for a drift measurement and the beam gunner unstraps a smoke float – or a flame float if it is night - inserts a wooden mushroom-shaped device into the ignition tube and hits it smartly with the palm of his hand, then immediately ejects the flare down the flare chute. The gunner in the upper turret has activated his turret and trains the centre pip of his dimmed illuminated sight on the flame, now a tiny speck on the sea surface behind us. The co-pilot reads its relative bearing from a calibrated ring around the turret rim while the captain keeps the aircraft as steady as possible... the longer the float is visible and the steadier the aircraft, the more reliable the drift reading. The bearing is then passed to the navigator who, after some calculations, instructs the pilot to alter course. This will be repeated many times during the flight, although the navigator will use other methods to chart the winds, including using the drift sight installed on the starboard side of his compartment in the nose – this allows him to estimate drift from the wave pattern on the ocean surface.

Remember, we are heading out into the middle of the Atlantic. We have no satellites or the super electronics of today. Our navigator has only his drawing instruments, a sextant, magnetic and gyro compasses, a very accurate watch, and his crewmates' faith that, for perhaps the next 12 to 13 hours, his math and the drawing of lines on a chart will remain accurate.

We expect to meet the convoy at 09:00 which, at an indicated air speed of 150 knots, is something like 600 nautical miles from base. We are instantly alert to any 'click' and exchange over the intercom so only essential instructions are given to one another. This is absolutely vital because if any crew member has reason to call for instant action, be it an enemy sighting or something involving the integrity of the aircraft, unnecessary chatter could kill us all.

Every 15 minutes after take-off, the navigator gives the duty radio operator the aircraft's position in latitude and longitude for transmission to base. Since base knows our take-off time, the message fixes our last ¼-hour position so our likely position any time in the next 15 minutes can be calculated."

Long-range communications were based on wireless telegraphy ('W/T') using Morse code. The SCR-287 'liaison radio' required a weighted, braided copper wire aerial – approximately 100 yards (90m) long – which was paid out by the wireless operator after take-off from a powered drum in the radio cabin and out through a short tube on the lower port side of the fuselage. In flight the aerial and weight described lazy circles astern of the Fortress and the operator had to remember to reel in the wire prior to reaching the landing circuit.

Short-range voice communication for flying control, convoy escort, and talking between aircraft used two state-of-the-art, American-built VHF transmitters and three receivers collectively known as the 'command radio' ('R/T' or radio telephony). These sets were used by the pilots and flight engineer and controlled from a panel on the cockpit ceiling. Although not official practice, the flight engineer was often left to talk to ground control when approaching an airfield and

Fortress IIA FK190 'J' captured while flying out of Lagens in the Azores while serving with 206 Sqn, as indicated by the squadron code '1'. It was previously the prototype LRASV radar trials aircraft for which it was fitted with the 'stickleback' aerial arrangement for the search transmit component of ASV Mark II radar – for some reason this was never removed and a nose astrodome never fitted. Perhaps because of these anomalies, FK190 only flew as a trainer with 206 Sqn and there is no record that it flew operationally with 220 Sqn after it was officially transferred to the unit in April 1944. Note the traces of White along leading edges back to the wing roundels, remnants of an earlier wrap-around application of the under surface colour. via Bryan Yates

during landing, especially during pilot training and when the workload was high. Ted Hedges continues his mission narrative:

"*We should be within sighting distance of the convoy but the weather is changing with the clouds down to low-level and rain squalls blotting out much of the sea surface. The navigator and captain briefly discuss that we are where the convoy should be but there is no sign of it. It's decided to undertake a search so we fly a square pattern with so many minutes for each leg, but with no success. The captain then calls for a radar search which, in theory, should cover a 60 mile pattern... but again, nothing. There is only one more chance and we call on our senior radio operator [W/O Joseph E Roch] 'Rocky' Boudreault.*

'Rocky' had already taken over the radio equipment as we were running up to the convoy's assumed position and is now given permission to break radio silence and make contact with the aircraft currently protecting the convoy. He transmits our call sign with an encoded request for an air-to-air homing, feeding bearings back to the pilot as he succeeds in making contact. He can tell we are approaching the holding aircraft as the signal strength increases and we at last make visual contact with the other Fortress, then using the trigger-operated Aldis lamp to communicate in Morse code.

We join the convoy at 09:45, some 4¾ hours after takeoff. Our relief aircraft is due to arrive at 13:00 so for the next three hours we fly escort as requested. Our first task is to circle the convoy and count the number of ships to see whether they have had any losses and if there are any stragglers. We then communicate with the convoy commander and are instructed to carry out the type of cover required. We learn that the convoy changed course after we took off to avoid a U-boat concentration and

W/O Officer B L 'Taffy' Baldwin takes a sunshot from the astrodome of an Azores-based Fortress. IWM CA.81

that for more than four hours it has been steaming at over 15 knots some 70 degrees to port of its original course."

Convoys were designated 'slow' or 'fast', 'slow' being dictated by the slowest vessel in the group while 'fast' was perhaps up to 15 knots (28km/h), although the speed of the slowest ship still applied. Most convoy escort work was based on Creeping Line Ahead (CLA) or the same astern, depending on where the U-boats were thought to be, although there were other search patterns such as Cobra, Crocodile 30 and Dog Lizard 60 that could be assigned by the convoy commander as needed. For creeping lines, the aircraft swept a swath of ocean 90 degrees to the convoy's course for a given distance and time, then turned onto the convoy's course to 'creep' ahead before repeating the pattern over several hours. The lines were more often flown some distance from the convoy with the majority of the ships' captains unaware of the aircraft's presence.

PRECIOUS PETROL

Fuel management was of critical importance throughout the flight since every gallon was precious in terms of maximising the length of the patrol and ensuring a safe return to base. The flight engineer maintained an operational log and was required to monitor all temperatures, pressures and fuel mixture settings, ensure that the engine speeds were reduced by 100 RPM every hour on the hour, and calculate the fuel state so it was available to the captain at all times. He also had to be prepared to advise the captain on how to resolve any problem with the aircraft. Ted Hedges describes the fuel management routine:

"We were expected to have about 350 to 400 gallons or around 100 gallons per engine remaining when we landed at Lagens and my log would be scrutinised in detail… woe betide us if the fuel consumption figure was not 1.1 air miles to the gallon or better.

Two sets of supplementary fuel tanks required fuel transfer: the two tanks in the bomb bay and the so-called 'Tokyo tanks' in the outer wings of some of the Fortress IIs. The transfer pump and cocks were located on the sill at the base of the door between the cockpit and bomb bay, just aft of the top turret.

Transfer of fuel from the 'Tokyo tanks', which held a total of 540 US gallons each side, required the tank or tanks for any one engine to be holding less than 300 gallons. The shutoff cocks for the 'Tokyo tanks' were turned full on for 20 minutes, then closed before the process was repeated twice more, each time the engine tanks were down to 300 gallons. The transfers were done on a timed basis and one erred on the low side as any tank overfill was immediately obvious from fuel pouring out of the overflow outlets and believe me, every gallon mattered. The transfer operation was very dangerous as it filled the aircraft with petrol fumes… once completed the bomb doors were opened and the fumes blown clear. No smoking was allowed during transfers and the flight engineer's word was law!"

Ted Hedges returns to his description of a typical mission:

"We have now been airborne for nearly eight hours and are expecting a relief aircraft to arrive. The weather is still deteriorating and it's getting very rough in the aircraft. The power of the sea terrifies me. I've looked down on a convoy and seen 40,000-ton vessels buried up to their bridge structure by sea water and then seen the whole length of their bilge keels… smaller ships seem to disappear completely. While I've been slung from side to side and up and down, in and out of cloud at 300ft in severe turbulence with both pilots working the controls, I've looked down and said to myself how sorry I am for the

poor devils below. At least I would be home in the next eight hours... they could have 14 more days of that weather with no opportunity to change course.

The radio operator calls the captain to report he has received a signal that our relief aircraft has been recalled to base, as have we. The weather at Lagens is closing in and we may have problems getting down. The convoy commander is told we are departing and will not be replaced... we ask for a latitude and longitude position, given over the Aldis signal light so this critical information is not intercepted, and turn for base.

The fact that we are on our way 'home' does not alter the need for constant attention to individual tasks, nor lessen the necessity of watching over areas of sea and sky. We fly in silence except for the navigator's course adjustments, given to the captain at regular intervals. The weather is getting worse and there is a constant need to use one hand for support. In the tail gun position, every up, down and sideways movement is amplified by the length of the rear fuselage and it is difficult for the occupant to stop his head from being smashed against the Perspex during his hour-long stint.

One's awareness level is suddenly boosted to a very high level when the pilot and navigator hold a conversation regarding the latter's inability to accurately determine wind and drift for the last 90 minutes. He has maintained two plots since we left the convoy, one based on his plot of our position when we found the convoy, the second on the position given to us by the convoy's navigator. The latter should be the more accurate but the lack of a drift estimate applies to both plots and our actual position is now suspect, although both plots suggest that we should be around 60 nautical miles from base.

The captain orders 'Rocky' to have the ASV radar manned, with the operator concentrating on our forward track to hopefully pick up the beacon at Lagens... there is silence as we await his report. It's been 12 hours since takeoff and our fuel is getting low... what feels like a year goes by before there is the click of a mic switch and the report: 'Radar to skipper, beacon ahead, 10 degrees to port.' The operator calls for a slow turn to the left until the beacon's glow is dead on the centreline of the radar screen.

We know Lagens is 60 miles ahead but we are in solid cloud at 3,000ft and approaching our base with its 3,000-foot mountains on one side of the runway and a 500-foot hill on the other... we have to arrive in line with a runway or it could be very nasty. So we will conduct a BABS approach, a demanding procedure that requires absolute co-operation and trust between the pilot and senior radio operator.

We arrive over Lagens, invisible below us, at our safe height of 4,000ft and enter a circular pattern. 'Rocky' begins receiving signals from BABS while Brian flies the aircraft in accordance with a stream of instructions from the radio operator and with reference to a small instrument with two cross needles. Meanwhile the crew take up landing positions while I perform a final security check to ensure there are no loose items to fly around in the event of a rough landing... I then take my position standing between the pilots.

All is now set. 'Rocky' has guided the captain directly over the island and at a certain point the cross needles tell him we have over flown over the centreline of the airfield. The co-pilot starts a

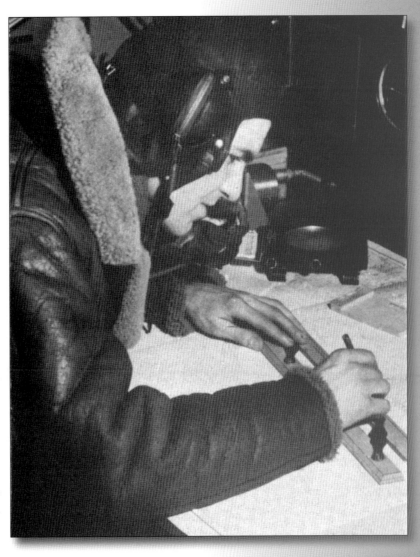

The navigator was in many ways the most important member of a Fortress crew. His diligence and skills were critical to the crew locating the convoy to be protected and finding their way home at the end of a 14-hour patrol. via Ted Hedges

stopwatch at that instant and we are now fully reliant on the skills of 'Rocky' and Brian. They must follow a precise pattern, timed to the second and adjusted constantly to Rocky's instructions.

A final turn should put us in line with the centre of the runway and we begin our descent at timed intervals. At the captain's order, it's 'Undercarriage down' as the co-pilot strains for a glimpse of the runway. Next come: 'Flaps down' and 'Airspeed' and from this point on I constantly call out the airspeed. We pass through 1,000ft and are still in cloud. On through 700ft... 500ft... but still no sight of the airfield. 'Rocky' gives a slight heading correction at 400ft and at any second we will have to apply full power to climb to safety.

Then, just off line to the right, we spot the runway lights. With a slight right bank and correction we are lined up, then it's throttles right back and the airspeed bleeds off. Brian has the control wheel pulled right back and we are just a few feet up. A slight forward and back movement of the wheel and there's a thump followed by the immense clatter of the planked runway as we roll out and brake to a standstill. Touchdown is at 17:45 hours, 12 hours 45 minutes after we took off, 15 hours 15 minutes after we were woken up.

We taxi to dispersal, shut down the engines and secure all switches and controls. Our ground crew helps us unload our equipment and put it into a truck. They ask if we have had any faults with 'their' aircraft and are pleased that we have no complaints and that we have brought it back in one piece. As we climb into the truck, our captain speaks for us all: 'Thanks, 'Rocky'' No one has anything to add.

We're taken to ops for debriefing followed by our operational meal of bacon, eggs and so on... we're then free for the next 24 hours. At 20:00 tomorrow night our captain's name will appear at the bottom of the flying list and in perhaps three days will be called on to fly another operation in one of the many forms possible."

220 Sqn crew led by Canadian P/O Herman M Johnson in the Azores with Fortress IIA FL464 'C'. Fourth from the left is WOP/AG and Radar Op F/Sgt Joe F. Ayling. Joe was a tireless champion for preserving 220 Sqn history and traditions until he passed away on February 20, 2004. via Joe Ayling

ATTACKING A U-BOAT

Very few operations like the one described resulted in the sighting of a U-boat, let alone an engagement. Indeed most Fortress crew members never saw a U-boat throughout their tour. Nevertheless, crews constantly trained for the possibility that their attack skills would be needed.

Surprise was the key element. Crews needed to spot a U-boat and manoeuvre unseen into position, to cross over the submarine on the surface or soon after it had submerged and its telltale swirl was still visible. Any reduction in the distance at which the aircraft was spotted gave the attacking crew precious seconds to position and run in before the submarine had dived too deep. Thirty seconds was considered the maximum time between the U-boat diving and the launching of depth charges, so aircraft usually patrolled at relatively low level, often just below the cloud base, sometimes climbing into cloud and positioning for an attack position once a submarine was spotted.

An alert submarine watch was more likely to see an aircraft first while a faster aircraft was more likely to make a successful attack. Since depth charges had to explode close to the submarine to inflict fatal damage, an attacking aircraft had to fly over its target at low level to deliver its weapons while absorbing return fire if the U-boat commander decided stay on the surface and fight. Aircraft camouflage therefore mimicked that of predatory sea birds with white undersides, increasing the chances of making a successful attack. Ted Hedges:

"The instant a U-boat was spotted, the captain called the sighting over the intercom while activating an alarm bell. The duty radio operator then sent an immediate Morse transmission to base, starting with the code letters 'O - A' followed by the last 15-minute position. On receiving the transmission, base plotted the last known position and establish an estimated position based on the flying time since the last report. The standby crew would already be on its way to their aircraft, armed with the estimated attack position and the knowledge that they had to be airborne within 15 minutes. If the attacking aircraft survived, the senior radio operator would subsequently send an updated position report. If the aircraft had been shot down, the standby crew would know where to look, subject to the usual navigational errors.

Time was of the essence and the aircraft would normally go straight into the attack... so it would be tracking over the target long before the navigator could get into position to use the low-level bombsight. The normal way to drop the depth charges was for the pilot to aim by eye... this was practised using dummy targets at between 50 to 150ft.

The top turret was always used on an attack run. The twin .50s were within two or three inches of the cockpit roof and the noise and vibration were incredible... it shook the cockpit occupants like jelly

Swirl left by a submerging U-boat under attack by a Bristol Blenheim of 1404 Met Flight on October 5, 1941. via Peter Rackliff

Successful attack on Type VIIC U-boat U-243 by Sunderland III W4030 'H' of 10 Sqn RAAF flown by F/O William Tilley on July 8, 1944. Note the track of machine gun fire from the rear turret. IWM C.4603

and dust and other debris appeared from every nook and cranny. As the attack progressed, the gun muzzles came progressively closer to the cockpit roof until the gunner became unsighted. If appropriate, the top gunner would re-open fire as soon as the aircraft banked to view the results of the attack.

When a U-boat gunner kept his head and aimed his four 20mm cannon slightly above the attacking aircraft he could not fail to get strikes. One 20mm shell could and did blow off an engine or demolish a gun turret... or blow off the foot of a rear gunner as was the case with a good friend of mine who I last saw being loaded into a C-54 on the Azores runway after being shot while attacking a U-boat in a Wellington of 172 Sqn... although they did give him a DFC to take home with him!

Aircraft were not always used to attack U-boats. We were escorting a 121-ship east-west convoy in mid-1944 and had identified a possible contact directly in its path. We started to position for an attack, informed the convoy escort's commander, and arrived over the target after it had submerged. But the convoy commander ordered our captain not to attack as the escorts were approaching at speed to use their Hedgehog spigot mortar and we were ordered to leave the area. The reason was that the target remained on shipboard sonar devices right up to instant of launching the mortars and the mortar bomb only exploded on contact... if we had dropped our DCs the water would have been too badly disturbed. When we were at least 20 nautical miles from the scene we saw the escorts using a naval weapon which sent out shock waves past our position... I believe these to be depth charges of perhaps 2,000 pounds. This didn't get entered into my logbook because Hedgehog, the similar Squid, and very large depth charges were not for mention or discussion for security reasons."

(See Appendix F for a more detailed, official description of the techniques to be used in attacks on U-boats).

Unidentified U-boat attack, possibly taken from a Fortress operating from the Azores. via Charles Lockwood

DESIRED EFFECT

By December 1943, 247 Group's constant patrols from the Azores were beginning to have the desired effect, to the point where 179 Sqn's detachment of Wellingtons returned to Gibraltar early in the month after sinking two U-boats in November. The Group ORB records:

"The conspicuous absence of the U-boats between the 6th and 28th of the month, may, no doubt, be due to the rude "shaking up" which was given the enemy by aircraft of 247 Group during November and the first six days of December, when U-boats apparently dispersed or limped out of the area almost entirely. Without appearing over optimistic therefore, it may be assumed that U-boat commanders have now recorded the Azores area on their danger list and are negotiating these waters with greater caution. It is significant, too, that while Fortress and Hudson aircraft may be keeping the U-boats "down" during daylight and attacked whenever opportunity presents itself, Leigh Light Wellington aircraft have been successful in locating and attacking the U-boats as they surface at night, giving the enemy no cover even under darkness."

On December 18, 220 Sqn's popular and much-respected commanding officer, 31-year old W/Cdr Patrick Hadow, left the Azores for interviews with HQ Coastal Command on crew policies. The aircraft in which he was returning, Douglas Dakota III FD903 of 512 Sqn, was reported missing en route to Gibraltar from Lyneham, Wiltshire, one week later. In 1950, Air Marshal Sir John Slessor, who had been Commander-in-Chief Coastal Command at the time, later talked to Ted Hedges about Hadow:

"He asked me who had commanded 220 in my time. He was visibly moved when I said: 'Hadow, Sir'. He replied: 'What a pity I lost him, he was one of the brightest and most promising of my young men... we could really do with his type now.' So Hadow was remembered by a great man, as he still is by those of us that remain."

In mid-December word came through that Germany was attempting to run a supply ship from the Far East to a port on the Bay of Biscay via the eastern Atlantic. From December 19, Fortresses of 206 and 220 Sqns flew continuous patrols in very poor weather to intercept the blockade runner and one aircraft from 220 Sqn had its bomb bay tanks replaced with bombs and kept on constant readiness in the event of a sighting. In the end, no sightings were made by Azores-based aircraft and the vessel was eventually sunk by 19 Group on December 27.

Fortress II FA710 'M' of 206 Sqn about to take off for a night sortie from Lagens. Until the arrival of Fortress IIIs equipped with improved ASV Mk III radar, most night patrols from the Azores were flown by Leigh Light-equipped Wellingtons. IWM CA.45

TRANSIT POINT

As well as functioning as a vital anti-submarine base, Lagens airfield was beginning to fulfil a new and equally important role as a transit point for aircraft ferried across the Atlantic, most importantly new American types being delivered to Allied forces in Europe and Africa. During December 1943, no less than 43 Liberators, 25 Douglas C-54 Skymasters, 13 Dakotas, three Fortresses, two Catalinas, one Hudson and one Lockheed Ventura passed through Lagens. East-bound destinations included Prestwick and Portreath in the United Kingdom; Rabat-Sale, Casablanca and Port Lyautey in Morocco; Yum-Dum in The Gambia; and Gibraltar, while west-bound destinations included Gander, Dorval, Torbay and Stephenville in Canada; Presque Ile, Maine and Washington in the United States; Bermuda; and Puerto Rico. Ted Hedges recalls there was another good reason for aircraft to stage through Lagens:

"We had all types of aircraft visiting the Azores. There were airships, every type of American aircraft in use, including the B-29, and every type of British aircraft which had the range. Before leaving, they were all filled up with five-star brandy, wine, fruit and whatever other scarce goodies could be found."

Night operations from Lagens during the four months after the new runway was opened relied on the use of flare pots for runway lighting. These primitive wick-based units burned with a smoky flame and needed to be laid out on the airfield at the beginning of each period of night flying. They proved to be totally inadequate in poor weather, as proved by an incident involving Fortress II FA697 'T' of 220 Sqn on the evening of December 19, 1943.

F/O John Ireland and his eight-man crew had departed Lagens at 04:59 and soon ran into problems. Their ASV radar, on which crews often depended for locating coastlines and bases in bad visibility, went unserviceable, while a cold front and associated deteriorating weather moved in sooner than expected. Nevertheless, Ireland started his patrol as planned at 08:06, coming 'off patrol' at 14:37. Two hours into the return leg to Lagens, FA697 received a message from base advising Ireland he should land at Santa Ana, but after setting course for the diversionary airfield he decided that, without the benefit of radar, the weather was simply too bad.

Despite Lagens being closed for operations, Ireland committed to a landing after nearly 14 hours aloft and requested a 'QGH' or BABS approach. He finally broke cloud at 300ft (90m) over the sea and crossed the coast at just 100ft (30m) in cloud with zero visibility, a no doubt tense situation given the proximity of the 500-foot ridge alongside the runway. Flying Control sent up

Flarepath crew organising oil lamps in preparation for night operations from Lagens. IWM CA.86

a green Verey light on FA697's starboard quarter and when he estimated he was at the end of the runway, Ireland closed the throttles. Ted Hedges witnessed the resulting arrival:

"I was standing just two hundred yards from what was the aircraft's starboard side of the runway and half way along its length. Ireland broke cloud in line with the runway but exactly over my head... he therefore had less than half of the runway left and at its end there was a deep quarry. He chopped the power and lost that 50ft like a lift, banged it onto the runway and ordered his co-pilot [Sgt] Norman Brooks to raise the undercarriage. This was Norman's third crash, having had two as a Wellington captain... he had reverted to co-pilot pilot duties when he joined 220 [Sqn] as part of his recovery period."

If Norman Brooks was wondering about his string of bad luck, so too must have been Canadian P/O William G Cameron. Part of the crew of FA697, he was also on board FA708 during its crash landing at Lagens during a training flight less than three weeks earlier.

The damage to FA697's fuselage was considered too great to be repaired and it was written off and disassembled for spares. John Ircland survived that war but was lost on January 24, 1946, when Anson I EG113 of 1380 TCU disappeared over The Wash on a flight out of Rearsby, Leicestershire.

Ted Hedges remembers that the growing volume of traffic at Lagens and a variety of unconventional landings had begun to take its toll on the steel plank runway:

"When we woke up on the Christmas morning of 1943, our lovely planked runway had a Wellington sitting on its belly on top of its crushed depth charges. The accident occurred because the runway had already developed a very long dip along its length and it was possible for an aircraft to become prematurely airborne. The Wellington pilot had been too hasty in raising the 'gear' and the aircraft had dropped back down onto its belly. When I was 'duty dog' one day I actually had my hand on the alarm button as an American C-54 took off and dropped so low that I could not see daylight under its belly... it only just made it. They were always adding to the steel planking but its inevitable humps and bumps were never operated on."

Fitters salvage the fin of Fortress II FA697 '2-T' following its write-off on landing at Lagens on December 19, 1943. The photo provides good views of the rear crew entry doors, LRASV transmit-and-receive aerials and style of the 48-inch 220 Sqn code letters. via Brian Speirs

Fortress II FA705 '1-U' of 206 Sqn takes off from Lagens airfield in late November or early December 1943. It was shot down on January 6, 1944, while attacking U-boat U-270 with S/Ldr Anthony J Pinhorn in command (see colour three-view, pages 232-234, and Pinhorn's profile page 178). The Liberator B.VI in the foreground is BZ978 (formerly B-24J-2-CF 42-64074), en route from Dorval to India for service with 159 Sqn. The code letters '30-13' identify it as an early example prepared for RAF service by the Louisville Modification Center, Kentucky. IWM CA.85

The new year began with another tough loss for the Fortress crews at Lagens. On January 6, S/Ldr Anthony J Pinhorn of 206 Sqn was flying an anti-submarine patrol northeast of the Azores in Fortress II FA705 'U'. It was his eleventh 'op' since his transit flight from St. Mawgan in Fortress IIA FK190 'J' on October 25. At 18:12 the duty radio operator sent a submarine sighting report followed, six minutes later, by a position report at 43°53'N 23°32'W – nothing more was heard from FA705. According to U-270's KTB ('*Kriegstagebuch*' or war diary) Pinhorn made two strafing runs on the U-boat before beginning a third run at 19:18. Anti-aircraft fire from the U-270 had by now found its mark, setting fire to the inner starboard engine. The Fortress began losing height and Pinhorn released his four depth charges some 100 to 130ft (30 to 40m) from the U-boat. The aircraft then plunged into the ocean some 1,000ft (305m) further on, engulfed in flames. All nine crewmembers were lost, including 206 Sqn's navigation officer, S/Ldr Ralph Brown, who was travelling as a passenger.

The U-boat, captained by *Kapitänleutnant* Paul-Friedrich Otto, was sufficiently damaged to have to return to St Nazaire for repairs. Five months later, on June 13, 1944, the crew of U-270, also captained by Otto, shot down a second attacking Coastal Command aircraft after being damaged in an attack by Wellington XIV MP789 'Y' of 172 Sqn. Liberator GR.V BZ818 'C' of 53 Sqn was seen to dive into the sea and explode after passing over the U-boat with an engine on fire. The damage inflicted by the Wellington ended U-270's operational career but she was sunk while in transit on August 12 by Sunderland III ML735 'A' of 461 Sqn, RAAF while under the command of *Oberleutnant* Heinrich Schreiber.

Despite the loss of Pinhorn and his crew, the Group ORB remained sanguine about the impact of its operations:

"*While reckless optimism is a dangerous thing, it can be said nevertheless that in the three months of active operations in the Azores, aircraft of 247 Group have driven the U-boats further afield and certainly broken up the concentration of submarines which may have found these waters a happy hunting ground in the past.*"

The balance of January 1944 proved to be relatively quiet in terms of contact with the enemy, mainly due to bad winter weather and the withdrawal of some U-boats to the Northwest Approaches and other areas. Fortress crews regularly encountered severe fronts 350 to 400 miles

(565 to 645km) away from Lagens, even when the weather at base appeared quite flyable, and daily Met flights by a Hudson of 233 Sqn proved to be indispensable in planning safe operations. The Group escorted eleven convoys during the month for a total of 121 hours, an average of a little over 10.5 hours per sortie, and undertook 125 anti-submarine sorties for a total of 1,229 hours, or 9.8 hours per sortie. Of the two Fortress squadrons, 206 Sqn flew 590 operational hours plus another 135 on training while 220 Sqn flew 442 plus another 101 on training.

There had been some sightings of enemy aircraft during the first two months of operations from Lagens – and one noteworthy combat, described earlier – but there was no enemy aircraft activity during January, although encounters or even token raids by Heinkel He 177s, Blohm und Voss Bv 222s, Focke-Wulf Fw 200s or Junkers Ju 290s were always expected.

THE AMERICANS ARRIVE

While the U-boat campaign was proving to be fairly low key, big changes were afoot at Lagens. These were heralded on January 9, 1944, by the arrival of the 96th Naval Construction Battalion who were to prepare for the arrival of a British-controlled USN Liberator squadron, together with improved facilities for transiting aircraft, to be managed by 74 Staging Post, RAF Transport Command, and the construction of an oil pipe line from the port at Angra to the airfield at Lagens. Ted Hedges recalls the impact of their arrival:

"The Americans arrived in two LSTs. On the night of January 15 the entire crew of LST-282 went ashore for some 'light refreshment'. Unfortunately, the LST broke its anchor cables and drove itself ashore… then, ten days later, it caught fire and burned happily for some time, destroying its load of earth moving equipment.

A replacement shipment of equipment arrived a couple of weeks later and they then set about building a proper airfield. The 500-foot hill was doomed from the start and we thought at the time that if they could have a go at the mountains too, they would. Their first two operational tents were for the cinema and ice cream making respectively… we felt they most certainly had their priorities right."

A new runway was urgently needed as the strong Atlantic winds were rarely aligned with the steel plank surface and regularly put landing aircraft at risk when they suddenly changed direction.

Douglas C-54A-DO Skymaster 41-37280 of the USAAF taxies past a flooded section of Lagens airfield. Transiting British and American transport aircraft such as the Skymaster, together with aircraft on delivery to the Allies like the RAF-bound Liberator in the background, were common visitors once the steel plank runway was completed. Judging by the piles of dirt and the image identification number, this photograph was taken in late 1943. The Skymaster, the 21st built, had a short career and was consigned to the Reconstruction Finance Corporation, presumably for scrapping, in January 1946. IWM CA.107

Ted Hedges recalls watching in awe as a resident Supermarine Walrus landed *across* the matting while actually moving backwards relative to the ground. Construction of the first of three new runways began in February.

U-boat sightings during February were rare and completely absent during the day and it was clear that enemy submarines were keeping outside the operational range of the Fortresses and moving northeast to exploit areas west of the British Isles. 206 and 220 Sqns were tasked with patrols up to 450 miles (725km) out to the west and northwest of the Azores and, on one occasion, to an area 800 miles (1,290km) to the northeast. The effectiveness of these relentless medium- and long-range patrols resulted in 233 Sqn's detachment of six Hudsons returning to Gibraltar on February 18 after completing 1,895 operational hours over 329 sorties, including 93 Met flights totalling 522 hours.

Close-up of Fortress IIAs FL459 '2-J' (see colour profile page 231) and FK200 '2-B' viewed from the hill at Lagens in late 1943. FL459 shows signs of repair to its fabric-covered rudder, the result of damage sustained during the sinking of U-boat U-707 on November 9. The 220 Sqn code '2' was replaced by the letters 'ZZ' in late 1944. IWM CA.1

ACTION AND DEPARTURE

The dearth of U-boat activity finally came to an end on March 13 when a Wellington, two Fortresses, American carrier-borne Grumman Avengers, two American destroyers and a Canadian frigate were credited with sinking U-575. The Wellington crew picked up the first radar contact at 01:51 while escorting convoy ON 227 and attacked with depth charges, leaving markers to indicate the U-boat's last known position.

Next on the scene was F/Lt A David Beaty in command of Fortress II FA700 'R' of 206 Sqn. He spotted the U-boat as it surfaced at around dawn but was faced with a dilemma. It was standard practice to advise base of a sighting and pending attack so reinforcements and, if necessary, rescue aircraft could be launched. Unable to make contact, he canvassed his crew and they collectively agreed to press home an attack. Beaty dived to 50ft (15m) and used his previous experience testing

the Fortress to corkscrew the aircraft, avoiding a single hit from the U-boat's guns. His four depth charges left the U-boat stationary in the water and it then submerged stern first while emitting two large patches of oil.

The third aircraft to tackle U-575 was Fortress IIA FL459 'J' of 220 Sqn flown by F/O Wilfred R 'Pip' Travell. He spotted the trail of oil left by the submerged and slow-moving U-boat and dropped two depth charges which produced an even greater flow of oil. At this point, Travell was instructed to leave the area while the attack was concluded at 46°18'N, 27°34'W by surface ships supported by three Avengers of VC-95 from USS *Bogue*. Dönitz's war diary noted: *"Last report* [from U-575] *on 13.3 concerning attack by aircraft. Orders to report weather and position on 15 and 16.3 were not answered. Possibly lost by air attack."*

This was the third confirmed U-boat sinking involving FL459 'J', making it the most successful of Coastal Command's Fortresses. Mk IIA FK195 'L' of 206 Sqn, with two sinkings and one damaged, was the next most successful. The loss of U-575 was the only U-boat sinking involving Coastal Command Fortresses where there were survivors, in this case 37 of the 55 submariners on board.

The next day, March 14, 1944, Coastal Command authorised 206 Sqn to be taken 'out of line' in the Azores and to move to Davidstow Moor in Cornwall for conversion to Liberator VIs. The squadron's final operation with Fortresses took place on March 16 when Mk IIAs FK186 'X' and FK198 'W' provided escort to convoy HX 282. F/O Frank Rigg, who had flown the squadron's first sortie from the Azores some five months earlier, flew the last escort in FK198 'W', landing at St Eval in Cornwall at the end of the sortie. 206 Sqn had flown 3,052 operational hours from Lagens, of which over 2,200 had been on anti-submarine operations.

On March 19, five 206 Sqn aircraft – Mk IIAs FK186, FK198, FK213 and FL460, and Mk II FA710 – and 65 personnel were transferred to 220 Sqn, bringing it up to an establishment of 16 operational plus four spare aircraft. Beginning the night of March 19, nine others – Mk IIAs FK199, FK211, FL451 and FL455 and Mk IIs FA695, FA696, FA699, FA700 and FA707 – were ferried by 206 Sqn crews to Bircham Newton in Norfolk for storage pending overhaul at Thornaby and reassignment within Coastal Command. The air test and ferrying unit established at Bircham Newton was made up of Fortress squadron personnel from the Azores and designated 247 Group Detachment. Airmen with 8206 Servicing Echelon (SE) moved with 206 Sqn, although some of its personnel transferred to 8220 SE in support of 220 Sqn at Lagens.

Fortress II FA700 'R' of 206 Sqn while based at Lagens in the Azores – it is equipped with the definitive ASV Mk II aerial arrays in the nose and on the fuselage sides. This aircraft contributed to the sinking of U-boat U-575 on March 13, 1944, while under the command of well-known author and aviation safety pioneer, David Beaty (see profile page 171). via Bryan Yates

Unidentified march past at Lagens. In the background are Fortress IIA FL462 '2-W' of 220 Sqn, Walrus 'A' of 269 Sqn and a Hudson from the same unit. RAF Museum PC71-19-1180

March of 1944 proved to be the worst month for weather so far, resulting in a dramatic reduction in flying activity. Operational hours slumped to 1,240, half of the total for November, and the runway was closed for three days due to flooding. Winds of up to 75 mph (121km/h) resulted in three diversions to St Eval in Cornwall and seven to Santa Ana. Four 220 Sqn Fortresses remained marooned at the diversionary airfield at month's end because the airstrip's surface was too soft to allow take-offs. These diversions were very costly in terms of lost operational availability and over the first three months of the year, a dozen diversions to St Eval, Casablanca and Gibraltar had cost the two squadrons 100 aircraft-days absence or 1½ aircraft per day based on normal utilisation rates.

Ted Hedges recalls his visits to Santa Ana:

"The weather on São Miguel was generally better than on Terceira but the airfield was soft and treacherous. On February 7, 1944, we took [FK193] 'H' to do some practice approaches onto the grass strip and on March 29 diverted there due to poor weather at Lagens in [FL464] 'C' following a 12-hour operational patrol. Once down we had to taxi onto boards as the aircraft was sinking into the mud. Up to eight aircraft were there and most crews were billeted in hotels in town. We were once stuck there for five days."

Bill Blackwell recalls an earlier diversion:

"On December 13, 1943, we took off at 09:00 hours in 'H for Harry' [FL460] on an anti-shipping sweep… we were looking for a German raider camouflaged with neutral flags. After a few hours we were recalled as the weather at Lagens was closing in. We turned for home and within minutes of

Maintenance crew tackles repairs to a flooded Lagens airfield. Taxiing to the rear right is Fortress II FA700 '1-R' of 206 Sqn with FL460 '1-H' parked behind. Visible to the left behind the crew members are, left to right, FK200 '2-B', FK188 '2-Z' and FL462 '2-W' of 220 Sqn. RAF Museum PC71-19-1179-6

arriving overhead were informed that base was closed and we would not be able to land. The alternatives discussed included bailing out but we were eventually instructed to proceed to Santa Ana on São Miguel. We did so but the cloud base was down to the deck, so we continued flying in the right direction, always trying to get below the cloud.

When we were within 20 miles of São Miguel something happened that I can only describe as a miracle. We finally managed to break through at only 100 to 200 ft and as we did I remember seeing an opening in the cloud with the sun shining through this one little gap right on the island. We gained height and saw the aerodrome completely lit by the sun's rays, landed and I think another B-17 and a Hudson managed to as well. But within half an hour the island was completely closed in... one Hudson didn't make it."

Given these challenges, facility improvements at Lagens were greeted with great enthusiasm. By early 1944 these included a much-needed temporary runway lighting system, installed by the Americans and featuring sodium lighting for the so-called 'northeast funnel', and a new runway with a volcanic ash surface for emergency landings.

To provide the much-needed meteorological information formerly provided by 233 Sqn – and to address growing concerns over the rescue of downed crews – a composite unit began to take up residence at Lagens from March 18. 269 Sqn operated six Hudson IIIAs for long range Met flights, two Spitfire VBs for local PRATA Met flights, two Walrus air-sea rescue aircraft, and a pair of Miles Martinet target-towers. The Hudson Met reconnaissance operation was given the codename MILESTONE with sorties averaging 9 ½ - 10 hours in duration and extending to 38°W. They provided valuable data for Atlantic synoptic charts, especially during the week preceding D-Day and Operation Overlord. Some of the Hudsons were fitted with air-droppable lifeboats, a new air-sea rescue capability that was to prove a wise investment a few months later.

W/Cdr James M N Pike, DSO, DFC, replaced W/Cdr Peter E Hadow as commanding officer of 220 Sqn effective January 1, 1944. This photograph of 'B' Flight, with Pike at its centre, was taken at Lagens in March 1944 with Fortress II FA713 'E' as backdrop. via Charles Lockwood

206 Sqn personnel in the Azores with Fortress IIA FK211 'Z'. via Bryan Yates

Maintaining the Guard

Under the terms of the agreement to use the islands, aircraft were not allowed to fly within three miles (5km) of any island within the Azores, with the exception of Terceira, without permission. Although impractical, this restriction included the diversionary airfield at Santa Ana. Ted Hedges remembers that anti-aircraft guns supplied to the Portuguese forces under the agreement were used with great abandon, regardless of the type of aircraft involved:

"The Portuguese forces appeared to take great delight in demonstrating how well they could use the radar-controlled equipment. We had been briefed to take some photographs of the Azores coastline and it was my task to take pictures from the starboard beam window using the large hand-held camera we always carried. It was about a 15-inch cube, weighed a ton, and needed two hands to lift and operate. Skipper Brian Reuter pushed his luck and we went in close... needless to say we got shot at for our pains by anti-aircraft guns supplied by the British!

Our crew was later given the task of photographing a very large oil tanker anchored in the bay at Pria da Vittoria, off the end of our metal runway. I was again elected to take pictures from the beam window. Brian flew some very steep circles and figures of eight and on one of his manoeuvres he had me on my way out of the window! Fortunately for me he had immediately reversed the bank so that I and the camera made an intimate connection with the beam gun mount on the other side of the fuselage, a mite preferable to the deck of the tanker."

Improved weather in April resulted in an increase in flying hours for all units based at Lagens, the Fortresses of 220 Sqn flying 1,219 operational hours over 105 sorties. The well-established pattern of anti-submarine operations was maintained until mid-month, as described in the Group ORB:

"Fortress aircraft had well maintained the air offensive by keeping the U-boats submerged during daylight and thus enabled Leigh Light Wellingtons to attack the enemy during darkness when he was forced to the surface [to charge their running batteries]."

Significant equipment changes were to take place during the month that were intended to improve to 247 Group's ability to locate and destroy U-boats at night. On March 26, 1944, a Fortress III arrived direct from 45 Group at Dorval for service with 220 Sqn. Serialled HB786, the modified B-17G sported a natural metal finish and was equipped with Mk X centimetric radar operating on the 10cm wavelength. Known in Coastal Command as ASV Mk III, it boasted far greater range and resolution than ASV Mk II. It featured a rotating scanner in a radome located in the opening previously occupied by the ball turret and a 360-degree tactical display called a Plan Position Indicator (PPI) in place of the direction and range indicator of the earlier system. It was also undetectable by U-boats.

Given the arrival of this new capability, 172 Sqn's Leigh Light Wellingtons were withdrawn to the United Kingdom on April 14, the first examples departing on April 16. Unfortunately, the newly-arrived Mk III HB786 'V' was damaged two days later when it was taxied into parked Mk IIA FK198 'R' following an *"alleged brake failure"*. FK198 was considered beyond economical repair while HB786 would not be serviceable again until early September. Meanwhile, two additional Fortress IIIs, HB791 and HB792, arrived at Lagens on June 14 and were taken on strength by 220 Sqn on June 29. Coded 'T' and 'U' respectively, they would fly their first sorties one month later.

June 6, 1944, saw the opening of the second front as Allied troops went ashore in France. The flight crews at Lagens naturally felt somewhat left out and AVM Bromet attempted to allay this feeling, neatly summing up the Group's role in the process.

"Remember, we are guarding an important flank and giving security to our ocean convoys as well as adding to the discomfiture of the U-boats: we have established a Staging Post for Transatlantic air traffic, which is an added insurance that reinforcements - aircraft and urgent equipment particularly - reach the theatres of war in the UK and Italy quickly."

A week later, on June 14, *poliomyelitis* (polio) broke out for the second time following a warm, dry period. Four of the first five cases died from respiratory failure and as there was initially no iron lung available on the Azores, ten British cases were flown to the United Kingdom between June 14 and 20 while Fortresses were kept on standby to evacuate patients at a moment's notice. Two iron lungs were subsequently flown out to the Azores but the evacuation flights remained in the plan in case this equipment failed. Heavy rains in early July brought an end to quarantine restrictions as the dust which carried the disease was no longer an issue.

Meanwhile, the Fortress crews of 220 Sqn continued searching the seaways north and north-east of the Azores, but the U-boat trade in June proved to be non-existent. There were just three convoy escorts and two independent vessel escorts that month requiring eight sorties totalling 92 flight hours.

The expansion of the facilities at Lagens by the Americans continued in high gear with three new runways underway including 29/11 of 6,720ft (2,050m) almost complete, 34/16 of 8,153ft (2,485m) and 21/03 at 6,600ft (2,010m), all 200ft (60m) wide. The British forces, who had used relatively primitive equipment to refine the original surface for the steel plank airstrip, were in constant awe of the American's equipment and progress, especially their mighty Caterpillar D.7 and D.8 bulldozers. These and other equipment effortlessly moved 300,000 cubic yards (229,370 cu m) of material for runway 34/16 and made a 45-foot (14m) cut in a hillside for runway 21/03. Black volcanic rock for runway surfacing was blasted daily using 300 to 500 pounds (135 to 225kg) of dynamite.

The need for new, into-wind runways was indelibly underlined when F/Lt Wilfred Travell made an extraordinary landing in Mk IIA FL462 'W' on July 23. Travell returned from a 12½-hour anti-submarine patrol to find a 90mph (145km/h) wind blowing at nearly right angles to the planked runway. There was a second, very short landing strip, suitable for only nosewheel types, that ran across the head of the main runway and the narrow airfield, and into the raging wind. Beyond and parallel to the planked runway were two rows of parked Fortresses, noses into wind and towards the main runway and perhaps two aircraft lengths apart.

Knowing he had no hope of stopping on the short strip, Travell touched down at the threshold but kept enough airspeed to haul FL452 through 60 degrees to the left, to end up stopped and essentially undamaged between the two rows of parked aircraft. The only physical evidence of the feat was two feet of missing white paint under the port wing tip. Awed by his accomplishment, Travell's fellow squadron members awarded him the following unofficial 'Illuminated Address':

Presented to F/Lt W. R. Travell by 220 Sqn on 23-7-44 for achieving the aerodynamically impossible in that he, on the aforesaid date, did successfully complete a Rate 4 turn through 60° at 15 feet well below stalling speed and maintained both aircraft and self intact. "Man is Not Lost."

Monitoring shipping was an important secondary role for the Lagens-based Fortresses. Here the Swedish vessel Sarek is photographed from a Fortress of 220 Sqn on May 18, 1944. It had earlier been incorrectly identified as a German blockade runner. via Bryan Yates

A Rate 4 turn represents a heading change of 720 degrees per minute or 12 degrees per second. Travell's turn to line up and land his 104ft (31.65m) wingspan aircraft between the two rows of parked aircraft 150ft (45.7m) apart in a 90mph (145km/h) crosswind therefore took just five seconds.

In addition to the improvements made by the American engineers, British forces erected some "giant" steel hangars, while extra Marston matting had been laid to accommodate the hundreds of east- and west-bound aircraft now transiting Lagens each month, volume having increased from 88 aircraft in December to 813 in June.

ENGINE FAILURES

Dry conditions together with strong winds returned to the Azores in late July 1944, turning the airfield into a choking storm of red volcanic dust. A normal month of hard flying resulted in perhaps one aircraft returning to Lagens with a failed engine, but over the next four months 220 Sqn was to suffer 19 such failures. The first incident, unrelated to the dusty conditions, occurred on July 26.

P/O Eric B McIlwrick was flying Fortress II FA707 'Z' at 1,200ft (365m) on a night anti-submarine crossover patrol to the east of São Miguel when his No. 1 engine began to overspeed. Within 50 minutes, the No. 3 and No. 4 engines had also overspeeded and all three propellers had been feathered. Unable to maintain height on one engine, McIlwrick had no choice but to ditch at 01:36, some 70 miles (115km) east of São Miguel. What followed is described in the 247 Group ORB as *"the perfect air sea rescue"*.

Fortress II FA709 'A' (or, according to flight engineer Eric Fretwell, FA701 'F') was on a night tactical exercise to the east of Terceira under the command of S/Ldr Hugh Warren and was ordered by base to proceed to the downed Fortress' estimated position and search along its intended track. On reaching the area, Warren put on his landing lights and was immediately rewarded by the sight of a Verey flare some 15 miles (24km) to the southwest. He flew to the source and dropped two flares which were quickly answered by two more Verey flares. Hudson 'F' of 269 Sqn, fitted with an airborne lifeboat, duly arrived overhead and, after two dummy runs, dropped its lifeboat 150 yards (135m) from the downed crew, who paddled across and clambered aboard.

In the meantime, Fortress 'A' was relieved by Fortress II FA699 'K', flown by F/Lt Frank E G Melener. He and Hudson pilot F/O Smith homed in the Portuguese vessel *Lourenco Marques* by

Fortress IIA FK208 '1-B' of 206 Sqn leaves a cloud of red volcanic dust as it takes off from Lagens for an anti-submarine sweep. Its fuselage-mounted LRASV aerials have been deleted by the wartime censor. IWM CA.87

dropping a trail of smoke floats and occasionally diving towards the lifeboat to indicate its position. The ship picked up the survivors at 09:43, some eight hours after McIlwrick had ditched FA707.

The loss of a Fortress to three overspeeding propellers pointed to a failure of the constant speed units (CSUs). Without an airframe to inspect, the cause of the loss could only be speculative, but the consensus among maintenance personnel at Lagens was that FA707, which was on its second operational flight after returning from overhaul at Thornaby, had not been fitted with replacement CSU quill drives due to a shortage of spare parts.

220 Sqn would lose a second aircraft on July 26, after Canadian pilot F/Lt Laurence H Croft experienced a fire in the starboard outboard engine of Fortress IIA FK189 'Y' during take-off at 06:35 for an anti-submarine patrol. Croft shut down the engine and feathered the propeller prior to landing and a USAAF fire crew extinguished the blaze, but the aircraft was considered beyond economical repair and written off. The main cause of the fire was overboosting of the engine caused by a blockage of the turbo regulator control due to carbon build-up. Other contributing causes included broken piston compression rings, which allowed oil to splash and ignite on the exhaust system, and a fractured petrol line to the carburettor pressure gauge, which also caused a fire.

Taxiing accidents involving the Fortress were not uncommon and on July 29, F/O Berwyn White was involved in a mishap following an anti-submarine patrol when he taxied Fortress IIA FL464 'C' into a tractor. Four days later, F/Lt Laurence Croft was unfortunate to be involved in a second write-off while taxiing Fortress II FA706 'S' to dispersal. Alone in the cockpit, he forgot to switch on the batteries and so lost brake pressure. He overlooked the brake pressure warning light and taxied into an unidentified aircraft, terminally damaging the starboard side of FA706.

WITHDRAWAL

220 Sqn flew 94 patrols in July 1944, producing just one U-boat sighting and attack at the end of the month. The first regular night patrols since the departure of the last Wellingtons started at the beginning of the following month, when 114 Sqn US Navy began operations with Leigh Light-equipped Liberators fitted with Mk X centimetric radar. 220 Sqn began its contribution on the night of July 28/29, 1944, when F/O Eric H Smith lifted Fortress III HB792 'U' off at 19:47 following a week of training flights for the new ASV Mk III radar.

Four hours into the patrol the ASV operator made radar contact with a possible target and

A no-doubt relieved crew watch as a Fortress over-flies their air-droppable lifeboat. Since the photograph came from 220 Sqn sources, it may well depict P/O Eric B McIlwrick and his crew who were forced to ditch Fortress II FA707 'Z' on July 26, 1944, following multiple engine failures off the Azores. On that occasion the lifeboat was dropped from a Hudson of 269 Sqn. via Brian Speirs

in the light of flares and return flak this proved to be a surfaced U-boat. Smith attacked immediately from 50ft (15m) with six depth charges, spaced at 55ft intervals, and at a ground speed of 200mph (321 km/h). Blue flashes were seen on both sides of the hull and the aircraft experienced severe shuddering as it passed overhead.

Contact with the U-boat was then lost so a square search was begun, resulting in radar contact being re-established at 01:42. Smith attacked again with two depth charges at an attack angle of 90 degrees while the U-boat replied with heavier flak from three guns with deep red tracer. HB792 remained in the area, making spasmodic radar contact with the U-boat, and at 05:55 was joined by Mk II FA699 'K'. At 07:18 Smith advised base he had lost contact and was returning to Lagens, where he landed at 09:27 with flak damage to the port elevator. Since the U-boat

P/O Eric B McIlwrick began flying Fortresses as a co-pilot while serving with 206 Sqn at Benbecula. His unit subsequently moved to the Azores and on March 19, 1944, McIlwrick transferred to 220 Sqn when 206 Sqn returned to the United Kingdom. As captain, McIlwrick was alone in the cockpit of FA707 'Z' when he was forced to ditch in the open ocean during the early morning hours of July 26 after experiencing three overspeeding propellers. McIlwrick struggled to remove his headphones and helmet and was finally able to wrench them off and squirm through a side cockpit window into the pitch black and drizzle. The other seven crew members came through unscathed at their crash positions in the radio compartment. In typical understatement, the accident report notes that the 'Pilot did well under difficult conditions.' No doubt frequently drawing on this harrowing experience, McIlwrick became a search and rescue instructor. He returned to the banking industry in Scotland at the end of hostilities. Maurice McIlwrick via John Lowe

was accurately targeted during the first run and made no effort to avoid Smith's second attack, the vessel was assessed by the Admiralty Assessment Committee as "*probably slightly damaged.*"

Fortress III operations finally got into their stride in early August with two aircraft typically dispatched every two or three nights. The repaired Fortress III HB786 'V' undertook its first night patrol on September 17 with F/Lt Frank Melener as pilot. F/O Eric Smith was to be involved in another exchange of fire when, on the night of September 23, he attempted to attack a surfaced U-boat while flying HB791 'T'. Smith released some flares but could not get into position to attack before the Fortress was hit in the outer port wing and the U-boat had dived.

It fell to accident-prone Fortress IIA FK191 'P' to make the final U-boat sinking by a Fortress of RAF Coastal Command. This took place on September 26, 1944 with squadron Navigation Leader, F/Lt Arthur F Wallace, in command – the pilot was F/O Eric C W Fielder. The Fortress

Disabled motor vessel from convoy CU 41 under the protective wing of Fortress IIA FK188 'Z', captained by F/O Ken Speirs of 220 Sqn on October 6, 1944. via Brian Speirs

was providing daytime escort to convoy CU 40 northwest of the Azores when the crew learned around 14:00 of a U-boat sighting by FK193 'H' at 42°55'N 36°05'W. FK191 arrived overhead a marker at 14:53 and began circling with FK193 and FA701 'F'. Nine minutes later co-pilot F/O Alexander Paruk spotted a periscope wake and Fielder attacked, dropping three depth charges from 50ft (15m). One weapon had hung up. These straddled the conning tower just as it was breaking the surface, destroying the schnorkel-equipped U-871 at 43°18'N 36°28'W. The submarine was on her maiden voyage under the command of *Kapitänleutnant* Erwin Ganzer. This successful attack brought to eleven the total of U-boats destroyed by Coastal Command's Fortresses while a further six had been assessed as damaged.

On September 29, 220 Sqn was notified that it was to re-equip with Liberator VIs fitted with Leigh Lights, auxiliary wing tanks and sono-buoys. Eight Fortresses were taken out of line, the first seven departing Lagens on October 12th for St Davids in Pembrokeshire, Wales, at which time the squadron had four aircraft at Thornaby undergoing Major Inspections. Onward assignment of the aircraft from St David's became the responsibility of the Fortress Disposal Flight, commanded by former 220 Sqn pilot, F/Lt Laurence Croft. Transit flights from Lagens to the United Kingdom resumed in early November with FK188 'W' the first to depart for RAF Lyneham in Wiltshire on November 6.

220 Sqn flew 27 operational sorties in November, including nine anti-submarine patrols, one convoy escort, one convoy cooperation, two searches for survivors, six Met flights and eight "*transit-recce*" patrols to the United Kingdom. Liberator crews began arriving towards the end of the month and the first Liberator VIs flew in from St Eval on December 4. The first Liberator sortie, a Met flight, was flown on December 8. Six more Fortress IIAs and IIs departed for St Eval on December 11, with the final pair leaving on December 18. Canadian pilot F/O Kenneth Speirs lifted Mk IIA FK210 'G' off at 06:02 arriving at 13:46, while fellow Canadian F/Lt Robert D Thompson took Mk II FA699 'K' aloft at 06:09, arriving at St Eval at 13:34.

This left the three Fortress IIIs, now wearing the new 220 Sqn code 'ZZ', to soldier on alongside the Liberators. HB791 'T' departed for Gosport in Hampshire via Chivenor on March 24 in the hands of F/Lt Francis S Johnson while F/O Eric Smith flew HB792 'U' to Gosport four days later. Coastal Command's use of the Fortress in the dedicated anti-submarine role finally came to an end on April 26, 1945, when F/O George Austen and W/O Jack Hobbs delivered HB786 'V' from Lagens to Gosport.

F/O Eric Smith, rear left, and crew with Fortress III HB791 'T' at Lagens. Smith was one of two 220 Sqn pilots who pioneered the use of ASV Mk III centimetric radar for night time anti-submarine operations from the Azores. Note the AN-65B receiving aerial for the SCR-521 homing system (the American version of ASV Mk II), as later fitted to RAF meteorological reconnaissance Fortresses. via Roger Smith

With the withdrawal of the Fortress from anti-submarine operations, Coastal Command began storing the type at Gosport under the care of 3502 Servicing Unit. Aircraft began arriving at what was known as the Gosport Pool from October 1944, with the majority flown in either directly from the Azores or from Thornaby following overhaul. A handful were transferred from Lichfield after storage with 51 MU.

Gosport was a relatively small aerodrome, a contributory cause of two accidents involving Fortresses. The first occurred on December 28, 1944, when long-suffering Mk IIA FK191 arrived with Canadian pilot F/O Walter C Reynolds at the controls. Failing to appreciate that a short landing was necessary, Reynolds approached too fast, to discover that the brakes were non-effective on the icy surface. FK191 left the runway and collided with target-towing Vultee Vengeance T.T.IV KG810 of 667 Sqn. The Fortress was flown to Prestwick in mid-February for repairs by Scottish Aviation but, like other Fortresses located at Prestwick, it was later recategorised as scrap – Cat. E – and struck off charge.

The second accident occurred on January 22, 1945, and involved Fortress IIA FL462 and pilot F/Lt Alexander T Lovell, who had been at the controls during FK191's first mishap. Visibility was poor in failing light as Lovell and two other crew members flew in from Thornaby with the freshly-overhauled Fortress. Gosport's small dimensions again caught the pilot unawares and Lovell elected to groundloop the aircraft to port as he found himself running out of runway, the starboard wing striking some trees. The aircraft was flown to Prestwick in March for repairs but by June the Fortress was unwanted and it too was consigned to scrap.

FINAL ROLE

Although now superseded by the longer-legged Liberator in the anti-submarine role, Coastal Command's Fortresses still had a key role to play in the defeat of Germany, that of meteorological reconnaissance.

Accurate weather chart analysis and forecasting depend on a reliable network of observations, particularly from oceanic areas. With the start of WWII, meteorological reports from ships and enemy-occupied territory virtually ended but data was still urgently needed for producing synoptic charts and special graphs displaying vertical atmospheric profiles as input for operational planning. The loss of data sources was solved by the introduction of long-range weather reconnaissance flights.

Royal Air Force Meteorological Flights were formed early in 1941 and upgraded to squadron status as each unit expanded. Their primary task was to fly regular weather reconnaissance sorties with secondary air-sea rescue and anti-submarine patrol roles. Each squadron operated a variety of types to undertake different Met flight profiles. Six RAF Met squadrons were equipped with long-range aircraft towards the end of the war in Europe. 517, 518 and 520 Sqns operated Halifaxes while 519, 521 and 251 Sqns were allocated Fortress IIAs, IIs and IIIs retired from the anti-submarine and training roles. (See Appendix J for a map of Met profiles performed by Coastal Command Fortresses.)

The Fortress was particularly well-suited to the meteorological reconnaissance role. A stable platform when flown on instruments, it could climb comfortably to the required altitude of around 23,000ft (7,010m) and, unlike the Liberator, which the USAAF had discovered tended to stall when its wing picked up ice, performed well in the often-present icing conditions. George Fox was a W/O when he converted to the Fortress at 1674 Heavy Conversion Unit prior to joining 519 Sqn:

"The Fortress was a wonderfully easy aircraft to fly with no vices at all. So easy was it that I was flying without an instructor after only three hours of dual instruction. This compares with the 5½ hours of instruction needed before I was ready to fly solo on the Hudson, which was not a particularly likeable plane."

W/O Leslie Hart flew with both 519 and 521 Sqns:

"Before joining a squadron, all Coastal Command pilots and navigators had to pass a six-week General Reconnaissance Course [on Oxfords]. *Pilots had to study and practice considerable navigation*

Wintry scene at Wick as Fortress II FL464 'Z9-B' of 519 (Met) Sqn is refuelled for a sortie. via Eric Jones

skills including astro-navigation, various search patterns, meeting and escorting convoys, ship recognition and so on, while the navigators did similarly. Bomber Command pilots and navigators did not undergo this extended training."

The eight-man Fortress crew consisted of captain and co-pilot, navigator, flight engineer, three Wireless Operator/Air Gunners and a Met Air Observer (MAO). Each aircraft retained the two bomb bay fuel tanks installed for operations from the Azores plus the ability to carry four depth charges on underwing racks for the secondary anti-submarine role. The ASV Mk II radar systems were retained for homing purposes while the nose-mounted Yagi arrays and the fuselage-mounted dipoles for submarine detection were removed. The homing aerials were replaced by pairs of AN-65 or AN-66 antenna, with one aerial on each side of the nose. The ASV system's transmit and receive switching function allowed one to be used for transmitting and both for receiving.

Met Fortresses were equipped with a variety of precision instrumentation, mostly installed at the MAO's station in the nose. This included a large aneroid barometer, an external strut psychrometer (wet and dry thermometer) mounted on the starboard side of the nose and visible to the MAO

519 (Met) Sqn crew with Fortress II FA700 'K' at Wick. Left to right: WOP/AG W/O L Loudfoot, MAO Sgt A B Parry, co-pilot F/Sgt J M Kinnear, captain F/Lt Nigel G S Marshall, navigator F/O W J Dingwell, flight engineer F/O L H Cowley, WOP/AG F/O C Liley and W/O J E F Leclerc. The codes are of the correct colour, Light Slate Grey. via Nigel Marshall

through one of the nose windows – a hand pump allowed the MAO to keep the reservoir for the wick feeding the wet-bulb thermometer topped-up – a Mk XIV altimeter with a sub-scale in millibars, and an airspeed indicator. The latter allowed the MAO to correct his temperature readings for pressure and airspeed. Additional cockpit instrumentation included a radio altimeter for calculation of accurate sea-level pressure readings. The instrument was wired to two tee-shaped aerials located on the underside of the rear fuselage and featured an altitude limit switch with three coloured lights: red, green and amber. Red indicated the aircraft was below a pre-set altitude while amber indicated it was too high. The Fortresses were also equipped with Gee, LORAN and an Air Position Indicator (API) to assist with navigation over the ocean.

Eric Jones was a navigator with 519 Sqn and describes a typical Met flight:

"Met flights were flown at a set pressure altitude. The outbound and return legs were flown at 950 millibars, or around 1,500 to 1,800ft, with a 250 nautical mile top leg at the terminal position flown at 500 millibars. The box climb prior to the top leg actually went up to 400mb – about 23,000ft (7,620m) – with a descent along the leg to 500 millibars, followed by a box descent at the end of that leg for the homeward trip. This requirement often meant flying in cloud for long periods. While within range of Gee this was no problem. LORAN was also a godsend under these conditions but signal reception was often less than ideal. During much of our time on 519, the LORAN signal from Iceland was weak or could not be received… I believe the main aerial was damaged by storms and it was using a temporary aerial. The other transmitters, based in the UK, gave a narrow angle of intercept of their position lines, reducing the accuracy for the navigator. Skywaves could be difficult to measure due to fading or rising up on the horizontal time base, but after flying in cloud or between layers for perhaps hours, it was the best, and sometimes the only available navigation aid.

A Met Log was completed by the Met Air Observer and handed to the radio 'op' ready for transmission. It consisted of three sets of figures in horizontal rows, arranged one above the other. The top line consisted of five-figure groups inserted by the cypher section prior to the flight. The second line was inserted by the MAO and recorded the observed weather using International Met Code, also in five-figure groups. The bottom line was obtained by subtracting the second set of figures from the top, resulting in a ciphered version of the Met information, which was handed to the radio operator at intervals during the flight for transmission to base.

We were encouraged to maintain radio silence as much as possible, except when transmitting Met information to base. On the twins - Venturas and Hudsons - we usually allowed ourselves the luxury of calling for a bearing from the DF station at Kirkwall in the Orkneys soon after we set course for home, as that was virtually the track we had to achieve. We may have done the same on the B-17 but it was far less important as we had LORAN, which was often far from perfect, and Gee, which was very good, for the last, say, 100 miles, depending on altitude, to straighten us up if we were off track."

519 (Met) Sqn Fortress II with, anticlockwise from nose top to bottom, psychrometer, AN-66 homing aerial, airspeed pitot and drift sight. Also visible, to the rear of the ADF loop fairing, is what appears to be an underwing depth charge rack. via Eric Jones

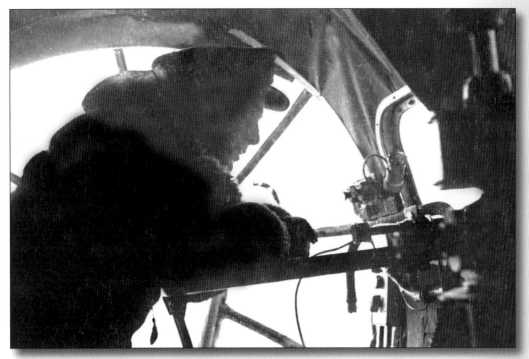

WOP/AG P/O M Stanley 'Blackie' Rundell of 519 (Met) Sqn looks out at the psychrometer from the MAO's position in the nose of a Fortress. via Eric Jones

MET SQUADRON

519 (Met) Sqn (code 'Z9' and motto 'Undaunted by weather') was the first Met unit to operate the Fortress. It had originally been formed at Wick near the northern tip of the Scottish mainland on August 15, 1943, from 1406 (Met) Flight, taking over the latter's Hampden Is and Spitfire VIs and later flying the Ventura and Hudsons. It moved to nearby Skitten on December 13, 1943. The squadron flew two types of Met sortie. The RECIPE sortie extended northwards beyond the Arctic Circle and was flown twice each day with takeoffs planned around midday (RECIPE I) and midnight (RECIPE II). With the arrival of the Fortress the mission was extended to become a four-leg track with turning points at 59°15'N 00°25'W, 67°10'N 04°30'E, 65°50'N 05°30'W and Noup Head, and then around the western side of the Orkney Islands to base. The RHOMBUS sortie was a two-leg operation out over the North Sea to a point 100 miles (160km) southwest of Kristiansand, Norway, at around 57°07N 05°43E and then on to Langham in Norfolk. Peter Rackliff flew as an MAO with 518 (Met) Sqn and the Radar Met Flight. He recently co-authored the book 'Even the Birds Were Walking', an account of the Met squadrons' wartime operations, and describes the RHOMBUS sortie thus:

"The aim was to fly two RHOMBUS sorties each day, one taking off around 06:00 and the second taking off at noon or soon after. This operation was shared between 519 and 521 Sqns but it was a flexible arrangement, depending primarily on aircraft serviceability. Typically a 519 aircraft would take-off from Skitten at around 06:00 and fly to the terminal position near southern Norway, then complete the Met climb and set course for 521's base at Docking, Norfolk, or nearby Langham effective the beginning of November 1944. The next sortie, taking off around noon would be operated by a 521 Sqn crew. They would fly the track in reverse and having completed their Met climb, head for 519's base at Skitten, or Wick starting late November 1944. The duration of these sorties was about 4½ hours. After an overnight stay, the 521 crew would be able to operate the 06:00 or the 12:00 sortie, returning to their base at Langham. Similarly, OC Operations would arrange for the 519 crew to operate the other RHOMBUS sortie, returning to their base at Wick or Skitten."

519's first Fortress arrived at Skitten from 1674 HCU on October 26, 1944, and not a moment too soon according to pilot Les Hart:

"In the autumn of 1944, as more ageing Hudsons arrived to replace our equally ageing Venturas, there was a general view among crews that we did not have aircraft suitable for our task. Another crew had been lost with no distress signal being picked up, a probable casualty of the complex fuel system with its overload tanks and susceptibility to frightening airlocks when changing tanks. The knowledge

519 (Met) Sqn at Wick.
via Bryan Yates

Fine study of Fortress
II FA695 'Z9-C' of 519
(Met) Sqn at Wick. It had
previously served in the
anti-submarine role with
206 Sqn from Benbecula
and the Azores. via Eric
Jones

Fortress II FA695 'C' of
519 (Met) Sqn at Wick. via
Don McNeil

Unidentified 519 (Met)
Sqn Fortress II at Wick.
via Eric Jones

that a ditching in the Arctic waters or even the North Sea held little hope of being picked up – even if one got into a dinghy and survived the freezing temperatures – was ever present.

Then, unexpectedly, the CO announced that the squadron was to be visited by the Air Officer Commander in Chief of Coastal Command, Sir W Sholto Douglas, KCB, MC, DFC. We listened attentively as he talked about the war and Coastal Command's increasing success. When he came to Met Flights, how vital they were and what a splendid job we were doing, it proved too much for some of the Australian and Canadians – they began interrupting him with: 'Why can't we have better aircraft?' and 'We want four engines like 518 [Sqn].' The AOC had a brief aside with our Station Commander and CO before telling us he was aware of our problems, that there were many other demands for aircraft, but that he would personally see that priority was given to our need. Less than two months later, the CO told us that we were shortly to be re-equipped with four-engined Boeing B-17 Fortresses – and in a matter of days the first few arrived. We could hardly believe our good fortune and were absolutely delighted."

The squadron's first RECIPE sortie was attempted on November 26 using Fortress IIA FL455 'A' under the command of S/Ldr Harry W G Andrews. The Fortress took off at 04:40 but was forced to return to base at 05:30 after the blind flying instruments failed, along with the DR compass master unit and repeater. Andrews circled the airfield to burn off fuel and eventually landed at 08:37. The unit moved back to Wick on November 28 and better fortune awaited the same aircraft and crew when, on December 2, Andrews flew a RECIPE I sortie after taking off at 01:27. The Fortress reached the top of its climb, around 17,200ft (5,245m) or 500 millibars at 68°26'N 02°58'W and then, following the high-level leg, descended to near sea level at 65°08'N 03°07'W before resuming the low-level leg at 950 millibars. This was soon changed to a four-leg track with a climb to 400 millibars.

W/Cdr Nigel G S Marshall was a Fortress captain with 519 Sqn:

"The RECIPE sortie took us well into the Arctic Circle and we sometimes witnessed wonderful displays of Northern Lights (Aurora Borealis), like hundreds of shafts of light sweeping across the sky. Another phenomenon was the setting and rising of the sun. I remember on one sortie seeing the sun sink below the horizon slightly to the west and then watching it appear again soon afterwards slightly east of north.

If there was thick cloud, rain, turbulence or icing it was just too bad – one 'pressed on regardless' to use an expression from those days. I remember one occasion when flying at night in heavy cloud and rain on the high level leg and suddenly bursting through what was probably a sharply-defined cold front into a marvellous clear, starry night. The transition was so incredible that I gazed in wonder at the beauty and vastness of the scene and thought: 'God is in his Heaven and all is well with the World'.

The Fortress was very comfortable, a steady and stable aircraft with a most efficient automatic pilot – made by Minneapolis Honeywell, with a lot of winking lights – which controlled the aircraft remarkably well."

Derek Willis served as an MAO with 519 Sqn:

"The Fortress was very comfortable to work in with a large table in the nose with a built-in ash tray and a nice swivel chair. Although it could get cold on the high level leg of a RECIPE – the lowest

outside air temperature I recorded was minus 50 degrees F – the heating in the nose for the Fort was much better than in the Halifax, although I used to fly with my fur-lined jacket draped over my knees."

Ted Hedges was one of several former 220 Sqn personnel assigned to training new Fortress crew members:

"I became an instructor at 1674 HCU at Aldergrove from mid-August 1944 and flew with trainee crews as staff engineer on both Fortresses and Liberators. My time there involved more near misses than I can bear to think about plus frequent burst tyres and burnt brakes. I spent a number of weeks with W/O [John L] Gullen, a tour-expired former 206 Sqn captain. We were based at Skitten and Wick in Scotland, providing conversion training for crews from 519 and 521 Met Sqns. This came to an end on December 31, 1944, when a former 220 Sqn captain, F/Lt [Charles H] Lockwood, RCAF, and I were flown from Aldergrove to Wick in an Oxford to collect Fortress 'M' the same evening. But it took seven days to find out why No. 3 engine wouldn't start... we had no kit, no money and I ended up spending my 21st birthday in the ice and snow.

But that was not the half of it. When we finally did get airborne and flew our first course, we found we were not where we should have been and eventually discovered that the compass had a massive error. The weather was atrocious and, with blizzard conditions over the Irish Sea, we could not locate Belfast Lough... when we did find some clear air we were over an airfield in Eire. Lockwood debated putting us in there but we would have been interned so we flew back north and very luckily located Belfast. Lockwood then started some very intensive time procedures as we had to climb into the 'clag' to clear the mountains.

We approached Aldergrove with me watching the airspeed like a hawk. When we asked flying control for landing instructions they refused, saying they were closed in and we couldn't possibly make it. Lockwood disregarded this and we made a timed approach, letting down completely blind over Lough Neagh. At just 150ft I caught sight of the runway, incredibly, dead ahead. We slammed down, stopped just short of the end of the runway and taxied clear. After shutting down, we simply walked off, leaving the aircraft to the blizzard. Lockwood saved our hides... it was a brilliant piece of flying. The irony of it all was that one of my old crew mates from the Azores, F/Sgt Ken Day, was killed in a blizzard just three weeks later when 519 Sqn lost FL455."

Detail view of a Met Sqn Fortress II with Met assistant Lucy Alder in the nose. The original mounting location for the ADF loop fairing is visible slightly to port of the aircraft centreline while the drift sight fairing is alongside to starboard. Also visible are the two pitot tube masts in the foreground and the psychrometer (wet and dry bulb thermometer) on the extreme left of the photograph. The two smaller probes are AN-65 aerials for the SCR-521 homing system. via Mike Diprose

FORTRESS DOWN

By early 1945, 519 Sqn had ten Fortress IIAs and IIs on strength but on February 1 tragedy struck. FL455 'Z9-A' took off from Wick at 10:45 on a RECIPE II Met flight with a crew of nine led by F/Lt F Keith 'Bluey' Humphreys and co-pilot F/O George H Pullan. The flight northwards into the Norwegian Sea proved uneventful, the Norwegian coastline was bathed in sunshine and the crew went about their various tasks. Third pilot F/O Tom G Wrigley, who had just joined the squadron, flew FL455 for a couple of hours to gain experience on type.

The Fortress reached the end of the outward leg, climbed to over 18,000ft (5,486m) for the top leg and then descended again for the long flight home. At about 16:00 the Fortress flew into a snowstorm and began picking up ice. Conditions were still bad when contact was made with flying control at Wick four hours later, with gusting snowstorms and low cloud. All other flying had been cancelled. At 20:08 the Fortress was heard passing over the airfield and was given a course to bring it back but at 20:13 radio contact was lost. The crew had been flying for almost ten hours, the last four of which had been in the storm. Humphreys reported that his radio altimeter was unserviceable and that he was having trouble with the carburettor icing controls.

At 20:40, while circling to find the airfield, the Fortress flew into level, marshy terrain near Halsary, some 12 miles (19km) southwest of Wick. It then slid along the surface and broke in two at the radio compartment before coming to rest. Four men died in the crash, two more were badly injured but the three pilots survived, only the unsecured Wrigley sustaining injuries. The survivors were sighted the following morning by the crew of one of several search aircraft, a Vickers Warwick of 279 Sqn, and at 13:00 were reached by the Mountain Rescue Unit and evacuated. Of the two injured men, one died the following day, the second nine days later.

Crash site of FL455 'A' of 519 (Met) Sqn. The three pilots occupying the cockpit in the nose section survived, but the remaining six crew members died. via Mike Diprose

The subsequent enquiry identified a number of contributing causes. After over ten hours of often demanding flying F/Lt Humphreys was clearly fatigued. This was aggravated by a "*bad feeling*" between the pilot and flying control at Wick, which prompted Humphreys to use an ASV beacon for his descent through cloud rather than request a QGH approach procedure (where the aircraft transmits, the ground station determines the direction of the signal and then gives the pilot a course to fly to the airfield).

Unfortunately, the ASV reading was apparently erroneous and Humphreys turned too far by 180 degrees. He also failed to request the airfield altimeter setting (QFE), instead relying on an incorrect reading provided by his MAO and did not use the Gee navigation set to cross-check his navigation. Compounding these ill-fated decisions, the pilot's R/T was set on 'send' and then turned off as it was assumed to be unserviceable. This prevented Humphreys from keeping in touch with flying control and receiving diversion information. Their fate was sealed when the aircraft could no longer climb after the engineer applied carburettor heat to counter possible carburettor icing following failure of the carburettor icing indicators. (Although no longer used for homing on U-boats, Met squadron Fortresses retained their ASV Mk II radar systems for navigational purposes.)

A memorial to 519 Sqn crewmembers lost in this and other accidents was dedicated at Halsary on August 29, 1992. It reads: 'We shall remember them and their comrades of 519 Met Recce Sqn, RAF Wick, "who flew beyond the storms, into the sunset".'

Navigator Eric Jones recalled:

"*Our crew never had occasion to use a QGH approach. But we did do a couple of VERY low flights from the north coast to Wick airfield to stay under low cloud and avoid doing the procedure. Quicker and safer that way!*"

Adversity of a very different kind befell F/O Don S MacNeil, RCAF, and the crew of Fortress IIA FK213 'G' on March 29, 1945. F/O Bevan Smith was the navigator:

"*We had surprised a convoy coming back from Russia… they were about 100 miles from where we had been told to expect them. We had just taken a sea level pressure reading and turned on our IFF, which hadn't warmed up, when we suddenly found all hell around us. As we came to a break in the cloud cover I could see flashes from the guns of the convoy below us. We took a hit in the right wing between fuel tanks and another one which went through the corner of my 'nav' table and exploded between the oxygen tanks. Our flight engineer 'pooped' off the colours [of the day], then started putting out the resulting fire [in the main fuse box]. I put one out in my cabin and I remember one of the WOP/AGs came down for what was left in my extinguisher and I believe they beat out the remaining fire with their gloves. With only 2½ engines left, the battery was running low so we had no lights and were down to 200ft for a while. The searchlights came up around Scapa Flow and 'depressed', pointing south. We found Wick… and MacNeil put us down beautifully.*"

Above: FK213 'Z9-G', formerly with 519 (Met) Sqn, in store at 51 MU, Lichfield. It had survived being shot at by the Royal Navy and was sold to International Alloys Ltd. for scrap on March 11, 1947. J D R Rawlings via Andy Thomas

Left: Personnel from 519 (Met) Sqn and Meteorological Office assistant Lucy 'Sue' Alder pose for the camera. To the extreme left is a relatively clear view of a later style of depth charge rack. via Mike Dipose.

Memorial to the 519 Sqn crew members killed in the crash of Fortress IIA FL455 'A' and in other Sqn losses. Left to right: Lord Thurso JP, FL455's co-pilot George Pullan and Dr Michael Diprose, the driving force behind the project. via Peter Rackliff

MacNeil and WOP/AG F/Lt Marc F Brunelle, who was manning the radio during the crisis, each received the Air Force Cross, while Bevan Smith and flight engineer 'Dicky' Day were Mentioned in Dispatches. FK213 was repaired on site and rejoined the squadron in mid-June.

WEARY WARRIORS

By now Coastal Command's Fortresses were showing considerable wear and tear from their long-range maritime operations and an increasing number of engine failures forced crews to return to base on three engines. Fortress IIA FL463 'C' of 1674 HCU suffered an engine failure on June 7 while W/O George Fox, who subsequently joined 519 Sqn, was undergoing type conversion at Aldergrove as part of 3 Fortress Met Course:

"Shortly after setting course from Rhinns of Islay on the first leg of the exercise, a distinct vibration of the engine cowling on No. 4 engine was observed, immediately followed by fluctuating RPM on this engine. Boost in use at time was 29" and RPM 1750 for all engines. Revs on No. 4 engine fluctuated between approximately 1600 and 2000 per minute and distinct snatching at the rudder control showed that the engine, and not the instruments, was at fault. Pressures, temperatures and fuel contents were all normal, and the ignition switch was fully 'on'. The mixture control was moved from 'weak' to 'auto rich' position. The fluctuation of RPM and vibration continued, the cowling was shuddering and blue smoke was seen streaming from the cowling gills, while black smoke was observed from the exhaust in short puffs every 15-20 seconds. No. 4 engine was then immediately feathered and course set for base where a successful three-engine landing was made."

An exacting flight profile, constant changes in altitude and often poor weather conditions made it highly unlikely that Met squadron crews would make contact with enemy U-boats, let alone initiate attacks. However, on April 17, 1945, F/O George Pullan of 519 (Met) Sqn made what is believed to have been the only attack by a Met squadron Fortress. Pullan had taken off from Wick at 00:30 for a RECIPE II sortie in Fortress IIA FL464 'B'. At 11:06 his crew sighted two wakes with 'smoke' – schnorkelling U-boats – at 59°50'N 03°21'W and 59°49'N 03°20'W respectively, to the north of Scapa Flow. The wake from the first sighting disappeared before an attack was possible but Pullan manage to launch his four underwing 250lb (113kg) Torpex-filled Mk XI depth charges at the second. Pullan recalled:

German Navy E-boat flies a white flag after surrendering to Fortress IIA FK211 'H' of 519 (Met) Sqn on May 2, 1945. via Bryan Yates

S/Ldr Gerry J Chandler, fourth from right, and crew of 519 (Met) Sqn with a Fortress IIA at Wick. The crew consisted of five members from the RAF, two from the RAAF and one RNZAF. via Bryan Yates

519 (Met) Sqn's final RECIPE sortie, flown from Leuchers, Scotland by W/Cdr Ian N M Mac-Donald in Halifax Met Mk III NP960 'C' on May 30, 1946. via Derek Willis

521 (Met) Sqn flight personnel with Fortress IIA at Langham. via Sheila Hart Simpson and Howard Simpson

"With reference to the 'long' RECIPE, meaning a RECIPE in Forts, we spotted and attacked a schnorkel. No result was observed so I guess we missed it. Afterwards we were instructed to circle until our PLE [Prudent Limit of Endurance], *waiting for a Sunderland to relieve us."*

519 Sqn was destined to fly its last Fortress sortie on June 23, 1945, when S/Ldr Gerry J Chandler took Fortress FL459 'M' on a night-time RECIPE II sortie. On that day Coastal Command temporarily grounded its Fortress fleet following discovery of corrosion in a tailplane spar during an inspection. All aircraft had to be inspected before the fleet was put back on line, effective July 12. 519 Sqn's role was initially undertaken by a detachment of crews from 518 Sqn at Tiree flying the Halifax Met. Mk III. On August 17-18, 1945, 519 Sqn and the 518 Sqn detachment moved to Tain where 519 Sqn crews converted to the Halifax Met. Mk III, flying their first sortie on 11 September. The squadron subsequently moved to Leuchars and was finally disbanded on May 31, 1946.

OTHER MET SQUADRONS

521 (Met) Sqn (code '5O', no motto) was the second Met unit to operate the Fortress. It was formed at Bircham Newton, Norfolk, on August 1, 1942, from 1401 Flight for meteorological duties over the North Sea and Europe. Hudsons and Blenheims carried out RHOMBUS sorties over the North Sea, Spitfires and Mosquitoes were used over enemy territory and Gloster Gladiators flew local Met climbs – or soundings – to around 25,000ft (7,620m). On March 31, 1943, the squadron divided into 1401 and 1409 (Met) Flights, 1409 being the Mosquito element, which was appropriated by Bomber Command for their Pathfinder Force and transferred to Oakington.

On September 1, 1943, 521 Sqn reformed at Docking in Norfolk with Hampdens, Hudsons and Gladiators. Venturas became the main type by the end of the year and Hurricanes arrived in August 1944 to supplement the Gladiators which, despite their age, continued to fly sorties until March 1945. Hudsons reappeared in September 1944 as the Venturas were required by other units.

The squadron moved to Langham on November 1, 1944, and beginning later that month was assigned a total of eight Fortresses, including Fortress IIAs and IIs and a single former 220 Sqn Fortress III. Pilot training was conducted from mid-December to the end of February 1945 by F/Lt Laurence Croft, initially using Mk IIA FL463 'P' on detachment from 1674 HCU at Aldergrove.

The first Fortress operation, a RHOMBUS II, departed Langham for Wick on February 2, 1945, using Mk II FA710 as a component of the shuttle arrangement with 519 Sqn. These two-day round trip operations continued twice-daily until the end of September. In October 1945, some Fortress crews were detached to Brawdy in South Wales, to fly the ALLAH Atlantic sortie with a terminal position of approximately 51°N 22°W and on November 3, 1945, 521 Sqn moved to Chivenor in Devon.

251 (Met) Sqn (code 'AD' and motto 'However wind blows') was the third Met unit to use the Fortress. Based at Reykjavik for meteorological flights and air-sea rescue duties around Iceland using Hudson IIIs, the former 1407 Flight attained squadron status on August 1, 1944. Conversion to the Fortress began with the arrival of Mk IIA FK184 'A' on March 26, 1945, although the Hudsons were not replaced until August when Warwicks arrived for the ASR role. Fortress IIA FK185 arrived on April 5 following conversion back to standard configuration and storage on completion of the 40mm cannon trials. The squadron's Fortress IIAs, IIs and two former 220 Sqn Fortress IIIs flew the MAGNUM sortie, a standard out-and-return track radiating some 650 miles (1,045km) southwest of Reykjavik out over the Atlantic. The squadron's first MAGNUM sortie, using Fortress IIA FL451 'D', was flown on May 6. Because of the increased range offered by the Fortress, the sortie was later extended to a triangular track that could be flown clockwise or anti-clockwise.

Stanley Holmes flew as an MAO with 251 Sqn and had reason to experience both the Liberator and Fortress in the Met role:

"251 Sqn's Hudsons were grounded at the end of March 1945 after two aircraft were lost and some flights were aborted for engine and equipment failures. The Met recce task was assumed temporarily by 53 Sqn who were also based in Iceland, flying anti-sub Liberators. 251's MAOs flew with 53 until

Top: F/O Les Hart about to touch down at Langham in a 521 (Met) Sqn Fortress IIA following a RHOMBUS sortie across the North Sea. via Sheila Hart Simpson and Howard Simpson

Middle: Interesting shot captures FK184 'A' while at Reykjavik with 251 (Met) Sqn. FK184 was the RAF's first Fortress IIA and served briefly with 206 Sqn before 'disappearing' for an extended period from operational records. Note that former Sqn codes, possibly 'VX' of 206 Sqn, have been painted out to the right of the roundel. Here Sgt Gracie is supervising the recharging of the oxygen system on the nearer aircraft while Aircraftsman Benson peers from the hatchway. Danny MacDonald via Peter Rackliff

Bottom: 251 (Met) Sqn crew at Reykjavik in May 1945 with an unidentified Fortress IIA. Left to right: Unknown, WOP/AG Sgt Archie E Clark, navigator Sgt Ron A Lee, captain F/Sgt Gray E Melville, WOP/AG Sgt Charlie Walker, co-pilot F/Sgt George Kirby and MAO Sgt Norman Thomas. Note that the supercharger cold air intake has been blanked off and the cowling tops painted, the latter as part of an upper surface repaint in Extra Dark Sea Grey. Norman Thomas via Peter Rackliff

Post-war view of Fortress II FA712 'C' Keflavik Cutie of 251 (Met) Sqn taxing for a MAGNUM sortie from Keflavik, Iceland. The large 48-inch underwing serials were applied around late July-August 1945. Note that the upper turret has been removed. Stanley Robins via Peter Rackliff

Former 519 (Met) Sqn Fortresses in transit from Wick to Reykjavik on July 23, 1945, to join 251 (Met) Sqn. Closest to the camera is Fortress IIA FL464 'B' with Fortress II FA696 'J' behind. Derek Willis

Former 220 Sqn Fortress III HB792 at Keflavik with 251 (Met) Sqn, still marked as 'ZZ-U' – it became 'AD-D'. The top turret and tail guns have been removed. Stanley Robins via Peter Rackliff

135

251 re-equipped with the Fortress. *Conditions in the 'Lib' were not very pleasant as it was very cold and drafty behind the front turret! What a pleasure it was when we moved into the rather grand nose section* [of the Fortress], *shared with the navigator."*

As noted earlier, the temporary grounding of Fortresses on June 23, 1945, had resulted in 519 Sqn relinquishing its aircraft and on July 24, seven examples were ferried to Reykjavik to join 251 Sqn. The unit continued to operate Fortresses from Iceland until it was disbanded on October 30, 1945. F/Lt Stanley Robins flew the final Met flight in Fortress II FA701 'J' *Jokull Jessie* on October 23.

251 Sqn experienced two significant incidents with its Fortresses. On April 18, 1945, F/Lt Gregory A MacMahon and his crew of six were ferrying Mk IIA FK188 from Gosport to Iceland while still under the care of 3502 SU. Just under three hours into the flight the RPM and boost for the port inner engine began to fluctuate violently and severe swirl vibration threatened to wrench the engine from its mount. MacMahon feathered the propeller and landed safely at Wick, the aircraft subsequently being written off. And on August 29, F/Sgt Gray E Melville approached too high and too fast while landing at Aldergrove in Mk IIA FL451 'D'. The aircraft was damaged when it ran off the end of the runway and no attempt was made to repair it. The veteran of the sinking of U-boat U-710 was offered to the Ministry of Aircraft Production but, unwanted, it was recategorised as scrap.

At 01:00 on January 8, 1946, Mk II FA703 of 521 Sqn, by now the only active Coastal Command Fortress unit, was undertaking an ALLAH II sortie from Chivenor when pilot F/O Peter M Williams began experiencing RPM fluctuations from the No. 3 engine. These returned to normal after 15 minutes. At 02:00 the RPM for the same engine dropped to 1500 RPM and could not be increased while the oil temperature had begun to rise. Williams ordered the engine shut down and co-pilot F/Sgt V C 'Tinker' Taylor reported that he pressed the feathering button for No. 3 engine but it was the No. 4 propeller that feathered. With its feathering button stuck in and the No. 3 propeller windmilling, the aircraft rapidly lost height as both pilots struggled to keep up the starboard wing. Williams was obliged to give the ditching order with the aircraft under only partial control and, tragically, only three crew members, pilots Williams and Taylor, together with engineer W/O Peter

Fortress IIA FK197 'AD-E' served briefly with 251 (Met) Sqn following 2-½ years with Scottish Aviation dedicated to LRASV radar trials. A Type C red, white and blue roundel can just be seen on top of the starboard wing although the Upper camouflage scheme is still Temperate Sea rather than the specified Extra Dark Sea Grey. It is seen in formation with a unit Hudson. via Mike Diprose

Fortress III HB786 'Q' of 521 (Met) Sqn being refuelled at Chivenor, Devon, in late 1945. It retains its upper turret, less guns, but the chin turret has been removed. It previously served with 220 Sqn in the Azores as 'ZZ-V' and was last recorded at Gatwick in March 1946. Note the large serial under the starboard wing and Gee whip aerial above the nose. Les Hart via Sheila Hart Simpson and Howard Simpson

W Collett, managed to escape, to be rescued from their dinghy seven hours later by the vessel SS *Harriet Tubman*.

This proved to be Coastal Command's very last operation with the Fortress and the type was grounded. 521 Sqn's aircraft were replaced by Halifax Met. Mk IIIs. The unit continued to fly the ALLAH sortie until the squadron was disbanded on 1 April, 1946, shortly after converting to the Halifax Met Mk VI.

521 (Met) Sqn crew with Fortress IIA Nanette (see Appendix M for another photograph of the artwork). Standing left to right: flight engineer F/Sgt Alf R Shoebottom, co-pilot W/O Jack E Ward, captain F/O Les F Hart, navigator P/O Bronte G Hayes, RAAF, and WOP/AG F/O Bob C Innes, RCAF. Kneeling left to right: WOP/AGs F/Os William G Bennett and R W 'Red' Mulligan, both RCAF. Les Hart via Sheila Hart Simpson and Howard Simpson

CONSIGNED TO SCRAP

The original intent of the Lend-Lease agreement was that all aircraft were to be returned from Britain to the United States. But with storage sites in both countries crammed with surplus aircraft, this was obviously impractical and, since the Fortress was already heading into retirement, the Air Ministry decided to scrap the entire fleet.

Of the 67 'Lend-Lease' Fortresses delivered to Britain for maritime reconnaissance operations with Coastal Command – 45 Fortress IIAs, 19 Fortress IIs and 3 Fortress IIIs – 48 survived service before being struck off charge in the period 1945-47. Of these, 16 were in storage at Gosport, 13 were at Prestwick for repair and overhaul by Scottish Aviation, 16 were under the care of 51 MU at Lichfield – known locally as Fradley – and three were at other locations. Four examples at Lichfield were 'Offered to MAP' (Ministry of Aircraft Production), presumably as flying test beds for which the Fortress was well-suited, but in the end all the Fortresses at Lichfield were scrapped, mostly by International Alloys Ltd. of Aylesbury, Buckinghamshire. Bryan Yates, a nearby resident and Fortress enthusiast, recalls their sad fate:

"Amazingly, the Fortresses were not stripped out but simply wrecked with cranes, power shovels or by simply driving tractors through them. International Alloys had a mobile smelter on site and the aircraft were reduced to ingots and trucked out."

Those at Prestwick and Gosport were similarly written off and scrapped. Regrettably, not one of Coastal Command's unsung Fortresses survived.

Fortress III HB792, formerly with 220 Squadron as 'ZZ-U' and later with 251 (Met) Squadron as 'AD-D', awaits scrapping at 51 MU, Lichfield. The open hatch behind the cockpit once contained a life raft. J D R Rawlings via Andy Thomas

Forlorn and weathered Fortress IIA FL463 awaits its fate at 51 MU, Lichfield. It wears code letter 'C' from its final service with 1674 HCU at Aldergrove and is equipped with both ASV Mk II radar and nose-mounted psychrometers for aircrew training. John M Rabbets

Fortress III HB791, still showing the partially erased USAAF serial 42-98021, retains the natural metal finish it wore with 220 Sqn in the Azores (see colour profile page 236) and 251 (Met) Sqn while based in Iceland as 'AD-L'. Note that the chin and upper turrets were removed for service in the Met role. It is pictured at 51 MU, Lichfield, awaiting the attention of International Alloys. MAP

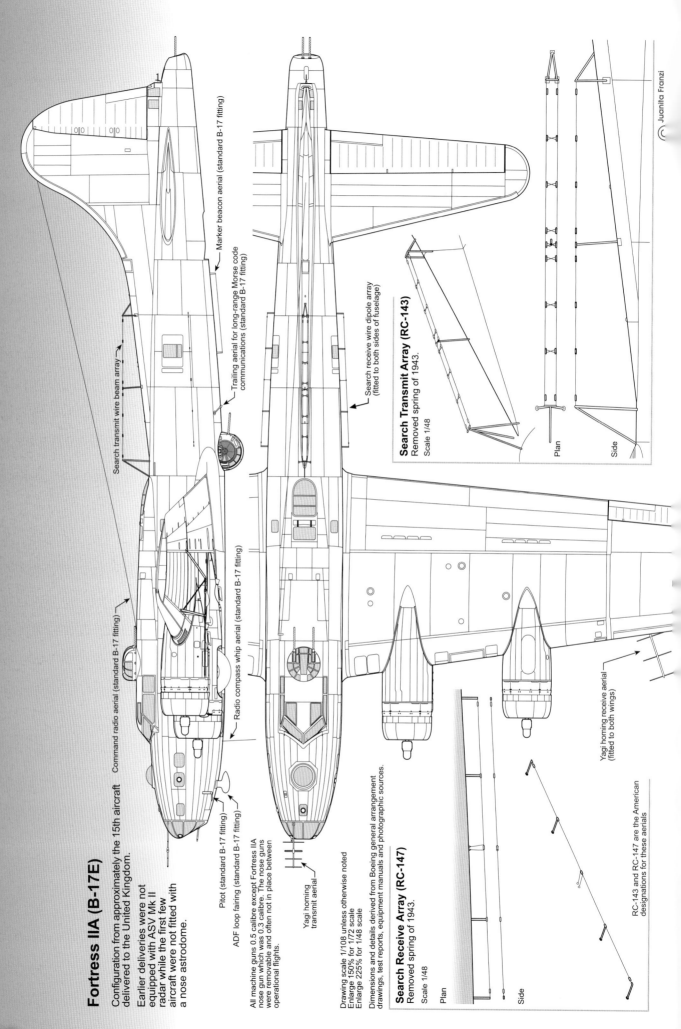

Fortress IIA (B-17E)

Configuration from approximately the 15th aircraft delivered to the United Kingdom.

Earlier deliveries were not equipped with ASV Mk II radar while the first few aircraft were not fitted with a nose astrodome.

All machine guns 0.5 calibre except Fortress IIA nose gun which was 0.3 calibre. The nose guns were removable and often not in place between operational flights.

Drawing scale 1/108 unless otherwise noted
Enlarge 150% for 1/72 scale
Enlarge 225% for 1/48 scale

Dimensions and details derived from Boeing general arrangement drawings, test reports, equipment manuals and photographic sources.

Command radio aerial (standard B-17 fitting)

Marker beacon aerial (standard B-17 fitting)

Search transmit wire beam array

Trailing aerial for long-range Morse code communications (standard B-17 fitting)

Search receive wire dipole array (fitted to both sides of fuselage)

Radio compass whip aerial (standard B-17 fitting)

Pitot (standard B-17 fitting)

ADF loop fairing (standard B-17 fitting)

Yagi homing transmit aerial

Yagi homing receive aerial (fitted to both wings)

Search Transmit Array (RC-143)
Removed spring of 1943.
Scale 1/48

Plan

Side

Search Receive Array (RC-147)
Removed spring of 1943.
Scale 1/48

Plan

Side

RC-143 and RC-147 are the American designations for these aerials

Juanita Franzi

140

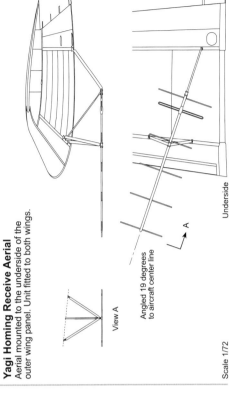

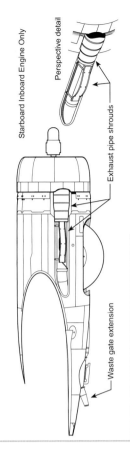

Yagi Homing Receive Aerial
Aerial mounted to the underside of the outer wing panel. Unit fitted to both wings.

View A

Angled 19 degrees
to aircraft center line

A

Underside

Scale 1/72

Flame Damping and Glow Suppression
Tested on Fortress IIA FK187 and known to have been fitted to FK202 'B' of 59 Squadron.

Starboard Inboard Engine Only

Perspective detail

Exhaust pipe shrouds

Waste gate extension

Waste gate extension

Port Outboard Engine
(Starboard side similar)

Exhaust pipe shroud

Front View

Scale 1/72

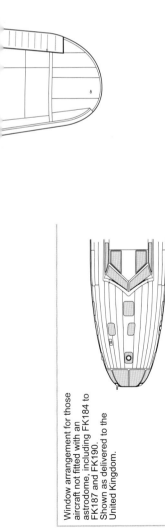

Window arrangement for those aircraft not fitted with an astrodome, including FK184 to FK187 and FK190.
Shown as delivered to the United Kingdom.

Prototype British-designed ASV Mk II Radar Search Arrays
Tested on Fortress IIA FK190. Sideways-looking search function also referred to as 'broadside'

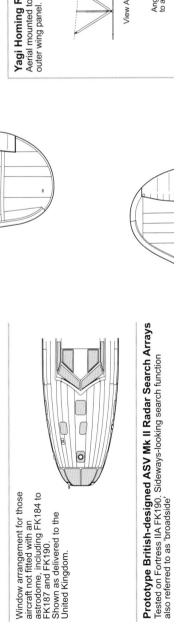

Search transmit dipole array
('stickleback')

Search receive dipole arrays
(fitted to both sides of fuselage)

Scale 1/108

Supercharger Cold Air Intakes
A few photographs show the supercharger cold air intake for each engine blanked off and overpainted. The supercharger was used on operations and no explanation for covering the intakes - and presumably disabling the superchargers - has been found.

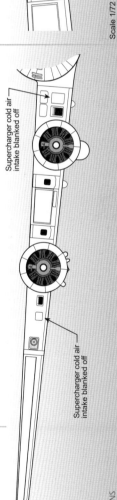

Supercharger cold air
intake blanked off

Supercharger cold air
intake blanked off

© Juanita Franzi
AERO ILLUSTRATIONS

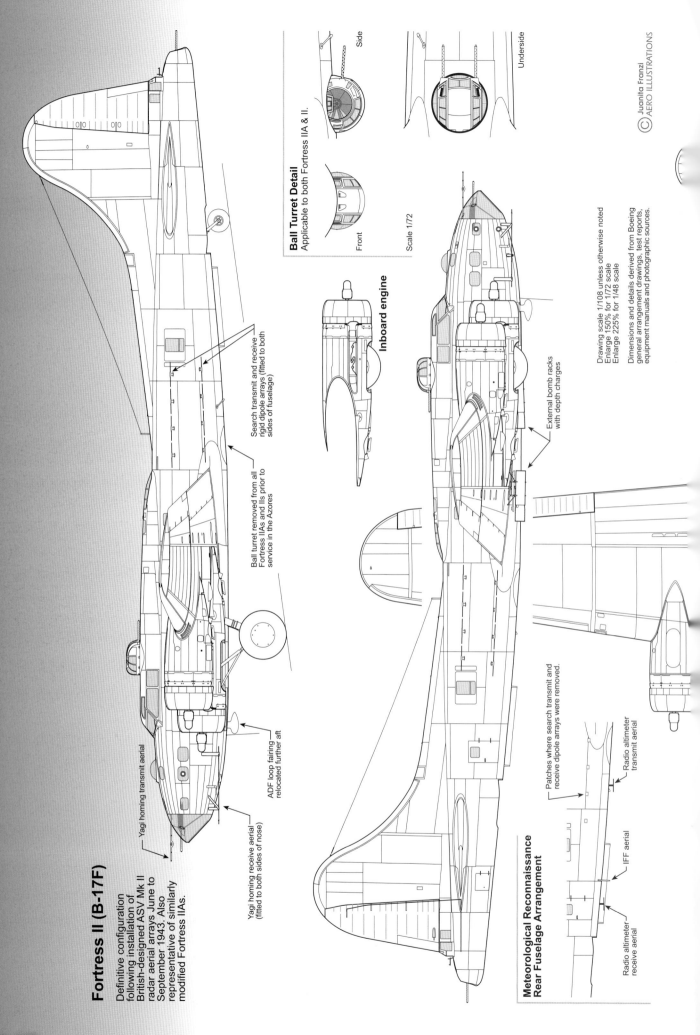

Fortress II (B-17F)

Definitive configuration following installation of British-designed ASV Mk II radar aerial arrays June to September 1943. Also representative of similarly modified Fortress IIAs.

Yagi homing transmit aerial

Yagi homing receive aerial (fitted to both sides of nose)

ADF loop fairing relocated further aft

Search transmit and receive rigid dipole arrays (fitted to both sides of fuselage)

Ball turret removed from all Fortress IIAs and IIs prior to service in the Azores.

Ball Turret Detail
Applicable to both Fortress IIA & II.

Side

Underside

Front

Scale 1/72

Inboard engine

External bomb racks with depth charges

Drawing scale 1/108 unless otherwise noted
Enlarge 150% for 1/72 scale
Enlarge 225% for 1/48 scale

Dimensions and details derived from Boeing general arrangement drawings, test reports, equipment manuals and photographic sources.

© Juanita Franzi
AERO ILLUSTRATIONS

Meteorological Reconnaissance Rear Fuselage Arrangement

Patches where search transmit and receive dipole arrays were removed.

Radio altimeter transmit aerial

IFF aerial

Radio altimeter receive aerial

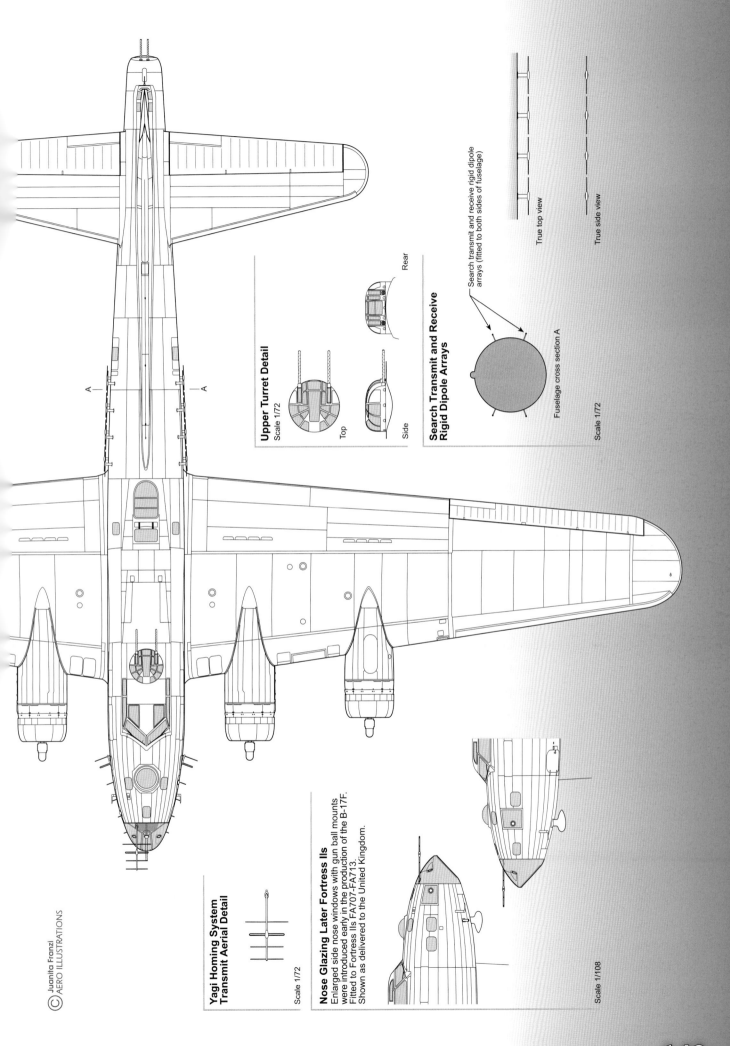

Upper Turret Detail
Scale 1/72

Rear

Top

Side

Search Transmit and Receive Rigid Dipole Arrays

Search transmit and receive rigid dipole arrays (fitted to both sides of fuselage)

Fuselage cross section A

Scale 1/72

True top view

True side view

A

A

Yagi Homing System Transmit Aerial Detail

Scale 1/72

Nose Glazing Later Fortress IIs
Enlarged side nose windows with gun ball mounts were introduced early in the production of the B-17F. Fitted to Fortress IIs FA707-FA713. Shown as delivered to the United Kingdom.

Scale 1/108

© Juanita Franzi
AERO ILLUSTRATIONS

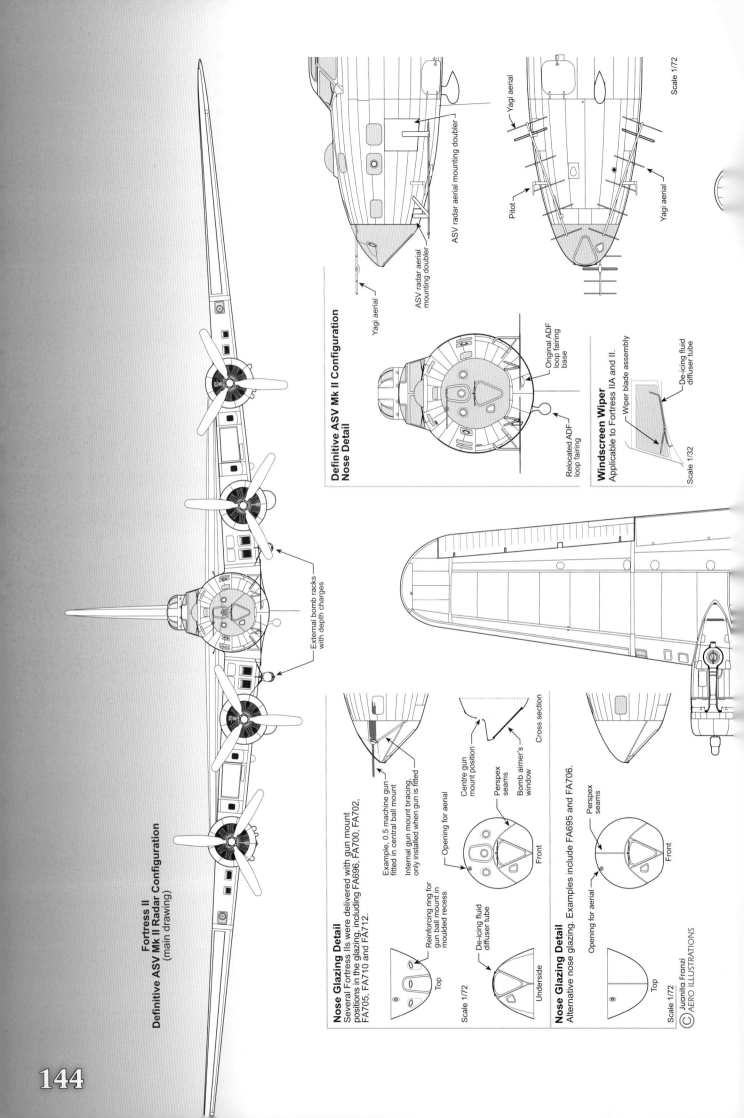

Fortress II
Definitive ASV Mk II Radar Configuration
(main drawing)

External bomb racks
with depth charges

Definitive ASV Mk II Configuration Nose Detail

Yagi aerial

ASV radar aerial mounting doubler

Yagi aerial

ASV radar aerial
mounting doubler

ASV radar aerial mounting doubler

Yagi aerial

Pitot

Yagi aerial

Scale 1/72

Original ADF
loop fairing
base

Relocated ADF
loop fairing

Windscreen Wiper
Applicable to Fortress IIA and II.

Wiper blade assembly

De-icing fluid
diffuser tube

Scale 1/32

Nose Glazing Detail
Several Fortress IIs were delivered with gun mount
positions in the glazing, including FA696, FA700, FA702,
FA705, FA710 and FA712.

Example, 0.5 machine gun
fitted in central ball mount

Internal gun mount bracing,
only installed when gun is fitted

Opening for aerial

Reinforcing ring for
gun ball mount in
moulded recess

De-icing fluid
diffuser tube

Top

Centre gun
mount position

Perspex
seams

Bomb aimer's
window

Cross section

Front

Underside

Scale 1/72

Nose Glazing Detail
Alternative nose glazing. Examples include FA695 and FA706.

Opening for aerial

Perspex
seams

Top

Front

Scale 1/72

Juanita Franzi
© AERO ILLUSTRATIONS

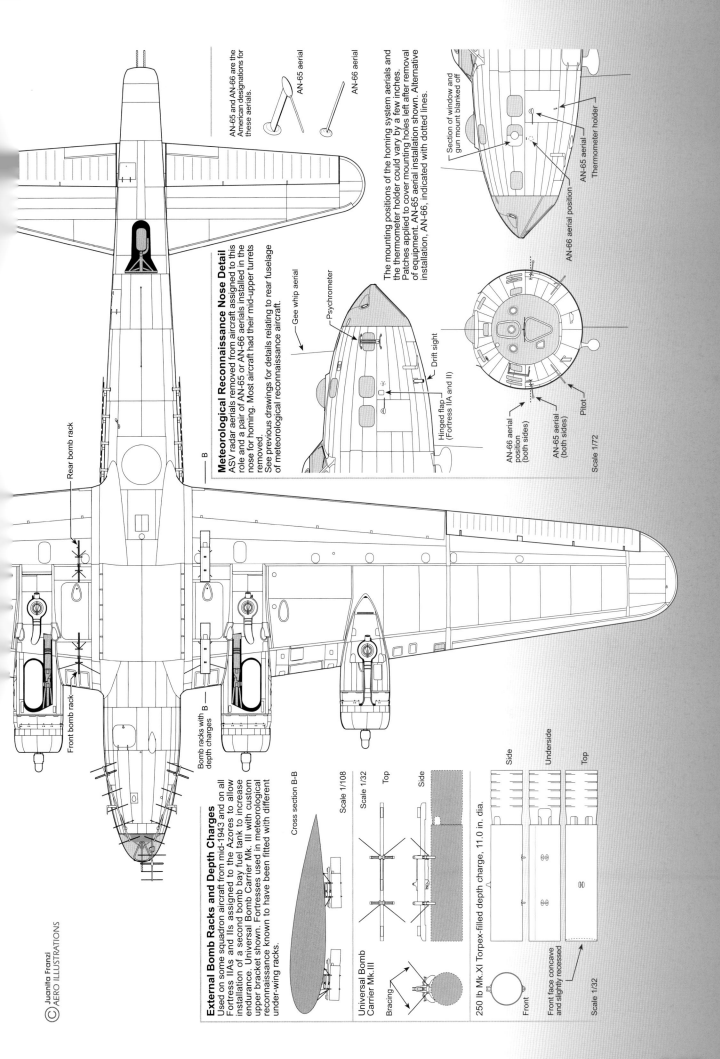

AN-65 and AN-66 are the American designations for these aerials.

AN-65 aerial

AN-66 aerial

Meteorological Reconnaissance Nose Detail

ASV radar aerials removed from aircraft assigned to this role and a pair of AN-65 or AN-66 aerials installed in the nose for homing. Most aircraft had their mid-upper turrets removed.

See previous drawings for details relating to rear fuselage of meteorological reconnaissance aircraft.

Gee whip aerial

Psychrometer

Drift sight

Hinged flap (Fortress IIA and II)

B

The mounting positions of the homing system aerials and the thermometer holder could vary by a few inches. Patches applied to cover mounting holes left after removal of equipment. AN-65 aerial installation shown. Alternative installation, AN-66, indicated with dotted lines.

Section of window and gun mount blanked off

AN-65 aerial

Thermometer holder

AN-66 aerial position

AN-66 aerial position (both sides)

AN-65 aerial (both sides)

Pitot

Scale 1/72

Rear bomb rack

Front bomb rack

Bomb racks with depth charges

B

External Bomb Racks and Depth Charges

Used on some squadron aircraft from mid-1943 and on all Fortress IIAs and IIs assigned to the Azores to allow installation of a second bomb bay fuel tank to increase endurance. Universal Bomb Carrier Mk. III with custom upper bracket shown. Fortresses used in meteorological reconnaissance known to have been fitted with different under-wing racks.

Cross section B-B

Scale 1/108

Universal Bomb Carrier Mk.III

Bracing

Top

Side

Scale 1/32

250 lb Mk.XI Torpex-filled depth charge, 11.0 in. dia.

Side

Underside

Top

Front

Front face concave and slightly recessed

Scale 1/32

© Juanita Franzi
AERO ILLUSTRATIONS

145

APPENDIX A: BOEING B-17 FORTRESSES OF RAF COASTAL COMMAND

INDIVIDUAL AIRCRAFT HISTORIES

Fortress I (B-17C): Two former 90 Sqn Detachment aircraft transferred to 220 Sqn Detachment, Middle East, Shallufa, Egypt.

Air Min	USAAC	Post-90 Squadron Service and Fate/Disposal
AN518	40-2043	220 Sqn, Det. M.E. 'B', Shallufa, Egypt 3.2.1942. To FEAF, India 1.7.42. Returned to USAAF (Tenth Air Force) 25.9.42.
AN532	40-2069	220 Sqn, Det. M.E. 'J', Shallufa, Egypt 3.2.1942. To FEAF India 1.7.42. Returned to USAAF (Tenth Air Force) 25.9.42.

There is confusion over the identities of these two aircraft following their return to the USAAF in India. Record cards for 40-2043 and 40-2069 do not indicate transfers back to the USAAF while those for 40-2066 and 40-2079 do – the latter were the former identities of AN530 and AN537 which never left the United Kingdom (see next table). The aircraft recorded as 40-2066 was written off in India on September 3, 1944, while 40-2079 was returned to the United States where it became an instructional airframe under the designation RB-17C It was scrapped effective May 6, 1945. Transfer of AN518 and AN532 from 90 Sqn Det. to 220 Sqn Det. M.E. recorded as 1.12.1941 in the 220 Sqn, Detachment ORB; 1.2.42 in the 220 Sqn ORB; and 3.2.1942 on Air Ministry Movement Cards (quoted in the table).

Fortress I (B-17C): Six former 90 Sqn aircraft transferred to Coastal Command

Air Min	USAAC	Post-90 Squadron Service (base as at allocation date) and Fate/Disposal (storage, overhaul & repair periods omitted)
AN519	40-2044	A&AEE 20.8.41. 206 Sqn '?', Benbecula 16.7.42. 59 Sqn 'V', Thorney Island 28.12.42. 1 (C) OTU '?', Thornaby 1.10.43. SOC 12.12.43.
AN520	40-2051	220 Sqn 'D', Nutts Corner 1.4.42. CCDU, Ballykelly 20.6.42. 206 Sqn 'X', Benbecula 27.7.42. 214 Sqn, Cheaburgh 19.2.44. SOC 14.8.44.
AN527	40-2061	220 Sqn 'A', Nutts Corner 12.2.42. SOC 15.9.43.
AN530	40-2066	220 Sqn 'F', Nutts Corner 12.2.42. CCDU, Ballykelly 20.6.42. 206 Sqn '?', Benbecula 29.7.42. SOC 11.9.43 & buried Benbecula airfield.
AN531	40-2068	220 Sqn 'O', Nutts Corner 12.2.42. CCDU, Ballykelly 20.6.42. 206 Sqn 'V', Benbecula 4.8.42. RAE 15.5.44. SOC 17.1.45.
AN537	40-2079	220 Sqn 'L', Nutts Corner 12.2.42. CCDU, Ballykelly 20.6.42. 1674 HCU '?', Longtown 24.12.43. 214 Sqn, Cheaburgh 19.3.44. SOC 1.9.44.

Aircraft allocated to CCDU 20.6.42 believed pooled with 220 Squadron as AN531 'O' and AN537 'L' were operational with the latter unit until mid-to-late July 1942.

Abbreviations
A&AEE: Aeroplane & Armament Experimental Establishment, Boscombe Down. Cheyenne: Cheyenne Modification Center, Cheyenne, Wyoming. Dorval: Dorval Airport, Quebec. Canada. FEAF: Far East Air Force. HCU: Heavy Conversion Unit. n/k: Ferry captain not known. 1 (C) OTU: 1 (Coastal) Operational Training Unit. RAE: Royal Aircraft Establishment, Farnborough. SOC: Struck off charge. '?': Aircraft code letter unconfirmed.

Fortress IIA (B-17E-BO): Forty-five aircraft delivered to the United Kingdom

Air Min	USAAF	Delivery to Britain (RAF Ferry Command captain)	Testing, Service (base as at allocation date) and Fate/Disposal (storage, overhaul & repair periods omitted)
FK184	41-2513	Dorval 24.3.42. Gander-Prestwick 31.3-1.4.42 (n/k)	206 Sqn 'K', Benbecula 14.8.42. 251 Sqn 'A', Reykjavik, Iceland 11.3.45. SOC 26.7.45.
FK185	41-2514	Dorval 24.3.42. Gander-Prestwick 23-24.4.42 (S/Ldr Donald G Ross)	220 Sqn 'E', Ballykelly 14.7.42. A&AEE: 40mm gun trials 31.1.44. 251 Sqn '?', Reykjavik 11.3.45. SOC 10.7.45.
FK186	41-2515	Dorval 8.4.42. Goose Bay-Reykjavik 9.4.42. Reykjavik-Prestwick 25.6.42 (Dillon M Teel)	220 Sqn 'S', Ballykelly 23.7.42. 206 Sqn 'X', Benbecula 12.8.43. To Azores 2.44. Transferred to 220 Sqn 'X' 19.3.44. SOC 13.6.45.
FK187	41-2516	Dorval 24.3.42. Gander-Prestwick 5-6.4.42 (Richard B Stophet)	A&AEE: type trials 24.4.42. SOC 4.7.45.
FK188	41-2517	Dorval 19.3.42. Gander-Prestwick 6.4.42 (S/Ldr Donald G Ross)	59 Sqn '?', Thorney Island 15.12.42 – damaged 30.12.42 & no ops. 220 Sqn, 20.8.43 – believed held in reserve Thorney Island. To Azores coded 'Z' 2.44. Re-coded 'W' 9.44. Engine failure 18.4.45 while under care of 3502 SU & SOC 10.9.45.
FK189	41-2518	Dorval 18.10.42. Gander-Prestwick 4.11.42 (n/k)	59 Sqn 'S', Thorney Island 11.1.43 – no record of ops. 220 Sqn, 26.8.43 – believed held in reserve Thorney Island. To Azores coded 'Y' 3.44. Engine fire take-off Azores 27.7.44, Capt: F/Lt Laurence H Croft. SOC 15.8.44.
FK190	41-2519	Dorval 1.4.42. Gander-Prestwick 15-16.4.42 (n/k)	RAE: LRASV trials 3.5.42. 206 Sqn 'J', Benbecula 18.3.43. To Azores 25.10.43. SOC 13.6.45.
FK191	41-2522	Dorval 20.4.42. Gander-Prestwick 27-28.4.42 (n/k)	206 Sqn 'N', Benbecula 13.9.42. 220 Sqn 'P', Benbecula 9.8.43. To Azores 1.44. SOC 8.3.45.
FK192	41-2615	Dorval 14.4.42. Gander-Prestwick 15-16.5.43 (William J Vanderkloot)	A&AEE High Altitude Flight: high altitude & meteorological research 11.6.43. SOC 18.9.45.
FK193	41-2526	Dorval 22.4.42. Gander-Prestwick 9-10.5.42 (S/Ldr Donald G Ross)	220 Sqn 'H', Ballykelly 16.7.42. To Azores 24.10.43. SOC 12.6.45.
FK194	41-2620	Dorval 8.7.42. Gander-Prestwick 20-21.7.42 (Dillon M Teel)	206 Sqn 'M', Benbecula 21.8.42. 251 Sqn '?', Reykjavik 30.5.45. Fate not recorded.
FK195	41-2608	Dorval 20.4.42. Gander-Prestwick 27-28.4.42 (n/k)	206 Sqn 'L', Benbecula 19.8.42. SOC 27.4.44.
FK196	41-2623	Dorval 24.4.42. Gander-Eglinton-Prestwick 7-9.5.42. (F/Lt Walter E Edser)	220 Sqn 'C', Ballykelly 13.7.42 – n o record of ops, used for training & transportation. 1 (C) OTU '?', Thornaby 30.8.43. 1674 HCU '?', Aldergrove 26.10.43. 251 Sqn '?', Reykjavik 1.4.45. SOC 21.6.47.
FK197	41-2625	Dorval 8.5.42. Gander-Prestwick 19-20.5.42 (Robert E Coffman)	Scottish Aviation: trial installation special wireless 18.7.42. 251 Sqn 'E', Reykjavik 3.5.45. SOC 21.6.47.
FK198	41-2622	Dorval 18.10.42. Gander-Prestwick 29.10.42 (Stewart A Reiss)	59 Sqn 'M', Thorney Island 9.1.43. 206 Sqn 'W', Thorney Island 15.8.43. To Azores 1.44. Transferred to 220 Sqn 'R' 19.3.44. Struck by taxiing Fortress III HB786 & SOC 19.4.44.
FK199	41-2614	Dorval 19.6.42. Gander-Prestwick 24-25.6.42 (Louis Bisson)	220 Sqn 'R', Ballykelly 23.7.42. 1 (C) OTU '?', Thornaby 31.8.43. 1674 HCU '?', Aldergrove 26.10.43. 220 Sqn 'L', Azores 22.8.44. SOC 14.6.45.
FK200	41-2619	Dorval 15.6.42. Gander-Prestwick 20-21.6.42 (n/k)	220 Sqn 'B', Ballykelly 11.7.42. To Azores 25.10.44. SOC 25.4.45
FK201	41-2618	Dorval 25.6.42. Gander-Prestwick 4.7.42 (n/k)	220 Sqn. 'T', Ballykelly 23.9.42. 1674 HCU '?', Longtown 25.12.43. Left runway Aldergrove after engine fire 22.6.45 & SOC 4.9.45.

Air Min	USAAF	Delivery to Britain (RAF Ferry Command captain)	Testing, Service (base as at allocation date) and Fate/Disposal (storage, overhaul & repair periods omitted)
FK202	41-9138	Dorval 23.6.42. Gander-Prestwick 4.7.42 (Paul E Zimmerman)	RAE: LRASV trials 11.7.42. 59 Sqn 'B', Thorney Island 13.12.42. 220 Sqn 'L', Benbecula 4.8.43. To Azores 23.10.43. Flew into sea off Azores 25.10.43, Capt: S/Ldr Harry A A Webster. All eight crew lost.
FK203	41-9195	Dorval 1.7.42. Gander-Prestwick 10.7.42 (Earl H Ortman)	220 Sqn 'M', Ballykelly 25.7.42. 251 Sqn '?', Reykjavik 19.5.45. SOC 22.12.45.
FK204	41-9136	Dorval 17.6.42. Gander-Prestwick 25.6.42 (n/k)	RAE: backup LRASV trials 1.7.42. 220 Sqn 'N', Ballykelly 25.7.42. Abandoned & crashed near Acklington, Northumberland 10.10.42, Capt: W/Cdr Richard T F Gates. All crew safe. Total time: 47 hr 45 min.
FK205	41-9135	Dorval 30.11.42. Gander-Prestwick 2-3.1.43 (Richard D Carlet)	59 Sqn 'B', Thorney Island 1.2.43 – re-coded 'P' by 6.2.43. 1674 HCU 'D', Longtown 21.1.44. Sold to International Alloys 11.3.47.
FK206	41-9202	Dorval 17.6.42. Gander-Prestwick 4.7.42 (Richard J Ralph)	220 Sqn 'K', Ballykelly 18.7.42. To Azores 18.10.43. Crashed into sea following night take-off Azores 4.12.43, Capt: F/O Desmond E Morris. All eight crew lost.
FK207	41-9204	Dorval 25.6.42. Gander-Prestwick 30.6.42 (Henry Morley)	220 Sqn 'J', Ballykelly 17.7.42. Crashed near Nutts Corner 10.8.42, Capt: W/O Gordon A Sanderson. All six crew lost. Total time: 86 hr 35 min.
FK208	41-9198	Dorval 28.6.42. Gander-Prestwick 11-12.7.42 (n/k)	206 Sqn 'B', Benbecula 4.8.42. To Azores 23.10.43. Crashed near Gibraltar 29.11.43, Capt: F/Sgt Denis J A Mitchener. All eight crew lost. Total time: 672 hrs 5 min
FK209	41-9203	Dorval 25.6.42. Gander-Prestwick 26-27.8.42 (Robert J Leeward)	59 Sqn 'J', Thorney Island 31.12.42. Shot down over Bay of Biscay by Ju 88C flown by Oblt Hermann Horstmann of 13/KG 40 23.3.43, Capt: F/O Richard J Weatherhead, RCAF. All eight crew lost.
FK210	41-9200	Dorval 1.7.42. Gander-Prestwick 9-10.7.42 (n/k)	206 Sqn 'E', Benbecula 12.8.42. 220 Sqn 'G', Benbecula 20.8.43. To Azores 23.10.43. 519 Sqn 'A', Wick 23.3.45. 521 Sqn 'W', Langham 12.5.45. Sold to International Alloys 11.3.47.
FK211	41-9199	Dorval 24.6.42. Gander-Prestwick 2-3.8.42 (George Oberdorf)	A&AEE: attitude, IFF & gun trials 10.11.42. 206 Sqn 'Z', Benbecula 3.8.43. To Azores 25.10.43. 519 Sqn 'H', Wick 22.1.45. SOC 31.7.47.
FK212	41-9237	Dorval 28.6.42. Gander-Prestwick 10-11.7.42 (n/k)	220 Sqn 'V', Ballykelly 31.7.42. Shot down over Bay of Biscay by Ju 88C flown by Lt Lothar Wolff of 15/KG 40 14.6.43, Capt: F/Lt Charles F Callender. All nine crew lost. Total time: 602 hr 10 min.
FK213	41-9232	Dorval 30.6.42. Gander-5-6.7.42 (n/k)	206 Sqn 'C', Benbecula 4.8.42. To Azores 24.10.43. Transferred to 220 Sqn. 'L' 19.3.44. 519 Sqn 'G', Wick 30.12.44. Sold International Alloys 11.3.47.
FL449	41-9243	Houlton 11.7.42. Gander-Ballykelly-Prestwick 10-12.8.42 (George Oberdorf)	220 Sqn 'O', Benbecula 26.8.43. To Azores 24.10.43. 519 Sqn 'F', Wick 18.12.44. SOC 31.7.47.
FL450	41-9240	Dorval 2.7.42. Gander-Prestwick 22-23.9.42. (Robert E Perlick)	59 Sqn 'A', Thorney Island 15.12.42. 220 Sqn 'U', Benbecula 7.4.43. 1 (C) OTU '?', Thornaby 30.8.43. 1674 HCU '?', Longtown 11.11.43. 519 Sqn 'D', Wick 2.12.44. 521 Sqn 'V', Langham 11.5.45. SOC 23.9.46.
FL451	41-9231	Houlton 6.7.42. Gander-Prestwick 11-12.7.42 (n/k)	206 Sqn 'D', Benbecula 4.8.42. 251 Sqn 'D', Reykjavik 13.4.45. Offered to MAP. SOC 29.5.46.
FL452	41-9242	Houlton 7.7.42. Gander-Prestwick 10-11.7.42 (Richard E Coffman)	206 Sqn 'G', Benbecula 30.7.42. To Azores re-coded 'F' 24.10.43. 521 Sqn 'U' 3.2.45. Sold to International Alloys 11.3.47.
FL453	41-9228	Dorval 1.7.42. Gander-Prestwick 11-12.7.42 (Dillon M Teel)	206 Sqn 'A', Benbecula 30.7.42. Crashed on take-off avoiding taxiing Fortress IIA FL457 6.10.42, Capt: P/O Jack E Delarue, RAAF. Five of seven crew lost. Total time: 303 hr 55 min.

Air Min	USAAF	Delivery to Britain (RAF Ferry Command captain)	Testing, Service (base as at allocation date) and Fate/Disposal (storage, overhaul & repair periods omitted)
FL454	41-9245	Houlton 7.7.42. Gander-Prestwick 14-15.7.42 (n/k)	206 Sqn 'J', Benbecula 15.8.42. Missing 14.12.42. Capt: F/O John Owen. All of seven crew lost. Total time: 65hr 45min.
FL455	41-9225	Dorval 4.7.42. Gander-Silloth-Prestwick 15-16.8.42 (Stewart A Reiss)	RAE: LRASV mods & trials 11.11.42. 206 Sqn 'N', Benbecula 12.7.43. To Azores 12.43. 519 Sqn 'A', Skitten 14.11.44. Flown into high ground near Wick 1.2.45, Capt: F/Lt F Keith Humphreys. Six of nine crew lost.
FL456	41-9230	Dorval 14.7.42. Gander-Prestwick 17.7.42. (Stewart A Reiss)	220 Sqn 'N', Ballykelly 20.8.42. To Azores re-coded 'N' 18.1.44. 521 Sqn '?' 22.1.45. SOC 14.7.47.
FL457	41-9229	Dorval or Houlton unconfirmed. Arrived Prestwick 12.7.42 (n/k)	206 Sqn 'F', Benbecula 30.7.42. 251 Sqn 'P', Reykjavik 2.5.45. 521 Sqn '?', Langham 29.11.45. Sold to International Alloys 11.3.47.
FL458	41-9197	Dorval or Houlton unconfirmed. Arrived Prestwick 17.7.42 (n/k)	A&AEE: gun firing trials 13.8.42. 220 Sqn 'A', Benbecula 23.3.43. To Azores re-coded 'Q' 2.44. SOC 14.6.45 & sold 15.9.47.
FL459	41-9241	Dorval 10.7.42. Gander-Silloth-Prestwick 21.7.42 (n/k)	220 Sqn 'J', Ballykelly 20.8.42. To Azores 25.10.43. 519 Sqn 'M', Wick 23.3.45. 251 Sqn 'A', Reykjavik 24.7.45. SOC 22.12.45. Noted 51 MU mid-1946.
FL460	41-9201	Dorval 1.7.42. Gander-Prestwick 14-15.7.42 (Ralph H Shulze)	206 Sqn 'H', Benbecula 12.8.42. To Azores 23.10.43. Transferred to 220 Sqn 'D' 19.3.44. SOC 13.6.45.
FL461	41-9234	Retained by the USAAF for service with the 5th Air Force 6.8.42.	Crash-landed near Wau, New Guinea 8.1.43. Capt: Lt Ray Dau. Two of eight crew died from wounds. Wreck extant.
FL462	41-9239	Dorval 11.7.42. Gander-Prestwick 17.7.42 (n/k)	59 Sqn 'C', Thorney Island 31.12.42. 220 Sqn 'W', Benbecula 7.4.43. To Azores 25.10.43. SOC 4.7.45.
FL463	41-9236	Dorval 8.7.42. Gander-Prestwick 16-17.7.42 (Merrill E Phoenix)	59 Sqn 'D', Thorney Island 31.12.42. 220 Sqn 'D', Benbecula 21.4.43. 1674 HCU 'P', Aldergrove 3.2.44 – re-coded 'C' by early-mid 1945. SOC 31.7.47.
FL464	41-9238	Dorval 6.7.42. Gander-Prestwick 17.7.42 (Edward B Newkirk)	59 Sqn 'E', Thorney Island 31.12.42. 220 Sqn 'Y', Benbecula. To Azores re-coded 'C' 23.10.43. 519 Sqn 'B', Wick 9.12.44. 251 Sqn 'E', Reykjavik 1.8.45. SOC 22.12.45.

B-17Es allocated to Britain but retained by the USAAF (16 aircraft): 41-2520, 41-2521, 41-2523, 41-2524, 41-2525, 41-2527, 41-2610, 41-2611, 41-2612, 41-2613, 41-2616, 41-2624, 41-9196, 41-9234 (see FL461 in table), 41-9235 and 41-9244. (Source: British Air Commission records). In addition, 41-9097 is noted in USAAF records as allocated to Britain but is known to have been retained by the USAAF. Other B-17Es allocated to Britain in 'Error' (4 aircraft): 41-9095, 41-9099, 41-9104 and 41-9109. (Source: USAAF aircraft movement cards).

149

Fortress II (B-17F-BO): Nineteen aircraft delivered to the United Kingdom

Air Min	USAAF	Delivery to Britain (RAF Ferry Command captain)	Testing, Service (base at allocation date) and Fate/Disposal (storage, overhaul & repair periods omitted)
FA695	41-24594	Dorval 11.11.42. Gander-Prestwick 22.11.42 (W F Sheldon Luck)	206 Sqn 'V', Benbecula 28.6.43. To Azores 24.12.43. 519 Sqn 'C', Wick 2.12.44. SOC 31.7.47.
FA696	41-24595	Dorval 2.2.43. Gander-Prestwick 14.2.43 (n/k)	206 Sqn 'Y', Benbecula 28.6.43. To Azores 25.10.43. 519 Sqn 'J', Wick 12.12.44. 251 Sqn 'B' *Borganes Bess*, Reykjavik 1.8.45. 521 Sqn 'B', Langham 19.11.45. Sold International Alloys 11.3.47.
FA697	41-24596	Dorval 28.10.42. Gander-Prestwick 6-7.11.42 (n/k)	220 Sqn 'T', Benbecula 26.8.43. To Azores 24.10.43. SOC following deliberate wheels-up landing Azores 19.12.43, Capt: F/O John M Ireland. Crew all safe.
FA698	41-24597	Dorval 28.10.42. Gander-Prestwick 6-22-23.11.42 (S/Ldr Donald G Ross)	59 Sqn 'V', Chivenor 12.3.43. Flown into hill near Chivenor 26.3.43, Capt: F/Lt James L Heron. Three of seven crew lost. Total time: 76 hr 15 min.
FA699	41-24598	Dorval 28.10.42. Gander-Prestwick 6-23-24.2.43 (Donald M McVicar)	206 Sqn 'O', Benbecula 8.7.43. To Azores 24.10.43. 220 Sqn 'K', Azores 6.44. 519 Sqn 'L', Wick 3.2.45. 251 Sqn '?', Reykjavik 24.7.45. SOC 22.12.45.
FA700	41-24599	Dorval 11.2.43. Gander-Prestwick 20.2.43 (Merrill E Phoenix)	206 Sqn 'R', Benbecula 27.6.43. To Azores 23.10.43. 220 Sqn 'R', Azores 17.6.44. 519 Sqn 'K' 3.2.45. 251 Sqn '?', Reykjavik 20.7.45. SOC 22.12.45.
FA701	42-5065	Dorval 3.11.42. Gander-Prestwick 7.11.42 (John T Parkinson)	220 Sqn 'F', Benbecula 15.7.43. To Azores 23.10.43. 251 Sqn 'J' *Jokull Jessie*, Reykjavik 30.5.45. Sold International Alloys 11.3.47.
FA702	42-5066	Dorval 3.11.42. Gander-Prestwick 6-7.11.42 (n/k)	206 Sqn 'P', Benbecula 12.4.43. 1674 HCU '?', Aldergrove 23.4.44. Sold International Alloys 11.3.47.
FA703	42-5067	Dorval 1.11.42. Gander-Prestwick 10-11.11.42 (n/k)	59 Sqn 'T', Chivenor 28.2.43. 206 Sqn 'A', Benbecula 18.4.43. 1674 HCU '?', Longtown 18.1.44. 521 Sqn '?', Langham 18.1.45. Ditched 8.1.46, Capt: F/O Peter M Williams. Five of eight crew lost.
FA704	42-5073	Dorval 9.11.42. Gander-Prestwick 11-12.11.42 (Ralph E Adams)	59 Sqn 'R', Chivenor 7.3.43. 206 Sqn 'R', Benbecula 17.4.43. Shot down by U-boat U-417 11.6.43, Capt: W/Cdr Ronald B Thomson. All crew safe. Total time: 238 hr.
FA705	42-5074	Dorval 22.11.42. Gander-Limavady-Prestwick 6.12.42 (Ralph H Shulze)	206 Sqn 'O', Benbecula 27.3.43. To Azores re-coded 'U' 24.10.43. Shot down by U-boat U-270 6.1.44, Capt: F/Lt Anthony J Pinhorn, DFC. All nine crew lost. Total time: 343 hr 35 min.
FA706	42-5075	Dorval 23.10.42. Gander-Prestwick 7.11.42 (Merrill E Phoenix)	A&AEE: astrodome trials 31.12.42. 220 Sqn 'S', Benbecula 10.4.43. To Azores 24.10.43. Taxied into another aircraft Azores & SOC 2.8.44, Capt: F/Lt Laurence H Croft, RCAF.
FA707	42-5234	Dorval 11.12.42. Gander-Prestwick 6-7.1.43 (Charles A Rector)	206 Sqn 'S', Benbecula 27.7.43. To Azores 23.10.43. Transferred 220 Sqn 'Z' 14.6.44. Ditched off Azores 26.7.44, Capt: Plt Off Eric B McIlwrick. Crew all rescued.
FA708	42-5235	Dorval 8.12.42. Gander-Prestwick 22.12.42 (Hillier Thompson)	Allocated to 206 Sqn, Benbecula 10.2.43 – no record of service. 220 Sqn 'D', Benbecula 23.6.43. To Azores 23.10.43. Damaged following low approach while landing Lagens 30.11.43, cockpit crew: F/Lt G Peter Roberson, DFC, Lt Theodore W Case & P/O William G Cameron. SOC 7.11.44
FA709	42-5236	Dorval 8.12.42. South Atlantic route to Prestwick 13-24.12.42 (Arthur G Sims)	220 Sqn 'B', Benbecula 17.4.43. To Azores coded 'A' 25.10.43. Sold & SOC 15.9.47.

Air Min	USAAF	Delivery to Britain (RAF Ferry Command captain)	Testing, Service (base at allocation date) and Fate/Disposal (storage, overhaul & repair periods omitted)
FA710	42-5237	Houlton 22.2.43. Gander-Prestwick 25-26.2.43 (Donald M McVicar)	206 Sqn 'M', Benbecula 5.7.43. To Azores 18.10.43. Transferred 220 Sqn 'M' 19.3.44. 521 Sqn '?', Langham 18.1.45. SOC 26.11.46.
FA711	42-5238	Houlton 2.1.43. Gander-Prestwick 25-26.3.43 (Arthur G Sims)	206 Sqn 'E', Benbecula 20.7.43. To Azores 23.10.43. SOC 14.8.44.
FA712	42-5239	Houlton 3.2.43. Gander-Prestwick 25-10.2.43 (n/k)	519 Sqn 'E', Wick 22.12.44. 251 Sqn 'C' *Keflavik Cutie*, Reykjavik 26.7.45. Sold to International Alloys 11.3.47.
FA713	42-5240	Houlton 3.2.43. Gander-Prestwick 9-10.1.43 (n/k)	220 Sqn 'E', Benbecula 23.7.43. To Azores 25.10.43. SOC 14.6.45.

No record official record has been found for the application of reserved Air Ministry serials FA675-FA684. However, photographic evidence indicates that the following B-17Fs were marked with serials from this series: 41-24352/FA678, 41-24368/FA683 and 41-24369/FA684. In addition, 41-24370 was operated in RAF-style disruptive camouflage with an apparently overpainted Air Ministry serial, while 41-24363 was marked as FA672, a serial belonging to a Martin Baltimore V.

Fortress III (B-17G-BO-50): Three aircraft delivered to the Azores

Air Min	USAAF	Delivery to Britain	Service (base at allocation date) and Fate/Disposal (storage, overhaul & repair periods omitted)
HB786	42-102437	Gander-Lagens 10.3.44. Arrived Azores 26.3.44	220 Sqn 'V', Azores 9.4.44. 521 Sqn 'Q', Langham 9.6.45. Last recorded Gatwick 7.3.46.
HB791	42-98021	Gander-Lagens 6.6.44. Arrived Azores 14.6.44	220 Sqn 'T', Azores 29.6.44. 251 Sqn 'L' 31.8.45. Sold to International Alloys 11.3.47.
HB792	42-98022	Gander-Lagens 1.6.44. Arrived Azores 14.6.44	220 Sqn 'U', Azores 29.6.44. 251 Sqn 'D' 31.8.45. Sold to International Alloys 11.3.47.

Sources

USAAF/Air Ministry serial tie-ups: British Purchasing Commission files, published in The British Air Commission and Lend-Lease by Ken Meekcoms (Air-Britain).
Transatlantic ferry flight dates and captain's names: RAF Ferry Command crew assignment cards, compiled by Bob Bolivar.
Testing, Squadron Service and Fate/Disposal: Air Ministry Form 54 and Form 78s Movement Cards, unit Operations Record Books and aircrew logbooks.

Allocation Dates

Allocation dates are as indicated on each aircraft's Air Ministry Form 78 Movement Card. It should be noted that these are not necessarily the precise dates on which aircraft arrived at their allotted units. In a few cases, Form 78 entries have appeared to be in error as certain allocations have not been reflected in squadron Operations Record Books.

Aircraft Serial and Code Match-ups

Definitively matching aircraft serials and codes presented a considerable challenge. Squadron Operations Record Books (ORBs) were the starting point, these official unit documents confirming match-ups for most 59 Sqn and 206 Sqn aircraft, and for 220 Sqn aircraft up to June 1943, although these documents sometimes contained errors and contradictions. Verification of ORB entries and additional match-ups were achieved by reviewing some 36 aircrew logbooks in conjunction with Air Ministry Form 1180 Accident Cards.
Codes for all 519 (Met) Squadron aircraft were confirmed by reviewing aircrew logbooks, as were a proportion of those operated by 251 (Met) Squadron and 521 (Met) Squadrons. A number of codes for the latter two squadrons were confirmed with reference to notes made by John Rabbets at 51 MU in the summer of 1946. In addition, either FA699 or FA700 was 'H' *Hekla Hettie* with 251 Squadron while FA703 and FA710 were either 'R' or 'S' respectively with 521 Squadron.
Codes for 1674 HCU Fortresses, in addition to those listed, are known to have included 'L', 'M', 'N' and 'O' over the period November 1943 to March 1944.

Appendix B: RAF Ferry Command Pilot Profiles

The following profiles describe the careers of three Ferry Command pilots who participated in the delivery Fortress aircraft to the United Kingdom. The first profile relates to British-born Arthur Sims, who noted in a 1975 interview:

"In Ferry Command, American pilots outnumbered Canadians by about three to one. Comparatively few Canadian bush pilots were qualified to the standard required by Ferry Command as the great majority had only flown single engine aircraft. Most of my flights were fairly routine except for the delivery of Mosquitos. To enable them to be flown across that Atlantic they were given special bomb bay tanks. This was a sort of 'tied on' affair and modifications sometimes caused things to go wrong with the fuel system. I clearly recall one flight with a Mosquito when petrol was swishing about in the fuselage by the time we got to Prestwick. Some pilots refused to fly Mosquitos. They were a good aircraft but the modifications required for the transatlantic flights gave rise to serious problems.

Pilots received $1,000 per month but this was taxable and there were no fringe benefits such as a pension fund or insurance. Civilian pilots paid for their own insurance which was quite expensive. If a pilot was killed, there were no benefits payable to his wife and family, other than this insurance, and as a result there were a number of cases of hardship."

Arthur George Sims

Arthur George 'Tim' Sims was born in London, England in 1907. He emigrated to Canada in 1927 and spent the next four years in the employment of aircraft engine manufacturers Canadian Wright Ltd and British Aeroplane Engines Ltd, both of Montreal. Here he assembled, overhauled and tested engines and later became a technical representative. His extensive knowledge of low temperature engine operations placed him as a mechanic on the inaugural airmail flight from Fort McMurray, Alberta, to Aklavik on the Arctic Ocean in 1929. From 1937, Sims worked with Aero Engines of Canada at Montreal in support of air-cooled Bristol engines installed on the Blackburn Shark, Supermarine Stranraer and Bristol Bolingbroke. He joined RAF Ferry Command in June 1942 and delivered a variety of types across the Western hemisphere until resigning at the end of April 1945. Following the war he captained a Bristol Freighter on a 40,000-mile demonstration tour of North and South America and subsequently joined Canadair Ltd as a sales representative and test pilot, flying North Star, Sabre and T-33 aircraft. Sims eventually became director of world-wide military aircraft sales until his retirement from the company in 1964 – he then devoted himself to his historical aviation library and writing about aviation. Sims was inducted in the Canadian Aviation Hall of Fame in 1974 with the following citation: *"The application of his exceptional skills as an aero-engine expert and his laudatory service as a war time Ferry Command pilot, despite adversity, have been of outstanding benefit to Canadian aviation."* Arthur Sims died in January 1982.

Arthur G Sims was the ferry captain for Fortress IIs FA709 and FA711. This and other photographs in this appendix from individual aircrew assignment cards. Directorate of History and Heritage

Deliveries with RAF Ferry Command (main route waypoints indicated)

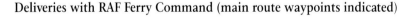

Departure	Type	Serial	Route
12-9-42	C-60 Lodestar	42-32173	Long Beach – Australia
28-10-42	B-26C Marauder	41-34844?	San Francisco – Samoa
13-12-42	Fortress II	FA709	Montreal – Prestwick (via South Atlantic route)
31-1-43	Fortress II	FA711	Houlton – Prestwick
17-2-43	Boston IIIA	BZ344	Montreal – Prestwick
8-4-43	Baltimore IV	FA395	Trinidad – Accra
23-4-43	Baltimore IV	FA423	Nassau – Accra
3-5-43	Baltimore IV	FA426	Nassau – Accra

Departure	Type	Serial	Route
19-5-43	Baltimore IV	FA573	Nassau – Accra
15-7-43	Dakota III	FD921	Nassau – Accra
26-7-43	Dakota III	FD883	Nassau – Accra
23-8-43	Marauder II	FB451	Nassau – Accra
18-9-43	Marauder II	FB472	Nassau – Accra
20-10-43	Dakota III	FL544	Montreal – Prestwick
9-12-43	Dakota III	FL563	Montreal – Prestwick via Azores
1-44 to 7-44	Liberators	Various	Series of flights between Montreal and N. Africa
13-7-44	Dakota III	KG771	Montreal – Prestwick
9-8-44	Mosquito B.25	KB421	Montreal – Prestwick
2-9-44	Mosquito B.25	KB434	Montreal – Prestwick
23-9-44	Liberator VI	KH283	Montreal – Prestwick via Azores, Rabat and Cairo
27-10-44	Mosquito B.25	KB498	Montreal – Prestwick
20-11-44	Mosquito B.25	KB524	Montreal – Prestwick
No recorded delivery flights until...			
7-4-45	Mosquito B.25	KA970	Montreal – Prestwick (belly-landed at Prestwick after in-flight explosion)

RAF Ferry Command pilot Edward L 'Les' Baxter. Directorate of History and Heritage

Edward Leslie 'Les' Baxter

Les Baxter was born in Cheshire, England on August 31, 1909. By the mid-1920s he had become captivated by the idea of becoming a pilot and, since Canada was seen as a vast country with many aviation opportunities, he emigrated across the Atlantic at the age of just 17 to pursue his passion. Baxter gained his license at the Toronto Flying Club in the early 1930s and in the years before the war built up his flying time through instructing and general flying. By the time the British Commonwealth Air Training Plan began operations in April 1940, Baxter was sufficiently qualified to be appointed as Chief Flying Instructor at Toronto's Malton Airport. However, teaching young 'hopefuls' to fly became somewhat tame compared to the possibility of ferrying aircraft to far-flung points around the world and in March 1942 he joined RAF Ferry Command, initially as a first officer. He was promoted to captain in mid-May following delivery of a Hudson as co-pilot and by the time Baxter left Ferry Command in February of 1945 had had completed 38 delivery flights to as far afield as Karachi.

After the war Baxter returned to instructing at Toronto Island and Malton airports while at the same time developing an aerial photography business that combined his expertise both as pilot and photographer. He operated his own two-seat Fleet 80 Canuck, flying with the door removed on the pilot's side, and provided services to the Toronto Telegram newspaper, the Toronto Harbour Commission and a variety of real estate companies. Les Baxter retired in his 70s and passed away in 1993.

Deliveries with RAF Ferry Command (main route waypoints indicated)

Departure	Type	Serial	Route (Captain unless marked FO – First Officer)
22-4-42	Hudson III	FH351	Montreal – Prestwick (FO)
23-5-42	Hudson III	FH168	Montreal – Prestwick
19-6-42	Ventura I	AE714	Montreal – Prestwick
10-7-42	Hudson VI	FK406	Montreal – Prestwick
31-7-42	Fortress IIA	FK211	Montreal – Prestwick (FO)

1942		Type	No.	PILOT, OR 1ST PILOT	2ND PILOT, PUPIL OR PASSENGER	DUTY (INCLUDING RESULTS AND REMARKS)	DUA. (1)
MONTH	DATE						
-	-	-	-	-	-	TOTALS BROUGHT FORWARD	
JULY	21	LIBERATOR	AL-627	W. MAY	SELF	GOOSE BAY, LABRADOR to DORVAL, QUE.	
JULY	30	BOEING B17E FORTRESS	FL-455	R. GUNN	SELF	SEQ. 3-7-8. (CO-PILOT CHECK).	
JULY	30	FORTRESS	FL-455	R. GUNN	SELF	SEQ. 7-8. MONTREAL + VICINITY.	
JULY	31	FORTRESS	FK-211	G. OBERDORF (CAPT.) SGT. HORNBY. A.W. (NAVIGATOR) K.J. O'BRIEN (RADIO OR) C. HALL (FLT. ENGINEER).	SELF	DORVAL, QUEBEC TO GANDER, NEWFOUNDLAND.	
						MONTHLY TOTAL	
						GRAND TOTAL	69:4
AUG 2 AND 3		BOEING B17E FORTRESS	FK-211	OBERDORF HORNBY O'BRIEN HALL	SELF	TRANSATLANTIC FLIGHT - GANDER, NFLD. TO PRESTWICK, SCOT.	
AUG	3	LIBERATOR	AL-587	P. EVES	SELF	PRESTWICK, SCOTLAND TO REYKJAVIK, ICELAND.	
AUG	4	LIBERATOR	AL-587	P. EVES	SELF	REYKJAVIK TO GANDER, NFLD.	
AUG	4	LIBERATOR	AL-587	P. EVES	SELF	GANDER TO DORVAL, QUEBEC.	
AUG	8	FORTRESS	FL-449	G. OBERDORF (CAPT.) C.F. JOHNSTON (NAV.) K.J. O'BRIEN (RADIO OR.) C. HALL (FLT. ENGINEER).	SELF	HOULTON, MAINE TO GANDER, NEWFOUNDLAND.	
AUG 10 AND 11		FORTRESS	FL-449	OBERDORF JOHNSTON O'BRIEN HALL	SELF	TRANSATLANTIC FLIGHT - GANDER TO BALLYKELLY, N. IRELAND.	
AUG	12	FORTRESS	FL-449	OBERDORF JOHNSTON O'BRIEN HALL	SELF	BALLYKELLY, NORTHERN IRELAND TO PRESTWICK, SCOTLAND.	
AUG	13	DC-3 DOUGLAS	U.S. ARMY 17817	PARKINSON	SELF	PRESTWICK TO BURTONWOOD, CHESHIRE	
AUG	13	DOUGLAS	17817	PARKINSON	SELF	BURTONWOOD TO HENDON, LONDON.	
						TOTAL - AUG. 3RD to AUG. 13TH.	
			GRAND TOTAL [Cols. (1) to (10)]			GRAND TOTAL TOTALS CARRIED FORWARD	69:4

Logbook for RAF Ferry Command pilot Les Baxter, showing familiarisation flights at Dorval in Fortress IIA FL455 and delivery of Fortress IIAs FK211 and FL449. Note that FL449 originated at Houlton, Maine and diverted to Ballykelly before proceeding to Prestwick. AL587 was a Liberator II of the Return Ferry Service. via Diane Harvey

Departure	Type	Serial	Route (Captain unless marked FO – First Officer)
8-8-42	Fortress IIA	FL449	Houlton – Prestwick (FO)
5-9-42	Catalina IB	FP193	Montreal – Prestwick (FO)
12-10-42	Halifax B.II	W7826	UK – Cairo (FO)
13-12-42	Baltimore IIIA	FA252	Nashville – Accra via South Atlantic
11-1-43	Baltimore IIIA	FA165	Nashville – Accra via South Atlantic
8-2-43	Baltimore IIIA	FA333	Nashville – Accra via South Atlantic
4-3-43	Baltimore IIIA	FA367	Nashville – Accra via South Atlantic
30-3-43	Dakota I	FD800	Nassau – Accra via South Atlantic
2-5-43	Baltimore IV	FA415	Nassau – Accra via South Atlantic
16-5-43	Baltimore IV	FA586	Nassau – Accra via South Atlantic
5-6-43	Dakota III	FD898	Nassau – Accra via South Atlantic
19-7-43	Liberator GR.V	BZ819	Montreal – Prestwick (FO)
17-8-43	Liberator GR.V	BZ868	Montreal – Yumdum via Prestwick
6-11-43	Liberator III	BZ929	Montreal – Cairo via Prestwick
22-12-43	Liberator GR.VI	BZ988	Montreal – Karachi via Azores and Cairo
8-2-44	Dakota III	KG365	Montreal – Prestwick
20-2-44	Liberator B.VI	EV943	Montreal – Prestwick
12-3-44	Dakota III	FZ691	Montreal – Prestwick
2-2-44	Liberator VI	EV973	Montreal – Prestwick
11-4-44	Liberator VI	EV970	Prestwick – Cairo
23-4-44	Liberator VI	EV987 'J'	Prestwick – Nassau via Goose Bay

Les Baxter with his Fleet 80 Canuck CF-EBE and the large-format camera used for his aerial photography business. Baxter flew with the pilot's door removed, hence his bulky insulating attire. CF-EBE (c/n 149) is preserved mounted on floats at the Canada Aviation Museum in Ottawa, Ontario. via Elaine Baxter

Departure	Type	Serial	Route
6-5-44	Liberator VI	KG835	Montreal – Algiers via Azores
21-5-44	Liberator VI	EW286	Montreal – Rabat via Azores
7-6-44	Lancaster B.X	KB771	Montreal – Prestwick
29-6-44	Liberator VI	KG939	Montreal – Algiers via Azores
31-7-44	Lancaster B.X	KB793	Montreal – Prestwick
27-8-44	Liberator VI	KH160	Montreal – Karachi via Azores and Cairo
16-9-44	Mosquito B.25	KB415	Montreal – Prestwick
1-10-44	Liberator VI	KH238	Montreal – Prestwick
27-10-44	Liberator VI	KH268	Montreal – Prestwick via Azores
17-11-44	Dakota IV	KK130	Montreal – BW1, Greenland
21-11-44	Mosquito B.25	KB489	Crash-landing at BW1, Greenland, due to undercarriage problems following test flight
31-1-45	Dakota IV	KN258	Montreal – Prestwick
24-2-45	Lancaster B.X	KB934	Toronto – Montreal

Total ferry flights: 38
Total first officer and captain time with RAF Ferry Command: 1,104 hours
Total return passenger time with RAF Ferry Command: 944 hours.

George Insley Bliss

George Insley Bliss was born in Pasadena, California, on November 17, 1909. His ambition was always to become a pilot and he eventually took flying lessons at a small private airport at Monrovia, California, while working for his father's painting business. He subsequently joined the Lockheed Aircraft Company where he built his flying time to 850 hours, notably on the Lockheed Hudson. His considerable multi-engine flying experience and eagerness to be involved in the war effort made Bliss a prime candidate for recruitment by Ferry Command and on September 20,

1941, he completed his flying check at Dorval. On his third delivery flight, George Bliss had the honour of being co-pilot aboard the first Fortress IIA delivered to the United Kingdom, FK184 (see page 33).

His son George Bliss Jr recalls his father's enthusiasm for flying:

"He told stories of flying just about everything in the air from RAF Mosquitos to B-17s and had tales of flying all over Africa, Europe and North America. He never dropped a bomb or fired a gun during the entire war. He said he once saw a German 'sub' in the Atlantic but had nothing but a cheese sandwich to drop on it.

He was interested in commercial aviation when he returned from the war but the competition was so intense among the many post-war pilots that he became a painting contractor, as his father had been. During Christmas of 1969, I joined Dad in England and we met his old co-pilot 'Kelly' in a pub. Boy, the stories they had to tell... I used to love hearing him 'hangar flying' with other pilots."

George Insley Bliss passed away in Los Angeles on February 21, 1970.

George Insley Bliss of Pasadena, California, was co-pilot for the first transatlantic delivery of a Fortress IIA, that of FK184 – he filled the same role for the delivery of FK185. Directorate of History and Heritage

Deliveries with RAF Ferry Command (main route waypoints indicated)

Departure	Type	Serial	Route (Captain unless marked FO – First Officer)
29-9-41	Hudson III	AM948	Montreal – Prestwick
30-12-41	Liberator I	AM582	Montreal – Prestwick (FO)
28-3-42	Fortress IIA	FK184	Montreal – Prestwick (FO)
21-4-42	Fortress IIA	FK185	Montreal – Prestwick (FO)
2-5-42	Ventura I	AE707	Montreal – Prestwick
14-6-42	Mitchell II	FL178	Montreal – Prestwick
10-7-42	Liberator III	FL908	Montreal – Accra – Montreal (FO)
31-7-42	Liberator III	FL908	Montreal – Accra – Montreal (FO)
26-9-42	B-25 (USAAF)	'973'	Long Beach – Australia
6-1-43	Boston IIIA	BZ236	Montreal – UK via South Atlantic
5-3-43	Liberator GR.V	FL974	Montreal – Prestwick
3-43 to 8-44	Liberator	Various	Series of flights between Montreal, Accra and the Middle East
30-8-44	Fortress III	KJ110	Montreal - Prestwick
8-10-44	Liberator VI	KH282	Montreal – Rabat via Azores and Cairo
3-11-44	Liberator VI	KH366	Montreal – Karachi via Azores, Cairo and Sheiba
19-11-44	Fortress III	KJ124	Montreal – Prestwick
21-1-44	Lancaster	?	Montreal – Prestwick
1-2-45	Fortress	?	Montreal – Prestwick
25-2-45	Liberator	?	Montreal – Middle East

APPENDIX C: FORTRESS AIRCREW CASUALTIES

A total of 82 Coastal Command aircrew died while flying in Fortress aircraft on anti-submarine and meteorological reconnaissance operations. These fatalities occurred over the loss of twelve aircraft, eight of which were lost with the entire crew.

The following information is based on records held by the Commonwealth War Graves Commission. Some ranks listed differ from those quoted in squadron records. The losses are presented in chronological order.

The majority of the attached aircrew photographs were drawn from a collection of 'escape and evade' passport-style portraits of 220 Sqn aircrew, taken in civilian clothing prior to posting to the Azores in October 1943. The images were 'liberated' for safekeeping by 220 Sqn pilot F/O Kenneth Speirs when he left the Azores in December 1944 and donated to the Author by his son, Brian Speirs.

Fortress IIA FK207 'N' of 220 Squadron

August 10, 1942: Lost speed in a turn and dived into rising ground near Nutts Corner airfield in bad weather while returning from a sortie originating from Ballykelly. All six crew members lost, as follows:

P/O Gordon Alan Sanderson age 23 (Captain).
Royal Air Force Volunteer Reserve, Service No: 742287.
Son of James and Ethel Maud Sanderson of Copnor.
Plot 101 (Jones), Row 14, Grave 15. Portsmouth (Kingston) Cemetery, Hampshire.

W/O Ernest William Bristow, age 26, (Co-pilot).
Royal Air Force Volunteer Reserve, Service No: 745118.
Son of William George and Blanch Ellen Bristow of Brighton, Sussex.
Sec. Z.I.D., Grave 70. Brighton (Bear Road) Borough Cemetery, Sussex.

Sgt David Farquhar Capel, age 22.
Royal Australian Air Force, Service No: 404602.
Son of Raymond Cecil and Irene May Capel of Goondiwindi, Queensland, Australia.
Sec. 23, Grave 8, Killead (St. Catherine) Church of Ireland Churchyard.

Sgt Victor Clarence Fretter, age 23.
Royal Air Force Volunteer Reserve, Serial No: 751381.
Son of Clarence and Mildred Fretter of Broughton Astley; husband of Joan Frette of Countesthorpe.
Grave 82, Broughton Astley Cemetery, Leicestershire.

Sgt Philip Gerard Foster, age 21.
Royal Air Force Volunteer Reserve, Service No: 1158929.
Son of Philip and Evelyn May Foster of Parkestone, Dorsetshire.
Plot 4, West Side, Grave 16, Glenavy Roman Catholic Churchyard, County Antrim.

Sgt Harry Garcia, age 20.
Royal Air Force Volunteer Reserve, Service No: 931532.
Son of Cecil Francis and Mabel Emma Garcia of Bickley, Bromley, Kent.Sec. 23, Grave 9, Killead (St. Catherine) Church of Ireland Churchyard, County Antrim.

Fortress IIA FL454 'J' of 206 Squadron

October 6, 1942: Stalled and crashed into the sea off Benbecula airfield after avoiding FL457 'F' on take-off. Five of seven crew members lost, as follows:

F/O Jack Edmond Delarue, age: 26. (Captain) (see profile page 175)
Royal Australian Air Force, Service No: 402322.
Son of Leopold Emile and Hilda Mariel Delarue of Lindfield, New South Wales, Australia.
Grave 1, West Wall Border, Nunton Old Churchyard, Benbecula.

Jack Edmond Delarue. via Edgar Delarue

Sgt James Cleveland Harold Rudolf Jaeger, age 31. (Co-pilot)
Royal Air Force Volunteer Reserve, Service No: 1382407.
Son of Cleveland and Ingeborg Jaeger of Kentish Town.
Square 162, Grave 46526, Highgate Cemetery, London.

F/Sgt Frederick Arthur Robinson, age 29.
Royal Air Force Volunteer Reserve, Service No: 1376615.
Son of Frederick and Elizabeth Robinson; husband of Winifred May Robinson of Ilford, Essex.
A.I.B. Panel 76, Runnymede, Surrey.

F/Sgt John Blatch Taplin, age: 27.
Royal Australian Air Force, Service No: 407607.
Son of Alfred Basil John and Estelle Christina Taplin; husband of Nancy Eileen Taplin of Largs Bay, South Australia.
Grave 2, West Wall Border, Nunton Old Churchyard, Benbecula.

Sgt John Flower Guppy, age: 20.
Royal Australian Air Force, Service No: 406452.
Son of George Edward and Nellie Guppy of Perth, Western Australia.
Grave 3, West Wall Border, Nunton Old Churchyard, Benbecula.

Survivors:
Sgt David Strang Coutts (died in the crash of Fortress IIA FK206 on November 29, 1943).
Sgt James Hunt (returned to operations with 206 Squadron and survived the war).

Fortress IIA FL453 'A' of 206 Squadron

John Owen. via David Clarke

December 14, 1942: Failed to return to Benbecula. Believed aircraft flew into the sea while establishing sea level barometric pressure. All seven crew members lost, as follows:

F/O John Owen, age 21. (Captain)
Royal Air Force Volunteer Reserve, Service No: 63800.
Son of Arthur and Beatrice Mary Owen of Wilmslow, Cheshire. Associate of the Institute of Bankers.
Panel 67, Runnymede, Surrey.

Sgt Robert Nockold Hildred, age 21. (Co-pilot)
Royal Air Force Volunteer Reserve, Service No: 1333535.
Son of Victor John and Constance Mary Hildred of Camberley, Surrey.
Panel 85, Runnymede, Surrey.

F/Sgt Eric Crowe, age 25.
Royal Air Force Volunteer Reserve, Service No: 964953.
Son of Ernest and Edith Mary Anne Crowe; husband of Freda Mary Crowe of Muswell Hill, Middlesex.
Panel 74, Runnymede, Surrey.

Sgt Rupert Bentley, age 32.
Royal Air Force Volunteer Reserve, Service No: 1115124.
Son of Arthur and Alice Bentley of Meols, Cheshire.
Panel 78, Runnymede, Surrey.

Sgt William James Parnell, age 22.
Royal Air Force Volunteer Reserve, Service No: 1163993.
Son of Thomas Hugh and Melinda Parnell; husband of Rosina Phyllis Parnell of Tuffley, Gloucestershire.
Panel 91, Runnymede, Surrey.

Sgt Walter Shanks, age 21.
Royal Air Force Volunteer Reserve, Service No: 1067932.
Son of Archibald and Agnes Shanks; husband of Margaret Stevens Shanks of Currock, Carlisle.
Pane 93, Runnymede, Surrey.

Sgt Garfield Charles Wilson, age: 21.
Royal New Zealand Air Force, Service No: NZ411113.
Son of Mr. and Mrs. David S. Wilson of Invercargill, Southland, New Zealand.
Panel 118, Runnymede, Surrey.

Sgts Rupert Bentley and Garfield C Wilson replaced regular crew members Sgts Donald Bryan and Charles Neill on this flight. Bryan later explained he was stood down following a sleepless night on orderly duty during a severe gale.

Fortress IIA FK209 'J' of 59 Squadron

March 23, 1943: Shot down at 47°42'N 06°55'W by Junkers Ju 88C of 13/KG 40 flown by Oblt Hermann Horstmann while based at Chivenor, Devon. All eight crew members lost, as follows:

F/O Richard John Weatherhead, age 30. (Captain) (see profiles pages 182 and 177).
Royal Canadian Air Force, Service No: J/6992.
Son of John Christopher Weatherhead and Florence Edith Weatherhead of Mission City, British Columbia, Canada.
Panel 175, Runnymede, Surrey.

F/O Robert Albert Phillips, age 31.
Royal Air Force Volunteer Reserve, Service No: 128609.
Son of Robert and Sarah Ellen Phillips of Bolton, Lancashire; husband of Margaret Fisher Phillips of Bolton.
Panel 128, Runnymede, Surrey.

F/O Willard Christian Zapfe, age 27.
Royal Canadian Air Force, Service No: J/7024.
Panel 175, Runnymede, Surrey.

P/O George Cojocar, age 22.
Royal Canadian Air Force, Service No: J/16374.
Panel 175, Runnymede, Surrey.

W/O Class II William James Arnold, age 20.
Royal Canadian Air Force, Service No: R/106166.
Son of C. H. and Ethel W. Arnold of Rainy River, Ontario, Canada.
Panel 179, Runnymede, Surrey.

W/O Class II Clarence Lummis Copping, age 25.
Royal Canadian Air Force, Service No: R/77233.
Son of William Carter Copping and Isabella Lummis Copping of Waterloo, Quebec, Canada.
Panel 179, Runnymede, Surrey.

W/O Class II Richard Glover Montgomery, age unknown.
Royal Canadian Air Force, Service No: R/106426.
Panel 180, Runnymede, Surrey.

W/O Class II Frank Spino, age 26.
Royal Canadian Air Force, Service No: R/75875.
Son of Mauro and Rose Spino of Hamilton, Ontario, Canada.
Panel 180, Runnymede, Surrey.

Fortress II FA698 'V' of 59 Squadron

March 26, 1943: Flew into hill at Luscott Barton near Chivenor during BABS approach. Three of seven crew members lost, as follows:

P/O Denis Macrorie Dunn, age 30.
Royal Air Force Volunteer Reserve, Service No: 141755.
Son of Wilfred Macrorie Dunn and Helen Dunn; husband of Eileen Hester Dunn, of Clapham, London.
Block 5, Grave 7941, Richmond Cemetery, Surrey.
Died of injuries: March 29, 1943.

W/O Class II Robert Simeon Sandelin, age 24.
Royal Canadian Air Force, Service No: R/82680.
Husband of Winifred Jane Sandelin of Cornwall, Ontario, Canada.
Grave 342, Gunnerside Methodist Chapelyard, Yorkshire.

Sgt Jeffrey Fage, age 23.
Royal Air Force Volunteer Reserve, Service No: 1172715.
Son of William Augustus and Ethel Mary Fage of Bushey.
Sec. R., Grave 25, Bushey (St. James) Churchyard, Hertfordshire.

Survivors:
F/Lt James L Heron (Captain), Sgt A Kenney (Co-pilot)
P/O D H McLeran, Sgt J F Clark

Fortress IIA FK212 'V' of 220 Squadron

June 14, 1943: Shot down by Junkers Ju 88 flown by Lt Lothar Wolff of 15/KG 40 while based at Chivenor, Devon, after transmitting position, course and speed report from 46°03'N 10°55'W. All nine crew members lost, as follows:

F/O Charles Francis Callender, age 36. (Captain)
Royal Air Force Volunteer Reserve, Service No: 68777.
Son of Andrew Martin Callender and Winifred Campbell Callender.
Panel 119, Runnymede, Surrey.

F/O James Way Verney, age 30. (Co-pilot)
Royal Air Force Volunteer Reserve, Service No: 80395.
Son of Frank Arthur and Malvina Verney of Kokstad, East Griqualand, South Africa.
Panel 130, Runnymede, Surrey.

F/Sgt James William Harbridge, age 32. (Navigator)
Royal Air Force Volunteer Reserve, Service No: 1220213.
Son of Charles Clifford Harbridge and Harriet Harbridge of Willenhall, Staffordshire; husband of Sadie Harbridge of Willenhall.
Panel 136, Runnymede, Surrey.

W/O Class I William Minor Comba, age 22.
Royal Canadian Air Force, Service No: R/59670.
Son of Minor and Lillian Comba of Killarney, Manitoba, Canada.
Panel179, Runnymede, Surrey.

F/Sgt Charles Percival Probst, age 33.
Royal Air Force Volunteer Reserve, Service No: 979949.
Son of Robert and Gladys Probst; husband of Mary Probst of Greenock, Renfrewshire.
Panel 138, Runnymede, Surrey.

F/Sgt Edward Wright, age 22.
Royal Air Force Volunteer Reserve, Service No: 978768.
Son of Tom and Gladys May Wright of Droylsden, Lancashire.
Panel 140, Runnymede, Surrey.

Sgt George Davison, age 22.
Royal Air Force Volunteer Reserve, Service No: 989245.
Son of Mrs. E. J. Davison of Newcastle-on-Tyne.
Panel 147, Runnymede, Surrey.

Sgt Shadrach Morton Frost, age 30.
Royal Air Force Volunteer Reserve, Service No: 1379682.
Son of Morton Bennett Frost and Eva Frost of Hayes, Kent.
Panel 150, Runnymede, Surrey.

Sgt George Scaife Patterson, age 23.
Royal Air Force Volunteer Reserve, Service No: 1051252.
Son of John and Irving Scaife Paterson of Cleghorn, Lanarkshire.
Panel 161, Runnymede, Surrey.

Fortress IIA FK202 'L' of 220 Squadron

October 25, 1943: Crashed into the ocean one hour out of Lagens, Azores, believed while crew was taking sea-level meteorological readings. All eight crew members lost, as follows:

S/Ldr Harry Arthur Andrew Webster, age 28. (Captain)
Royal Air Force, Service No: 37619.
Son of William Leckie Webster and Marjorie Webster (nee Pringle-Pattison); husband of Gillian Webster of Shawford, Hampshire.
Panel 119, Runnymede, Surrey.

Harry Arthur Andrew Webster

F/O Alfred William Dungate, age 24.
Royal Canadian Air Force, Service No: J/16441.
Son of Sydney and Annie Dungate of Vernon, British Columbia, Canada.
Panel 173, Runnymede, Surrey.

F/O William Henry Offler, age 33.
Royal Canadian Air Force, Service No: J/22508.
Son of William and Bessie Offler of Leamington, Ontario, Canada; husband of Margaret C. Offler of Leamington.
Panel 174, Runnymede, Surrey.

Alfred William Dungate

F/O James Walton, age unknown.
Royal Air Force Volunteer Reserve, Service No: 131472.
Son of Arthur and Susannah Walton; husband of Constance Lina Walton of St. Annes-on-Sea, Lancashire.
Panel 130, Runnnymede.

P/O William Thomas Potter, age 30.
Royal Air Force Volunteer Reserve, Service No: 143930.
Son of Thomas Henry and Maud Potter of Shoeburyness, Essex.
Panel 133, Runnymede, Surrey.

William Henry Offler

F/Sgt Alexander Baxter Christie, age 29.
Royal Air Force Volunteer Reserve, Service No: 1375581.
Son of John and Nellie Christie; husband of Jean Mary Christie of Barkingside, Essex.
Panel 135, Runnymede, Surrey.

F/Sgt John Smith Mckay, age 27.
Royal Air Force Volunteer Reserve, Service No: 1325202.
Son of John Smith McKay and Henrietta McKay; husband of Vera Dorothy McKay of Ealing, Middlesex.
Panel 137, Runnymede, Surrey.

William Thomas Potter

W/O Class I Maxwell Everette Varney, age 24.
Royal Canadian Air Force, Service No: R/71569.
Son of Archibald Stevens Varney and of Bertha Varney (nee Taylor); husband of Agnes Lindsay Varney (nee MacDougall) of Cambuslang, Lanarkshire.
Panel 179, Runnymede, Surrey.

James Walton

Fortress FK208 'B' of 206 Squadron

November 29, 1943: Crew attempted to divert to Gibraltar but found it closed by fog. Crashed off Carnero Point, ten miles south of Gibraltar, while trying to reach Port Lyautey, Morocco. All eight crew members lost, as follows:

F/Sgt Denis John Anthony Mitchener, age 21. (Captain)
Royal Air Force Volunteer Reserve, Service No: 1450109.
Son of John Rudolph Mitchener and Florence Mitchener.
Gibraltar Memorial.

F/O Arthur Edward Moule, age 24.
Royal Air Force Volunteer Reserve, Service No: 126145.
Son of Harry Arthur and Edith Moule; husband of Helene Veronica Moule of Blackpool, Lancashire.
Gibraltar Memorial

W/O Donald Brooke Brown, age 22.
Royal Air Force Volunteer Reserve, Service No: 1066461.
Son of Charles and Alice Brown of Handbridge, Chester.
Gibraltar Memorial.

W/O David Strang Coutts, age 29.
Royal Air Force Volunteer Reserve, Service No: 1023023.
Son of James and Jane Greig Coutts of Forfar, Scotland.
Gibraltar Memorial
David Coutts was one of two survivors of the crash of Fortress IIA FL454 'J' at Benbecula on October 6, 1942.

F/Sgt Robert Alfred Charles Burnett, age 21.
Royal Air Force Volunteer Reserve, Service No: 1270447.
Son of Leslie George and Kathleen Burnett; husband of Lilian Mary Burnett of Ernesettle Plymouth.
Gibraltar Memorial.

F/Sgt James Stones, age 23.
Royal Air Force Volunteer Reserve, Service No: 751932.
Son of James and Muriel Stones of Bell Green, Coventry.
Gibraltar Memorial

F/Sgt John Wilson, age unknown.
Royal Air Force Volunteer Reserve, Service No: 1120348.
Gibraltar Memorial

Sgt Ronald Andrew Senior, age 23.
Royal Air Force Volunteer Reserve, Service No: 1115843.
Son of Mr. and Mrs. C. H. Senior; husband of Betty Senior of Cloughton, Yorkshire.
Gibraltar Memorial.

Fortress IIA FK206 'K' of 220 Squadron

December 4, 1943: Crashed into ocean after night take-off from Lagens, Azores, en route to the United Kingdom. Official likely cause was loss of control following the change from visual flight to instruments on a very black night. All eight crew members lost, as follows:

F/O Desmond Edward Morris, age unknown. (Captain)
Royal Air Force Volunteer Reserve, Service No: 132320.
Panel 126, Runnymede, Surrey.

Desmond Edward Morris

F/Sgt Robert Noel Morrison, age 22. (Co-pilot)
Royal Air Force Volunteer Reserve, Service No: 1192004.
Son of Robert Leonard and Edith Leiper Morrison of Reading, Berkshire.
Panel 138, Runnymede, Surrey.

P/O Harold Lawson, age 23.
Royal Air Force Volunteer Reserve, Service No: 149162.
Son of William James Lawson, and of Gertrude Lawson of Whitestakes, Lancashire.
Panel 132, Runnymede, Surrey.

Robert Noel Morrison

P/O James Geoffrey Johnson, age 20. (Navigator)
Royal Australian Air Force, Service No: 408252.
Son of Alex Arthur and Amy Florence Johnson of Burnie, Tasmania, Australia.
Row A, Grave 6, Lajes War Cemetery, Azores.

P/O Arthur Pearce, age 25.
Royal Australian Air Force, Service No: 406868.
Son of Lionel and Phyllis Jean Edna Pearce of Busselton, Western Australia; husband of Jean Mearns Pearce of Glasgow.
Panel 191, Runnymede, Surrey.

W/O Class II Joseph Edouard Roch Boudreault, age 22 (see profile page 173).
Royal Canadian Air Force. Service No: R/125388.
Son of Elzear and Cecile Boudreault of Ottawa, Ontario, Canada
Row B, Grave 2, Lajes War Cemetery, Azores.

W/O Class II Carl Thomas Flack, age 23.
Royal Canadian Air Force, Service No: R/121119.
Son of Alex and Clara Flack of Saskatoon, Saskatchewan. Canada.
Row B, Grave 1, Lajes War Cemetery, Azores.

W/O Michael Patrick Campion, GC, age 27.
Royal Air Force, Service No: 536451.
Husband of Frances Rosina Campion of Battersea, London
Panel 134, Runnymede, Surrey.

W/O Michael Patrick Campion after being awarded the Empire Gallantry Medal in 1940. It was exchanged for a George Cross later that year. via Marion Hebblethwaite

W/O Michael Patrick Campion was awarded the Empire Gallantry Medal in 1940 – this was automatically exchanged for the George Cross under the terms of the institution of that award in September 1940. On March 12, 1940, Campion, a Leading Aircraftman at the time, and Aircraftman 1st Class Ernest Ralph Clyde Frost were among the first on the scene of a take-off collision between two Bristol Blenheims engaged in training at RAF Upwood, Huntingdonshire. Blenheim IV L8845 was under the command Sgt Alphonse Roger Hermels of 35 Squadron while Blenheim I L1396 of 90 Squadron was being flown by Sgt Blanks. Blanks was uninjured but Hermels was trapped in his cockpit with severe back injuries as his aircraft caught fire. W/O Campion worked to free the injured pilot while Frost, who did not realize there was only the pilot on board, looked for a radio operator in the rear fuselage. Despite the imminent danger of an explosion, Campion and Frost managed to extricate Hermels from the burning wreck before the petrol tanks exploded and the aircraft burned out. Unfortunately, Hermels died later that day from his injuries.

Fortress II FA705 'U' of 206 Squadron

January 6, 1944: Shot down near 43°53'N 23°23'W by U-boat U-270 during an attack that damaged the submarine. All nine crew members lost, as follows:

S/Ldr Anthony James Pinhorn, DFC, age 28. (Captain) (see profile page 178).
Royal Air Force, Service No: 42468.
Son of Harold J and G Maud Pinhorn of Victoria, British Columbia, Canada.
Panel 201, Runnymede, Surrey.

F/O Joseph Henry Duncan, age 24. (Co-pilot).
Royal Air Force Volunteer Reserve, Service No: 126994.
Son of George John and Ann Elizabeth Duncan of North Shields, Northumberland.
Panel 205, Runnymede, Surrey.

Anthony James Pinhorn.
via Wendy Hopkins.

S/Ldr Ralph Brown, age 33. (Squadron navigation officer)
Royal Air Force Volunteer Reserve, Service No: 78250.
Son of William Leck Brown and Florence Brown; husband of Irene Brown of Hebden, Yorkshire.
Panel 200, Runnymede, Surrey.

F/O Francis Dennis Roberts, age 34.
Royal Air Force Volunteer Reserve, Service No: 122972.
Son of William and Ester Roberts; husband of Violet Roberts.
Panel 209, Runnymede, Surrey.

W/O Ronald Norman Stares, age 25.
Royal Air Force Volunteer Reserve, Service No: 931486.
Son of Frederick Walter and Harriett Stares of Greenford, Middlesex.
Panel 214, Runnymede, Surrey.

W/O Class I Donald Luther Heard, age 35.
Royal Canadian Air Force, Service No: R/105458.
Husband of Carlotta Margaret Heard of Peterborough, Ontario, Canada.
Panel 253, Runnymede, Surrey.

W/O Class I Oliver Ambrose Keddy, age 24.
Royal Canadian Air Force, Service No: R/88434.
Son of Reginald C. and Reta M. Keddy of Kingston, King's Co., Nova Scotia, Canada.
Panel 253, Runnymede, Surrey.

Ronald Norman Stares.
via John Ashdown

F/Sgt Thomas Eckersley, age 31.
Royal Air Force Volunteer Reserve, Service No: 1533557.
Son of Thomas and Janet Ellen Eckersley of Bolton, Lancashire; husband of Ellen Eckersley of Bolton.
Panel 217, Runnymede, Surrey.

Sgt Robert Fabian, age 24.
Royal Air Force Volunteer Reserve, Service No: 1288265.
Son of Frederick and Ethel Fabian; husband of Alice Amy Fabian of Willesden, Middlesex.
Panel 229, Runnymede, Surrey.

Fortress IIA FL455 'A' of 519 Squadron

February 1, 1945: Flew into a gently sloping 700-foot hill near Halsary, 12 miles southwest of Wick airfield in bad weather. Six of nine crew members lost, as follows:

F/Sgt William Henry Payne, age 20.
Royal Air Force Volunteer Reserve, Service No: 1738660.
Son of Lilian Martha Payne, and stepson of Ernest Worley of East Kirkby.
Sec.A, Row A.H., Grave 4201, Kingsway New Cemetery, Nottinghamshire.

F/Sgt Geoffrey Arthur Francis Panzer, age 21.
Royal Air Force Volunteer Reserve, Service No: 1384480.
Son of Arthur Oswald Francis and Christina Panzer of Highbury, London; husband of Emily Edith Panzer of Minsterley, Shropshire.
Sec. 20, R.C., Grave 162, St. Pancras Cemetery, Middlesex.

F/Sgt Kenneth Anthony Ian Day, age unknown.
Royal Air Force Volunteer Reserve, Service No: 1234239.
Grave 1434, Wellingborough (Finedon) Cemetery, Northamptonshire.

Sgt Alexander Purdie Beatson, age unknown.
Royal Air Force Volunteer Reserve, Service No: 823242.
Sec. O, Grave 449, Wick Cemetery, Caithnessshire.

Kenneth Anthony Ian Day

Sgt Dennis Alfred Pressley, age 21.
Royal Air Force Volunteer Reserve, Service No: 1640545.
Son of William Alfred and Jessie Eveline Pressley of Cheam.
Sec. Y, Grave 116, Sutton Cemetery, Surrey.
Died of injuries: February 3, 1945.

F/Lt Edwin Arthur Wood, age 24.
Royal Air Force Volunteer Reserve, Service No: 109926.
Son of Edwin James Wood and Emily Wood; husband of Paddie Wood of Middlesbrough. Sec. A, Grave 1701, Middlesbrough (Acklam) Cemetery, Yorkshire.
Died of injuries: February 12, 1945.

Survivors:
F/Lt F Keith Humphreys (Captain)
F/O George H Pullan (Co-pilot)
F/O Tom G Wrigley (Third pilot)

Fortress II FA703 '?' of 521 Squadron

January 8, 1946: Ditched following engine failure and feathering of incorrect propeller. Five of eight crew members lost, as follows:

F/O Reginald George Cummings, age: 24.
Royal Air Force, Service No: 56649.
Son of Fred and Eliza Cummings of Tredegar, Monmouthsire.
Panel 285, Runnymede, Surrey.

F/O George Boyd Sharp, age: 23.
Royal Air Force Volunteer Reserve, Service No: 164868.

Son of James and Mary C. Sharp of Grove, Berkshire.
Panel 285, Runnymede, Surrey.

F/Sgt James Kendel Thrower, age unknown.
Royal Air Force Volunteer Reserve, Service No: 1435458.
Son of Arthur and Emma Elizabeth Thrower of Hucknall, Nottinghamshire; husband of Janet Thrower of Hucknall.
Panel 286, Runnymede, Surrey.

W/O Edgar Stanley Newark, age: 25.
Royal Air Force Volunteer Reserve, Service No: 1331073.
Son of James William and Alice Newark; husband of Doris Rose Newark of Enfield, Middlesex.
Panel 285, Runnymede, Surrey.

Sgt David Thomas Brown, age: 20.
Royal Air Force Volunteer Reserve, Service No: 3031563.
Son of David George and Margaret Eleanor Brown of Leytonstone, Essex.
Panel 286, Runnymede, Surrey.

Survivors:
F/O Peter M Williams (Captain)
F/Sgt V C Taylor (Co-pilot)
W/O Peter W Collett (Flight engineer)

The Air Forces Memorial at Runnymede is located in the District of Egham, Surrey, England, and overlooks the valley of the River Thames. It commemorates by name over 20,000 airmen who were lost in the Second World War during operations from bases in the United Kingdom, Iceland, the Faeroe Islands, Northern Ireland and the Azores, and from bases on the Continent of Europe and who have no known graves. They served in Bomber, Fighter, Coastal, Transport, Flying Training and Maintenance Commands, and came from all parts of the Commonwealth. Some were from countries in continental Europe which had been overrun but whose airmen continued to fight in the ranks of the Royal Air Force. The memorial was designed by Sir Edward Maufe with sculpture by Vernon Hill. The engraved glass and painted ceilings were designed by John Hutton and the poem engraved on the gallery window was written by Paul H Scott.

APPENDIX D: AIR MINISTRY BOMB DISPOSAL

Report on Incident at RAF Benbecula 28.10.42
(Fortress IIA FL454 'J' of 206 Sqn. As written by W/Cdr Stevens, Air Ministry Org.10)

On Wednesday, 14th October 1942, a call was received from HQ 43 Group to the effect that a Flying Fortress bomber had crashed when taking off from RAF Station Benbecula. The aircraft was lying just off shore in the bay and there were depth charges and anti-submarine bombs on board.

The disposal of these explosives was considered urgent and the A.O.C.s Nos. 15 and 43 Groups were extremely anxious that the matter should be dealt with as expeditiously as possible. (In addition there were bodies on board and it was believed that the relatives were aware of this).

It was pointed out to 43 Group that the crash was their responsibility.

Apparently, however, it was considered impossible to salvage the aircraft and it was thought that the only alternative was to counter-mine the charges. As valuable RAF property might be affected it was requested that an expert who was familiar with British munitions, bomb disposal techniques and was also an expert on probable effects following detonation, should be despatched to Benbecula to deal with the incident. 43 Group could not provide such an expert.

I consequently despatched S/Ldr J.S. Rowlands of this branch whose knowledge and experience would enable him to accept full responsibility for dealing with the incident.

He travelled by rail to Glasgow and by priority passage from Renfrew to Benbecula arriving at 12.30 pm - less than 24 hours since O.10 was contacted. [Air Ministry Org. 10 (Bomb Disposal)]

He found that the aircraft was in such a position in the bay that should the explosives (approximately 3,000 lbs of Torpex) on board detonate, that a considerable amount of damage would be caused as follows:-

(i) To all aircraft (15 Flying Fortresses, Air/Sea Rescue Flight, etc), hangars and other buildings on the airfield owing to the complete absence of screening.

(ii) Possible damage to the Operations Room through earth shock, since there was water logged soil (which approximates [sic] earth shock) between the crash and the Operations Room.

(iii) Damage to No.1 site consisting of Nissan Huts and housing a substantial number of station personnel.

(iv) Station sick quarters.

(v) The C.O.'s house.

The aircraft - a Flying Fortress - had crashed when taking off and had twelve 260 lb. depth charges fuzed XIII pistols and two 250 lb. anti-submarine bombs fuzed No.30 Mk.IV pistols.

The aircraft was upside down and about half the wheels were visible at low water. The tide rise was 6 to 8 feet.

The depth charges were set to function at 20 feet depth of water.

Reconnaissance of the plane (from an RAF dinghy) at low water revealed that at least some charges had broken away but that some were still in the bomb bay.

In such circumstances it was considered possible that the depth charges had become armed and in this case the level of the water, considering the nature of the seabed (rocky) was dangerously near the 20 ft mark. (S/Ldr Rowlands was prepared to dive in order to attempt to locate and defuze the charges under water, but it was ascertained that it was impossible for a launch of sufficient size to carry pumping equipment to be brought near the crash owing to the swell and proximity of reefs).

Despite the foregoing and bearing in mind all other considerations (including the fact that the meteorological forecast gave only 36 hours of the comparative calm) S/Ldr Rowlands decided to try to move the aircraft.

Several hundred fathoms of 2" wire rope were requisitioned from the contractors working on the airfield and work was carried out on the crash, even throughout high water, in affixing wire ropes to the wings and oleo legs of the aircraft.

After several breakages (repairs affected from the dinghy) the aircraft was towed some 20 yards on to a submerged reef and the surfaces of the wings were just awash at low water.

Low water was after black-out and S/Ldr Rowlands rowed out to the crash, climbed on to the plane and found that parts of two anti-submarine bombs were visible, one being on a bomb rack and the other one having become detached and wedged in the wreckage. (There was also one body visible - close to the bombs). It was seen that all the safety devices of the pistols of the bombs had been carried away by the sea and that the needle strikers of the tail pistols were merely floating on light creep springs, so that any slight movement of the striker would have brought about detonation. S/Ldr Rowlands carefully de-fuzed the two bombs by hand after having to force the tail off one bomb (using a hammer). The two fuzes were extracted using copper wire and thrown into deep water.

The following day the aircraft was pulled over on to its wheels and towed (using two 2" wire ropes) across the bay to the shore.

Examination there revealed that only one of the anti-submarine bombs remained on board, the other bombs and depth charges having apparently been forced off during moving and towing.

Between 9.30 and 11.30 p.m. the body was removed from the aircraft.

It was considered impossible to recover the depth charges owing to the nature of the sea bed.

The Station Commander was advised as follows: -

(i) It was considered unlikely that all the depth charges were now in the same place, but were in all probability distributed over the sea bed.

(ii) Should these depth charges detonate singly they would cause blast damage to glass, etc., but little material damage to property on shore.

(iii) The bay should be put out of bounds for boating and bathing (save perhaps for a short period each side of low water).

(iv) The beach should be patrolled each day at low water and an hour after high water to search for bodies or depth charges washed ashore.

(v) A general warning to be issued to all personnel concerned including civilian contractors on the station and local Police advising of the position and giving brief description of the depth charges. Any such objects discovered to be reported to the Station Armament Officer.

The Station Armament Officer was given full instructions regarding the disposal of any such charges and of the anti-submarine bomb on board the aircraft.

Finally I should like it recorded that F/O Thornburn (Station Armament Officer) and Mr Gush and Mr Higgins (63 Salvage M.U. Royal Air Force) at various times unhesitatingly rowed out to the crash with S/Ldr Rowlands though warned of the possibility of the depth charges detonating.

Air Ministry Org. 10 (B.D.) Wing Commander Stevens

APPENDIX E: FORTRESS AIRCREW PROFILES

David Beaty

Commercial aviation is safer now than it has ever been. Accident rates have fallen steadily over the past 40 years and are now, by one measure, less than one tenth of what they were in the early 1960s. Through his study of how human factors contribute to aviation accidents, former Coastal Command Fortress pilot David Beaty was to make a vital contribution to this dramatic improvement. Yet ironically he was almost prevented from pursuing a career in aviation by one of the very traits he would later identify: the desire for conformity.

David Beaty was born into a disciplined Methodist family in what was then Ceylon, on March 28, 1919. When about eight years old, he was sent to Kingswood Boarding School, Bath. He became an avid reader while also displaying a passion for writing, a vocation that would become a central pillar of his life.

An excellent student with a strong leaning towards the Arts, Beaty won an Exhibition to Merton College, Oxford, in the autumn of 1938 to study History. With war on the horizon, he applied to the join the University Air Squadron as a way of ensuring entry into the Royal Air Force but was turned down for lack of flying experience and mechanical knowledge. Following the outbreak of war, and as a last resort, Beaty applied to join the Army. During the recruiting board interview, he was labelled *"an Arts man"* by an attending RAF officer, implying he did not conform to the model required for service. His ambition was rescued by Chairman Lindsay, Master of Balliol, who noted Beaty's earlier interest in the RAF and who then helped cement the direction of his life by stating: *"… an Oxford man can do anything!"*

Beaty while at Oakington in 1945 with 206 Sqn. With the war in Europe over, the squadron's role changed from anti-submarine patrols to flying troops to the Far East.

Beaty began his flying training at Prestwick in Scotland with 12 EFTS on de Havilland Tiger Moths, followed by a move to 3 FTS, South Cerney to fly Airspeed Oxfords. It was around this time Beaty observed a 'laterality problem' that sometimes made it difficult for him to distinguish left from right. This common phenomenon would later cause him to study other human factors affecting a pilot's ability to fly an aircraft safely, especially when under stress or when fatigued. Beaty's next postings were to 3 School of General Reconnaissance at Blackpool flying Blackburn Bothas (where he selected the Short Sunderland as the type he would like to fly) and 1 (Coastal) OTU at Silloth for training on Lockheed Hudsons.

Beaty's first operational posting was to 221 Sqn based at Limavady in Northern Ireland in mid-1941. From here he flew anti-submarine sweeps over the Bay of Biscay in war-weary Wellingtons until selected to captain one of three aircraft to be detached to Malta. The so-called Special Duties Flight operated ASV Mk II-equipped Wellington VIIIs and was tasked with locating, shadowing and, on occasions, illuminating Italian supply convoys sailing from Naples and Palermo to Tripoli in support of Rommel's forces in North Africa. Vessels located by the Flight were then attacked by the cruisers and destroyers of 'Force K'. After six grueling but rewarding months, Beaty flew out of Malta on March 28, 1942, his 23rd birthday.

Tell-tale oil slick from damaged U-boat U-575, taken from David Beaty's Fortress II FA700 'R'.

His next posting was to the Coastal Command Development Unit (CCDU) at Tain in Scotland where he flight-tested every operational Coastal Command type, as well as their specialized equipment. He also operated from East Fortune, Thornaby and Ford and was responsible for developing fighting tactics for the Bristol Beaufighter, a type considered by squadron pilots as particularly demanding to fly. At the end of his term with the CCDU, Beaty received the rarely-bestowed pilot grading: 'Exceptional'.

In September 1943, Beaty was posted to Thornaby to begin training on the Fortress following which he was assigned to 206 Sqn. He flew out to the Azores to

Fortress II FA700 'R' at Lagens.

Beaty and his trooping Liberator crew at Oakington. Back row, left to right: Peter Laird and Jim Cunningham. Front row: Johnny Baugh, Beaty and Gerry Clements.

join the squadron in mid-January 1944 and on March 13 pressed home the second attack on the doomed U-boat, U-575 (see page 112). 206 Sqn left the Azores in March 1944 to re-equip with the Liberator and was then assigned to anti-submarine patrols over the Bay of Biscay, most notably during the period around the Normandy Landings in early June. The squadron moved to Leuchers, Scotland, in July to cover convoys bound for Russia and on the night of February 2/3 of the following year conducted a mass attack by 14 aircraft on U-boats in the Baltic Sea under code name Operation 'CHILI'. Beaty's Liberator VI was badly damaged by a defending destroyer during the attack but he successfully nursed it back to Leuchars on two engines and with some 600 holes in the airframe.

Following a series of trooping flights to India in Liberators at the end of hostilities in Europe, Beaty left the RAF to join the fledgling British Overseas Airways Corporation (BOAC). He initially flew grueling transatlantic passenger services on Liberators before switching to the more advanced and comfortable Lockheed Constellation. Beaty's first novel, *The Take-Off*, was published in 1949 and in 1954 he left BOAC to concentrate on writing full-time. Although he had left commercial flying, he remained active with the British Airline Pilots Association (BALPA), targeting flight safety issues such as pilot fatigue and flight time limitations.

His second novel, *The Heart of the Storm* (published in the United States as *The Four Winds*), was based on his experiences flying the North Atlantic and proved to be very successful. It was followed by *Cone of Silence*, inspired by the injustices suffered by pilots involved in a series of Comet take-off accidents – the book later became a film. Meanwhile, Beaty continued to develop his theories around human factors in aviation accidents and, as part of related studies in psychology and, as a psychologist on an Air Ministry team, devised a method to test pilot fatigue at the end of long flights.

While continuing to write, Beaty joined the Overseas Development Agency, first working in Africa and then taking responsibility for the Latin America desk. His next book, *The Human Factor in Aircraft Accidents*, pulled together his research work and was followed by *The Naked Pilot*. The latter title is widely considered by pilots to be one of the best books of its kind. It is often used during pilot training and is required reading for some university courses. In 1992, the study of human factors became compulsory for new pilots throughout the European Economic Community (now the EU) and Beaty's research has become the foundation for what is now known worldwide as Cockpit Resource Management (CRM). That same year he received the MBE for his services to aviation. Beaty continued to write and eventually penned five non-fiction books and 24 novels. Two of his novels became films while a third, *Village of Stars*, was purchased by 20th Century Fox for a film to be made by Alfred Hitchcock. David Beaty passed away on December 4, 1999.

Beaty and his crew at Leuchers with a Liberator VI. All photographs courtesy of Betty Beaty.

With special thanks to Betty Beaty, wife of David Beaty.

Joseph Edouard Roch 'Rocky' Boudreault

Roch 'Rocky' Boudreault was born on August 4, 1921, the fifth of eleven children of Elzear and Cecile Boudreault of Ottawa, Ontario in Canada. His father was a postman as well as a 'jack-of-all-trades' and his salary was always stretched thin during those difficult economic times.

Boudreault attended La Salle Academy, reaching Grade 10 and achieving his Intermediate School Certificate. At age 20, he applied secretly to join the Royal Canadian Air Force, only telling his parents after he had been accepted, and was assigned for training as a Wireless Operator/Air Gunner (WOP/AG). He received the rank of W/O.

His training began in early May 1942 at 4 Wireless School at Burtch, Ontario, where he flew 11:50 hours of W/T and D/F instruction on both Gypsy Major- and Menasco-powered de Havilland Tiger Moths and a Noorduyn Norseman. In late June he joined 9 Bombing and Gunnery School at Mont Joli, Quebec where he flew ten hours in Fairey Battles as part of an *ab initio* gunnery course. This was followed from the beginning of August by a stint at Debert, Nova Scotia where he accumulated 30:30 hours of wireless operator experience on Avro Ansons followed by 56 hours on Lockheed Hudson IIIs and Vs as a WOP/AG with 2 Squadron. His crew practiced dive bombing, cross-country flying, air-to-air firing, instrument flying, low-level bombing, anti-submarine patrols and searchlight cooperation. Towards the end of his training, Boudreault was assessed for altitude tolerance and, after a series of three two-hour tests "*blowing into tubes*", was recommended for flights above 35,000ft (10, 668m).

Boudreault was then posted overseas, arriving at the port of Greenock near Glasgow, Scotland, on December 1, 1942. Like most Coastal Command aircrew of the time, he was posted to 1 (Coastal) Operational Training Unit at Silloth, beginning February 22, 1943. Flying initially on Airspeed Oxfords, he accumulated an additional 12:40 hours of WOP/AG training before moving onto Hudsons. On March 9, he moved to Thornaby in Yorkshire to continue his training.

His first operational posting was to 220 Sqn at Benbecula in the Outer Hebrides. He arrived on April 27, 1943, and undertook his first operational flight, a Musketry anti-submarine patrol over the Bay of Biscay in Fortress IIA FL459 'J', on June 21 while

Roch Boudreault sits atop a target-towing Fairey Battle of 9 Bombing and Gunnery School at Mont Joli, Quebec during his ab initio gunnery course. Laurette Chagnon

Fortress FK206 'K' of 220 Sqn, the aircraft in which Boudreault and seven other aircrew died on December 4, 1943. It is seen over a convoy – there are three vessels just visible above the forward fuselage – while operating from Benbecula and is likely an unofficial photograph since the nose and underwing ASV homing aerials remain visible. Bryan Yates

Sgt Joseph Edouard Roch Boudreault. Laurette Chagnon

on detachment to St Eval in Cornwall. Five more operational flights from Benbecula followed before 220 Squadron was deployed to the Azores.

Boudreault's sister Laurette Chagnon recalls: "*Once Roch left Canada, we had no idea where he could be... his letters were all censored. He wrote in one of his first letters* [from the Azores]: "*...there are no electric lights, we're unable to shave for lack of water and have to walk to the closest farm to buy eggs and bread, etc.*"

Boudreault undertook his first patrol from the Azores, a 9½-hour convoy escort in Fortress IIA FL449 'O', on December 3 as part of Flg Off Desmond E Morris' crew. Four anti-submarine sweeps followed in November, bringing his total operational flights to eleven. Except for the handwritten titling: '*220 Squadron, Lagens, Azores*', the next two pages of Boudreault's logbook are ominously blank. He was lost in the early morning hours of December 4 when FK206 'K' dived into the ocean shortly after taking off from Lagens en route to the United Kingdom.

Laurette Chagnon: "*Roch sent most of his pay cheque to my mother to help her make both ends meet for our large family. Thanks to my big sisters and brothers, I could keep studying nursing and public health. In 1944, my mother received $354.00 that Roch had willed to her.*

In 1997, I received an invitation to attend the annual 220 Sqn reunion, this time held in Stratford-on-Avon. We had learned that Maureen Diehl, the caretaker of the cemetery in the Azores, was trying to trace our family... so we combined the trip to England with one to The Azores. At Stratford we met, for the first time, the courageous men of 220 Squadron. They reminisced about their World War Two experiences and gave us our first opportunity to find out what had happened to Roch.

We learned that his aircraft was packed with food, cigarettes and other things not available in England and there was a rumour in Canada that Roch was on his way to England to be decorated. The reunion organizer [former 220 Squadron WOP/AG] *Joe Ayling confided in me: 'You know that if Roch had lived you could have had links with my family.' It turned out Roch was very fond of Joe's sister and was hoping to visit her after the plane arrived in England.*

Roch loved flying so much. Aeroplanes meant adventure, challenge, a passion for something new and extraordinary. Although he died in an aeroplane, he was at the same time realizing his greatest passion."

With special thanks to Laurette Chagnon, sister of Roch Boudreault.

Jack Edmond Delarue

"That's Jack Delarue! A fantastic cricketer... bowled left-handed and batted with his right. A very good all-round sportsman and a good friend to have." That is how 91-year-old Group Captain Paul Metzler, RAAF retired, responded on being shown a photograph of his former school mate while visiting a new exhibit at the Historical Society Rooms, located at Old Gordon Public School where both were pupils in the 1930s.

Jack Edmond Delarue was born in Lindfield, New South Wales, Australia – some 12 miles north of Sydney – on March 24, 1916. He was the first child of commercial traveler Leopold Emile Victor Delarue and his wife Hilda Majel Cliff and had two brothers and one sister.

A keen sportsman who grew to love cricket and golf, Delarue attended the local primary school in the Ku-ring-gai District until his teachers tried to dissuade him from being left-handed. Outraged, his mother moved him to the main school at Gordon. On leaving school, Delarue joined the Rural Bank of New South Wales as a clerk.

Jack Delarue on gaining his Pilots Flying Badge, April 1941. via Edgar Delarue

On August 19, 1940, Delarue enlisted as an Aircraftman 2 at 2 Initial Training School at Bradfield Park, New South Wales, and joined Course 4(P). Two months later, he was posted to 8 Elementary Flying Training School at Narrandera to begin training on de Havilland Tiger Moths. Over 3,800 student pilots began their elementary flying training at Narrandera under the Commonwealth Air Training Plan.

His primary training complete after 51:40 hours of flying, Delarue departed Sydney for Canada on December 28, 1940, and on arrival was attached to the RCAF for training on Avro Ansons with 7 Service Flying Training School at RCAF MacLeod, Alberta. He received his Pilots Flying Badge on April 14, 1941, was promoted to Sgt Pilot, and recommended for flying bomber types. Remustered as an Airman Pilot, Delarue was attached to the RAF and moved to 31 General Reconnaissance School at Charlottetown, Prince Edward Island, to continue training on Avro Ansons in preparation for joining Coastal Command and the vital campaign against the U-boats. He flew a total of 131:40 hours on Ansons.

Delarue departed Halifax by ship for the United Kingdom on August 15, 1941, and was posted to 1 (Coastal) Operational Training unit at RAF Silloth on October 13, to begin training on Hudsons in advance of joining an operational squadron – two months later, on December 24, he was posted to 206 Sqn at Aldergrove, Northern Ireland. His first operational flight took place on February 20 when he flew as co-pilot with F/Sgt L A Goodson on an anti-submarine sweep in Hudson AM566 'F'.

The house at 3 Dangar Street, Lindfield, New South Wales, where Jack Delarue was born in March 1916. via Edgar Delarue

On February 28, Delarue was promoted to P/O and from March 7 to 18 was detached to Stornoway as part of a strategy of positioning the relatively-short range Hudsons closer to the convoy routes and U-boat operating areas. His first flight as captain took place on April 12, a six-hour sweep in AM711 'E', and on the night of June 25/26 he led one of twelve crews provided by 206 Sqn for the third so-called '1,000-bomber raid.' Taking off at 23:15 from Donna Nock, a satellite field for North Coates on the Norfolk Coast, he dropped his bombs on the city of Bremen, although it proved impossible because of heavy cloud for any of the squadron to identify their assigned target, the U-boat building yard of Deschimag AG Weser. Delarue landed AM792 'B' back at North Coates at 04:54.

206 Sqn moved to Benbecula in the Outer Hebrides on July 1 and by the end of the month Delarue had completed 32 operational flights on Hudsons, the last being a combined anti-submarine sweep and search-and-rescue sortie on July 29 in AM792. He was promoted to F/O on

Former 8 EFTS Tiger Moth A17-440 (US registration N17440), restored in its original wartime finish for United Airlines captain, Dave Harris. Dave Harris

August 28 and four days later the squadron ceased operational flying to focus on training for the Fortress. Delarue had flown 492:40 hours on Hudsons and would accumulate another 36:45 during the work-up period on the Fortress.

Delarue's first sortie on the new type was scheduled for the early morning of October 6, 1942. Well into his take-off roll, he was confronted with another Fortress taxiing towards him on the runway. F/O Jack Edmond Delarue died along with four of his crew members when Fortress FL454 'J' stalled and crashed into the sea as he attempted to fly over the other aircraft (see page 50 for more details).

With special thanks to Jo Harris and Edgar Delarue, brother of Jack Delarue

Some of the remains of Fortress IIA FL454 'J' after they had been towed to the beach. The long structure is the rear spar. via Chris Ransted

Right: F/O Jack Edmond Delarue's headstone in the Nunton Church cemetery near Benbecula airfield. Martin Briscoe

Hermann Horstmann

The air war over the Bay of Biscay, fought mostly over the passage of German U-boats and Allied aircraft transiting to and from the Atlantic from 1942 to 1944, was among the most unforgiving of the Second World War. Encounters between Luftwaffe and Allied airmen tended to be intense and, for those unlucky enough to be shot down over the cruel waters of the Bay, final.

V Group/*Kampfgeschwader* 40 (V/KG 40) was the Luftwaffe's only long range maritime fighter unit. Equipped with the formidable Junkers Ju 88C and latterly the Ju 88 R-2 twin-engined heavy fighter, or *Zerstörer*, it was tasked with protecting U-boats from the attentions of attacking Allied aircraft which, until mid-1942, had experienced little opposition. Success came quickly with a Wellington of 311 Sqn shot down on July 15 and two more from 15 OTU on July 20, although the attacking Ju 88 was in turn shot down during the latter engagement.

Twenty-four-year-old *Oblt* Hermann Horstmann joined 13/KG 40 on January 20, 1942. He had no previous fighter experience but quickly achieved his first aerial combat success on February 5, shooting down a Bell P-39 Airacobra from a flight of 346th Fighter Sqn /350th Fighter Group aircraft that had become lost en route from Cornwall to Gibraltar. His next two victims came a day apart. On March 23, Horstmann shot down Fortress IIA FK209 'J' of 59 Sqn (see profile for Richard John Weatherhead) while on the following day he brought down Halifax II BB277 'H' of 58 Sqn. In each case, all on board were lost. Horstmann was promoted to *Staffel Kapitän* of 13/KG 40 the same day after just two months with KG 40.

Air activity over the Bay continued to increase with the Ju 88s attempting to intercept Coastal Command's Liberators, Fortresses, Wellingtons, Whitleys and Sunderlands as well as aircraft of the USAAF and USN. They in turn were hounded by superior but nonetheless vulnerable Beaufighters of Coastal Command. On June 3, 1943, Grossadmiral Dönitz announced that U-boats transiting the Bay of Biscay would now do so in daylight in groups of two or three and, in the event of an attack by Allied aircraft, stay on the surface and fight back. Starting June 1, V/KG 40 ramped up its missions in support of this change, resulting in a greater number of encounters with Allied aircraft. In one of several combats that day, Horstmann shot down a Wellington of 420 Sqn.

His next two victories took place less than a week apart. On August 18, he dispatched Wellington HZ407 'K' of 547 Sqn while on August 24 he was credited with the destruction of Halifax DT636 'J' of 58 Sqn during an attack by no fewer than 14 Ju 88s. On November 29 he shared with three other pilots in the demise of Sunderland JM676 'P' of 461 Sqn.

By the end of 1943, Allied combat strength over the Bay of Biscay was in the ascendancy with Mosquitos starting to take an increasingly heavy toll on the German long-range fighters. On December 12, the respected and popular Hermann Horstmann was part of a six-aircraft group tasked with protecting aircraft returning from a reconnaissance operation. Less than 30 minutes

Oblt *Hermann Horst-mann. Chris Goss*

A Schwarm *of Ju 88C-6s belonging to 14/KG 40 about to take-off for a mission over the Bay of Biscay. Chris Goss*

177

Smoke and debris are all that remain of a V/KG 40 Ju 88C-6 shot down by Beaufighters of 248 Sqn on January 29, 1943. Chris Goss

into the sortie, one Ju 88 suffered an engine failure and had to be escorted back to base by a second. Ninety minutes later the four Junkers ran into eight Beaufighters from 143 Sqn led by W/Cdr Edric H McHardy. Outnumbered two to one, they nevertheless attacked, shooting down two Beaufighters, including one by Horstmann. The Allied pilots then regained the upper hand, sending three of the Ju 88s plunging into the water. Like so many other Luftwaffe and Allied airmen, Hermann Horstmann was lost forever in the Bay of Biscay.

With special thanks to Chris Goss.

Anthony James Pinhorn

Anthony James 'Tony' Pinhorn was born on September 3, 1915, in Hamiota, Manitoba, the only son of Harold and Maud Pinhorn – he had one sister, Gwendolen 'Wendy' Pinhorn. Tony Pinhorn was an ardent fisherman and hunter from an early age and pursued these interests after the family moved to Victoria, British Columbia in 1920. Here he attended what was then known

Anthony Pinhorn with a Fleet 7B of the Aero Club of British Columbia while taking private flying lessons.

Trainees at the de Havilland School of Flying, Hatfield, June 1939. Anthony Pinhorn is second from the right in the front row.

as University School, now St. Michaels University School, followed by some four years working in logging camps on Vancouver Island and the Mainland coast. His sister Wendy takes up his story:

"When Tony finished University School the Depression was in full swing. His options were either working in the logging camps, with the idea of eventually getting to the management level, or following a business course in Victoria. Either way, there were no jobs with any future at the time and as Tony was aware of the possibility of a four-year Short Service Commission in the RAF, our parents agreed he should follow the opportunity in aviation. Dad wanted him to gain some knowledge of flying first so off Tony went to take some training with Hal Wilson of the Aero Club of British Columbia on Sea Island [now Vancouver International Airport]. Almost immediately after that, he set out for England 'on spec' and in anticipation of passing his RAF entrance exams. I was already in England, training as a physiotherapist, and well recall meeting him as he arrived on the Queen Mary. *The ship was quite out-*

Anson Is and Harvard Is at 6 SFTS, Little Rissington

179

U-boat U-570 after its surrender to a Hudson of 269 Sqn on August 27, 1941.

standing in those days... it was comparatively new and so huge. Tony passed his RAF exams with flying colours and was accepted in the spring of 1939."

Tony Pinhorn began his formal flight training at the de Havilland School of Flying at Hatfield in Hertfordshire on June 12, 1939, flying civilian Tiger Moths. He soloed on June 24 and completed his training early in early August with an 'Above average' rating. A course of multi-engine training followed at 6 SFTS, Little Rissington in Glouscestershire, based on Avro Anson Is and this he completed on March 23, 1940, again with an 'Above average' grade. Now an Acting P/O destined for service with Coastal Command, he moved to 3 School of General Reconnaissance at Blackpool for two weeks of navigation training.

Pinhorn's first posting was to 269 Sqn on Hudsons, based from July 10, 1940, at Wick in Scotland and, from June of the following year, Reykjavik in Iceland. Notable operations in which he took part included a reconnaissance sortie on November 10, 1940, in Hudson I T9337 to search for the German heavy cruiser *Admiral Scheer* during its first cruise, and arriving on-scene in Hudson III T9452 'G' just as the battleship HMS *Hood* blew up after being hit by a salvo from the battleship *Bismarck* on May 24, 1941. Pinhorn radioed directions to British destroyers, speeding up the search for survivors. On August 28, he maintained watch over U-boat U-570 from Hudson III T9448 'X' following its surrender to a squadron aircraft the previous day and on September 14, while flying T9427 'B', he attacked U-boat U-552 in concert with a second squadron aircraft. Pinhorn left 269 Sqn on January 22, 1942, with the rank of Flight Lieutenant. His next move took place in February 1942 when he was posted to 1 (C) OTU at Silloth as an instructor. While there he took part in the '1,000-bomber raid' on Bremen on the night of June 25/26, flying a 1 OTU Hudson V coded '51'. The following month Pinhorn was promoted to Squadron Leader while, on a less auspicious note, he was pilot-in-command when Hudson V AM595 '6' of 1 OTU struck a wall after landing at Ronaldsway, Isle of Man, on August 26.

According to Pinhorn's logbook, his second operational tour was to have been with 59 Sqn based at Aldergrove flying Liberator Vs but for reasons unknown this was changed to a posting to 206 Sqn to fly Fortresses. He arrived at Benbecula on May 25, 1943, and began his conversion training four days later under the tutelage of F/O Robert Cowey, a veteran of two U-boat sinkings. Pinhorn's first operational flight took place on June 30 when he flew Fortress IIA FL457 'F' on a Creeping Line Ahead patrol off the southwest coast of Ireland. Three more operational flights followed before preparations began in earnest for the squadron's move to the Azores. This took place in late October with Pinhorn flying the squadron's dedicated trainer FK190 'J' from St Mawgan to Lagens on the island of Terceira on October 25, 1943. A notation in his logbook by the squadron's commanding officer, W/Cdr Ronald B Thomson, reads: "*Very experienced in bad weather flying.*"

Anthony Pinhorn, left, with the battle flag from U-boat U-570 at Reykjavik.

Pinhorn's operational flights in November included three more CLAs and one Met flight. In December he undertook one CLA, one convoy escort, two searches for a German blockade runner and two more anti-shipping patrols. His first operational flight of 1944 took place on January 6 in Fortress II FA705 'U'. The entry in his logbook was completed by W/Cdr Thomson with the added notation: '*Failed to return.*' S/Ldr Anthony James Pinhorn and his crew had been shot down while attacking U-boat U-270 400 miles (645km) north-northeast of the Azores. Searches over the next four days found no trace of the Fortress or its crew. (See page 110 for details)

Hudson I T9427 'B' with Anthony Pinhorn at the controls just after he had attacked U-boat U-552 on September 14, 1941. Photographed from the second squadron aircraft involved in the attack flown by P/O Colin D M Thompson.

Thomson, who with his crew had earlier survived being shot down by a U-boat, would later write to Pinhorn's family: "...*I realized what a magnificent officer and hard worker he was. His loss is deeply felt throughout the squadron, and I personally feel that his position as Flight Commander can never be as capably fulfilled.*"

On February 27, 1945, Pinhorn's parents received a telegram notifying them that their son had been posthumously awarded the Distinguished Flying Cross, effective January 5, 1944, the day before he had died. His sister Wendy, now a Lieutenant Nursing Sister in the RCAMC, accompanied by their aunt, Miss Anne Blackwell, MBE, received the decoration from King George VI at a Next of Kin Investiture held at Buckingham Palace on July 17, 1945. The citation read:

"*During his second tour of operational duty, S/Ldr Pinhorn has taken part in a large number of operational sorties, including anti-submarine patrols and bombing attacks on targets in Norway. Since May 1943 this officer has served as Flight Commander and in that capacity has displayed fine administrative and flying ability, setting a splendid example to all under his command.*"

On November 11, 1979, the Province of British Columbia, as part of an initiative to commemorate British Columbia residents lost in the Second World War, dedicated a 7,346ft (2,239m) peak in the north-west corner of the province as Mount Pinhorn. Its location, 57°13'N 130°04'W, lies near the junction of Burrage Creek and Iskut River in the snowcapped Cassiar Land District, 680 miles (1,100km) from his family home of Victoria. Its remote location is in many ways symbolic of a person being lost far from home.

In September 2005, Wendy and her daughter Judi set out to visit Mount Pinhorn.

"*We flew to Whitehorse and drove the Alaska Highway to Watson Lake, where we spent the night. The following morning we turned south down Highway 37 and were fortunate to find an airfield adjoining the road. It was a quiet Sunday and, as he was not busy, a helicopter pilot agreed to take us over 'our' mountain... it took just five minutes to get there in his Hughes 500. The clouds parted on our arrival, giving us a perfectly clear view of the peak and allowing us to enjoy the scene in all its beauty. The summit was quite flat and we could see the hoof marks of mountain sheep. Best of all there was a*

Newly-promoted S/Ldr Anthony Pinhorn, most likely at Silloth, shortly after the June 25/26, 1942, '1,000-bomber raid' on Bremen.

Wendy Hopkins in front of the mountain named after her brother.

Anthony Pinhorn's sister, Wendy, and their aunt Miss Anne Blackwell, MBE, after receiving his Distinguished Flying Cross at Buckingham Palace on July 17, 1945.

cairn of stones… it was gratifying to know that hikers had spent time there and had thought to leave a permanent marker. We agreed that as a memorial to an avid outdoorsman, this was ideal."

With special thanks to Wendy Hopkins, sister of Anthony Pinhorn.

Richard John Weatherhead

It is unlikely that residents of Weatherhead Court in Mission, British Columbia, know how their street came by its name. So named after passage of a municipal bylaw on December 4, 1995, it commemorates the life and sacrifice of a local young man who was lost with his crew 52 years earlier while on patrol in a Fortress over the Bay of Biscay.

Richard John 'Dick' Weatherhead was born in New Westminster, British Columbia, on November 1, 1912, the only son of John and Florence Weatherhead. His father was killed just six years later while serving with the ambulance corps in France, leaving his wife, daughter Nellie and son.

Dick Weatherhead attended elementary school in his home town of Mission from 1919 to 1925, moving to Mission High School and then West Vancouver High School for his secondary education. He was a member of the Mission Cadets and an enthusiastic marksman, participating in a February 1926 competition staged by the Dominion of Canada Rifle Association. From 1928 to 1929, Weatherhead took a Business Methods Course and, after being turned down for training in the army, joined the Wabasco Cotton Company in Vancouver. In 1934, he secured a sales and advertising position with the British-American Tobacco Company in Shanghai and served as a Private with the Shanghai Volunteer Corps (Armoured Car) and, after moving to Hong Kong towards the end of his tenure, with their Volunteer Corps as a Private (Anti-Aircraft).

Future Fortress pilot Richard Weatherhead attended Mission Public School. In this 1923/24 Grade 8 photograph the eleven year-old Weatherhead stands on the far right of the second row from the back. Mission Archives

Following the outbreak of war, Weatherhead returned to Vancouver and on September 3, 1940, was interviewed in Vancouver for service with the Royal Canadian Air Force. The recruiting officer described him as "*alert, keen as mustard... good natural ability... distinctly above the average and is recommended strongly.*" On October 28, 1940, Weatherhead enlisted in the RCAF and, after initial training at Regina, Saskatchewan, was posted back to Vancouver to begin his flying training on de Havilland Tiger Moths with 8 Elementary Flying Training School. He moved to 3 Service Flying Training School, Calgary, Alberta, on May 28 to begin multi-engine training on Avro Ansons and was graded as a pilot and promoted to Sgt on August 20 – he was commissioned effective that date. Weatherhead attained high marks throughout his training, in both flying and academic subjects, and was fifth in a class of 47 at 3 SFTS.

The RCAF assessed Weatherhead as best suited to maritime reconnaissance work so his next posting, on September 13, was to 31 General Reconnaissance School at Charlottetown, Prince Edward Island, flying Ansons. This was followed, from November 22, by a month with 31 Operational Training Unit at Debert, Nova Scotia, this time on the Lockheed Hudson.

Richard Weatherhead, front centre, with six of the 59 Sqn Fortress crew lost on March 23, 1943 – they most likely comprise the seven Canadian crew members lost. P/O George Cojocar is on the right end of the back row while F/O William Zapfe is believed to be seated to Weatherhead's left. The broken wheel to the rear is the main element in the 59 Sqn badge. Chris Goss

Weatherhead moved to Halifax on January 6, 1942, in readiness for service overseas and on January 21 disembarked in the UK. His first posting was to 6 (Coastal) OTU at Thornaby in Yorkshire on February 27, followed by 1 (Coastal) OTU at Silloth on March 10. His first squadron posting, on May 30, was to Hudson-equipped 407 Coastal Strike Sqn, based at Bircham Newton and charged with attacking enemy shipping along the Dutch and Belgian coasts. On August 21, Weatherhead was sent to RAF Lyneham in preparation for flying to Africa for service with 200 Squadron based at Geswang, The Gambia.

His service with 200 Squadron began on September 7 but proved to be brief. Just nine days after his arrival, Weatherhead was piloting Hudson III FH288 back to base at the end of an anti-submarine patrol when he found his track blocked by a large tropical storm producing heavy rain. His all-Canadian crew comprised observer Plt Off Willard C Zapfe, air gunner Sgt Frank Spino, and wireless operator Sgt Clarence L Copping. Turning south, Weatherhead attempted to fly up the beach at 200ft (60m) but encountered blinding rain and had to turn back, flying on instruments as water streamed in the windows. Back in the clear, he could see no break in the storm to the southeast, so proceeded northwest. He was unable to get radio bearings as the equipment had been rendered unserviceable in the storm. Another promising hole in the storm proved a disappointment and, as fuel was by now running low, Weatherhead jettisoned his depth charges and began looking for a safe place to force-land. He turned on the IFF while Copping sent out an SOS and established contact with his base at Freetown.

They were advised to put down in Portuguese territory and selected a field near Bolama in what is now Guinea-Bissau. Weatherhead made a successful wheels-up landing by which time only one tank had any fuel remaining – the crew subsequently set fire to the Hudson. The local administrator later led the crew on a long trek to the British Consulate in Bolama, by the end of which all four were suffering from malaria. Managing to avoid internment thanks to the efforts of the Vice-

Consul, they made their way to Lisbon and on October 21 were flown to the United Kingdom by flying boat.

The crew returned to 407 Squadron on November 8 and on December 12 was re-posted to 59 Squadron at Thorney Island to fly Fortresses on anti-submarine patrols over the Bay of Biscay from Chivenor in Devon. With a crew complement of seven, including Zapfe, Spino and Copping, Weatherhead flew his first patrol on March 12, 1943, in Fortress IIA FL462 'C'. The crew used their ASV Mk II radar, or Special Equipment (SE) as it was discretely recorded, to search for a convoy of 52 Allied vessels and were initially fired on by some of the outer ships in the formation when they arrived unexpectedly out of a cloud bank. Their second operation, on March 15 in the same aircraft, was fraught in a different way. The initial patrol was undertaken at just 200ft (61m) in very bad weather. In the convoy area, the cloud extended from sea level to 4,000ft (1,219m) and although ASV radar contact was made, no ships could be seen and the aircraft was recalled to base.

On his next operational flight, on March 17, Weatherhead captained FK205 'P' while escorting convoy KMF 11. A more routine sortie, the vessels were met in position 49°39'N, 13°54'W and escorted for the next 4¼ hours. Six days later, on March 23, 1943, Weatherhead took off from Chivenor at 04:30 for an anti-submarine patrol in Fortress IIA FK209 'J' with a crew complement of eight. At 13:10 hours base received the W/T message: "*Am being attacked by enemy aircraft.*" Shortly afterwards, FK209 was shot down by a Junkers Ju 88C-6 flown by *Oblt* Hermann Horstmann of 13/KG 40. (See page 177 for Horstmann's profile).

Later that month, W/Cdr Geoffrey C C Bartlett, 59 Squadron's commanding officer, sent the following letter to Dick Weatherhead's now-remarried mother:

"Dear Mrs. Solloway:

You will have had a telegram informing you that Dick has been reported missing on active service as a result of air operations on the 23rd of March. I want to convey to you the deep sympathy the officers and men of this squadron feel for you in this time of great anxiety.

Dick's crew were out to do one of our normal anti-submarine patrols down the Bay of Biscay, as they had already done several times before. They were homeward bound off patrol when at 1.10 p.m.

Fortress IIA FK209, the aircraft Richard Weatherhead was flying when shot down by Oblt *Hermann Horstmann. The photograph was taken at Dorval, Quebec, on August 24, 1942, during the aircraft's delivery to the United Kingdom. Department of National Defense*

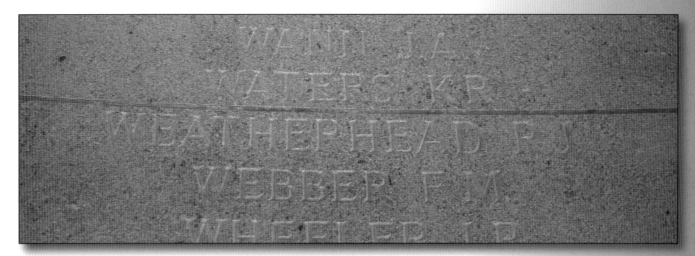

Inscription commemorating Richard John Weatherhead at the Air Forces Memorial, Runnymede. Terry Hissey

we picked up a message on the wireless from them, saying that they were being attacked by enemy aircraft. Since then, nothing has been heard. There were many other aircraft in the Bay of Biscay that day, and every day since they were instructed to look out for Dick's aircraft, but so far there is no news.

They must have been 120 miles off the French coast when attacked. If they were shot down into the sea they have, of course, their life-saving dinghies and there is every hope that they may either get picked up by our own or German seaplanes, or by fishing vessels, or even make shore themselves in their dinghies. Many wonderful voyages have, as you no doubt know, been made in these little rubber boats, which are fitted out with rations and water and all sorts of devices for assisting an unlucky crew. Some crews have spent many days (even weeks) on the sea and have come successfully to shore. If they are captured by the enemy, the news may take a month or more to come through, via the International Red Cross, and you will be notified immediately.

Meanwhile, your son's kit has been taken into safe custody and forwarded to the RAF Central Depository where it will be held until better news is received, or for at least six months, after which time it will be forwarded to you through the Administrator of Estates, Ottawa.

The other seven members of the crew were all Canadians, too, except one. Dick has had them as his crew ever since he joined the squadron, and under his leadership they made a very excellent team. He has been through several varieties of unpleasantness in his time with the RAF, and came through them well. He is an experienced captain and a very sound pilot, and I have been pleased with his operational results, although he has not had time to do anything spectacular yet. In our particular job, spectacular incidents are fairly rare, but I know he was going about the work in a methodical and resolute way, and it would have gone ill with any U-boat that came his way.

We are all longing for good news of him and feeling for you in this awful time of waiting. I have written to Mrs. Aldridge and will let both of you know immediately there is any news. Meanwhile if there is any way in which I can help you, or if there is any further information you would like that it is in my power to give, please do not hesitate to write."

Dick Weatherhead and his crew were never found.

With special thanks to Hugh Halliday and the Mission Community Archives.

APPENDIX F: COASTAL COMMAND
TACTICAL INSTRUCTION NO. 41

Coastal Command Anti-Submarine Tactical Instruction
C.C.T.I. No. 41

INTRODUCTION.

This Anti-Submarine Tactical Instruction is issued with the primary object of enabling aircraft to destroy U/Boats. All other results from attacks, such as killing members of the crew, superficial damage by machine-gun fire or forcing the U/Boat to dive, are of secondary importance.

A number of separate instructions on Anti-Submarine Tactics has been issued by this Headquarters from time to time and numerous amendments added. These instructions have been revised and consolidated into one, which cancels all Coastal Command Tactical Instructions previously issued on this subject i.e. Nos. 31, 33, 35, 36 and 40. In future, variations in tactical procedure will be issued as amendments or addenda. Amplification of the instructions contained herein will be found in Coastal Command Tactical Memoranda.

To kill U/Boats, crews must have a sound theoretical knowledge of:-
    (i) The best means of sighting U/Boats.
    (ii) The correct method of attack.
    (iii) The correct procedure after attack.

The successful application of this theoretical knowledge is dependent on continual practice. But neither theoretical perfection or practical proficiency will be of any avail if, when the critical moment comes in a real attack, the release mechanism for some reason or other fails to function correctly. All Junior Commanders and Captains of aircraft should, therefore, continually bear in mind:-

    (i) The vital importance of air crews being given continual training in delivering attacks.
    (ii) The absolute necessity for eliminating any possibility of failures due either to defective maintenance or faulty crew drill.

VISUAL LOOKOUT.

Good visual lookout by day and night is of outstanding importance in all A/S operations. In order to bring their crews to maximum efficiency, captains of aircraft must carefully organise a watch system and train individual members in both how and where to look.

There must always be at least two A/S lookouts who must keep a constant watch while on duty. They should cover a 180° sector, i.e. from ahead to 90° on either side of the aircraft and one of them must invariably be provided with binoculars. Lookouts should be changed every half hour whenever this is possible.

The area of sea to be searched must be at a sufficient range from the aircraft - dependent on height and visibility - to give the crew a good chance of sighting the U/Boat before the aircraft is itself observed.

Full details of how an efficient lookout can best be organised and maintained are given in Coastal Command Tactical Memorandum No.50.

A.S.V. **LOOKOUT.**

In addition to a visual lookout, it is essential that, subject to the restrictions detailed in para. 10 below, that an efficient A.S.V. watch should always be kept. The proper use of A.S.V. by day can be expected to increase appreciably the total number of U/Boats sighted and by night is indispensable.

MK. II A.S.V.

There is no restriction on the use of A.S.V. Mk II by night, but except when specially ordered it is not to be used by day on A/S patrols unless:-
    (i) Visibility is under three miles.
    (ii) Aircraft is flying above cloud in sufficient quantity to make sighting of U/Boat unlikely at over three miles.
        A.S.V. should be switched off at least 10 minutes before descending through cloud.
    (iii) Required for navigational purposes.

When a Mk.II A.S.V. blip fades and the operator is reasonably sure that it was caused by a U/Boat, the following procedure should be adopted, except (a) at night and (b) on convoy escorts:-
    (i) Switch off A.S.V.
    (ii) Leave area to a distance of at least 20 miles.

(iii) 20 to 30 minutes after leaving area, return without using A.S.V. at height which will ensure maximum degree of surprise.

(iv) Should no sighting follow, continue duty ordered.

MKS. III, IV, V and VI A.S.V.

There are no restrictions upon the use of A.S.V. Mks. III, IV, V and VI, and continuous watch by a trained WOP/AG must be maintained by day and night. In order to ensure maximum efficiency, the Captain of aircraft should carefully organise a tube watch system to enable operators to be changed at suitable intervals, and so avoid eye fatigue which results in inefficiency. Watch of the indicator should, when possible, not last more than 45 minutes, when a relief watch must take over. The operator relinquishing watch should then have a period of at least one hour on some other duty before returning to A.S.V. watch again.

HEIGHT AT WHICH TO FLY.

The best height at which to fly on an A/S patrol is that which gives the greatest chance of the aircraft surprising the U/Boat. In conditions of moderate or good visibility, A/S patrols should therefore, be flown as indicated below:-

(i) When there is no cloud or cloud is above 5,000 feet
Patrol height should be 5,000 feet. Pilots may, however, fly higher if they wish, when confident that they can lose height sufficiently quickly to make an effective attack.

(ii) When clouds are not more than 5/10th below 5,000 feet
Patrol above cloud, but not above 5,000 feet. Aircraft flying above cloud should not normally fly directly over the cloud tops, but preferably 500 to 1,000 feet above them.

(iii) When clouds are more than 5/10ths below 5,000 feet
Cloud cover to be used to the maximum to give concealment. Aircraft should normally fly as near the cloud base as possible.

In conditions of low lying haze with good visibility above, U/Boats will have only a limited horizontal view, while their view, upwards, will be little affected. Aircraft should, under these conditions, fly much lower and at a height calculated to reduce to the minimum the chances of being sighted, on the assumption that an aircraft flying high will be seen by a U/Boat sooner than one flying lower.

A/S WEAPONS.

The normal A/S weapons at present in use are the 250 lb. Torpex-filled depth charge and the 600 lb. Anti-Submarine Bomb.

HEIGHT LIMITATIONS.

The height limitations of these two weapons are as follows:-

	Maximum Height	Minimum Height
250 lb. Depth Charge	500 feet	No limitation.
600 lb. A/S Bomb	5,000 feet	500 feet.

Depth Settings

Pistols, in both the 250 lb. depth charge and the 600 lb. A/S Bomb should be set at the shallowest settings. These are as follows:-

250 lb. D.C.	25 feet.
600 lb. A/S Bomb	35 feet (Set during manufacture).

STICK SPACINGS.

When dropping a stick of 250 lb. depth charges by eye, the stick spacing to be used is 100 feet, which has been proved over a period to give the best all-round results.

When using the Mk.II(0)A and Mk.III Low Level Bombsight, stick spacings for the 250 lb. D.C. are to be as follows (as soon as the necessary computer charts have been issued):-

For sticks of six D.C.s	60 feet
For sticks of four D.C.s	100 feet
For sticks of two D.C.s imaginary	100 feet (Distributor to be adjusted so that these are dropped as Nos. 2 and 3 of an stick of four).

The 600 lb. A/S Bomb should be employed in conjunction with the Mk.XIV Bombsight, or the Mk.II(0)A or Mk.III Low Level Bombsights. It has not yet been cleared for stick spacings less than 80 feet and will normally be dropped in sticks of three, spaced 150 feet.

METHOD OF APPROACH TO ATTACK.

In a low level attack, height must be lost and the approach made in the quickest possible manner. In doing so, however, the pilot must appreciate:-
(i) Whether, if flying direct to the target, he has time to get the bomb-doors open (when applicable) and to get in all respects ready for the attack.
(ii) Whether a direct diving approach will increase the speed of the aircraft to a point which necessitates an adjustment to the bomb distributor setting.
(iii) Although the attack may be carried out from any direction, it should be delivered as near along track of the U/Boat as is possible in the circumstances.

On the run-up, the pilot should aim to be not higher than 300 to 500 feet, when three-quarters of a mile to a mile from the target.

Pilots should keep a sharp lookout during the approach for alterations in course by the U/Boat, whether it is diving or remaining on the surface.

METHOD OF ATTACK.

In view of the recent introduction of new weapons and new sighting devices, no standard method of attack can at present be laid down except for the low level attack, where depth charges are released by eye and in which considerable experience has now been gained.

The aim of the attack must be to make the centre of the depth charge stick explode within lethal range of the centre of the U/Boat. To do this, factors to be considered are, the estimated forward speed of the submarine, the time of flight of the D.C.s and their forward travel of 40 feet after entering the water.

In order to reduce errors to a minimum, depth charge attacks should be delivered from low altitude. The normal height of release is 50 feet, and if possible all depth charge attacks, when no sight is used, should be made from this height.

NOTE: The lethal range of the 250 lb. Depth Charge is 19 feet, and that of the 600 lb. A/S bomb 28 feet.

POINT OF AIM.

In order to be able to make the necessary calculations quickly, regarding the point of aim, the pilot or bomb aimer, as the case may be, must be fully conversant with the following data:-
(i) The time from the release of a depth charge from 50 feet to detonation at the shallow setting (25 feet) is approximately 5 seconds (2 seconds in the air and 3 in the water).
(ii) If the U/Boat is in process of crash-diving, her speed will be approximately 6 knots (10 feet per second). Therefore, if the U/Boat is attacked while some part of the hull is visible, the centre of the stick should be aimed 5 x 10 = 50 feet ahead of the conning tower (or its estimated position) at the time of release. (If the conning tower is itself in sight, however, at the time of release, it is desirable to make this the aiming point, although theoretically, the stick will then fall 50 feet behind it.)
(iii) If the U/Boat has dived before the depth charges are released, (see para. 32), the stick must be aimed a certain distance ahead of the swirl, the apex of which is made by the foremost end of the conning tower. This distance is, of course, that run by the submarine between its final disappearance and the time of detonation of the depth charges. Assuming that the speed of the U/Boat is 6 knots, the distances are as follows:-

Time of Submersion to release of D.C.s:-	5 secs.	10 secs.	15 secs.	20 secs.	25 secs.	30 secs.
Distance to aim ahead of swirl -	100 ft.	150 ft.	200 ft.	250 ft.	300 ft.	350 ft.

(iv) If the periscope only, is sighted, the speed of the U/Boat will probably be only about 2 knots, i.e. 3.4 feet per second, hence the stick should be aimed 5 x 3.4 = 17 feet ahead of the periscope at the time of release.
NOTE: An additional allowance must always be made for the under-water travel of the depth charges (40 feet).

The approximate length of a U/Boat's diving swirl is 100 feet and this can be conveniently used as a yardstick in estimating the distance ahead that the depth charges should enter the water.

The time lapse between submersion of the U/Boat and release of depth charges must be known exactly. It should preferably be recorded by stop-watch and counted over the intercom. by a member of the crew previously detailed for this duty.

WHEN TO ATTACK AND WHEN NOT TO ATTACK.

If the aircraft cannot deliver its attack until after the U/Boat has been submerged for some time, the question always arises as to whether to attack or whether the D.C.s should be saved for a probable second and better opportunity later.

The pilot must in these circumstances, always use his own judgement whether to deliver an attack or not; but it is most unlikely that an attack with 250 lb. D.C.s will be successful if the U/Boat has been submerged for more than 30 seconds at the time of detonation, unless it happens to have been seriously damaged previously.

A depth charge attack should not, therefore, usually be made after this time limit, unless there is conclusive evidence of slow submersion or the U/Boat is in the pilot's opinion, threatening a convoy or other surface craft, or unless the attacking aircraft is nearing the end of its sortie. In these circumstances, an attack may be made with a view to giving the U/Boat at least a bad shaking up, and in the case of a threat to shipping, preventing it delivering its attack.

Owing to the increased lethal range of the 600 lb. A/S bomb and its slightly deeper depth setting, this weapon has a good chance of being effective if detonation occurs within 40 seconds of the U/Boat submerging. When using this bomb, however, allowance must of course, always be made for the increase in time of fall. The time between release from 1,500 feet, for example, and detonation at 35 feet would be approximately 10 seconds. As a temporary measure, until sufficient data on which to assess the value of the 600 lb. A/S Bomb, is available, release may be made up to 40 seconds after U/Boat has submerged.

If a U/Boat is sighted and no attack has been made, "baiting tactics" are to be employed except when the aircraft is proceeding to escort a convoy, in which case it should continue on its way. For details of "baiting tactics", see paragraph 48 below.

Attacks are not to be made on oil streaks unless specifically ordered.

NUMBER OF DEPTH CHARGES TO BE RELEASED.

The number of depth charges to be released in any attack must always be left to the discretion of the Captain of the aircraft, according to the total load carried and other circumstances at the time, but the following is given as a general guide and should normally be adhered to:-

Aircraft on A/S Patrols or Sweeps -

(i) Aircraft carrying six or less depth charges should drop the whole load in one stick.
(ii) Aircraft carrying more than six depth charges should drop sticks of six leaving the remainder for subsequent use.

Aircraft on Escort Duty -

Aircraft on convoy or other escort duty should drop sticks of four depth charges, leaving the remainder for subsequent attacks, e.g., an aircraft carrying a total of six depth charges would drop four in the first attack leaving two for a possible second attack, and an aircraft carrying twelve depth charges will thus have sufficient for three attacks.

The Captain of the aircraft is, however, always at liberty to drop more than four depth charges if he considers the chances of a second sighting unlikely, e.g., when near his P.L.E. If he makes his first U/Boat sighting when returning to base, he should always drop at least a full stick of six.

When a U/Boat is sighted by an aircraft which is en route to escort a "threatened" convoy, an attack should be delivered only if a Class "A" Target is presented, i.e., if the U/Boat is on the surface or has submerged for less than 15 seconds, but not more than 50% of the depth charges, (and in any case a maximum of four) should be expended in these circumstances. When proceeding to a convoy not reported as "threatened", however, a full stick of four depth charges should always be dropped if the chances of a successful attack are considered good.

U/BOATS FIGHTING BACK.

It is evident that U/Boat Commanders are now tending, increasingly, to remain on the surface and fight back with their gun armament when attacked by aircraft. It is in fact, known that they have received orders to adopt these tactics if surprised on the surface, in such a way as to be unable to dive to a safe depth before the aircraft can deliver its attack.

When a U/Boat remains on the surface and fires at the attacking aircraft, the decision as to the method of attack must rest with the Captain of the aircraft who will take into consideration his armament, the degree of surprise achieved, the presence or otherwise of A/S surface vessels and the extent to which he is committed to the attack when the U/Boat opens fire. In general, however, he must remember that the primary reason for his existence is, for the time being, to kill U/Boats and that a U/Boat on the surface presents a much better chance of a kill than one submerged. It is no coincidence that recently, by far the larger proportion of certain or probable kills have been U/Boats which stayed on the surface and fought back.

It should also be borne in mind that even a big aircraft properly handled and using its guns well presents a difficult target for the gunners in the necessarily cramped positions of a U/Boat, which in any sort of a sea is a very poor gun platform and especially so if the sea is beam-on. While, therefore, the tactics to be employed must be left to the Captain's judgement the attack should, whenever possible, be pressed home at once, preferably from dead ahead, making full use of the front guns to kill the U/Boat's gun crews or at least to keep their heads down.

If, however, the Captain of aircraft considers the direct form of attack undesirable, alternative tactics are to circle the U/Boat at such a range as to bring accurate fire to bear, flying an irregular course with constant variations in height and firing with as many guns as possible, until the U/Boat's gunners are disabled or the U/Boat begins to dive; when the aircraft must be prepared to make an immediate attack. While adopting these tactics, a very careful watch through binoculars should always be maintained to ensure that the earliest possible warning is received of any intention on the part of the U/Boat to submerge.

ACTION AFTER ATTACK.

After carrying out an attack on a U/Boat by day, the aircraft must drop a marker beside the swirl. By night the site of the attack is to be marked by flame float, and whenever practicable, two flame floats should be dropped at the same time as the depth charges.

The aircraft should then keep the area of attack under observation long enough to observe results and if possible, determine the extent of the damage caused by the attack. Where there are indications, such as wreckage or persisting oil, or air bubbles, that the U/Boat may be forced to re-surface, the aircraft is to remain over the site and maintain position and height best suited for delivering another attack.

On other occasions, excepting, of course, when the U/Boat is definitely sunk, and except when the aircraft is on convoy escort duty, or at night, "baiting tactics", are to be employed. Aircraft proceeding en route to escort a convoy should not remain over the site of an attack for a period longer than fifteen minutes.

BAITING TACTICS.

In adopting "baiting tactics" the aircraft will set course from the position of the attack to a distance of at least 30 miles and will remain outside this range for not less than 30 minutes. The aircraft should then return to the scene of the attack, taking full advantage of cloud, sun and weather conditions for concealment, in the hope that the U/Boat will have again surfaced.

PHOTOGRAPHS.

Photographs are to be taken whenever possible and duties are to be allotted as necessary to individual members of the crew prior to take-off. The most important photographs are those recording the attack. The rear, or mirror camera is to be turned on at least five seconds before the release of the depth charges and must be kept on for a minimum of 15 seconds afterwards, throughout which period the pilot should make no alteration of course.

SIGNALS PROCEDURE.

The Captain of aircraft must always appreciate the situation relative to the task upon which he is engaged and bear in mind the order of precedence for the despatch of signals subsequent to the sighting and attack of a U/Boat. Whenever a U/Boat is sighted by an aircraft on an A/S patrol or sweep, if there is sufficient time and opportunity without interfering with the efficiency of the attack, the Captain of aircraft will instruct the W/T operator to transmit on his operational frequency the Group 465 from the Naval section of the Air Force code. The Group is to be preceded by his own aircraft call-sign and will indicate that an attack is about to be made on a U/Boat. If it is subsequently discovered that no U/Boat is present, a cancellation must be sent immediately and an acknowledgement obtained from W/T control. This procedure does not apply to aircraft on a convoy escort, who are to make initial reports of sightings by R/T to the S.O. Escort. It may also be suspended in special circumstances, when the risk from enemy fighters is considered such as to justify wireless silence.

When engaged on escort duty, the Captain of Aircraft must, as soon as possible inform the Senior Officer of the surface vessels of the presence of any U/Boat sighted, giving the position as a bearing and distance relative to the vessel(s) or in the case of convoys, relative to the centre of the convoy. This report is to be made by R/T, or V/S, if R/T communication cannot be established; co-ordinates for latitude and longitude positions are not to be used. The making of this report must not, however, be allowed to prejudice the efficiency of the aircraft's attack on the U/Boat and will usually be sent after the attack has been completed.

When an aircraft on convoy escort estimates that it has sunk a U/Boat, the report is to be made by V/S to S.O. Escort. Only if this is impossible is R/T to be used.

Aircraft on protective sweeps, when from a previous sighting the position of the convoy is known and the aircraft is within 20 minutes' flying thereof, will close on the convoy and inform the S.O. Escort of the presence of a U/Boat. Signals reporting sightings and attacks of U/Boats are to be sent to base as follows, unless special instructions have been issued to the contrary:-
    (i) Immediately after the attack, when on A/S patrol or sweep.
    (ii) Immediately after informing S.O. Escort when on escort duty, or on a sweep where the aircraft is in sight of or in R/T communication with S.O. Escort.
    (iii) While closing on a convoy, when on a sweep.

It is essential that the relevant information be passed to base in the correct form and without delay. The signals to be sent on the completion of an attack are as follows:-
    (i) The Groups 465 and 472 together.

(ii) The Group 511, denoting also the type of attack, but not giving an estimate of hits unless a direct bomb hit on the surface on a U/Boat is actually seen.

(iii) If the U/Boat is forced to the surface after the attack in an obviously damaged condition and remains there for an appreciable time, the Group 512 should be sent. If this happens immediately after the attack and before the Group 511 has been sent, the Group 512 may be sent in lieu.

(iv) If the U/Boat does not dive on being attacked, the Group 467 should be sent.

(v) If, after either 512 or 467 has been sent, the U/Boat subsequently dives, the Group 466 should be transmitted.

The first signal (Groups 465 and 472) should always be sent uncoded, i.e. as it appears in the Naval section of the Air Force Code. All subsequent signals and amplifying reports are to be sent in special "SYKO".

All future action either by S.O. Escorts or base depends on receiving accurate reports from the aircraft. No signal is to be sent claiming the destruction of a U/Boat unless there is complete and absolute certainty. Probable destruction calls for an amplifying signal giving accurate details. Amplifying reports on U/Boats disabled on the surface must be made at intervals of not less than 15 minutes.

Pilots and W/T operators must be fully conversant with homing procedures and must be prepared to home either surface vessels or other aircraft to the scene of the attack with the minimum of delay.

OBSERVATION AND REPORTING OF RESULTS OF ATTACK.

For purposes of assessment and so that all possible lessons may be learned from every attack, it is essential that the most complete and detailed account should be available. This is only possible, whether the attack is by day or night, if the crew drill is such as to ensure that no detail has been overlooked. Captains of aircraft must, therefore, allot tasks to respective members of the crew so that each knows his duty in this respect whenever an attack is made.

Crews, on landing must be interrogated by the Intelligence Officer, so that the Form Orange can be completed and at the same time, paras. 1 to 11 of C.C. Form Ubat should be compiled. The remainder of this form is to be completed by the Squadron Commander or his deputy, in conjunction with the Intelligence Officer, when the crew is rested; this should normally be done within 24 hours. The story should be complete to the smallest detail and even facts which may appear irrelevant should be included. The best way to obtain such information is by informal discussion and when the whole incident has been thoroughly investigated a connected account should be written down and read by the crew. If they are satisfied, the Form Ubat can then be completed.

It is appreciated that the Form, compiled in this way, may differ considerably from the Form Orange, but this is acceptable.

(Signed) J.C. SLESSOR
Air Marshal,
Air Officer Commanding-in-Chief,
Coastal Command.

12th June, 1943.

Courtesy Jeff Noakes

Appendix G: Convoy Code Letters

Appearing in Text

HX:	Halifax to United Kingdom
KMS:	United Kingdom to Gibraltar (slow)
MKS:	Gibraltar to United Kingdom (slow)
ON:	United Kingdom to Halifax
ONS:	United Kingdom to Halifax (slow)
SC:	United Kingdom to USA
SL:	West Africa to United Kingdom
UC:	United Kingdom to New York

APPENDIX H: AIR-TO-SURFACE VESSEL (ASV) RADAR INSTALLATIONS

FORTRESS IIA (FK & FL SERIALS) AND FORTRESS II (FA SERIALS)

Aircraft are listed in onward assignment sequence from the Cheyenne Modification Center where ASV Mk II radar equipment, including Yagi homing aerials and American search aerials, was installed. The three aircraft marked (x) served on early anti-submarine operations with 220 Squadron and were almost certainly equipped with ASV and an early aerial arrangement – there is uncertainty as to whether they were initially equipped in the United States or after arrival in the United Kingdom.

Air Ministry serials in assignment sequence	Delivered to UK without ASV	Fitted with ASV & homing aerials in UK	Delivered to UK with ASV, Yagi homing aerials & American search aerials	Delivered to UK with ASV & Yagi homing aerials only	Modified with 'production' LRASV from June 1943	Notes
FK184	X	See note				Not used for anti-submarine operations
FK187	X	See note			X	Not used for anti-submarine operations. Fitted with LRASV but not allocated to a squadron
FK185	X	See note				Assigned to 40mm cannon trials after very short operational service suggesting ASV never fitted
FK190	X	See note				UK trials aircraft for 'prototype' LRASV. Served as a trainer with 206 Sqn
FK186	X	See note			X	Photographic evidence suggests never fitted with early ASV installation
FK192	See note					Late delivery to UK in May 1943 and use in non-operational roles suggests aircraft was never fitted with ASV
FK191	X	X			X	
FK195	X	X			X	
FK193	X	X			X	
FK196	X	See note			X	Not used for anti-submarine operations but served as trainer with 1674 HCU after LRASV modifications
FK197	X	See note			X	Fitted with trial installation that included LRASV and additional dorsal aerials. Not used for anti-submarine operations
FK200	(X)	(X)			X	
FK204	(X)	(X)				Lost pre-LRASV modifications
FK199	(X)	(X)			X	
FK202			X		X	
FK211			X		X	
FK207			X			Lost pre-LRASV modifications
FK201			X		X	
FK206			X		X	
FK209			X			Lost pre-LRASV modifications
FK212			X			Lost pre-LRASV modifications
FK208			X		X	
FK213			X		X	
FK203			X		X	
FK210			X		X	
FL453			X			Lost pre-LRASV modifications
FL460			X		X	
FL458			X		X	
FL450			X		X	

Air Ministry serials in assignment sequence	Delivered to UK without ASV	Fitted with ASV & homing aerials in UK	Delivered to UK with ASV, Yagi homing aerials & American search aerials	Delivered to UK with ASV & Yagi homing aerials only	Modified with 'production' LRASV from June 1943	Notes
FL457			X			Not available for LRASV modifications
FL455			X		X	UK trials aircraft for 'production' LRASV
FL451			X		X	
FL464			X		X	
FL452			X		X	
FL454			X			Lost pre-LRASV modifications
FL463			X		X	
FK194			X		X	
FL459			X		X	
FL462			X		X	
FL449			X		X	
FL456			X		X	
FK198				Unlikely - see note	X	Held for reasons unknown at Wayne County Airport, Michigan. Known not to have been fitted with American search aerials
FK189			See note		X	Trials aircraft at Wright Field, Dayton, Ohio, believed for ASV. Likely delivered to UK with aerials installed
FA706				X	X	
FA697				X	X	
FA703				X	X	
FA704				X		Lost pre-LRASV modifications
FA701				X	X	
FA702				X	X	
FA695				X	X	
FA698				X		Lost pre-LRASV modifications
FA705				X	X	
FA699				X	X	
FK205			Possibly - see note		X	Retained for a period in the US on 'special duty', possibly for ASV trials
FA709				X	X	
FA707				X	X	
FA708				X	X	
FA712				X	X	
FA711				X	X	
FA696				X	X	
FA713				X	X	
FA700				X	X	
FA710				X	X	

Sources: Air Ministry Form 78 movement cards (with references to assignment to 218 MU, Colerne for modifications) and photographic evidence.

APPENDIX I: U-BOATS SUNK OR DAMAGED BY FORTRESS AIRCRAFT OF RAF COASTAL COMMAND OCTOBER 1942 TO SEPTEMBER 1944

Map Key	U-boat	Commander	Lat & Long	Date	Aircraft	Pilot	Sqn	Fortress Base, U-boat Details & Notes
S.1	U-627 VIIC	Kptlt. Robert Kindelbacher	59.14N, 22.49W	October 27, 1942	Fortress IIA FL457 'F'	P/O Robert Cowey	206	Benbecula. First patrol. All 44 crew lost.
S.2	U-265 VIIC	Oblt. Leonhard Aufhammer	56.35N, 22.49W	February 3, 1943	Fortress IIA FL456 'N'	P/O Kenneth Ramsden	220	Ballykelly. First patrol. All 46 crew lost.
S.3	U-624 VIIC	Kptlt. Graf Ulrich von Soden-Fraunhofen	55.42N, 26.17W	February 7, 1943	Fortress IIA FL459 'J'	P/O Peter Roberson	220	Ballykelly. Second patrol. All 44 crew lost.
S.4	U-384 VIIC	Oblt. Hans-Achim von Rosenberg-Gruszcynski	54.18N, 26.15W	March 19, 1943	Fortress IIA FK208 'B'	P/O Leslie Clark	206	Benbecula. Second patrol. All 47 crew lost.
S.5	U-469 VIIC	Oblt. Emil Claussen	62.12N, 16.40W	March 25, 1943	Fortress IIA FK195 'L'	F/Lt William Roxburgh	206	Benbecula. First patrol. All 47 crew lost.
S.6	U-169 IXC/40	Oblt. Hermann Bauer	60.54N, 15.25W	March 27, 1943	Fortress IIA FK195 'L'	F/O Ian Samuel	206	Benbecula. Second patrol. All 47 crew lost.
S.7	U-710 VIIC	Oblt. Dietrich von Carlewitz	61.25N, 19.48W	April 24. 1943	Fortress IIA FL451 'D'	P/O Robert Cowey	206	Benbecula. First patrol. All 49 crew lost.
S.8	U-417 VIIC	Oblt. Wolfgang Schreiner	63.20N, 10.30W	June 11, 1943	Fortress II FA704 'R'	W/Cdr Ronald Thomson	206	Benbecula.. First patrol. All 46 crew lost. Fortress shot down by U-417 - crew rescued.
S.9	U-707 VIIC	Oblt. Günter Gretschel	40.31N, 20.17W	November 11, 1943	Fortress IIA FL459 'J'	F/Lt Roderick Drummond	220	Lagens. First patrol. All 51 crew lost.
S.10	U-575 VIIC	Oblt. Wolfgang Boehmer	46.18N, 27.34W	March 13, 1944	Fortress II FA700 'R' / Fortress IIA FL459 'J'	F/Lt David Beaty / F/O Wilfred Travell	206 / 220	Lagens. First patrol. 18 survivors from crew of 55. Shared with other aircraft and vessels.
S.11	U-871 IXD2	Kptlt. Erwin Ganzer	43.18N, 36.28W	September 26, 1944	Fortress IIA FK191 'P'	F/Lt Arthur Wallace	220	Lagens. First patrol. All 69 crew lost. Pilot was Flg Off Eric Fielder.

Map Key	U-boat	Commander	Lat & Long	Date	Aircraft	Pilot	Sqn	Fortress Base, U-boat Fate & Notes
D.1	U-632 VIIC	KrvKpt. Hans Karpf	57.40N, 27.10W	January 15, 1943	Fortress IIA FL452 'G'	P/O Leslie Clark	206	Benbecula. Sunk April 6, 1943, by Liberator of 86 Squadron..
D.2	U-614 VIIC	Kptlt. Wolfgang Sträter	56.17N, 20.39W	February 9, 1943	Fortress IIA FK195 'L'	S/Ldr Richard Patrick	206	Benbecula. Sunk July 29, 1943, by Wellington of 172 Squadron.
D.3	U-666 VIIC	Kptlt. Herbert Engel	53.55N, 23.51W	March 19, 1943	Fortress IIA FK203 'M'	F/O William Knowles	220	Benbecula. Unexplained loss mid-February 1944.
D.4	U-450 VIIC	Oblt. Kurt Böhme	62.12N, 15.28W	June 6, 1943	Fortress IIA FL458 'A'	S/Ldr Hugh Warren	220	Benbecula. Sunk March 10, 1944, by British and US surface vessels.
D.5	U-338 VIIC	Kptlt. Manfred Kinzel	43.42N, 09.37W	June 17, 1943	Fortress IIA FL457 'F'	F/O Leslie Clark, DFC	206	St. Eval. Unexplained loss mid-September 1943.
D.6	U-270 VIIC	Kptlt. Paul-Friedrich Otto	43.53N, 23.32W	January 6, 1944	Fortress II FA705 'U'	S/Ldr Anthony Pinhorn, DFC	206	Lagens. Fortress shot down by U-270 – all crew lost. Sunk August 13, 1944, by Sunderland of 461 Sqn.

U-BOATS SUNK AND DAMAGED BY
FORTRESS AIRCRAFT OF RAF COASTAL COMMAND

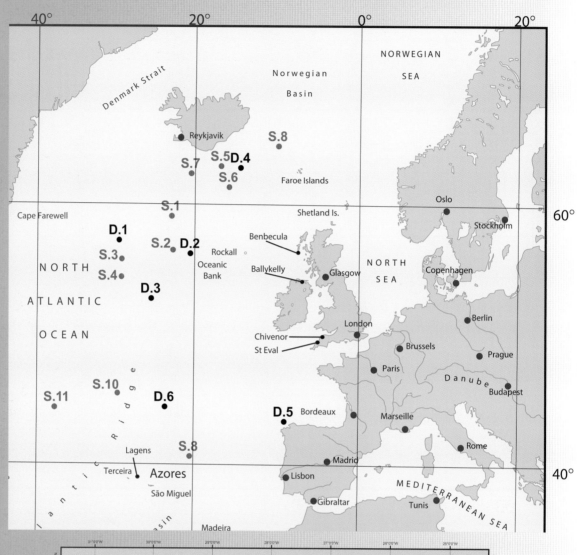

- Fortress base
S Location of sunk U-boat
D Location of damaged U-boat
See pages 194-195 for details

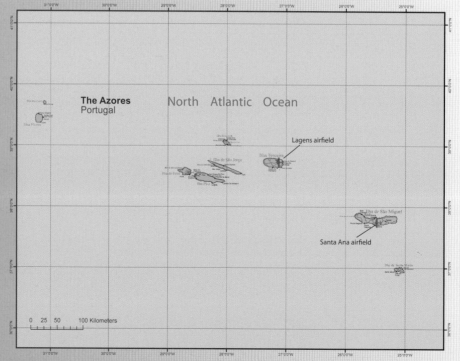

Appendix J: Meteorological Profiles Performed by Fortress Aircraft of RAF Coastal Command

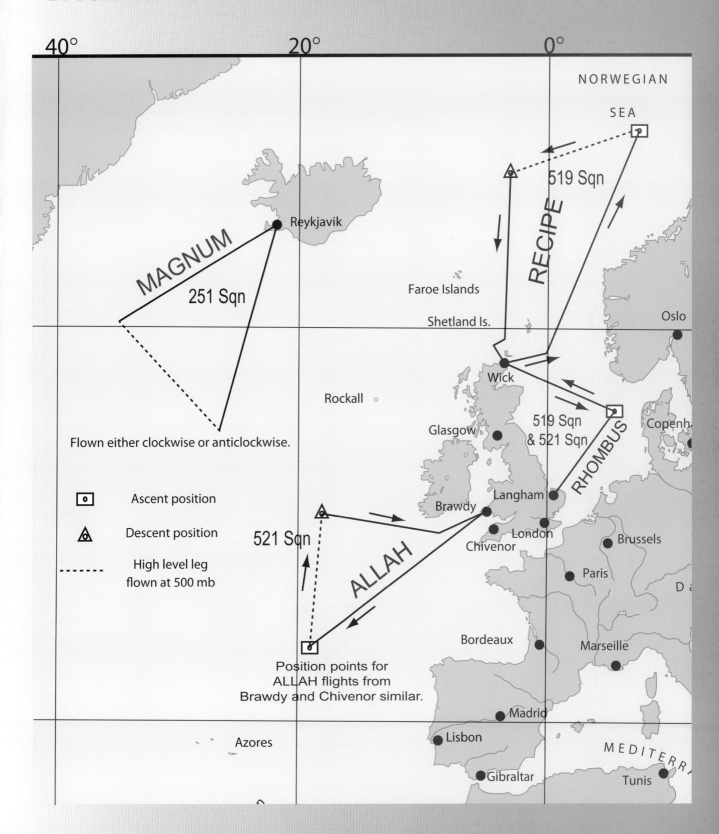

APPENDIX K: BOEING B-17E FORTRESS 41-9234, ALIAS FORTRESS IIA FL461

It has been nicknamed 'The Grey Ghost' and 'Mystery Ship' over the years. Many theories have been put forward regarding the origins of this puzzling Boeing B-17E Fortress yet it was only recently that the full story of this aircraft, perched broken and enigmatic on a remote ridge in Papua New Guinea, was finally revealed.

In the autumn of 1940, the United States government ordered 512 B-17Es under contract W-535 ac-15677. Production at Boeing's Seattle plant began on September 5, 1941, and on May 26 of the following year, the US Army Air Force accepted 41-9234 (constructor's number 2706), the 501st B-17E built – it had cost American taxpayers $280,135.00. Four days later, the Fortress was allocated to Britain under the US-UK Lend-Lease agreement and flown to the United Air Lines-run Cheyenne Modification Center at Cheyenne, Wyoming, to be modified as a Fortress IIA for anti-submarine operations with RAF Coastal Command. But with the USAAF's then urgent need for offensive capability in both Europe and the Pacific, 41-9234, along with 15 other B-17Es assigned to Britain, was taken back by to the USAAF. On August 6, it was flown to Hamilton Army Air Field in California for delivery to Australia under the shipping code Sumac.

The Fortress had spent approximately nine weeks at Cheyenne, four weeks longer than the typical five-week modification period for a Fortress IIA. From examination of its remains, it is known to have been fitted with an astrodome and ASV Mk II aerial arrays for service with the RAF. It was also painted in Coastal Command's Temperate Sea camouflage scheme of Extra Dark Sea Grey and Dark Slate Grey with Sky undersides, together with Type A1 fuselage roundels, equal-banded fin flash, Type B upper wing roundels and the Air Ministry serial FL461. In common with earlier RAF-bound B-17Es, the Fortress retained its yellow USAAF serial 19234 on the fin (see colour profile page 236). The fact that 41-9234 was fully modified and wearing an RAF serial, the only known instance involving a B-17E subsequently transferred back to the Army Air Force, suggests that a ferry flight to Dorval for onward delivery to the United Kingdom was imminent at the time of re-allocation. Supporting this conclusion, a British Air Commission (BAC) document notes FL461 at Cheyenne on July 7, 1942, five weeks after it arrived from Seattle – and therefore at the end of the normal modification period – and at the same time other Lend-Lease B-17Es in the same Army Air Force serial range were departing Cheyenne for Dorval. Shortly after the report to the BAC, 41-9234 was reconfigured for operations with the USAAF at Cheyenne – including removal of the astrodome and ASV Mk II radar aerial arrays – but retained its Temperate Sea with Sky finish.

When the Author visited the Fortress in 1977, the Dark Olive Drab finish had weathered away to reveal the Extra Dark Sea Grey and Dark Slate Grey camouflage pattern applied at Cheyenne although, after 35 years in the tropical sun and exposure to the occasional brush fire, the hulk appeared a uniform medium grey from a distance. The fuselage sides still carried remarkably sharp Type A1 RAF fuselage roundels while Type B blue-and-red roundels were evident on the upper wing. The serial FL461 was discernible in front of the port horizontal stabilizer while the yellow USAAF serial 19234 was still clearly visible on both sides of the bullet- and shrapnel-riddled fin.

41-9234 departed Hamilton Field in mid-August under Project X – the transfer of B-17s and B-24s to Australia – and arrived, most likely at Townsville in Queensland, on August 21. Once

Boeing B-17E Flying Fortress 41-9234, alias FL461, photographed near Wau, Papua New Guinea in April 1977. It crash-landed following a raid against a Japanese convoy off Lae on January 8, 1943. Of note is the large B-17F-style gun window on the port side of the nose, added in Australia with a similar starboard window after the Fortress had been reassigned to the USAAF.

in Australia, the nose section was fitted with large B-17F-style gun windows, a field modification applied to a number of B-17Es operated by the 5th Air Force. Allocated to the 28th Bombardment Squadron of the 19th Bombardment Group based at Mareeba, Queensland, it flew its first mission just four days after its arrival, still wearing its Temperate Sea and Sky finish (see colour profile page 237).

Trial by Fire

The war in the Southwest and Central Pacific was characterized by island-hopping campaigns that relied heavily on the availability and safe passage of shipping – targeting convoys engaged in invasion and resupply operations therefore became a critical role for the aerial forces of both sides. Boeing had designed its legendary Flying Fortress as a high-level strategic bomber. But its availability in the Pacific at the beginning of the war, and the prevailing belief that heavily-armed, unescorted bombers could fight their way to and from any target, meant that the large and less-than-agile B-17 was pressed into the tactical anti-shipping role, sometimes at low level.

Missions to New Guinea (the northern half of what is now Papua New Guinea) typically began with a late evening take-off at Mareeba and a risky night landing at 7-Mile Airdrome at Port Moresby. Departure for the mission was usually before sun-up and was followed by an unescorted leg to the target and bomb runs in flights of two or three aircraft, if not already separated by often marginal weather and frequent tropical storms. Once the bombing was complete, almost invariably after running the gauntlet of anti-aircraft fire and defending fighters, each pilot found his way back to Port Moresby where he refuelled before returning to Australia for another night landing.

Directing these operations were Major General George C Kenney, Commanding General of the Allied Air Forces in the South West Pacific Area (SWPA), and Brigadier General Kenneth N Walker, Kenney's key tactician for the growing bombing offensive. Kenney knew from intelligence sources that the Japanese planned to capture three vital airfields at Milne Bay on the extreme south-eastern tip of the New Guinea mainland, so the 19th Bombardment Group (BG) at Mareeba was ready to respond when an invasion convoy was spotted around noon on August 25, 1942. Major Felix Hardison of the 93rd Bombardment Squadron (BS) commanded a mixed force of nine Fortresses drawn from three squadrons: the 93rd BS, the 28th BS, and the 30th BS.

It fell to Capt. John W Chiles to take 41-9234 on its first mission of the war, the 27th mission out of Mareeba. 1st Lt. James Dieffenderfer was Chiles' co-pilot: "*On August 25th, we flew up from Mareeba to Milne Bay with Hardison leading… it was our indoctrination mission. We had just delivered a B-17F across the Pacific and the crew was not happy to change aircraft. We found a three-ship Australian convoy in Milne Bay and exchanged a few shots before flying to 7-Mile Airdrome.*"

The Fortresses had been two hours late leaving Mareeba and low ceilings and the growing darkness obscured the enemy convoy, allowing the Japanese troops to land. Eight aircraft returned to Milne Bay early the following morning. Jim Dieffenderfer recalls that August 26 began with a couple of bad omens: "*We got up in the dark early in the morning* [for a 4:45am take-off]. *We had a dead magneto on number 1 engine and blew a spark plug on take-off on number 2… but we went anyway. We assembled in the dark* [with our B-17 41-9234] *leading an unplanned three-ship formation.*"

The Fortresses arrived over Milne Bay around 6:45am, a little after dawn, and this time the crews had no difficulty spotting the convoy. John Chiles remembers their arrival. "*The weather was terrible. We were supposed to be bombing from 24,000ft but found ourselves in fighter territory at around 1,700ft. Clyde Webb was on my left wing* [in B-17F 41-24354]." The Japanese responded with intense and very accurate anti-aircraft fire and most aircraft were immediately hit. A radio transmission from 41-9234 described damage as: "*large A/A holes in nose, left wing, bomb bay.*"

Cpl. Wathen Cody was the flight engineer and describes what happened in the nose compartment. "*An ack-ack shell exploded just above the nose and left a hole in the Perspex the size of a basketball. The bombardier Sgt. Earl Snyder was hit in the back of his head by a piece of metal but man-*

Capt. John Chiles flew 41-9234 on its first two missions, to Milne Bay on August 25 and 26, 1942. Here he receives the Legion of Merit from General Francis H Griswold at HQ Army Air Forces in early 1946. The award was for his management of the project to arm the Boeing B-29 Superfortress with larger bombs, primarily the 1,000-pounder. via John Chiles

1st Lt. James Dieffenderfer was John Chiles' co-pilot for the two missions to Milne Bay in 41-9234. This photograph was taken in San Francisco the previous month, shortly before Dieffenderfer delivered a new B-17F to Australia. via James Dieffenderfer

Fortress 41-9234 shortly after landing at Mareeba, Queensland, following the harrowing mission to Milne Bay on August 26, 1942. The aircraft's identify was confirmed by enlarging the data block, visible below the rearmost nose window. Of note are two bullet holes in the fuselage, one at the bottom left corner of the large gun window and one behind the data block. Repairs to these and the distinctive paint demarcation line between the upper Temperate Sea and lower Sky helped confirm the identity of the aircraft in the colour image on page 212 as also being 41-9234. Damage to the Perspex nose panels was caused by shrapnel that killed bombardier Sgt Earl Snyder and injured the navigator, Lt. David Hirsch. Paul Cool, son of Capt. Paul E Cool.

aged to release four 500-pound demolition bombs before he died. The navigator, Lt. David Hirsch, was badly hit in one knee so I tied a tourniquet to try to stop the bleeding."

John Chiles' priority now became getting medical attention for his wounded crew, so he turned 41-9234 away from the convoy, salvoed the four remaining bombs into the sea and climbed into the clouds. "*I had a badly injured navigator, the radio operator was hurt and the right waist gunner had been hit in the eyes.*" With the navigator incapacitated, Chiles sent Dieffenderfer to his station

B-17E 41-9234 spent close to nine weeks at the Cheyenne Modification Centre in mid-1942. Here Lockheed Vega-built B-17F Fortresses are prepared for service with the USAAF at the United Air Lines – run facility in May of the following year. 42-23024 (foreground) served in the US throughout the war while 42-30139 was lost while participating in the costly Schweinfurt ball bearing plant raid of August 17, 1943. The main fin assembly was painted Medium Green by the subcontractor rather than Dark Olive Drab – this area would subsequently exhibit a characteristic red hue on weathered airframes such as 41-9234. Also of interest, the nose gun windows were narrower on Vega-built Fortresses than on those manufactured by Boeing and Douglas. United Air Airlines

in the nose to find a map. "*Chiles needed a course for Mareeba right away so we gave the navigator some morphine, hauled him up to the 'hole' behind the cockpit and stood him up. He then gave us a heading for home.*" The seven battered Fortresses made it back to Mareeba some three hours after leaving the target area. The newly-delivered 41-9234 and its fledgling crew had been well and truly tested in combat. The other crew members were radio operator Sgt. Marvin Berkowitz, waist gunners Pvt. Galen A Brown and Pvt. George D Browning, and tail gunner Gilbert R Tredway.

41-9234 Returns to the Fray

The Japanese army's thrust into Milne Bay proved to be a significant turning point in the Pacific War. Although able to land two more groups under cover of the prevailing poor weather, the invaders had underestimated the strength and determination of the Australian and American forces and by the end of the first week of September had been forced, for the first time in the Pacific War, to abandon a ground campaign.

Fortress 41-9234 had by then been repaired following the harrowing second mission to Milne Bay and on September 5 was one of six 28th BS B-17s dispatched from Mareeba to Port Moresby for an attack on the Japanese evacuation convoy. Five aircraft were refuelled and each loaded with four 500-pound bombs prior to departing 7-Mile Airdrome in two flights. Capt. Richard F Ezzard led 'A' flight with wingman Lt. Walter T Schmid in the camera-equipped 41-9234. Capt. Boris M Zubko in 41-9235 *Clown House* – another B-17E originally destined for RAF Coastal Command – led 'B' flight. As Zubko's mission report describes, the mission did not proceed smoothly.

"*I led a flight of three planes for reconnaissance north of Milne Bay. My aerial engineer, M/Sgt. Thrasher, broke his arm in [the] top turret so I returned to Port Moresby landing at 1345. Got another gunner and immediately took off again on [the] same mission. Searched areas off Milne Bay, Trobriand and D'Entrecastreaux Islands with remainder of my flight. Lt. Laubscher was forced to return due to a faulty flight indicator. Returning to Port Moresby by way of Milne Bay and the China Straits, we found [an] enemy cruiser and two destroyers in mouth of Milne Bay shelling [the] coast. Time was 1815 and it was almost dark. Before a run could be completed darkness and weather obscured the ships... returned to Port Moresby. Weather during mission bad. Ceiling 100 to 800 feet. Overcast. Visibility less than two miles.*"

The following day, Zubko led a flight of three Fortresses including 41-9234, again flown by Lt. Walter Schmid, on a 7½-hour armed reconnaissance to the east and north of Milne Bay, while on September 7, Capt. Richard Ezzard led a gruelling 10½-hour, three-plane search in the same area as pilot-in-command for Schmid's crew in 41-9234. There were no sightings on each occasion and all bombs and ammunition were brought back to Port Moresby.

Four days later, on September 11, word came through that two enemy destroyers had been spotted off the Japanese bridgehead at Buna on the north Papuan coast (Papua was the southern half of what is now Papua New Guinea). At 2:00pm, Major Elbert Helton, commanding officer of the 28th BS, departed Port Moresby in 41-9234 to lead a five-aircraft bombing strike. The mission report emphasizes the perils and challenges of attacking heavily armed vessels.

"*The two ships started firing upon the formation as soon as it was first spotted, using anti-aircraft fire as well as a broadside from their big guns, the shells of which fell into the water short of the formation... Helton's bombs hit quite a way short of the destroyer at 16:10.*"

Early the following day, Helton led another formation to Buna in 41-9234, this time to bomb the Japanese-held airfield.

Target: Rabaul

Rabaul was the centre of Japanese operations in the region and destroying shipping in its harbour before troops and equipment could be transported to forward positions became a pre-occupation for Kenney and Walker. The first mission to Rabaul involving 41-9234 took place on September 15, a 7¾-hour strike against Japanese shipping in the town's Simpson Harbour.

Three of 41-9234's crew members for its final flight

Pilot 1st Lt. Ray S Dau flew 18 B-17 missions over New Guinea. via Janice Olson

2nd Lt. Donald W Hoggan was Ray Dau's co-pilot. Donald Hoggan

Bombardier 2nd Lt. Albert V 'Bud' Cole was originally slated to serve with the 427th BS, 303rd BG in Europe but was reassigned to the Pacific Theatre. via Janice Olson

According to the mission report, 41-9234 carried a keenly interested but unauthorized observer, General Kenneth Walker.

"General Walker and Captain [Jerome] *Tarter* [Executive Officer for the 28th BS] *made the trip to Moresby in Captain Ezzard's ship. This ship developed engine trouble on the flight to Moresby and was found not to be in flying condition for the first mission. Consequently, Capt. Tarter and General Walker decided to fly the first mission in Capt. Zubko's ship* [41-9234], *Capt. Tarter as pilot and Capt. Zubko as co-pilot, and General Walker as Command Pilot.*

…Just before getting on the bombing run, the formation flew into a cloud while turning, and all ships of the formation became separated. When they broke out, each was in sight of the target, but widely separated, so each started an individual bombing run on various ships in the harbor… Approximately 15 Zeros were seen altogether. Five attacked Capt. [Jay] *Rousek… scored no hits… The other ships were not reached by the Zeros…"*

The following day, September 16, Capt. Boris Zubko was back over Rabaul in 41-9234 as part of a six-plane mission to attack the airfields at Lakunai and Vunakanau. All six aircraft survived the concentrated flak and returned to Mareeba the following day for a well-earned break. General Walker issued his next mission instructions to the 19th BG on September 21.

"Confirm verbal orders. Attack shipping Rabaul with one squadron on nights of 22nd to 25th September inclusive. First squadron arrive Seven Mile by 1500K [local time] *22nd September and perform two missions remain overnight and return Mareeba upon completion. Second squadron arrive by 1530K 24th September to perform second two missions."*

Nine B-17s of the 28th BS, including 41-9234 piloted by Capt. Jay Rousek, departed Mareeba for Port Moresby on September 22, arriving at 2:30pm that afternoon. Engine problems prevented Rousek and his crew participating in the first raid that evening, so it was the middle of the following night when they finally took off for Rabaul as part of the 28th BS's second mission. Rousek's mission report documents a routine and uneventful operation.

"Six planes depart SM at 0015 to 0030 [on September 24]. *#41-9234 in wing position in the "B" echelon… arrived about three o'clock at Rabaul… made one run at 10,500 feet and dropped four bombs*

B-17F 41-24381 Panama Hattie of the 63rd BS led B-17E 41-9234 to Lae for the January 8 attack. It was transferred to the 54th Troop Carrier Wing at Port Moresby in November 1943 and was scrapped in April 1947. Karl J Lonnquist via Lawrence J Hickey

on a ship at the new wharf on the northwest side of the harbour. Bombs observed to hit close to the boat... No enemy interception."

The next mission for 41-9234, again to Rabaul, followed on 27 September but it too failed to yield results due to poor weather. Only Lt. Richard T Hernlund in 41-9234 reached the target and he was forced to jettison his bombs. Lt. Thomas Parkinson faired no better on October 5 when he flew 41-9234 as part of a group sent to attack Lakunai Airdrome.

On October 9, 41-9234 returned to Rabaul, this time as a flare ship with Capt. Edward C Habberstad at the controls. The Fortress was loaded with seven 300-pound bombs and 20 parachute flares.

"[Our] *flare ship went across the target just ahead* [of the group] *and drew moderate A/A and heavy machine gun fire... Dropped two flares to make observation but found only water below. Flares were seen by other ships but no contact* [with the town of Rabaul] *was made.*"

Simpson Harbour, Rabaul under attack by B-17s of the 43rd BG and B-24s the 90th BG on January 5, 1943, the day before the Lae Convoy departed. USAF via Bruce Hoy/ Lawrence J Hickey

Close-up of a Lae Convoy transport - either the Chifuku Maru or the Brasil Maru - taken from a B-25 of the 38th BG on January 7, 1943. Note the deck cargo including landing barges and the bombs falling in the lower right corner. Roy L Grover via Lawrence J Hickey Collection

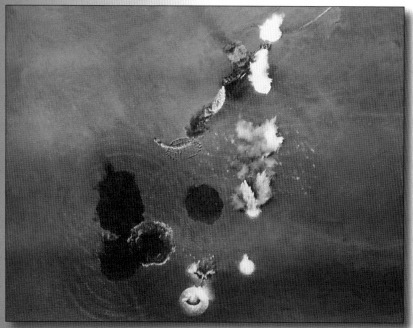

Medium-altitude attack on ships in Lae Convoy by 38th BG B-25s on Jan. 7, 1943. Note the ship is getting underway as a landing barge pulls away for the shoreline. Roy L Grover Collection via Lawrence J Hickey

A week later, on October 16, 1942, 5th Bomber Command sent the following radio transmission to the 19th BG:

"Dispatch 2 squadrons 7 Mile immediately. 1 squadron will attack Vunakanau Aerodrome night of 16th/17th October and night of 17/18th October. 1 squadron attack Kahili Aerodrome... night of 16/17 and night of 17/18 October."

At least seven aircraft from the 30th BS and ten aircraft from the 28th BS departed Mareeba for 7-Mile Airdrome, to be joined by a pair from the 93rd BS. Lt. Richard Hernlund was again the pilot of 41-9234.

"Six aircraft on mission. Attack was to be made starting at 0400 October 18, 1942, individually with the aid of flares... We were a flare ship and dropped two to three flares at a time alternately at intervals from 0400 to 0500. Flares were dropped from 9,500 feet. Four bombs were dropped on the town as no shipping was sighted. Results were unobserved. ... No enemy pursuit... Landed Port Moresby 0730... Departed AOB [Advanced Operating Base, Port Moresby] 0930 October 18, 1942 arriving home base [Mareeba] 1230 same date."

Fortress 41-9234 is known to have flown up to Port Moresby on October 21 and returned to Mareeba the following day in the hands of Capt. Jack Thompson but there is no record that the aircraft flew a mission on the night of the 21st.

On the next day, General Walker issued the following instruction:

"Return 3 aircraft of relieved [28th BS] to Port Moresby for reconnaissance special area. Aircraft have 1 bomb bay tank. Arrive Port Moresby 2100 Z 22... Walker."

Over the following three days, Lt. Walter Schmid took 41-9234 on armed reconnaissance missions over the waters between the New Guinea mainland and the Solomon Islands. The report for October 23 reads:

View of Fortress 41-9234 taken from 10,000ft (3,048m) by a B-17 of the 8th Photo Reconnaissance Squadron on January 26, 1943, 16 days after the crash-landing. The Fortress approached from the upper left over Kaisenik Creek and slewed 90° to the right after touchdown. Note how soil piled up at the port wing root as the aircraft slid sideways. via Donald Hoggan

View across Kaisenik Creek shows how pilot Ray Dau ran out of options as he wrestled to keep the Fortress in the air on two engines in rising terrain. Phillip Bradley

"Departed AOB [Port Moresby] 0930... to search area bounded by 157 degrees and 153 degrees meridians and 10 degrees-50' South and 11 degrees-40' South parallels, for enemy shipping etc...No sighting during patrol at low altitudes ... No A/A or enemy pursuit encountered."

The mission for October 24 repeated that of the previous day while that of October 25 covered an area bounded by 157 degrees to 153 degrees East and 9 degrees 20 minutes and 10 degrees 10 minutes South. Schmidt returned 41-9234 to Mareeba on October 26 without having made a single enemy sighting.

Records for the 28th BS now become sketchy, no doubt because the majority of the 19th BG crews had departed for the United States while the remaining crews from the squadron were about to be attached to the 43rd BG until they had earned enough rotation points to return home. Radio transmission reports confirm that 41-9234 participated in a raid by 28th BS crews on shipping in Tonolei Harbour, Bouganville on the night of October 29/30 and that 2nd Lt. Vincent

41-9234 sits in a tranquil field of kunai grass in August 1993, much as it would have appeared following the Lae Convoy mission 50 years earlier. The large break in port side of the fuselage coincided with the forward end of the radio compartment where several of the crew were located during the crash landing; radio operator Robert Albright was unable to secure himself and died of his injuries six days later. Bruce Hoy

J Roddy was the pilot. Twelve B-17s from the 28th and 30th BS returned to Bougainville the night of October 31/November 1 to attack shipping at Buin, Tonolei Harbour and Faisi Island, refueling at Fall River, Milne Bay. The unconfirmed crew of 41-9234, most likely Lt. Vincent Roddy's, claimed a possible hit on a destroyer.

Seven B-17s of the 28th BS were tasked with attacking an enemy convoy 20 miles (32km) south of Gasmata on the morning of November 2 but it is not certain that 41-9234 took part. It is known that the Fortress returned to Mareeba on November 3 with Lt. Roddy as pilot.

Fortress 41-9234 possibly flew one more mission with a 28th BS crew when, on November 13, it was part of a ten-aircraft operation by the 63rd and 65th BS for a pre-dawn attack on Tonolei Harbour. Around November 18, the last flight crews from the 28th BS left Mareeba and flew to Brisbane in their own aircraft. It is not known if 41-9234 made such a trip – if it did, it was subsequently returned to Mareeba and transferred to the 65th BS, 43rd BG.

View from the port wing tip showing the exposed Type B RAF roundel. The person to the right is sitting on the life raft stowage compartment. The heavy vegetation is shown in later photographs to have been burned away by brush fires. Author

Joining the Fight

On November 21, Replacement Crew # 66-X-1 received orders to move from Townsville to Mareeba where they were instructed to report to the commanding officer of the 43rd BG "*for assignment and duty*". They were assigned to the 65th BS, '*The Lucky Dicers*', the same day. The crew consisted of pilot 1st Lt. Ray S Dau, co-pilot 2nd Lt Donald W Hoggan, bombardier 2nd Lt Albert V Cole, navigator 2nd Lt Peter Hudec, radio operator Sgt Robert Albright, engineer SSgt Lloyd T Dumond, gunners Sgt Francis E Caldwell and Sgt Henry J Blasco, and tail gunner Sgt Henry Bowen.

Dau and his crew flew nine missions between their arrival at Mareeba in late November and the end of 1942. The last of these took place on December 24, when they were dispatched from Mareeba with five other B-17Es to attack two transports at Gasmata, New Britain. One of their most successful sorties, the crew scored a direct hit on the stern of the 623-ton *Koa Maru*, which subsequently sank.

The Lae Convoy

With their forces in Papua pushed back to the sea at the end of 1942 and forced to withdraw from Guadalcanal in early January, the Japanese Command resolved to hold onto the northern Solomons, New Britain and, most importantly, northern New Guinea. The necessary build up of strength was met by dispatching a convoy of six destroyers and five transports from Rabaul to the port of Lae on January 6, 1943, with a portion of the 51st Division under the command of Major General Tooru Okabe.

Anticipating this move, General Kenney ordered a major bombing raid on Rabaul for January 5, to destroy as much shipping as possible before it could be used to reinforce Japanese positions on the New Guinea mainland. Contrary to Kenney's direct orders, General Walker flew on the mission and was lost when B-17F 41-24458 *San Antonio Rose* was shot down by a combination of flak and attacks by Zero-Sen fighters.

Attempts were made to attack the Lae-bound convoy before dark without any results, although the crew of a solitary Consolidated Catalina of 11 Sqn, RAAF, A24-1, under the command of F/Lt David Vernon, achieved a remarkable success that night when they stalked and sank one of the transports, the *Nichiryu Maru*. The following day, the Allies launched a major aerial campaign to prevent the convoy reaching Lae. Starting in the early hours of the morning, American and Australian aircraft flew 154 sorties and dropped over 250 large bombs. Yet by 3:45pm, the four remaining transports had reached Lae harbour and only one, the *Myoko Maru*, was seriously damaged and subsequently ran aground. An estimated 4,000 Japanese soldiers and their equipment made it ashore.

With a substantial number of Japanese troops now landed at Lae, the focus for Allied operations on January 8 became disrupting their movements, destroying their supplies and sinking the ships before they left the harbour. As on the previous day, American and Australian units contributed a diverse force of aircraft that included B-17s, Consolidated B-24 Liberators, Martin B-26 Marauders, North American B-25 Mitchells, Lockheed P-38 Lightnings, Douglas A-20 Havocs and Bristol Beaufighters and Beauforts.

Ray Dau and his crew were assigned B-17E 41-9234 and tasked with bombing the escorting destroyers – this was to be their first mission originating from Port Moresby and their thirteenth in all. Donald Hoggan's diary captures the start of that fateful day.

"*Friday, January 8: Arrived at operations 5am, waiting to strike convoy at Lae. Took off about 10am, 7 ships to go. We circle over airdrome at 6,000 waiting for ships to form but* [they] *do not* [arrive] *so take off for Lae… in a two-ship formation.*"

Rau Dau formated 41-9234 on the right wing of B-17F 41-24381 *Panama Hattie*, flown by Capt. William M Thompson of the 63rd BS – the two unescorted bombers then set course across the Owen Stanley Range, arriving at Lae harbour at 11:45. Ray Dau describes the reception.

"*Prior to reaching the harbor we could see heavy ack-ack and a lot of fighters. It was the first time we'd encountered such heavy concentrations. Our other missions had been fairly routine… but this one was different. We came into the harbor area from the sea side and everything happened at once. I was concentrating on keeping on Thompson's wing for our run. The ack-ack was hitting us and the Zeros were coming in with head-on attacks and swerving up over the plane… we were getting hit from every direction. I knew that bombardier 'Bud' Cole was hit almost simultaneously with all this action… I knew too that our number 3 and 4 engines were shot out.*"

Despite the mayhem around him, Cole remained focused on dropping his bombs on the Japanese destroyers. As he squinted through the Norden bomb sight he became aware of an approaching Zero-Sen and at that instant was hit in the face by a cannon shell. About the same time an anti-aircraft shell smashed into the nose section, shattering the Perspex and filling both of Coles' knees with shrapnel – fortunately, the bomb sight protected the rest of his body. Though seriously wounded, Cole courageously insisted on staying at his post until he had released the bombs. The navigator, Peter Hudec, then pulled Cole away from the nose and attempted to block the catwalk so Cole could be shielded from the roaring wind.

After completing the run, the crew of 41-9234 found themselves separated from Thompson's Fortress and any mutual protection it could provide. Without fighter escort they had to fight their way out of the target area on their own, surrounded by a swarm of Japanese fighters and with two failed engines. Hoggan relates their retreat from Lae: "*We counted up to 20 fighters but just had to sit there, shouting directions at the gunners while lumbering along in our unescorted bomber. Lloyd DuMond in the upper turret was hit by a shell on the back of his head and stopped shooting. Dau shouted, 'What's wrong?' DuMond said, 'I can't see… I'm blind… I've been scalped!' Dau shot back, 'Well put it back on and start shooting. If you can't see, I'll tell you where to point the guns!'*"

Port side of the fin still bearing USAAF serial 19234 and vestiges of the British fin flash. The Temperate Sea camouflage pattern is visible in the original slide as is British serial number FL461, just below the intersection of the panel lines in front of and underneath the leading edge of the horizontal stabilizer Author

The running battle with the Japanese fighters continued for several minutes as 41-9234 headed south towards the Bulolo Valley and the Australian outpost of Wau. Dau's gunners later claimed four enemy aircraft destroyed though they received credit for only three, one by waist gunner Henry Blasco and two by tail gunner Henry Bowen. "*But it was the flak over Lae that brought us down,*" recalls Hoggan, "*not the attacking fighters.*"

Refuge at Wau

Looking out to his right at the failed number 3 and 4 engines, Hoggan asked Dau if he should feather the propellers. "*Ray said, 'If the fighter pilots see the props feathered they'll know our critical condition'. So we let them windmill. The fighters stayed with us but eventually dropped back out of shooting range.*" Dau then attempted to feather the number 3 and 4 propellers but was only successful with the inboard engine. "*With each ridge the aircraft got closer to the ground. We could maintain altitude but not climb. Ray was as cool as one could get… he made light of any crisis and was a superb leader. He asked for everything to be thrown out but was still not satisfied as the aircraft would not climb on two engines. He sent me back to check and I found everything including guns and ammunition boxes, had been jettisoned. I had just got back to the cockpit and sat down and was looking down at my lap strap to tighten the buckle when Ray said, 'We're going in!'*"

The stricken bomber came to a stop in less than 200ft (60m) as it ploughed up a 20° slope, slewing 90° to the right in the process. The sideways skid caused the fuselage to fracture at the front and rear spar attachment frames, the nose bending to the right while the rear fuselage was torn open on the port side at the front end of the radio compartment and wrenched though 45°, also to the right. Ripped from its mounting, the unoccupied ball turret rolled down the side of the ridge.

Without shoulder harnesses, pilots Dau and Hoggan had their upper bodies snapped forward on impact, striking their heads on the instrument panel shroud – in the nose, Albert Cole was thrown forward against the bombardier's chair and somehow threw himself out of a front window. The rest of the crew had moved to their crash positions in the radio compartment but Robert Albright was unable to secure himself prior to touchdown and was badly hurt. Rear gunner Henry Bowen had been gravely injured by the attacking Japanese fighters.

Australian soldiers based at Wau witnessed the crash-landing and, with the help of local villagers placed five of the nine aircrew, including Cole, Albright, Blasco and Bowen, on stretchers and

Hudsons of 1 OTU, RAAF at Wau airstrip on either January 8, 1942, the day of the B-17's crash-landing, or January 10, the day of the rescue mission. Note the steep downward slope of the airstrip behind the aircraft and that the engines have been left running for a quick departure. Owen Robinson Collection via David Vincent

headed back down the trail to their camp – sadly, Henry Bowen died during the trek.

Mercy Flight

Word had already been sent to Port Moresby that the crew needed immediate medical attention but little could be done until someone could get through by air. Port Moresby was only 250 miles (400km) away but a rescue operation across the Owen Stanley Range to Wau in the prevailing poor weather was by no means a simple task. Fortunately, the right person to lead such an mission was currently based at Port Moresby, an Australian pilot named F/Lt Archibald 'Arch' Dunne.

Dunne had flown commercially in New Guinea prior to joining the RAAF at the start of the war and was familiar with the demanding flying conditions around Wau. At the time

of the crash-landing he was flying Hudsons with the Special Transport Flight, a detachment of 1 Operational Training Unit tasked with flying resupply missions from Port Moresby to Allied troop outposts in New Guinea.

"*When we received word that a B-17 had crashed, the number of casualties was not known. I was asked to try and get in there on January 9 because I knew my way around the area and it was almost impossible to take a group of aircraft in at that time of day. However, I couldn't find any sort of break as the whole area was 'socked in', normal for New Guinea in the late afternoon. So early the next morning, January 10, I led a group of Hudsons to Wau in perfectly clear conditions.*"

The Hudsons flew 13 missions into Wau that day with 'Arch' Dunne leading the first group of six aircraft. With Japanese fighters only 30 miles (48km) away at Salamaua, the ground crews worked as fast as they could to load the injured while Dunne and the other pilots left their engines running for a rapid departure. Twenty-two wounded personnel were flown out, including the crew of 41-9234.

Aftermath

Despite the varied gallant efforts to stop the Lae Convoy, the majority of the Japanese troops had made it ashore. In reality, the Allied deployment of aircraft had been piecemeal and largely ineffective. But the principle of concentration of force had been hammered home and would soon be applied with decisive effect. On March 3, all eight merchantmen tasked with reinforc-

ing the Japanese garrison at Lae were sunk in what would become known as the Battle of the Bismarck Sea.

Ray Dau came through the crash landing of 41-9234 with only a concussion and temporarily blurred vision. After a few days in a hospital, he was reunited with two former crew members, engineer Lloyd DuMond and ball turret gunner Francis Caldwell. On the return leg of his 18th mission, his first to Rabaul, he was forced to ditch B-17E 41-9193 *Gypsy Rose* after running low on fuel. He later returned to the United States and flew B-17s for radar development. At the end of

F/Lt Archibald 'Arch' Dunne flew 75 hours over 48 missions on Lockheed Hudsons while based at Port Moresby with the Special Transport Flight. He is pictured at Darwin on June 3, 1942, seven months before the rescue mission to Wau. Australian War Museum neg. 012436

Palm Springs, California, October 29, 2001. Donald Hoggan (left) is reunited with Albert Cole (centre) and Ray Dau for the first time in 58 years. Ray Dau

Careful examination of the upper nose section reveals the circular repair made at Cheyenne following removal of the astrodome, installed at the same location to meet Air Ministry requirements for RAF Coastal Command operations. Tim Vincent

the war, Dau returned to the Dupont Company, later making a career change to advertising.

Donald Hoggan eventually returned to operations, flying Douglas C-47s with the 40th Troop Carrier Sqn, 317th Troop Carrier Wing based at Port Moresby and Hollandia in northern New Guinea. He too returned to the United States and after a period flying navigators around in Cessna AT-17 Bobcats, became a project pilot for the APQ-44 missile guidance system using the B-17. He left the Air Force in May 1947 to join his father's building company and later became a surveyor and a teacher, finally retiring to a start a cattle ranch in northern California.

Gunner Henry Blasco spent several months in hospital following the crash landing and received credit for downing one Japanese fighter – he became a tool and die maker. Ball turret gunner Francis Caldwell remained with the 65th BS after the May 24 ditching of B-17E *Gypsy Rose* but was lost on August 3, 1943, when B-17E 41-2634 *Red Moose Express* was shot down over the sea near Bogadjim. Engineer Lloyd DuMond returned to combat but was wounded again and sent home – he later served in the Korean War. Navigator Peter Hudec married a young woman from Townsville – he passed away in his native New York in November 1994.

Hudson pilot 'Arch' Dunne joined British Commonwealth Pacific Airlines, flying Douglas DC-4s and DC-6s, and subsequently moved to Quantas as a Lockheed Super Constellation captain on the company's round-the-world service. He participated in route-proving flights for the Boeing 707 and completed his career flying Lockheed Electras on the Australia-New Zealand run.

Flying Fortress 41-9234 still rests where it crash-landed, a local landmark located 6.5 miles (10.5km) ESE of Wau in an area called Black Cat Pass. There has been considerable discussion over the years about salvaging and restoring the 'Grey Ghost', but in all likelihood, the most complete of all the Boeing B-17 Flying Fortresses intended for RAF Coastal Command will remain where it crash-landed over 65 years ago.

Researched with the invaluable assistance of Janice Olson, principal of the Pacific Theatre B-17 Project. Special thanks to former 41-9234 crew members John Chiles, Jim Dieffenderfer, Ray Dau and Donald Hoggan, former RAAF Hudson pilot Archibald Dunne, and researchers Steve Birdsall, Lawrence J Hickey and Bruce Hoy.

Small repairs on the dorsal fin fillet coincide with the mounting points for the US-designed ASV Mk II broadside receive aerial masts, installed and then removed at the Cheyenne Modification Center. Tim Vincent

Ted Fulton served with the Australian Sixth Division and, following service in the Middle East and Greece, was posted to New Guinea to conduct forward intelligence behind Japanese lines. While stationed at Wau, he helped crew members from Fortress 41-9234 negotiate the tortuous track from the crash site to Wau. Elizabeth Thurston, daughter of Ted Fulton

Above: Rare image of 41-9234, one of the four B-17Es allocated to Britain but taken back by the USAAF and assigned to the 5th Air Force in the South West Pacific Area – the other three aircraft were 41-9196, 41-9235 Clown House and 41-9244 Honi Kuu Okole. The photograph was taken at Mareeba between September and November 1942. Pilot Capt. Paul E Cool of the 28th BS, 19th BG stands alongside the aircraft. The view confirms that middle-period B-17Es destined for Britain were painted with Sky under surfaces in addition to the Temperate Sea upper camouflage scheme. Former aircrew recall the aircraft being 'blue' on top and 'white' underneath, an understandable interpretation of the Extra Dark Sea Grey and Sky colours. Paul Cool, son of Capt. Paul E Cool.

Right: Staff Sgt Henry 'Billy' Bowen, photographed shortly after joining the US Army Air Force at Fort Lewis in Washington state. A private pilot before the war, Bowen became a tail gunner. He died of his wounds while being carried to Wau following the crash-landing of 41-9234. via Charles Bowen

Revealing view of 41-9234's rear starboard fuselage and fin taken in 1977. The Dark Olive Drab upper finish, applied for service in the Pacific, has mostly weathered away to reveal the Temperate Sea camouflage scheme and early Type A1 RAF roundels, applied prior to the intended delivery flight to the United Kingdom. Note the colour transition at the 11 o'clock position above the RAF roundel from what was Extra Dark Sea Grey (left) to Dark Slate Grey. The RAF fin flash and USAAF serial are visible on the fin. Author

APPENDIX L: CAMOUFLAGE AND MARKINGS

The following discussion on Fortress camouflage and markings expands on what has been outlined in the main text while laying out the documentary evidence. Page numbers in parenthesis indicate where related photographs and colour profiles may be found throughout the book.

Fortress I

United Kingdom-based Fortress Is serving with RAF Coastal Command fulfilled two functions: convoy escort and type training. 220 Sqn was the only unit to use the Fortress I in the former role with just two aircraft, AN531 and AN537, equipped to carry depth charges and employed on convoy escorts. AN520, AN527 and AN530 were used briefly by the unit as trainers and hacks.

The first four former 90 Sqn aircraft arrived at 220 Sqn's base at Nutts Corner on February 13, 1942, in finishes previously applied for the high-level bombing role. There may well have been some variation in the colours as 90 Sqn's Fortress Is wore a number of finishes to reflect changing operational requirements. These finishes have been the subject of much research and conjecture and the actual schemes worn by these aircraft on delivery to 220 Sqn will likely never been known for certain. The most consistent scheme appears to have been 'grey and green' upper surfaces with either, depending on the evidence, PRU Blue or Sky Blue under surfaces, fin and rudder. Interpreting other written accounts, themselves based in part on first-hand observations made by Michael J F Bowyer, the 'grey and green' was most likely the Temperate Sea scheme of Extra Dark Sea Grey and Dark Slate Grey although it could have been the original Dark Green with the Dark Earth overpainted Dark Sea Grey.

Gerry Haggas was a pilot with 220 Sqn and flew convoy escorts in both AN531 and AN537. He had a clear recollection when asked recently whether the unit's Fortress Is were operated in a

Staged scene featuring public relations officer F/O L W Taylor, RAAF, in the dark blue uniform and crew members drawn from 206 Sqn in front Fortress IIA FL462 'W' of 220 Sqn, taken at Benbecula mid-1943. Other identified personnel include navigator F/O Leslie 'Sid' Banks to the rear and WOP/AG 'Razz' Bury on the extreme right. Bury later became president of the RAF Air Gunners Association. The Author had previously identified the location as Lagens in the Azores. This cannot be so as the Fortress is still equipped with its ball turret, removed before the aircraft departed Benbecula, and is not yet fitted with ASV Mk II radar, installed on FL462 by 218 MU, Colerne between September 4 and October 2, 1943, in advance of deployment to Lagens. The photograph provides an accurate rendition of a weathered Temperate Sea camouflage scheme. IWM TR.1082 with thanks to Sid Banks

different camouflage scheme from that applied to the later Fortress IIAs and IIs: "*Quite right. Both aircraft were operated with the Bomber Command camouflage scheme from their days with 90 Sqn.*" It is clear from the well-known photograph of AN537 'NR-L' flying over a convoy that this aircraft was at some point repainted in the Coastal Command scheme of Temperate Sea with White undersides, fuselage sides, fin and rudder while in service with 220 Sqn (see pages 24 and 229). Other evidence, presented below, indicates that AN531 also acquired Temperate Sea upper camouflage, either while with 90 Sqn or after joining 220 Sqn.

It would appear that all five Fortress Is assigned to 220 Sqn – the fifth example, AN527, arrived in April 1942 – retained their former 90 Sqn individual aircraft codes with AN520 'WP-D', AN530 'WP-F' and AN531 'WP-O' confirmed as 'NR-D', 'NR-F' and 'NR-O' respectively at the end of July 1942 when 206 Sqn took delivery of these aircraft. Of the other two, AN527 'WP-A' is known to have become 'NR-A' while AN537, which became 'NR-L', has been quoted as 'WP-L' with 90 Sqn, a code that does not appear to have been allocated to another squadron aircraft.

Following service with 220 Sqn and brief assignments with the Coastal Command Development Unit, also at Ballykelly, three aircraft – AN520, AN530 and AN531 – were allocated to 206 Sqn at Benbecula for use as conversion trainers and hacks, a role they fulfilled until early-to-mid-1943. AN520 is known to have been re-coded 'VX-X' while AN531 became 'VX-V'.

On March 27, 1943, Michael Bowyer noted AN531 'VX-V' at Cambridge prior to undergoing overhaul by Marshall following service with 206 Sqn. His period sketch shows the Fortress painted with faded and worn Temperate Sea camouflage and Night under surfaces – Bowyer recently recalled: "*The black was so much in contrast.*" According to Bowyer's sketch, AN531 had also acquired a White fin and rudder and White code letters and serial (page 228). Quite when and why the Night finish was applied is a mystery, although Bowyer recalls that the rumour at Cambridge was that the Fortress had been used in a service film. The aircraft is known to have been wearing blue under surfaces at the time it was delivered to 220 Sqn (page 23) and the addition of black while in service with either 220 Sqn or 206 Sqn for operational reasons seems highly unlikely.

Adding to its predilection for wearing unusual finishes, Bowyer noted AN531 departing Cambridge for 51 MU at Lichfield via Driffield on July 5, 1943, with Extra Dark Sea Grey upper surfaces and, again, Night under surfaces (page 229). While not providing any form of explanation, Extra Dark Sea Grey upper surfaces with Night under surfaces was a standard scheme for Coastal Command aircraft engaged in nocturnal operations while Marshall was applying Extra Dark Sea Grey to the upper surfaces of Coastal Command Whitley GR.VIIs at the time. After a period of storage with 51 MU, AN531 served with the RAE at Farnborough before being struck off charge in January 1945.

AN520 'VX-X' is known to have been painted in what appears to have been an overall white finish prior to joining 214 Sqn as a trainer (page 47). Nothing is known of the appearance of AN519 while with 59 and 206 Sqns, although logbook entries confirm that it did serve with 59 Sqn as a hack and trainer (coded 'V') long after the squadron had relinquished its operational Fortresses for Liberators.

Fortress Is serving with the Middle East detachment retained the 90 Sqn finishes applied at the time of their departure for Egypt, including blue under surfaces (page 17). They received the unit codes 'MB' when reassigned to 220 Sqn but retained their 90 Sqn individual aircraft code letters (page 18).

Fortress IIA and II

Camouflage and markings applied to Fortress IIA and II aircraft destined for service with RAF Coastal Command fell into three broad categories. The following notes apply to descriptions of these finishes.

1. 'Delivery Scheme' is not an official term.
2. The terms 'Type A1', 'Type B', etc., commonly used to define roundel types, were not official Air Ministry nomenclature. However, due to their widespread use, they are included here, together with the official terms. The official term for the so-called 'Type A1' roundel is not known.
3. Camouflage Pattern No. 1 consisted of a disruptive camouflage scheme over all upper surfaces, the fin and rudder, and down the fuselage sides with a separate under surfaces colour. On Pattern No. 2, the disruptive scheme was limited to the upper surfaces of the wings and horizontal stabilizer and the upper part of the fuselage with the under surfaces colour wrapping up the fuselage sides and over the fin and rudder.

Delivery Scheme 1

Finish: Standard USAAF finish of Bulletin 41 Dark Olive Drab No. 41 with Neutral Gray No. 43 under surfaces.

Markings: 'Type A1' fuselage roundels, pre-May 1942 fin flashes and National Marking I ('Type B') upper wing roundels. USAAF five-digit serial in yellow on the fin.

Application: The first ten or so aircraft delivered to the United Kingdom. The only marking added to these aircraft while passing through Cheyenne was an Air Ministry serial, painted in 8-inch black characters on the rear fuselage sides.

Evidence:

1. B&W photo of FK184 (2nd aircraft delivered to Dorval, March 19, 1942) on arrival at Prestwick on April 1, 1942. This was the first aircraft modified at Cheyenne and the first delivered to the United Kingdom (page 33).
2. B&W photo of FK187 (4th aircraft delivered to Dorval, March 24, 1942) under test by A&AEE, Boscombe Down (page 28 and 38).
3. B&W photo of FK190 (5th aircraft delivered to Dorval, April 1, 1942), under test at RAE Farnborough (page 42).
4. B&W photo of FK193 (10th aircraft delivered to Dorval, April 22, 1942) at Dorval, Montreal, on delivery to the United Kingdom (page 29).
5. B&W photo of 41-2610 and 41-2611 at Seattle, allocated to Britain but became two of the 16 B-17Es retained by the USAAF (page 27).

Delivery Scheme 2

Finish: Temperate Sea (Extra Dark Sea Grey and Dark Slate Grey) upper surfaces with Sky under surfaces, to Pattern No. 1. These colours would have been the American equivalents of British paints and may have been of slightly different hues. Dark Slate Grey was actually a sickly shade of green rather than a grey, the Temperate Sea scheme inspiring such unflattering nicknames as 'slime-and-sewage' and 'sea-sick'.

Markings: National Marking III ('Type C1') fuselage roundels, post-May 1942 fin flashes and National Marking I ('Type B') upper wing roundels. Air Ministry serial painted in 8-inch black characters on the rear fuselage sides and USAAF serial in yellow on the fin. One aircraft, FL461 (see later), which was one of the 16 B-17Es allocated to Britain but retained by the USAAF, is known to have been marked with the earlier style 'Type A1' fuselage roundel and pre-May 1942 fin flashes. (See Appendix K for the history of this aircraft plus related photographs).

Application: Unconfirmed number of Fortress IIAs, estimated at around 20.

A comparison of the Temperate Land upper surface finish on pattern Lancaster I R5727 and Fortress IIA FK209 demonstrate that the latter is finished in the more subtle and less 'contrasty' Temperate Sea camouflage. The mouth-watering collection of mostly United Kingdom-bound aircraft in the background includes Hudsons, Harvards, Venturas, and Mitchells plus a second Fortress IIA (FL450), a Marauder, a Catalina and a Havoc. Department of National Defense Photo Unit PL-11070

Evidence:

B&W photographs of FK209 (21st aircraft delivered to Dorval, June 25, 1942) and FL450 (29th aircraft delivered to Dorval, July 2, 1942) at Dorval, Montreal, on delivery to the UK (pages 34 and 184).

From August 10, 1941, the official Coastal Command scheme for large land-based General reconnaissance types – Wellington, Whitley and Liberator – was Temperate Sea with White under surfaces to Pattern No. 2. The Fortress was officially added to this list in July 1942 under Air Ministry Order AMO A.664/42. However, as already noted, this second group of Fortresses delivered to the United Kingdom was painted to Pattern No. 1, perhaps reflecting the scheme defined by a Boeing drawing of July 1941, if not the actual colours (see next section for a discussion of this drawing).

At the same time, smaller types being delivered to the United Kingdom for Coastal Command service – including Hudsons, Venturas and Catalinas – were finished with Sky under surfaces, also to Pattern No. 1. These factors open up the possibility of Sky being applied to the under surfaces of this group of Fortresses.

Regarding the upper surfaces, the full image of FK209 with UK-built Lancaster I R5727 alongside, above, shows a clear difference between the upper camouflage colours of the two aircraft, the contrast between the Dark Green and Dark Earth on the Lancaster being far greater than that between the Extra Dark Sea Grey and Dark Slate Grey on the Fortress.

As for the under surfaces, the white of the fuselage roundel and fin flash on the Fortress – as well as on the Hudson and A-20 to the rear – is clearly lighter and brighter than the comparable areas of the undersides which have a darker, 'creamy' appearance, consistent with the look of Sky in black and white photographs. However, the possibility remains, based on the evidence so far, that the under surfaces *could* have been painted grey.

Returning to the upper surfaces, colour transparencies of FL461, taken by the Author during a visit to the crash site in Papua New Guinea in April 1977 (page 212 and next page) clearly show

the Extra Dark Sea Grey and Dark Slate Grey disruptive pattern on the starboard side of the fuse-lage, the Dark Olive Drab applied in-theatre having been weathered away. The under surfaces were not observed but are assumed to have displayed remnants of the corresponding Neutral Grey. The camouflage pattern observed on the fuselage matches that applied to FK209 and FL450, noted ear-lier. Had FL461 not been retained by the USAAF, it would have been around the 35th aircraft de-livered to Dorval.

The colour image of 41-9234 in Appendix K (top of page 212) provides the definitive evidence that Sky *was* the under surface colour applied to middle-period B-17Es allocated to Britain. The aircraft is shown while being flown by the 28th BS, 19th BG from Mareeba, Australia, and Port Moresby, Papua, on operations over New Guinea. It still wears the Temperate Sea scheme applied in the United States prior to its intended delivery to the United Kingdom. The under surfaces – which it has been established were *not* painted White and which can be seen in this photograph not to be grey but slightly off-white with a bluish-green hue – are Sky or its American equivalent. 41-9234 was later repainted in standard Dark Olive Drab and Neutral Grey. (See colour profiles for of all three finish and marking combinations applied to 41-9234, pages 236 and 237).

Related Topic: Boeing camouflage drawing for RAF-bound B-17Es and photographs of B-17Es 41-9141 and 41-9131

As noted in the main text, Britain placed an order for 300 aircraft B-17s, nominally B-17Es, in June of 1941. The following month Boeing prepared a drawing for the application of camouflage to these aircraft on the understanding that they would be used in the high-level bombing role. The scheme consisted of Temperate Land upper surfaces (Dark Green and Dark Earth) with 'deep sky blue' under surfaces to Pattern No. 2 and was, not surprisingly, very similar to that initially worn by Fortress Is of 90 Sqn for daytime bombing operations over Northern Europe. The camouflage pat-tern, Scheme 'A' as defined by Air Ministry drawing AD 1161, was the same as that later applied to RAF-bound Fortress IIAs finished in Temperate Sea for maritime reconnaissance.

Starboard side of B-17E 41-9234 showing the colour demarcation between the Extra Dark Sea Grey and Dark Slate Grey of the Temperate Sea upper camouflage pattern. Although the photograph is strongly backlit, the colours and their division are clearly visible two thirds of the way from the left along the open dinghy storage hatch. Author

The Boeing drawing is dated July 2, 1941, although the reference to 'deep sky blue' is believed to have been added after October 1941 when the colour's name was first coined in the United Kingdom. The first ten Fortress IIAs were delivered to the United Kingdom in USAAF Dark Olive Drab and Neutral Gray finish between April 1 and May 12, 1942, while the first aircraft known to have been painted with Temperate Sea upper surfaces, Fortress IIA FK209, was assigned to Cheyenne from Boeing on May 16, 1942. Given the requirement for Temperate Sea camouflage for Coastal Command's Fortresses dating back to August 1941, it seems highly unlikely that Boeing would have started to routinely apply the now obsolete high-level bombing scheme to aircraft destined for Britain.

Remarkable formation, captured near Seattle in April 1942, featuring B-17E 41-9141 finished in a high-level daytime bombing scheme similar to that applied to RAF Fortress Is. 41-9131, to the rear, wears standard USAAF Dark Olive Drab and Neutral Grey. Both aircraft served exclusively in the United States. Boeing

That said, there is a well-known series of photographs of B-17Es 41-9141 and 41-9131 flying in formation near Seattle, dated April 1942. 41-9141 is painted in a pattern identical to the one described by the Boeing drawing, although the darker camouflage colour appears to match the Dark Olive Drab worn by 41-9131. According to its record card, 41-9141 was never intended for release to Britain and is not included in a British Air Commission listing of 16 B-17Es allocated to Britain but retained by the USAAF. It was delivered to the USAAF in an unknown finish on May 1, 1942, and never left the continental United States. Although not known for certain, it appears likely that 41-9141 sported a one-off application of the Temperate Land and 'deep sky blue' scheme, possibly applied in error at the time of the changeover from Dark Olive Drab to Temperate Sea and perhaps combined with an anticipation on Boeing's part that the aircraft would be allocated to Britain.

Of related interest, the overhead view of 41-9141 (page 220) shows that, contrary to normal practice, USAAF roundels have been applied to both the port and starboard upper sides of the wing, suggesting that RAF Type B roundels were previously applied and have been at least partially over-painted. This conclusion is reinforced by the fact that the red '*meatballs*' in the centre of these markings are proportionately larger than normal. The RAF fin flash remains unaltered.

Delivery Scheme 3

Finish: Temperate Sea with White under surfaces to Pattern No. 2. Again, these colours would have been the American equivalents of the British paints.

Markings: National Marking III ('Type C1') fuselage roundels, post-May 1942 fin flashes and National Marking I 'Type B' upper wing roundels. Air Ministry serial in 8-inch black (later, grey) characters on the rear fuselage sides.

Application: Later Fortress IIA arrivals at Dorval, around 10, and all 19 Fortress IIs.

Evidence:
1. B&W photo of unidentified Fortress IIA at Dorval, mid-1942 (not reproduced).
2. B&W photo of FA705 (53rd aircraft delivered to Dorval, November 22, 1942) at Burtonwood, United Kingdom, shortly after delivery from Dorval (page 31).
3. B&W photo of FA711 (59th aircraft delivered to Dorval, January 2, 1943) at Wayne County Airport, Detroit, on delivery to Dorval (page 30).

In-Service Finishes

Those B-17Es delivered in USAAF Dark Olive Drab and Neutral Gray – Delivery Scheme 1 – and allocated for squadron service were repainted in the Temperate Sea and White scheme at the Burtonwood Repair Depot.

B-17Es arriving painted in Temperate Sea with Sky under surfaces – Delivery Scheme 2 – were also repainted at Burtonwood. It seems likely that only those areas to be White were repainted and that the American paints used for the Temperate Sea scheme, with any slight colour differences they might have had from British paints, were left 'as delivered.' In the case of Delivery Scheme 1 and Delivery Scheme 2, the USAAF data block on the port side of the nose was masked off so it remained visible after application of the White finish. Photographs suggest that the second line of the data block was longer than usual and possibly read, for example: AIR CORPS SERIAL NO. A.D. 41-9234. The meaning of the additional letters 'A.D.' is not confirmed but they may have stood for Article of Defense, a variation on the term 'Defense Articles' found throughout the Lend-Lease Act in reference to military equipment destined for the United Kingdom.

Fortress IIAs and IIs delivered in Temperate Sea and White – Delivery Scheme 3 – almost certainly served in their US-applied finish. Aircraft subsequently overhauled in the United Kingdom after accumulating 800 flight hours were routinely repainted.

The August 1941 requirement for the Temperate Sea and White scheme also included specific instructions for the application of white on larger land-based General Reconnaissance types. Aircraft 'sides', which included the fuselage sides to Pattern No. 2 and the fin and rudder, were to be painted matt white while the remaining under surfaces were to be painted gloss white. The rationale for this instruction was that the under surfaces would be in shadow when viewed from a U-boat under attack and thus relatively dark unless some reflectance could be gained from the sea surface by the glossy finish. The matt and gloss white requirement remained in effect well into 1945 although operational and supply constraints make it unlikely the instruction was routinely, if ever followed.

In a further attempt to blend an attacking aircraft with what was assumed to usually be a predominantly cloudy background, instructions to operational units also included a requirement to

Colour transparency of Fortress IIA FK186 'S' of 220 Sqn, taken during the mid-1943 air-to-air photo sessions from Benbecula. The Dark Slate Grey ('green') of the Temperate Sea upper camouflage scheme appears a little washed out on the nose while the serial and code letter 'S' on the fuselage side and nose appear to have been applied in a grey darker than the specified Light Slate Grey. Note the absence of an astrodome on top of the nose. IWM TR.1084

Overhead view of the
same formation shows the
over-painted upper wing
roundels with oversize red
"meatballs". Boeing

paint the entire engine cowlings with white stoving enamel, which is assumed to have had a glossy finish, and to apply a special flexible white paint to de-icing boots on the wing, horizontal stabilizer and fin leading edges.

While Fortress cowlings were certainly painted white, there is no definitive evidence that stoving enamel was ever used, although the cowlings in some photographs appear to have a slightly glossier finish than the adjacent nacelles (page 61, top). Similarly, no evidence has been found for the application of white paint on de-icing boots.

Coastal Command's Fortresses served in the Temperate Sea and White finish throughout the critical years of the Battle of the Atlantic, from September 1942 to March 1943, and on into service in the Azores from that October. Yet as early as December 30, 1942, HQ Coastal Command had proposed changes to the scheme.

Their first recommendation was the elimination of Dark Slate Grey from the disruptive Temperate Sea camouflage, leaving the upper surfaces in just Extra Dark Sea Grey, as the pattern offered no operational benefits and required substantial effort to apply. An instruction to this affect was issued by the Air Ministry on February 2, 1943. Yet ironically, given that Coastal Command had made the recommendation, photographic evidence suggests that the instruction was not acted on while the type was serving in the anti-submarine role with the possible but undocumented exception of the few aircraft temporarily returned to the United Kingdom from the Azores for Major Inspections.

In fact, photographic evidence also confirms that some Fortresses retained their Temperate Sea upper surfaces while serving in the meteorological reconnaissance role from late 1944 although most, if not all, were eventually repainted with Extra Dark Sea Grey upper surfaces, including the tops of the formerly white cowlings. John Rabbets noted the following examples at 51 MU, Lichfield following their retirement: Mk IIAs FK210 '5O-W', FK211 'Z9-H', FK213 'Z9-G' (page

130), FL449 'Z9-F', FL452 '5O-U', FL457 'AD-P' and FL463 'C' (latterly with 1674 HCU, page 139), and Mk IIs FA696 '5O-B' (page 235), FA701 'AD-J' and FA712 'AD-C' (page 135).

Returning to the Air Ministry instruction of February 2, 1943, one change that was generally implemented, again to help reduce aircraft visibility, was the painting of all de-icing boots with aluminium paint. This finish can be seen in a number of photographs including those on pages 61 (top), 63, 74 and 101. The instruction also included requirements to paint propeller spinners and cowlings matt white and in cases where de-icing equipment was not fitted – which, in theory, did not apply to the Fortress – to wrap the white under surface finish up over the leading edges of the wings and horizontal stabilizer to a line where, when viewed from ahead, the flying surfaces appeared white. This last instruction led to the application of some interesting finishes on operational Fortresses.

Both Mk IIA FK202 'B' of 59 Sqn (page 58) and Mk II FA704 'R' of 206 Sqn (page 68), previously with 59 Sqn, were painted with the required White upper wing leading edges and nacelle sides. FA704 also featured a very narrow band of Temperate Sea camouflage along the top of a predominantly white fuselage while its forward cowlings were not painted White as specified. FK202 featured a non-standard disruptive camouflage finish although its cowlings were painted White. Mk II FA709 'B' of 220 Sqn is also known to have been finished with a thin band of Temperate Sea camouflage atop an almost entirely white fuselage (page 64).

Fortress IIA FK190 became a dedicated trainer with 206 Sqn following its ASV Mk II radar trials with the RAE at Farnborough and received the same finish as FA704, appearing to be all-white when viewed from slightly below but still showing a thin band of Temperate Sea along the upper fuselage centreline. It was repainted in full Temperate Sea and White some time prior to service in the Azores although traces of White on the upper wing leading edges remained visible (pages 63 and 101).

The origins of the thin and, presumably, ineffective band of Temperate Sea camouflage along the fuselage top are not known although the same finish, with white wing and horizontal stabilizer leading edges, was worn by some Coastal Command Bristol Beaufighters. One possibility is a requirement in the original Temperate Sea and White scheme instruction of August 1941 that defined the white being applied on any visible surface 8 degrees below the horizontal.

At least two aircraft are known to have been painted with a wavy demarcation line between the upper surface Temperate Sea camouflage and the White fuselage sides, likely applied at the unit level. These were the already noted Mk IIA FK202 'B' with 59 Sqn and Mk IIA FL462 'W' with 220 Sqn while based at Benbecula, later repainted with the more normal straight demarcation line (page 66). Like FA704, FL462 had previously served with 59 Sqn, further suggesting that this unit applied non-standard Temperate Sea and White schemes to its aircraft.

Fortress III
The three Fortress IIIs delivered to RAF Coastal Command – HB786, HB791 and HB792 – remained in natural metal finish throughout their anti-submarine and meteorological reconnaissance duties.

Code Letters and Serial Numbers
On April 30, 1942, the Air Ministry issued an instruction that codes letters and serials were to be painted Light Slate Grey. However, there was a

Fine detail shot of the nose of Fortress IIA FL462 'W' of 220 Sqn, taken at Benbecula with public relations officer F/O L W Taylor, RAAF, to the fore. Of note is the extended second line of the masked off data block. This would normally read 'AIR CORPS SERIAL NO. 41-9239' but in this case is believed to include the additional text 'U.K. GOVERNMENT' immediately before the serial. Another example, FL451, appears to have had a shorter, three-character addition before the serial, possibly 'R.A.F.' It is also interesting to observe that the demarcation between the Extra Dark Sea Grey and the Dark Slate Grey of the Temperate Sea camouflage above the forward window, clearly visible in the colour group photograph taken on the same occasion, (page 213), is invisible in this black and white image. IWM CH.11119 via Steve Birdsall

brief period while this change was being implemented when squadron and individual aircraft code letters were authorised to be displayed in Red (often referred to as 'Dull Red') with serial numbers painted Night (black). This coincided with the introduction to service of the Fortress I by 220 Sqn and it is known that AN537 was at some point repainted in the Temperate Sea and White scheme with codes 'NR-L' in Red.

The change to Light Slate Grey appears to have been adopted by 220 Sqn for its Fortress IIAs and IIs, the unit applying the required 48-inch high letters such as seen on FL459 'J' (page 61) and FA709 'B' (page 64). However, photographs of 206 Sqn aircraft suggest that this unit applied 36-inch high codes letters in a darker grey while 59 Sqn did the same using 48-inch characters, examples being FA704 'R' of 206 Sqn (page 69) and FK202 'B' of 59 Sqn (pages 58).

Light Slate Grey was only intended to be used for codes and serials and it is apparent that the colour was either not always available at the unit level or not too much attention was paid to the actual colour applied as long as it was a shade of grey.

As permitted by the applicable Air Ministry Order, unit codes were sometimes applied forward of the fuselage roundel, for example FL451 'VX-D' of 206 Sqn (page 45), or behind the roundel, for example FK185 'E-NR' formerly of 220 Sqn (page 69), looking at the port side in both cases. Fortress IIAs were initially painted with both unit and individual aircraft code letters. When unit codes were subsequently removed from Coastal Command aircraft for security reasons, effective November 1, 1942, the individual code letters remained in their original positions, either before or after the roundel, even within the same squadron. For example, FL459 'J' of 220 Sqn was left with its code letter after the roundel on the port side (page 75) while FK212 'V' of the same unit had its code letter remaining before the roundel on the port side (page 74).

This situation appears to have become standardised as part of the preparations for 206 and 220 Sqns moving to the Azores in October 1943. To help differentiate squadron aircraft operating from a common base, Coastal Command implemented a practice of allocating single digits at the base level. For the Azores deployment, 206 Sqn aircraft received the unit code '1' (pages 99 and 118) while those of 220 Sqn were marked with the code '2' (pages 98 and 99). In each case the unit code was applied forward of the roundel on both sides of the fuselage while the individual letter was positioned behind the roundel. Both squadrons applied 48-inch high characters in a shade of grey darker than Light Slate Grey.

206 Sqn departed the Azores in March 1944 followed by the bulk of 220 Sqn's Fortresses between October and December of the same year. The re-application of squadron codes for General Reconnaissance aircraft was approved in mid-1944 and it is known that 220 Sqn's three Fortress IIIs received the new unit code 'ZZ' applied in black prior to their departure in April 1945 (page 135). It is not known if any of the unit's Fortress IIAs and IIs received new squadron codes before to leaving the Azores.

Fortresses assigned to the three meteorological reconnaissance squadrons were marked with 48-inch squadron codes and individual letters, in the case of 519 Sqn, in the required Light Slate Grey (pages 123 and 126), while serial numbers were painted in the same colour. The three unpainted Fortress IIIs wore black codes and serials.

In addition to the previously mentioned Extra Dark Sea Grey upper surfaces, Met Fortresses received two further modifications to their paint schemes in 1945. In an attempt to address concerns that RAF aircraft might be misidentified and shot down by Allied aircraft, a January 7, 1945, instruction required that the red and blue upper wing roundel be modified with the addition of a white ring between the two colours. This revised roundel was known as National Marking IA ('Type C') (page 136). The second change concerned the identification of low flying aircraft, the cause of an increasing number of accidents. A July 26 order, AMO A.766, required that the aircraft serial number be painted on the outboard section of the underside of each wing in large characters. In the case of the Fortress, the prescribed formula translated into 48-inch high black characters (pages 135, top, 137 and 235).

Interpreting Black and White Photographs

There are relatively few photographs of Fortresses in Coastal Command service. Their bases tended to be remote and, perhaps because of this and the greater limelight given to bomber and fighter units, formal photographic sessions seem to have been infrequent. The two best known series are held by the Imperial War Museum in London. The first, the 'CH' series, depicts a Fortress being prepared for an anti-submarine patrol at Benbecula while its crew are being briefed for the operation – this is followed by shots of the aircrew and aircraft and a series of air-to-air photographs of Fortress IIAs FK186 'S', FK212 'V' and FL459 'J' of 220 Sqn. The second set, the 'CA' series, is part of a larger collection taken in the Azores from the time of the opening of the base at Lagens in October 1943 through to photographs issued as late as 1945.

Black and white photographs of aircraft painted in Temperate Sea camouflage are challenging to analyse in terms of colours and patterns. The constituent colours, Extra Dark Sea Grey and Dark Slate Grey, are subtle and each can change from being the dominant hue to the less dominant hue depending on the age of the finish, the contour of the aircraft surface, the ambient lighting and the type of film used. The in-flight shot of the recently repainted FK190 '1-J' (page 101) is an excellent example, with the hues of the disruptive pattern on the port wing changing back and forth from dominant to less dominant.

There are two known colour photographs of Coastal Command Fortresses, both of 220 Sqn aircraft taken at Benbecula mid-1943: a transparency of FK186 'S' of 220 Sqn flying near Benbecula (page 219) and a colour print of a staged crew briefing with FL462 'W' to the rear (page 213). These were very useful in helping interpret available black and white photos for production of the colour profiles.

Colour Profiles and Scale Drawings

Great care went into researching the colour schemes depicted in the colour profiles. The Author and illustrator Juanita Franzi cross-referenced the colour images and available black and white photographs with the applicable Air Ministry Orders (AMOs), other written accounts of Fortress colour schemes, input from acknowledged experts, and first-hand accounts from two respected enthusiasts who were 'there' at the time and who methodically recorded the appearance of wartime aircraft: Michael J F Bowyer and John Rabbets.

It soon became apparent that, in spite of the directions contained in the AMOs, the exigencies and practicalities of war meant that camouflage and markings varied considerably from the written standards and that in the absence of colour images of the aircraft being depicted, there would always be a degree interpretation when analysing black and white photographs.

The base drawings for the colour profiles and scale drawings were prepared using dimensioned Boeing general arrangement drawings supplied by the company.

The Author extends special thanks to Paul Lucas for his invaluable guidance in the preparation of this appendix.

APPENDIX M: ARTWORK

As far as is known, Fortresses in service with 59, 206 and 220 Sqn in the anti-submarine role were never painted with artwork. However, it would appear that regulations were relaxed with the allocation of the type to 1674 Heavy Conversion Unit at the end of August 1943 and certainly by the time the type was reassigned to the meteorological reconnaissance role in October 1944.

Fortress IIs *Borganes Bess* (FA696 'AD-B'), *Hekla Hettie* (FA699 or FA700, 'AD-H') and *Keflavik Cutie* (FA712 'AD-C') are all 251 (Met) Sqn aircraft based at Reykjavik, Iceland. Each aircraft retains the doubler plates, installed immediately behind the bottom of the nose cone and below the rearmost window to support the receiving aerials for the forward-looking homing component of ASV Mk II radar. The upper whip aerial is for the Gee navigation system while the lower whip aerial is part of the original radio compass system, paired with the faired ADF loop. The small AN-65 aerial below the rearmost window is one of a pair fitted for homing purposes and linked to the ASV Mk II radar system. The probe below it is believed to be an outside air temperature thermometer pocket.

(All photos: Stanley Robins, seen below, via Peter Rackliff)

Kitty (middle), modelled on the Varga pin-up in *Esquire* magazine for July 1943, is painted on an ASV-equipped aircraft. *Lucy Lastic*, a Fortress IIA (see photo page 78), is also equipped with ASV and both were likely trainers with 1674 HCU.

Of the remaining photographs, *Cleopatra*, *Gna*(?) and *Suzy* are unidentified.

Nanette (see also photo page 137) is also known to have been applied to a Fortress IIA of 251 (Met) Sqn. Based on the other examples from the unit noted above, the first letter of the artwork name, 'N', is likely to have been the same as the aircraft's individual code letter. This pattern would very likely apply to the other examples.

Elizabeth adorns a Fortress II while *Ferdinand* and *Queenie* are also unidentified.

(All photos via Bryan Yates except as noted).

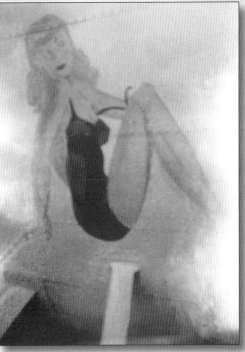

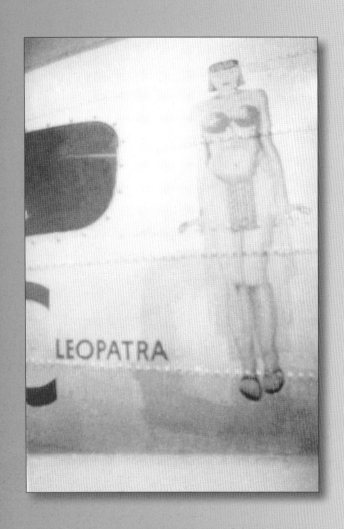

LEOPATRA

Gna

Nanette

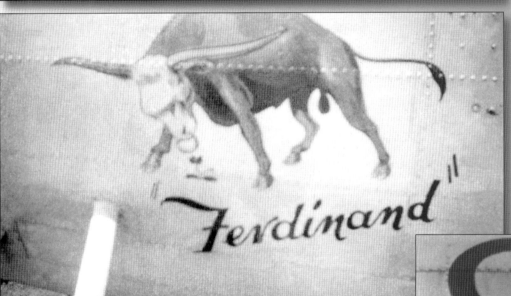

Fortress I AN537 'NR-L' recorded by John Rabbets at 51 MU, Lichfield, late 1942. As evaluated by Coastal Command Development Unit, Bal-lykelly, following service (without ASV radar) with 220 Sqn. (See pages 24-25).

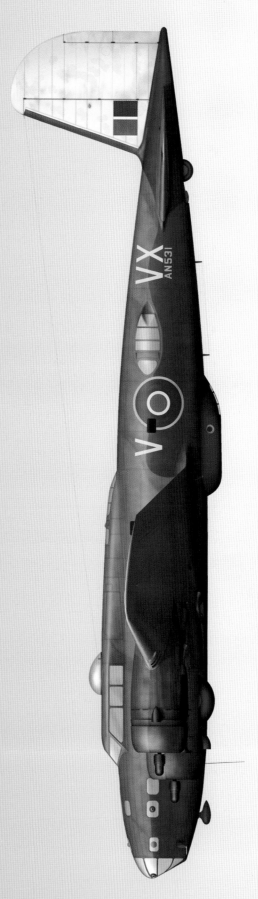

Former 206 Sqn Fortress I AN531 'VX-V', as recorded by Michael J F Bowyer at Cambridge airport on March 27, 1943, prior to overhaul by Marshall. (See page 214).

Fortress I AN531, recorded by Michael J F Bowyer at Cambridge on July 5, 1943, prior to delivery into storage at 51 MU, Lichfield. (See page 214).

Fortress IIA FK190 configured for trials of the prototype British-designed ASV Mk II aerial arrays at A&AEE Boscombe Down, May to August, 1942. (See pages 41-42).

Fortress IIA FL450 recorded at Dorval, Montreal, on August 24, 1943, prior to delivery by RAF Ferry Command to the United Kingdom. (See page 34).

Fortress IIA FK202 'B' of 59 Sqn while based at Chivenor, Devon, early 1943. Fitted with American-designed ASV Mk II search arrays on the rear fuselage and shrouds on the engine exhaust systems. (See page 58).

Fortress IIA FK195 'L' of 206 Sqn as marked and equipped during the sinking of U-boat U-469 on March 23, 1943, with F/Lt William 'Willis' Roxburgh in command and U-169 just four days later with F/O A C Ian Samuel as captain. (See pages 63-65).

Fortress IIA FL459 '2-J' of 220 Squadron, Azores, as flown during the sinking of U-boat U-707 on November 9, 1943, with F/Lt Roderick P Drummond in command. (See pages 85 and 89).

Former 220 Sqn Fortress IIA FK185 'E' recorded at A&AEE Boscombe Down, January 1944, during trials of the 40mm Vickers 'S' gun. (See pages 69 and 71-74).

Fortress II FA705 '1-U' of 206 Sqn as lost on January 6, 1944, while attacking U-boat U-270 with S/Ldr Anthony J Pinhorn in command. (See page 110).

Upper plan view of Fortress II FA705 '1-U'. Representative of aircraft operated in the anti-submarine role.

233

Underside view of Fortress II FA705 'L-U'. Representative of aircraft operated in the anti-submarine role from mid-1943 with four externally-mounted depth charges.

Fortress II FA696 'SO-B' of 521 (Met) Sqn, Langham, Norfolk, late 1945 with scrap views of outer port wing. Serial on lower starboard wing read from the rear. (See page 220).

Fortress III HB791 'ZZ-T' of 220 Sqn, based at Lagens in the Azores, late 1944. (See pages 116 and 120-121).

Fortress IIA FL461 (41-9234) following modification for the RAF at the Cheyenne Modification Center, early July 1942. (See pages 29 and 198).

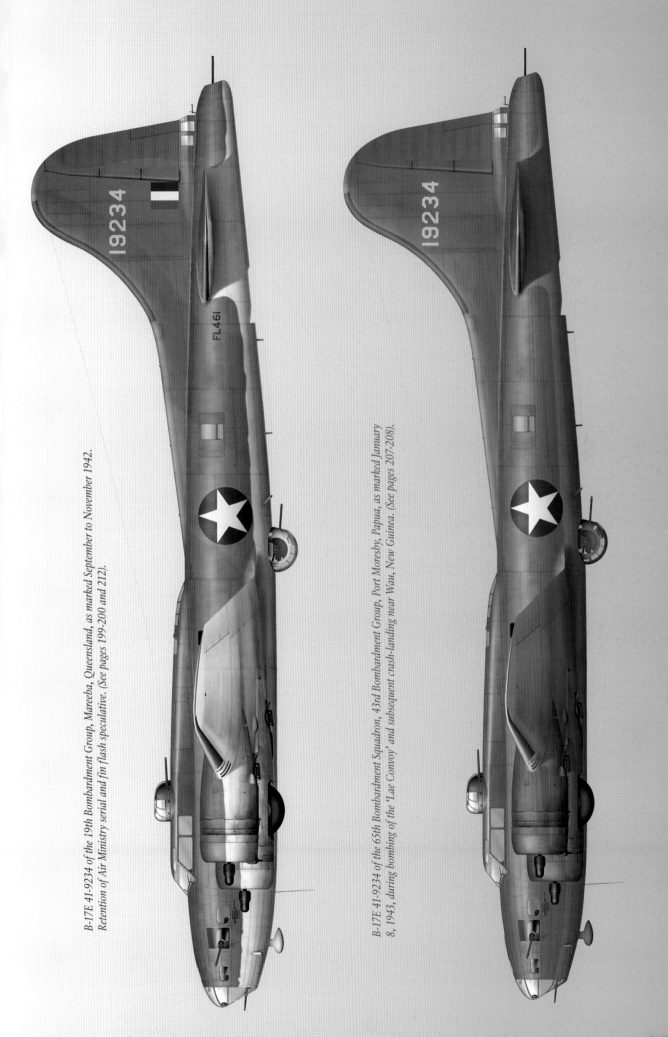

B-17E 41-9234 of the 19th Bombardment Group, Mareeba, Queensland, as marked September to November 1942. Retention of Air Ministry serial and fin flash speculative. (See pages 199-200 and 212).

B-17E 41-9234 of the 65th Bombardment Squadron, 43rd Bombardment Group, Port Moresby, Papua, as marked January 8, 1943, during bombing of the 'Lae Convoy', and subsequent crash-landing near Wau, New Guinea. (See pages 207-208).

INDEX

Seasoned 220 Sqn aircrew, including P/O Kenneth Ramsden to the right. Ramsden flew the first convoy escort performed by the Fortress I and made the first U-boat sinking using the Fortress IIA. via his son, Edward Ramsden

About the Author

Robert Stitt was born in Kent and spent much of his youth plane-spotting at airports around south-east England. Following technical training with Hawker Siddeley Aviation at Brough in Yorkshire, he spent five years managing projects among the former battlefields of the South-West Pacific where he developed a keen interest in aviation archaeology. After moving to Canada, Robert worked in the aerial forest firefighting industry where he began chronicling the fascinating variety of 'retired' types employed in specialty aviation. In-depth articles on other rarely-covered aviation topics followed, totaling some twenty published works to date. Robert lives with his wife on Vancouver Island.